The Ancient Port Of Whitby And Its Shipping: With Some Subjects Of Interest Connected Therewith

Richard Weatherill

THE

ANCIENT PORT

OF

WHITBY

AND ITS SHIPPING,

WITH SOME SUBJECTS OF INTEREST CONNECTED THEREWITH.

PLANS AND ILLUSTRATIONS.

Compiled from Various Registers of Shipping, Periodicals, Local Newspapers and Histories, etc.

BY RICHARD WEATHERILL.

WHITBY:
HORNE AND SON, Bridge Street.
1908.

ABBEY PRESS

WHITBY.
From a Drawing by Geo. Weatherill, 1843.

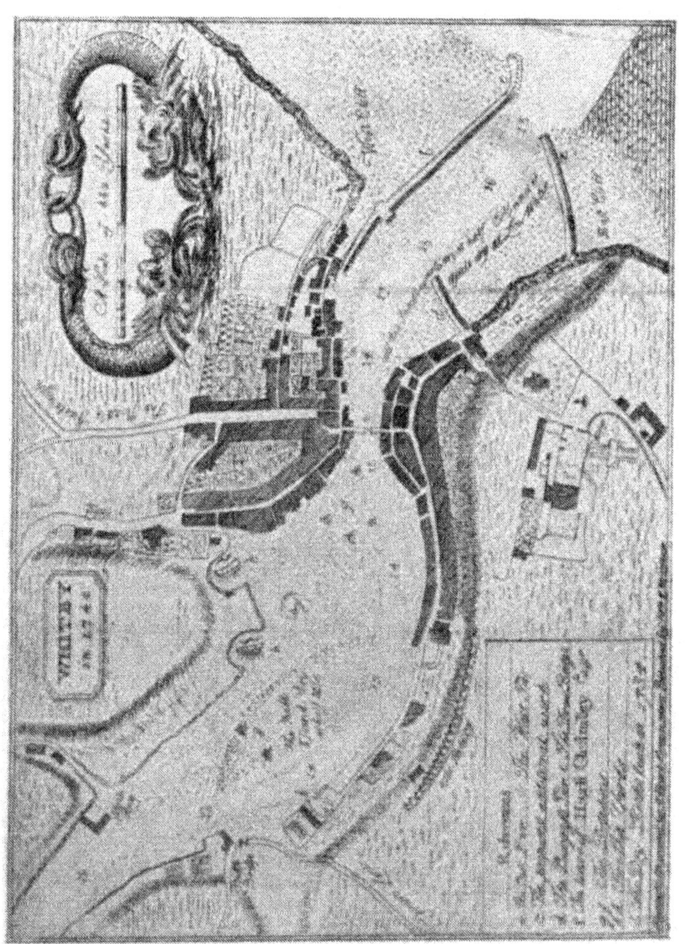

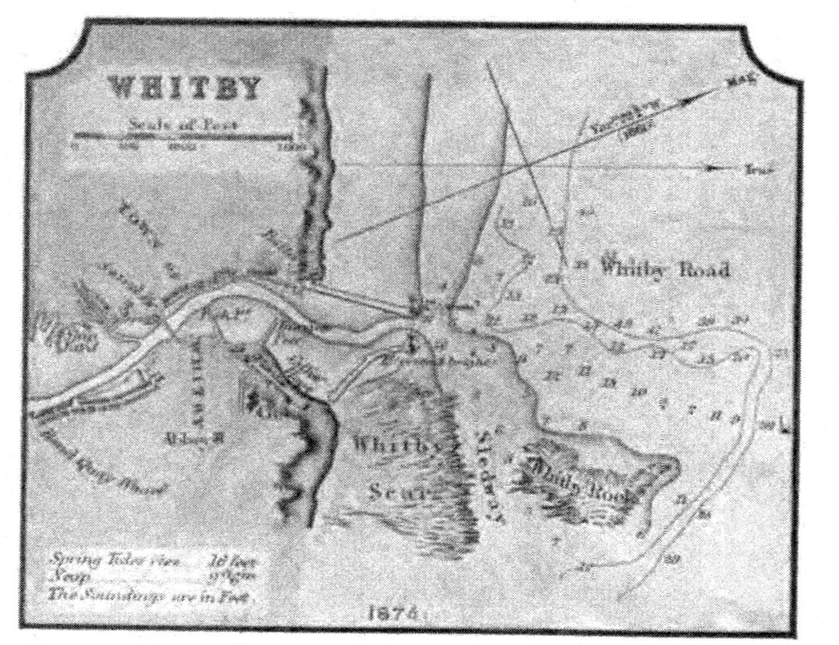
WHITBY
Scale of Feet
Whitby Road
Whitby Scar
Sledway
Whitby Rock
WHITBY
TOWN
Spring Tides rise
Neap
The Soundings are in Feet
1874

PREFACE.

THESE records originated from conversational reminiscences, whilst enjoying the sociable pipe with an esteemed friend, at whose hospitable fireside gentlemen of seafaring experience, and captains, both of wooden sailing ships and of the modern steamers, meeting together, would tell their varied experiences. At such times, the name, date, and owners, &c., of some vessel would often be a matter of debate and difference of opinion. The wish for accuracy in these details resulted in the records. Whilst thanking all who have kindly helped me in various ways, the knowledge and splendid memory of the above friend having been of invaluable assistance, I acknowledge my indebtedness to him by inscribing the records to John Stonehouse, Surgeon.

1908. R. W.

CONTENTS.

"Forsan et hæc olim meminisse juvabit."

WHITBY.

ITS PIERS, LIGHTHOUSES, HARBOUR, BRIDGE, &c.

So long ago as soon after the Conquest, the port of Whitby was of considerable importance, and at the period of the dissolution of the monastery (about 1539) it was a fishing town of some note. About that time the harbour received great improvements, by the erection of a new quay, and the enlargement of the pier. How long a pier has existed here, on which side of the river it lay, or whether it was on both sides, is not known, but it was then repaired, or rather rebuilt with stone that had fallen from the cliff, as well as with timber. A Custom House was established here in the reign of Charles II. It was at first on the West side of the town, but was afterwards removed to the East side. Nevertheless, nothing effectual was done to put the piers and harbour into anything approaching a satisfactory condition until the year 1702, when in consideration of the utility of this port as a harbour of refuge for colliers and other coasting vessels, an

Act of Parliament was passed providing funds for that purpose. Several Acts were afterwards obtained to continue or increase the revenues then provided. These revenues, known as the "Passing Tolls," arose from a duty of one halfpenny per chaldron (a measure of 12 sacks) on all coals shipped at Newcastle, Sunderland, Blyth, and their dependencies, except in Yarmouth vessels, with duties on coals, salt, corn, &c., landed at Whitby; on butter and fish shipped at Whitby, and on ships entering the port—every English ship 1s. and 4d. for each top (a semi-circular platform at the junction of the lower mast and the topmast in square-rigged vessels)—every foreign ship 2s. with 4d. for each top. The first of these duties was the most productive. The whole revenues about the year 1800 averaged some £2,000 annually, but later they produced considerably more. These passing tolls were abolished in 1861; and subsequently the harbour was managed by Trustees, who had, however, very small revenues to work with. In 1906, the Trust was abolished, and the control of the harbour was taken over by the Urban Council. The improvements in the harbour of Whitby, during the period of the above Acts of Parliament, have been great and extensive. The East Pier has been wholly built, and the West Pier repeatedly enlarged and repaired, smaller piers inside built to break the force of the waves, rock and immense beds of sand removed. In 1734 the West Pier was lengthened 100 yards, that the sand banks accumulating round its head might be washed away. Some years later about 230 yards of the old part of it was rebuilt, and later still the whole pier was faced with dressed stones, and afterwards the East Pier also. The length of the West Pier beyond the Scotch Head, as finished in 1814, is 338 yards, and the length from the bridge to the pier end is 795 yards. It is not known when the projection called the Scotch Head was built, or whence it obtained its name. A lighthouse was built on the West Pier end in 1831. A fluted Doric column 75 feet high, including a rusticated base below, and an octagonal light room above which terminates in a dome and is surrounded by a gallery. Lat. 54°30′0″N. Long. 0°37′0″W. The East Pier Lighthouse was built in 1854, after the final extension of the pier was completed, and which was begun about 1845. They are for harbour lights only, which are exhibited two hours before till two hours after high water. Both green lights, but that on the East Pier is shaded red over Whitby Rock, and the entrance is between the two green lights.

Two lighthouses were built at High Whitby in 1857-8, for the guidance of coasting vessels to clear Whitby Rock, but the North one was discontinued on the night of the 30th Dec., 1890, and was taken down. The remaining one has a white light, 240 feet above the sea, occulting every 30 seconds, shaded red over Whitby Rock, and visible 22 miles. A fog-horn was established in 1903, built on the site of the old North lighthouse. It came into use in Dec., 1903—four blasts of 2½ seconds each, three intervals of 2 seconds, and a rest of 74 seconds; in all 90 seconds.

Time out of mind there had been a drawbridge at Whitby, and bridge masters, who collected tolls from vessels passing through, and rents of tenements erected on the frame works. In 1628 it underwent considerable repairs, but the cumbrous buildings which projected over it at both ends were not wholly removed till 1766, when it was entirely rebuilt, with stone pillars, at a cost of £3,000. Although greatly superior

to its predecessor, it was found to have several defects. The passage in the centre was only 32½ feet, too strait for large ships, and the leaves and tackle were often going wrong,

and much damage frequently done by their getting entangled in the rigging of vessels. A new bridge was commenced in January, 1834, but the preliminary work of taking down the old bridge, excavating foundations, driving piles, &c., had occupied the time since the previous 20th June. It was completed in 1835, at a cost of £10,000, and opened for traffic on 25th March. It is entirely different in construction to the old one, having two swivel leaves meeting in the middle, and a waterway of 45 feet 3 inches on the plan, slightly increased a few years ago by reducing a stone projection on the bridge piers. Preliminary operations are now proceeding for the building of a new bridge in the same situation, but broader, and with a 70 feet waterway.

A beacon buoy, or buoy with staff and globe, was placed in 1845 to mark the position of Whitby Rock, as a guide to coasters, as well as to those vessels entering or leaving the harbour. It is about ¾ of a mile, and about N.N.E. true, from the West Pier end. A beacon bell buoy was substituted in 1879.

The Dudgeon Sheal in lat. 53°14′35′ N., and long. 0°57′0″ E., lies right in the fairway of the colliers and coasters passing along the East Coast, and was for years a danger to them. In 1736 a light vessel was placed to mark its position by the exertions and at the expense of Whitby shipowners. It shows a flashing light, white and red alternately every 30 seconds, that is in the present day. A Captain Taylor, writing in 1811, says, "About 100 years ago a few gentlemen of Whitby of the names of Chapman, Stockton, Walker, and Kitchingman did place and maintain the Dudgeon light." He also says "that so long

as the light was a cause of expense the Whitby gentlemen were left to support it, but when it began to be profitable the Trinity House took it out of their control."

DISTANCES.

The nautical or geographical mile or knot is the 21,600th of the earth's circumference, and is estimated to be about 6,087 feet, or 2,029 yards. It is roughly taken to be 1,000 fathoms (fathom = 6 feet), and hence a cable's length is the tenth part of a knot and equals 100 fathoms.

A more scientific definition of a knot is the 60th of a mean degree of the earth's circumference, and is equal to 6,076·818 feet, or 2,025·6 yards.

The knot is to the statute mile as 15 to 13. The distance from Whitby to the Naze of Norway is about 111 leagues, and about N.E. true. The nearest part of Norway to Whitby is Midbrodo light.

The Dogger Bank is about 76 knots N.E. by E.¾E. true from Whitby at its nearest part. It extends Southward nearly parallel with the land to about off the Spurn 64 knots, and stretches 120 knots E. by N.¾N. It narrows from N. to S. There are 7 to 17 fathoms of water over it.

Whitby to the Dudgeon light ...	... 92	knots.
Whitby to Flamboro' Head ...	... 28	,,
Whitby to Scarborough ...	... 14½	,,
Whitby Rock Buoy to the Tyne	... 42	,,

Whitby is said to be one of two places only on the East Coast of England where the sun can be seen to rise and set apparently out of and into the sea, on the same day, the other place being Cromer.

On the 21st June the sun sets a little West of North West from the pier end.

GENERAL SKETCH OF WHITBY AS A SHIP-OWNING PORT.

In the year 1700 the number of vessels owned here was 130, two or three of them of 20 keels (400 tons) or more. About the middle of the 18th century they were over 200 in number, and in 1790 there were 260 vessels of 48,647 tons combined. After this time there was an apparent falling off both in number and tonnage for many years, the reason being that several of the larger vessels, adapted to the transport service, were, for the convenience of the owners, registered at London. But in 1828 Whitby was well to the front, for in a complete list of the shipping of the United Kingdom for that year, procured and published by the authority of Parliament, Whitby, in the amount of tonnage registered at the Custom House—that is, owned in the port and neighbourhood—ranked as the seventh in England, and the eighth in the United Kingdom. The only English ports exceeding it in registered tonnage were London, Newcastle, Liverpool, Sunderland, Hull, and Whitehaven; no Irish port came near it, and of the Scottish ports Aberdeen alone exceeded it by the trivial amount of 500 tons. Whitby then owned 280 vessels of 46,086 tons gross.

After this, for a few years, the shipping interests of Whitby were again on the decline, national affairs being in a disturbed condition. It was at this time, 1828 to 1834, that several Whitby ships sailed from the port direct for the St. Lawrence, carrying emigrants from the district. The "Crown" in 1828; the "Intrepid," the "Addison," "Gulnare," "Earl Stanhope," and "Jackson" in 1830; the "Ida" and the "King William" in 1831; the "Columbus" in 1832; and the "Hindoo" in 1834. (All these vessels will be found in these records.)

About 1835 a revival set in, and in 1850 the number of vessels had increased to 390 of 62,000 tons. About 1866 the sailing vessels of Whitby reached their highest point in numbers and tonnage. The "Shipping Gazette" of Jan. 1st, 1866, gives the following statement about them:—51 vessels under 50 tons, and of 1,801 tons register; 360 above 50 tons and of 73,058 register; and 3 steamers of 558 tons aggregate; together 414 vessels registering 75,417 tons.

About 1870 the wooden ships began to decline before the increasing competition of iron and steam, and by the end of the 19th century the wooden sailing ships were nearly extinct at this port, only some smaller coasters remaining. So these beautiful and picturesque structures are gradually passing away, and with them the wonderful old romance of the sea.

"*Tempora mutantur.*" "*Vestigia nulla retrorsum.*"

Nevertheless Whitby does not disappear as a ship-owning port—far from it—but the conditions are changed. According to "Turnbull's Shipping Register" (published at Newcastle, Jan. 1st, 1901) the steamers registered here had increased from the three of 1866 to 75, their net register ranging from 722 to 2,409 each, and their combined tonnage amounting to 112,449, with a carrying capacity of nearly

300,000 tons. Much Whitby capital is invested in steamers registered at other ports, and many steamers registered here are partly owned elsewhere. But all this is outside of these records. Whitby, although continuing to increase its shipping after 1828, never afterwards held the same forward position, compared with the other ports of the United Kingdom, they having increased in a much greater ratio, and especially so since the advent of steam.

Our harbour has a deserted appearance, whilst our steamers trade to and from all parts of the world.

"*Fuimus et Sumus.*"

OUTLINES AND REMINISCENCES OF THE DAYS OF THE WOODEN SAILING SHIPS.

Great numbers of the smaller craft owned at Whitby were employed in the coasting and coal trades, which found occupation for immense fleets from other ports as well as from Whitby. Mr. James Rayment, a Whitby captain, was, about 1850, in one of some 800 arriving in the Thames on one tide. Six hundred vessels have been seen to pass Whitby on one day. I myself have counted 400 in sight at one time from our cliffs.

Far greater numbers still have been known to take shelter in Yarmouth Roads and Bridlington Bay from contrary or stormy winds.

In these days of steamers a 5,000 ton vessel will have perhaps 25 men for a crew, but 5,000 tons carried by the old sailing coasters required some 30 vessels and about 200 men.

The larger Whitby vessels traded to the Baltic, Mediterranean, and America, the largest of all going to India, China and Australia. Several of these latter were licensed Indiamen, carrying passengers as well as cargo, and were known as strong, comfortable vessels, though, of course, much smaller than the regular East India Company's ships. They all carried guns, and had to be prepared to resist the pirates in the China seas.

Through the period (1753 to 1837) when the whale fishery was carried on from Whitby, many large vessels were employed in that business. (Further details of this in the section on the whale fishery.)

During the long French war, and the American war, numbers of Whitby owned ships were hired by the Government for the transport service, no vessels of that day being better adapted for it. In a register of shipping for 1814 there are 92 Whitby built ships then in the service The Admiralty also bought several large vessels, built here, for the Navy.

It was the custom for the vessels in the Baltic, and also for some in the coasting trade, to "lie up" during the winter months. Mr. Geo. Milburn, lately Lloyds' agent at Whitby, stated that the Insurance Clubs would not take the risk between December 20th and March 1st without a considerably enhanced premium, even for one day. This custom caused our harbour, at those times, to appear a "forest of masts." Opportunity was taken during this time of enforced idleness to repair hulls, sails, rigging, &c. It also gave the town a lively appearance from the number of young sailors passing their spare time in the

streets and on the quay and pier. These sailor lads being full of high spirits indulged in somewhat unruly pranks, especially about Christmas-time, but their presence about the town incited the younger lads to become sailors, and at a very early age. It was quite common for boys to be apprenticed at 12 or 13 years of age, and some were younger still, and they were usually bound for a period of seven years.

Then some weeks before the 1st March the ships had to be got ready for sea, sails bent, and water and provisions

filled up. Numbers of old bulls were brought in from the country to be killed and salted down to supply the sailors' beef casks. These matters gave active employment all round, and about the 1st March, if the weather were favourable, there was a general unmooring and putting to sea to proceed to the loading ports to begin the year's work.

Sometimes on account of bad weather, or contrary winds, there would be many vessels detained in the harbour. They were moored in "tiers" to posts and buoys, and to "dolphins," so close together at times that it was a common saying, "you could have walked across them from one side of the harbour to the other." Even below bridge four or five small vessels were occasionally moored between the bridge and the Custom House.

Owing to the immense numbers of coasters constantly in the North Sea, a sudden gale arising always resulted in many wrecks and casualties all along the sea board. Whitby had its full share of these, and "ship ashore" was a frequent and rousing cry, whether by day or night, to the inhabitants, who rapidly gathered in crowds. Very frequent also was the

news of the loss of some member of a sea-faring family, or of the whole crew of a vessel. But the very fact of the dangers of the North Sea from gales, sand banks, and strong currents, among which our sailors mostly spent their early years, or perhaps their whole lives, produced such splendid seamen that they became known as the most capable, reliable, and hardy of our British marine.

The industries of Whitby were mostly dependent on or connected with the shipping, such as block and mast making, boat building, sail making, and rope manufacturing. Much timber was imported from the coast, the Baltic, and from America, for the ship-building and repairing. Whitby, being isolated by its environment of sea and moorland, was prevented from doing much trade with inland towns, so the exports were comparatively small. After the railway to Pickering (worked by horse power) was opened for traffic in 1836, a considerable amount of ironstone was sent away from here. It was a general practice of the smaller colliers and coasters, on their passage to the North, to call in at Whitby, and take whole or part cargoes of ironstone to the Northern ports. Freestone and alum were also exported. But as time went on the ironstone mines became more difficult to work, richer deposits were found nearer to the coal fields, and railway communication being greatly extended, this export ceased. Somewhat similar conditions affected the export of freestone. As to the alum, a new and cheaper method of manufacturing it superseded the very costly method previously adopted in this district, the last load of alum being sent away from Sandsend about 1867.

In the palmy days of the wooden sailing vessels the graving docks on both sides of the river were seldom unoccupied, whilst there were usually several vessels in the harbour waiting "turns" for dry dock repairs. Before the ships went into the docks, the ballast, generally chalk when they were from the Thames, was discharged into lighters till they came out, when it was re-shipped. At the Church Street docks the vessels' massive bows and figure heads standing out over the palings with the bowsprits and jibbooms stretching across the street were always an interesting sight, and the sound of the carpenter's calking hammers was a local characteristic. The ship carpenters and others worked from 6 a.m. to 6 p.m., the Town Hall bell ringing at those times for them to begin and finish the working day. When leaving work they took home as much firewood as they could carry under an arm. One or two large vessels arrived each year from the St. Lawrence with heavy timber, bowsprit and mast pieces. The deck cargoes were often partly or wholly discharged in the "roads," there not being sufficient water on the bar for these larger vessels to enter the port with all their

cargo. They had two bow ports, one in each bow, the higher one for discharging the timber from the "'tween decks," and the lower one for discharging from the main hold. The timber was rafted under the ship's bows. When hauling it out the sailors made use of a "chanty" so as to pull all together.

THE BUILDERS OF THE WOODEN SAILING VESSELS AT WHITBY, AND THEIR SHIP-YARDS.

Ship-building has been carried on at Whitby from time immemorial, though formerly the vessels were small. It was not till the harbour began to be improved through the revenues provided by the Acts of Parliament already referred to that regular ship-yards were formea, and ships of considerable size were built.

1. The earliest of these was commenced by a Mr. Jarvis Coates, whose name first appears in the rate book in 1697. In the Whitby registers there is a ship of the name of "William and Jane," built at Whitby in 1717. This ship must have been built by him, but he may have built others previously. The vessel was 237 tons, three masts, and 92 feet in length by 25 beam. The ship-yard was at a place formerly called the "Walker Sands," adjoining Bagdale Beck, which was then often named the Slike. The beck was open up the valley then, and cobles have taken grain, at high tide, as far up as the brewery, which was formerly above the present old Bagdale Hall.

Mr. Jarvis Coates died in the year 1739. His second son, Benjamin Coates, succeeded him. He died in 1756.

According to Dr. Young this yard "was divided about the year 1763," and Mr. Thos. Hutchinson began building in the North part. He erected the residence adjoining—now occupied by the station master. After he gave up business Mr. Robt. Barry was the next occupier of this part. The first vessel in the Whitby registers as built by John and Francis Barry, shipwrights, and Robt. Barry, gentleman, is in 1787; but they may have built vessels before this.

Mr. Robt. Barry was born in 1719 and died Jan. 20th, 1793. His son, John Barry, who continued the ship-building, was born in 1763, and died May 24th, 1826. His son, Robert Barry, succeeded him; but in 1830, shipping being much depressed and ship-building unprofitable, he gave up business. In 1845 the York and North Midland Railway Co., having bought the Horse Railway from Whitby to Pickering and extending their system to Whitby, bought this yard and built there the station and made approaches thereto.

The Southern part of Mr. Coates' ship-yard was taken possession of by Mr. Henry Barrick. The first mention of his name as a ship-builder in the Whitby registers is in 1786, but he also may have built ships before this.

Mr. Thos. Barrick succeeded him, and died May 1st,

1827, aged 57. His son Henry continued the ship-building; but the York and North Midland Railway Co. bought part of his yard, as well as the whole of Mr. Barry's, as already stated. He continued building in the remaining portion, with one "slip," and the dry dock for repairing, which had been constructed by Mr. Thos. Barrick in 1812. Both these premises formerly had each several building "slips." Mr. Henry Barrick finally gave up business in 1866, being quite blind. So this oldest ship-building yard was abandoned.

The N.E.R. Co., having bought this land in 1865, they afterwards filled in the dry dock and entirely obliterated all signs of the ship-yard.

2. A second ship-building yard was commenced by the eldest son of Mr. Jarvis Coates, whose name was also Jarvis, and appears in the rate book in 1717. The date of his commencing work is not known, nor how long he continued; he became a bankrupt. The situation of this yard was further up the river than the first one. The present Goods Station is upon part of its site. Dr. Young says that Mr. Thos. Fishburn, whose first mention in the rate book is in 1742, took possession of this yard about 1748, and that he bought it about 1759. He built Esk House as a residence, and a dry dock at Boghall in 1757. He had previously built one close to his ship-yard, but when it was nearly completed, it sank down in one night, as the foundation was on soft ground. His son, Thos. Fishburn, succeeded, with whom Mr. Thos. Brodrick was partner. The first vessel in the registers built by them is in August, 1795, those before being built by Mr. Thomas Fishburn alone; he died February 24th, 1826, aged 72; and Mr. Brodrick died April 7th, 1829, aged 63; and in 1830 the yard was closed. The terminus of the Whitby and Pickering Railway being in these premises, the office of Messrs. Fishburn and Brodrick became that of the Railway Company in 1836, and then in 1845 the York and North Midland Railway absorbed and obliterated this ship-yard also. The dry dock was not filled in until 1902, as it was held on lease till then by Messrs. Turnbull and Son, ship-builders.

The firm of Fishburn and Brodrick built many large vessels both for local owners and for other ports. The "Esk," built in 1781, is said to be the largest wooden sailing vessel ever built at Whitby. The "Cullandsgrove," built in 1802, was another large ship. They also built three of the vessels selected by, but not specially built for, Capt. Cook for his historical voyages.

3. According to Dr. Young it was about the year 1730 when a Dock Company was formed at Whitby. The premises included a considerable extent of ground on the East side of the river, extending from the foot of Green Lane to the opening called Boyes' Staith, commonly known as "Abraham's Bosom." It was in four shares held by William Barker, John Holt, John Reynolds, and John Watson; but Mr. Watson's share was obtained soon after by Mr. John Kildill. In 1816 the three shares first mentioned were owned by Messrs. Peter Barker, Robt. Campion, and William Reynolds; the share of Mr. Kildill by Messrs. G. J. and N. Langborne and Mr. Jameson. The Company built a double dry dock in 1734, and a single one later. There were also ship-building slips at each end of the premises. There is no mention in the registers of any vessels built by the Company. But in 1790 there is a vessel built by Reynolds and Co., and in 1792 and 1796 others by Messrs. William Reynolds and Wm. Holt. These were perhaps built in the Company's premises. And from 1804 to 1819 there are vessels built by Messrs. Holt and Richardson, who, according to Dr. Young, were the occupiers of the Company's yard in 1816. From 1828 to 1865 vessels were built there by Messrs. Henry and George Barrick, when they unfortunately became bankrupt. During some years previous to 1829 Mr. Peter Cato occupied the Northern part of this ship-yard, opposite to Saltpan Well. He was accidentally killed by falling over the quay into a lighter. He died July 29th, 1829, aged 54. In 1861 three shares of the Dock Company were held by Messrs. Henry and George Barrick, and the fourth by the Rev. John Thos. Barker. On February 24th, 1862, this latter share

was purchased by Messrs. Smales Bros. The portion bought by them is at the North end of the premises, and included the single dry dock, now filled in. They built here—1866-1871—three vessels, the last two composite, *i.e.*, iron frame with wood planking. The "Monkshaven," launched 1871, was the last "sea-going" sailing vessel built at Whitby. Many small craft, fishing boats, &c., were built at Whitby after this, but they do not come under this description. The remaining portion of the Dock Company's premises was afterwards bought by the "Whitby and Robin Hood's Bay Ship-building and Graving Dock Co., Ltd.," who built several smacks. The Urban Council now own this part, and have built there an Electric Power Station.

So ends this ship-building yard.

4. Another yard was begun after this by a Mr. William Coulson, from Scarborough. It was above Spital Bridge, and is now known as the Whitehall Ship-yard. There are no records of the vessels built there previous to 1790, the Whitby registers not giving the builders' name before that date. The first name is Ingram Eskdale; later Messrs. Eskdale, Smales and Cato; Messrs. W. S. Chapman and Co.; Mr. Robt. Campion; and in February, 1842, Messrs. J. and W. Campion, who were then the builders, unhappily became bankrupt. In 1851 Messrs. T. Turnbull and Sons became the owners of this property, and built wooden ships there till 1870. After this time they built iron steamers. A dry dock built in the yard by Mr. R. Campion in 1818 was filled in after the period of these records.

5. About the year 1760 a Mr. Wm. Simpson began a building yard on the West side of the river, on land apparently gained from the harbour, and built a dry dock there. "It appears," says Dr. Young, "that his father had built a dock on the East side of the river, near the house of Mr. Chapman in Church Street, about the year 1755, but the ground being spongy, it could not be kept dry, and it was, therefore, after a few years, abandoned and filled up, the materials being taken to build the dock on the West side,"

as above. Mr. Simpson was followed by a Mr. Wm. Hustler, and he by Messrs. Langborne. In 1774 they built the ship "Diligence" for Mr. Herbert, of Scarbro', which vessel was bought by the Government to accompany the "Resolution" in Capt. Cook's third voyage. It was re-named "Discovery." Messrs. Langborne occupied this yard till 1837. In 1838 Mr. Wm. Hobkirk began work in this yard, but the dry dock was in the occupation of Mr. Henry Barrick. After the retirement of Mr. W. Hobkirk in 1850, his son Thomas continued the building till 1862, when he became a bankrupt. Soon after this the N.E. Railway Co. bought the whole of these premises, filled in the dock, and the yard, as such, disappeared.

The above were the principal ship-building yards at Whitby.

In 1800 Mr. Jonathan Lacey commenced building vessels below Larpool. He gave up in 1803. Mr. John Spencelayh afterwards occupied this place; vessels are in the registers as built by him from 1819 to 1827. Mr. T. Turnbull afterwards—1840 to 1844—built six ships in the same yard before he removed to the Whitehall premises as before stated.

Mr. James Wake built some small vessels, not far from Mr. Lacey's yard, 1802 to 1806; he then relinquished it.

Mr. Gideon Smales built a brig in 1816 above the oil house at Boghall.

Many other places about the harbour were used for a time for building small craft. Mr. Thos. Hutchinson occupied the place where the Angel Inn yard now stands before he removed, as already stated, to Mr. Coates' yard in 1763. Even below bridge small vessels were built. One place was behind the Custom House, whence they were launched along the sands, which then occupied the back of Sandgate.

There were many other builders of small sailing craft and cobles, &c., at Whitby as well as those already mentioned :—

Falkingbridge, Thos. Coates, Wm. Webster, Marshall Copley, John Skelton, Robt. Marshall, Thos. Newbitt, Thos. Gale, Valentine Pinkney, Mark Dring, Robt. Holmes, &c.

ILLUSTRATIONS.

Ship.

Sailing vessels were described by the style of their rigging. The name "ship" did not mean any vessel, but one of a particular rig—always a three-masted vessel, with yards on each mast, or in other words "square rigged."

Barque.

Square rigged foremast and mainmast, with fore and aft rigged mizzenmast.

Brig.
Two masts only, both square rigged.

Brigantine.
Two masts, one only square rigged.

Schooner.

Similar to Brigantine, but with small structural differences.

CATALOGUE OF THE SAILING VESSELS OF WHITBY.

In Three Sections.

SECTION I. covers the period from 1717 to 1789, and includes vessels built and owned here; built here but owned elsewhere; and owned here but built elsewhere. It is alphabetically arranged to first two letters.

SECTION II. contains vessels built at Whitby, and their builders, for both local owners and for other ports. Chronologically arranged from 1790 to 1871, with an alphabetical index at the end.

SECTION III. List of vessels owned at Whitby, but not built here, from 1790 to 1900.

EXPLANATIONS.

The following catalogue of vessels is arranged as under.

1. Name of vessel — Achilles.
2. The vessel's rig — Bn.—Brigantine.
3. The registered tonnage — 180.
4. Where and when built — bt. Wy.—built at Whitby—1764
5. Owners or owner — ow, or owner.

All vessels were owned in 64 shares, therefore the figures, where given, after the owner's name indicate the number of 64ths held by him.

ABBREVIATIONS.

S., Ship. Bk., Barque. Bg. Brig. Bn., Brigantine. Sch., Schooner. Slp., Sloop. Bqtn., Barquentine. Lug., Lugger. Smk., Smack. Reg., Registered. Lad., Launched. Capt., Captain. M.M. or m.m., Master Mariner. Sq. st., Square stern. Bd., Builder. Voy., Voyage. Bt. Built. Wy., Whitby. Ports spelt without vowels, as Lndn.—London.

FIRST SECTION.

During this period exact particulars are given when possible, and when not the earliest date when a vessel is mentioned is stated, and any known particulars or matters of interest connected with it.

ACHILLES.—Bn.; 180; bt. Wy. 1764; Owner, Thos. Barker; Owners later, T. B. Kilton, m.m., Matthew Storm and Jn. Chapman. Sold to Sndld., July, 1793.

ACTIVE.—Slp.; 59; bt. Wy. 1785; Owner, Jn. Anderson and Co. Captured by enemy, 1800.

ACTIVE.—Bn.; 240; bt. Wy. 1786; Owner, James Harrison; two masts, 91 by 25. Lost after 1804.

ACTIVE.—Slp.; 42; bt. Stcktn., 1781; Owner, Wm. Weatherill, Staithes. Reg. Sndld., 1790.

ACORN.—Sq st. S.; 276; bt. Wy. 1787; Owners, Levi. Wm. and Elisha Preston, of Sneaton; Reg. Lndn. after 1796.

ADVENTURE.—S.; Owner, Benj. Chapman, 1747. Lost at sea, 1763.

ADVENTURE.—S.; Owner, Henry Clark, 1750; Mate, Miles Conyers. Lost, 1755.

ADVENTURE.—S.; Owner, Wm. Swales, first mention, 1772.

ADVENTURE.—Bg.; 110; bt. Wy. 1783; Owner, Lawson Fleck.

ADVENTURE.—In 1770 a vessel was built at Wy. by Mr. Thos. Fishburn for Mr. Wm. Hamond, of Hull. It was bought by the Government as a consort to the "Resolution" for Capt. Cook's second voyage of discovery. It was named the "Adventure."

ADVENTURE.—Owner, 1785, Mr. Robt. Barry. Sold.

ADVENTURE.—Bk.; 251; bt Wy. 1785; Owners, Mr. Hy. Anderson, m.m., Jos. Barker and Peter Middleton; Registered at Hull March, 1795.

ADVENTURE.—S.; 369; bt. Wy. 1786; Owners, Jos. Clark, Isaac Stockton and Jn. Chapman; 103 by 29, Reg. Lndn., 1795. Lost.

ADDISON.—Owners, 1769-1772, Jn. Addison and Co.; a Whaler; Owner later, Hy. W. Yeoman. Lost, 1783.

ADVICE.—1772; Owner, Richard Watkins.

ADVICE.—1772; Capt., Jn. Galilee.

ADVICE.—Bn.; 110; bt. Wy. 1783; Owner, Charles Noddings; 69 by 19; Pink Stern. Sold to Sndld., 1803.

ADVICE.—S.; 210; bt. Wy. 1784; Owners, Geo. Brodrick, m.m., and Thos. Brodrick, gentleman; three masts, 82 by 25; Reg. Hull May, 1799. Sailed 26th July, 1784.

ADAMANT.—S.; 222; bt. Hull 1759; Owner later, Thos. Scarth; to Greenland; Reg. Wy., 1787.

ADAM PARKER.—1781; Owner, John Addison.

ADMIRAL BARRINGTON.—1781; Owner, Thos. Hall.

ADMIRAL PAKENHAM.—Bg.; 200; bt. Wy. 1787.

AGREEMENT.—1756; Capt. Sam. Campion. Sold to Shlds.

AGENORIA.—S.; 260; bt. Wy. 1787; Owner, Henry Barrick, Shipwright, and Geo. Barrick, m.m. Sold to Lndn. about 1788. Owner, Jn. Clarkson, linen draper; Transport, 1814.

AISLABY.—Owner, Chris. Franklin, 1777.

AID.—S.; 327; bt. Wy. 1781; bd., Thos. Brodrick; Owners, Chris. and Wm. Richardson and Hy. Stonehouse. Rebuilt 1817 to 352 tons by Thos. and Hy. Barrick; Owners, 1818, Richard Kneeshaw and Henry Barrick; Owners, 1825, Hy. Barrick 16/64, Rd. Kneeshaw 16/64, Jn. Bedford, of Kirkheaton, 16/64, and Jn. Harrison, Wakefield, 16/64. Lost at Miramichi, 1834.

ALBION.—Owners, Dock Company. Lost, 1768.

ALBION.—Owner, Thos. Scarth, 1767. "About March, 1774, sailed from Hull the good ship 'Albion,' of Whitby (Thos. Porritt, master), for Nova Scotia, with woollens, drapery, linen, ironmongers' ware, &c., and 188 emigrants."—"Yorkshire Gazette," 1886. Owner later, Thos. Willis.

ALICIA.—Owner, William Reynolds, 1768.

ALFRED.—S.; 342; bt. Wy. 1783; Owners, Jos. and Thos. Holt and Chris. Richardson; Sq. st.; quarter deck and forecastle 101 by 28; Lad. Sept. 27th, 1783. Lost, 1788.

ALICE AND JANE.—Bk.; 241; bt. Wy. 1784; Owners, Wm. Skinner, senr. and junr., and Alice Skinner; three masts, 90 by 26. Sailed August, 1784. Captured by the enemy, 1796.

ALLIANCE.—S.; 256; bt. Wy. 1784; Owner, Sam. Galilee.

AMITY.—Bt. Wy. 1753; Capt. and Owner, Robt. Chapman.

AMITY.—1764; Owner, Wm. Frankland, Staithes.

AMITY.—Capt., Thos. Hall.

AMPHITRITE.—Bg.; 229; bt. Wy. 1783; Sold; Transport in 1814.

ANN.—Owner, Ralph Dodsworth; first mention, 1747; to Greenland. Sold, 1762.

ANN.—Capt., Wm. Gaskin, 1756.

ANN.—Capt. Garbutt, Staithes. Lost at Sndld., 1762.

ANN.—Owner, Jn. Gibson, 1766.

ANN.—Slp.; 49; bt. Scrbr. 1765; Owner, North Avitt. Lost, 1799.

ANN.—Charles Jackson. New ship sailed 31st March, 1783.

ANN.—S.; 359; bt. Wy. 1779; Owners, Chris., Benj. and Wm. Harrison; 10 guns; 103 by 29. Sold to Lndn.

ANN.—Bg.; 123; bt. Wy. 1787; Owner, Wm. Usherwood; two masts; 68 by 20; Capt., Cornelius Usherwood; Owners, 1796, Stephen Brown, Wy., and Jn. and Ja. Burn, Sneaton.

ANN AND ELIZABETH.—Owner, Mr. Pressick, 1747. Sold, 1763.

ANN AND ELIZABETH.—S.; 323; bt. Wy. 1776; Owners, Chris., Ben. and Wm. Harrison; Reg. Nwcstl., 1795.

ANN AND MARY.—Bt. Wy. 1749; first mention, 1750; Dodsworth.

ANN AND MARY.—Owner, Thos. Harrison, 1751-6; later, Mr. Dent.

ANN AND DOROTHY.—Owner, Wm. Dobson, 1759. Sold.

ANTELOPE.—S.; 280; bt. Wy. 1757; Owners, Sam. and Chris. Pressick and Richard Moorsom; pink stern; quarter deck and forecastle; six guns; Transport in 1814; Reg. Nwcstl., 1835; Timber ship.

ANT.—259; bt. Wy. 1757.

ANATOLIA.—Bg.; 180; bt. Wy. 1789.

APOLLO.—Bk.; 327; bt. Wy. 1774; Owner, J. C. Coates; Owners, 1787, J. Chapman, Jn. and Jos. Holt; Quarter deck carried before mainmast; ten guns; Reg. de novo, 1797, for alteration of tonnage to 372. Destroyed in Basque Roads, 1809.

AQUILLON.—Bg.; 179; bt. Wy. 1788.

ARCHER.—S.; 275; bt. Wy. 1762; Capt., J. Hudson, 1765-7; pink st. Lost, 1796.

ARIEL.—Bk.; 331; bt. Wy. 1780; Owner, Henry Stonehouse; 100 by 28; later owners, Hy. Stonehouse, Chris. and Wm. Richardson. Sold to Sndld., 1796.

ARGO.—S.; 360; bt. Wy. 1774; Owner, Henry Clark, ropemaker; later owners, Thos. and Jos. Holt, and Chris. Richardson; Owner, 1801, Jos. Holt, J. C. Coates and Margaret Mellar, widow. Taken by the enemy.

ASELBY.—Capt., Jos. Allely; Owner, Wm. Noble; later owner, Mrs. Noble; first mention, 1747-9. Lost, 1758.

ASTREA.—Bk.; 286; bt. Scrbr. 1766; Owner, Thos. Chilton; six guns; later owners, John Mellar and Henry Clark; Reg. Nwcstl., April, 1795.

AUGUST.—Bn.; 64; bt. Wy. 1787; Owners, Geo. and Nath. Langborne. Sold to Stcktn., 1791.

AUGUST.—Owner, Mr. Carnaby.

AUTUMN.—Slp.; 59; bt. Wy. 1784; Owners, J. Atty and Robt. Farndale. Sold to Bstn., May, 1789.

AURORA.—S.; 300; bt. Wy. 1789; Owner, F. Easterby.

AURORA.—Bn.; 108; bt. Shlds. 1786; Owner, Cockerill Deighton. Sold to Fvrshm., 1790.

BARBARA.—Capt., Jackson Prudom. Stranded at Falmouth, 1752. Re-floated. Lost about 1756.

BAY PACKET.—Slp.; 43; bt. Sndld. 1775; Owner, Geo. Estill; later owner, Wm. Jowsey, 1786 (Agent to Saltwick Alum Works); Owners, 1794, Robt. Turnbull, m.m., and Wm. Clarkson, hardwareman.

BARRICK.—S.; 304; bt. Wy. 1786; Owner, Hy. Barrick, shipwright; three masts; 97 by 27; Transport in 1814.

BETTY.—Capt., Robt. Feard, 1747-9. Sold, 1753.

BENJAMIN'S CONCLUSION.—Owner, Benj. Coates, 1756-7.

BENJAMIN'S GOODWILL.—Capt., Jarvis Gowland. Sold, 1762.

BETSY.—Bg.; 283; bt. Wy. 1776; Owner, Hy. Dowsland; Lad. 15th July, 1776.

BETSY.—Bk.; 276; bt. Wy. 1778; Owners, Robt. Clark, Wm. Jackson and Francis Skinner; eight guns; Reg. Lndn., Nov., 1794.

BETTY.—Bn.; 250; bt. Wy. 1787; Owners, M. Cockerill and Benj. Gowland; two masts. Taken by the enemy.

BETSY.—Bg.; 158; bt. Wy. 1789; Owners, Wm. Oxley, m.m., Robt. Burbank and Hy. Barrick, shipwright. Sold.

BETSY AND SALLY.—New, 1777; Owner, Thos. Brodrick. Taken by the enemy.

BENJAMIN AND MARY.—Bk.; 330; bt. Nwcstl. 1782; Owners, Jn. and Ingram Chapman; Reg. Lndn. April, 1821.

BENJAMIN AND ELIZABETH.—Bk.; 278; bt. Wy., 1786; Owners, Benj. Gowland and Mich. Cockerill; Reg. Lndn. March, 1798.

BELLONA.—Owner, Chas. Jackson, 1775-80.

BELSAY.—Slp.; 13; bt. Stcktn. 1756; Owner, Wm. Bedlington. Lost.

BENJAMIN AND ANN.—1775-9; Owner, Benj. Harrison. Lost, 1782.

BIRD.—Owner, Henry Clark, 1754.

BLESSING.—1747-9; Owner, John Marshall, Staithes. Voyage to Lndn.

BLESSING.—Owner, Jn. Webster. Voyage to Cadiz. Lost, 1758.

BLESSING.—Owner, Geo. Skinner, 1751-6. Lost, 1762.

BLESSING.—Bn.; 53; bt. Sndld. 1786; Owner, Geo. Estill, R.H.Bay; Owner 1824, Wm. Estill. Lost, 1829.

BOREAS.—Bk.; 420; bt. Wy. 1783; Owner, Thos. Milner; quarter deck and forecastle; launched March; ten guns; 111 by 30. Sold to Nwcstl., 1791.

BONITO.—Sq. st.; Snow; 296; Owners, Jn. and Abel Chapman and Wakefield Simpson; bt. Wy. 1788; Capt. Cockburn. Lost at Anticosti, Oct., 1829.

BROTHERHOOD.—Owner, Jonth. Lacy, 1748-50. Voyage to Maryland.

BROTHERLY LOVE.—Owner, Thos. Ellerington, 1747-9.

BROTHERLY LOVE.—Owner, Matthew Wright, R.H. Bay, 1747-9; later, J. Pearson. Sold.

BROTHERLY LOVE. Capt., I. Woodhouse, 1751-6.

BROTHERLY LOVE.—Capt., Wm. Jefferson, 1765-7.

BROTHERLY LOVE.—Lug.; 48; bt. Staithes 1770; Owner, Brown. Broken up, 1803.

BROTHERLY LOVE'S INCREASE.—Owner, — Dent.

BRITAIN.—New ship, 1748; Owner, Hy. Clark. Sold, 1752. Transport, 1748-9.

BRITAIN OR BRITON.—Owner, Mark Dring, 1756-7.

BRITANNIA.—Capt., Wm. Coates, 1747-9.

BRITANNIA.—Capt., Paul Harrison. Sold, 1752.

BRITANNIA.—S.; 364; bt. Wy. 1781; Owners, Lacy Lotherington and Catherine, widow of Thos. L. and Jn. Lacy; deep waisted; ten guns; detained by the French; afterwards purchased by the Commissioners of the Navy; Reg. Lndn., 1796.

BROTHERS.—Slp.; 54; Leith, 1762; Owner, John Johnson, 1786. Lost.

BRITISH KING.—1767-8; Owner, Wm. Swales. To Greenland.

BRITISH QUEEN.—Bk.; 292; bt. Wy. 1785; Owners, Wm. Rymer, Geo. and Nath. Langborne, shipwrights; Reg. Nwcstl., Feb., 1800. Transport in 1814.

BROTHERS.—S.; 364; bt. Wy. 1775; Owners, Abel and Jn. Chapman, and Isaac Stockton; round stern. Lost, 1803, or after.

BROTHERS.—Owner, Anthony Ridley. Sandsend, 1782-5.

BROTHERS.—Bg.; 266; bt. Wy. 1788; Owners, Jos. and Wm. Barker; two masts; Reg. Nwcstl., 1800.

BROTHERS.—Slp.; 54; bt. Leith, 1762; Owner, J. Johnson; Reg. W., 1786.

BRILLIANT.—S.; 256; bt. Wy. 1760; Owner, Rd. Watkins and Robt. and Cornelius Clark, 1786; sq. st.; three masts. Lost.

BRIDGET.—Bg.; 256; bt. Wy. 1786.

CATHARINE.—1747-9; Capt., Miles Mewburn.

CATHARINE.—Bg.; 148; bt. Cork 1788; Owner, Thos. Chilton; Reg. Lndn., 1807.

CAROLINA.—1767; Owner, Jonas Brown.

CALYPSO.—Bn.; 298; bt. Wy. 1787; Owners, Dan. Stevens and Benjamin Gowland. Sold to Lndn. after 1803.

CAMPION.—S.; 297; bt. Wy. 1789; Owners, Harrison Chilton, m.m., Staithes, Sam. Campion and Jn. Campion; Owners, 1835, Thos. and Harrison Chilton; 96 by 27. Lost, June 22nd, 1841; Reg. Liverpool, 1837.

CENTURION.—S.; 333; bt. Wy. 1749; Owner, Cornelius Clark; Owners, 1786, Robt. Clark, T. Middleton and Isaac Hunter; three masts; 107 by 28. Lost after 1805. Cat built.

CERES.—S.; 288; bt. Wy. 1789; Transport in 1814.

CHARLES AND ELEANOR.—Capt., Ch. Gray, R.H. Bay. Sold, 1762-3.

CHRISTOPHER AND DOROTHY.—1756-7; Capt., Ch. Marshall, Staithes.

CHARMING JENNY.—Owner, Jn. Blackburn. Sold, 1759.

CHARLOTTE.—Capt., Richard Andrew, 1761-5. Lost, 1766.

CHARLOTTE.—Owner, Lord Dundas, 1765-7.

CHARLOTTE.—Owners, Dock Company.

CHARLOTTE.—S.; 199; bt. Sweden 1771; Owner, 1788, Jn. Ridley, Stow Brow, and Jn. Peacock, Wy.; three masts; 83 by 21. Lost, 1791.

CHARLOTTE.—S.; 216; bt. Grovehill 1783; Owner, Newark Andrews, Staithes; sq. st.; 83 by 25½; lengthened to 279 in 1790.

CHRISTOPHER.—Bk.; 282; bt. Wy. 1762; Owner, Jn. Clifton; later, Wm. Hustler; 14 guns; Reg. Lndn., 1801. Bought by Jn. Boyes, April, 1803, and Reg. Wy. Made a brig, 1804. Lost after 1812.

CHARLOTTE'S INCREASE.—New ship, 1780-1; Owner, Newark Andrews. Sold.

CHANCE.—S.; 326; bt. Wy. 1760; Owners, 1780, Wm. Swales and Co.; Owners, 1787, Jonathan Lacey, Jonathan Saunders and Jas. Atty. Lost, 1788.

CHANCE.—Owner, Ralph Strong, 1782-5.

CHANGEABLE.—Bk.; 235; bt. Wy. 1780; Owner, Thos. Porritt and Robt. Hunter, and Wm. Whitehous, Tallow Chandler; Launched March 22nd, 1780.

CHAPMAN.—S.; 558; bt. Wy. 1777; bd. Thos. Fishburn; Owner, Abel Chapman; Owner, 1851, King and Co., Lndn.; 116 by 33; Reg. Lndn. Launched 1776.

CHOLMLEY.—S.; 224; bt. Wy. 1788; Owner, Edward Cayley, attorney, Wy. Sold to Nwcstl., 1795. Wrecked near Bridlington, May, 1832.

CLEVELAND.—Owner, Wm. Sympson, 1747-9. Voyage to Dantzick. Sold, 1756.

CLEVELAND.—Owner, Richard Fenwick, 1772-6.

CLIFTON.—Capt., Jn. Cranston, 1761-5.

COMPANY.—Capt., Jos. Wright, R.H.Bay, 1749-51.

CONCLUSION.—Owner, Benj. Coates, 1756-7.

CONCORD.—Capt., Wm. Chapman, 1747-9; Transport, 1748-9.

CONCORD.—Capt., Chris. Ellis, 1747-9. Sold.

CONCORD.—S.; bt. Wy. 1779.

CONCORD.—S.; 380; bt. Wy. 1783; Owners, Robt. Chapman, m.m., John Chapman, gent., Wm. Chapman, sailmaker; pink st.; 105 by 30. Lost after 1794.

CONCORD.—Capt., Wm. Addison, 1749-51.

COMMERCE.—Owner, Jn. Yeoman, 1768-72.

COMMERCE.—Owner, Wm. Swales, 1782-5, New.; Owner later, Thos. Weatherill.

COMMERCE.—Slp.; 51; bt. Wy. 1783; Owners, Jas. Atty and Chris. Yeoman, 1786; Owner, 1813, Wm. Usher, Lofthouse; round st.

COMMERCE.—Owners, Messrs. Jn. Price and Co., 1789.

CONQUEST.—Capt., Nathan Pickering, 1756-7.

CONTENT.—Owner, Thos. Benson, 1747-9.

CONTENT.—Capt., Wm. Swales, 1758-61.

CONTENT.—S.; 332; bt. Wy. 1761; Owners, Walter Carr, Jas. Atty, and Jonathan Lacy, in 1787; Captured by the enemy, 1797.

CONTENT'S INCREASE.—S.; 288; bt. Wy. 1750; Owner, Thos. Benson; later owner, Ann, widow of Thos. Benson; Cat built; Pink st.; quarter deck and forecastle; Owners, 1792, Thos. Willis, Jn. Chapman, and Jas. Atty; Reg. Nwcstl., 1797.

CONSTANT FRIEND.—Owner, Dorothy Benson, 1747-9; Owner later, Wm. Benson; Capt., Robt. Chapman. Taken by the enemy.

CONSTANT MARY.—Capt., Richard Jackson, 1747-9; Transport, 1748-9.

CONSTANT BETTY.—Capt., A. Rickinson, R.H.Bay. Lost, 1758-9.

CONSTANT MATTHEW.—Owner, Taylor Storm, R.H. Bay, 1747-9.

CONSTANT ANN.—Slp.; 44; bt. Blythnook 1740; Owner, 1786, John Tulf; Reg. Wy., 1786; Owners, 1791, Jn. Cuthbert, cabinet maker, Jas. Hutchinson, stonemason, and Jas. Wake, lighterman. Lost, 1800.

CONSTANT JOHN.—Owner, Francis Easterby, 1747-9; Owner later, Geo Brodrick. Lost, 1763.

CONSTANT JANE.—Owner, Richard Jackson.

CONSTANT ANN.—Owner, North Avitt, 1777; Owner later, Wm. Taylerson.

CONSTANTINE.—Slp.; 57; bt. Wy. 1783; Owners, Lord Mulgrave and Jn. Addison; Launched Dec., 1783; Reg. Wy. 1786; Owner, 1815, Jn. Frank, Wy. Lost, April, 1815.

CUPID.—Slp.; 49; bt. S. Shlds. 1778; Owner, 1786, Jas. Farquharson; Reg. Wy. 1786; 63 tons in 1794; Owner, 1810, Lord Dundas. Broken up, 1819.

DARLING.—Owner, Jn. Jefferson, 1747-9.

DAIRY MAID.—Owner, Chas. Noddings, 1775-9.

DART.—Owners, Messrs. Swales and Co., 1780-1.

DART.—Bn.; 51; bt. Fishlake, 1781; Owners, Messrs. Atty and Co.; Reg. Wy. 1787; Owner, 1810, Thos. Keld; Reg. Scrbr., 1811.

DELIGHT.—Owner, Richard Moorsom, 1751-6; Owners, 1774, Thos. Scarth, Jn. Yeoman, and R. Moorsom. To Greenland.

DESIRE.—Capt., Wm. Blackburn, 1751-6. Lost, 1762.

DESIRE.—Capt., Thos. Galilee, 1772-6.

DESIRE.—Bn.; 81; bt. Wy. 1786; Bd., T. Barrick. Sold. Owner, 1787, Lawson Hesk, Redcar; Reg. Wy. Feb. 17th, 1795, from Dover, being sold there, 1793. Sold to Sndld. later.

DEPENDENCE.—Robt. Easterby, 1765-7.

DIAMOND.—Owner, Jn. Yeoman, 1747-9. Lost, 1766.

DIAMOND.—Owner, Sam. Campion, 1756-7.

DIANA.—Owner, Jos. Hunter, 1765-7.

DILIGENCE.—S.; 340; bt. Wy. 1748; Owners, Isaac Stockton, Jonth. Lacy and John Mellar, the two last ropemakers; 100 by 28; Cat built. Lost.

DILIGENCE.—Capt., Ch. Peacock, Lofthouse, 1749-51; Mate, Francis Emlington; A Seaman, Sam. Barry. Sold, 1757.

DILIGENCE.—Slp.; 48; bt. Wy. 1772; Owners, Alex. Bagwith, m.m., and Jn. Seaton, gentleman. In 1803, a Bn., 50 tons. Lost, March, 1824; Owner, Matthew Ord.

DILIGENCE.—S.; 295; bt. Wy. 1774; Bd., Geo. and Nath. Langborne; Owner, Wm. Herbert, Scrbr. Purchased by Government for Capt. Cook's third voyage as consort to the "Resolution," and renamed "Discovery."

DOLPHIN.—Owner and Capt., Will. Clark, 1747-9; Capt. later, Benj. Chapman; later, Geo. Brodrick, 1756. To Greenland, Capt. Thos. Cornforth. Docked at Wy., 1759.

DOLPHIN.—Capt., Wm. Watson, R.H.Bay, 1747-9.

DOLPHIN.—Owner, Jn. Yeoman, 1761-5.

DOVE.—Capt. Phatuell Harrison, R.H.Bay, 1747-9.

DOVE.—Bn.; 58; bt. S. Shlds. 1777; Owner, 1786, Jn. Sanderson, Staithes; Reg. Wy., 1786; Lengthened 1789 to Bn.; 92 tons; Owner, Dan. Cole. Sold.

DOROTHY.—Bn.; 64; bt. Scrbr. 1768; Owner, Ed. Turner, cabinet maker, 1787; Reg. Wy., 1787; Reg. Sndld., 1790.

DOROTHY.—Capt., Jn. Blackburn, 1761-5.

DOROTHY.—Owner, Francis Barry, 1780-1.

DOROTHY AND ESTHER.—Owner, Adam Boulby, 1751-6.

DOROTHY AND CATHARINE.—Owner, Robt. Galilee, 1765-7.

DORIS.—Bn.; 141; bt. Wy. 1789; Owner, Wm. White, m.m., and Jas. Atty; two masts. Sold.

DUKE OF RICHMOND.—Capt., Jn. Crow, 1747-9.

DUKE OF CORNWALL.—Capt., Jn. Stephenson, 1756-7. Sold.

DUKE.—Capt., Jn. Blackburn, 1751-6.

DUNDAS.—Owner, Lord Dundas, 1768-72. Sold to T. Williamson.

DUNDEE PACKET.—Slp.; 68; bt. Wy. 1787.

DUTIOUS.—Bn.; 103; bt. Lymmington 1765; Owner, 1786, Wm. Arnott; Reg. Wy. 1786. Lost after 1803.

EAGLE.—S.; 257; bt. Wy. 1778; Owners, Jn. Brignell and Mr. Pressick; 92 by 26. Sailed April 1st, 1779. Lost, 1789.

EAGLE.—S.; 310; bt. Wy. 1788; Owner, Jn. Brignell; Reg. Lndn., Nov., 1813.

EASTROW.—Owner, Thos. Adamson; Crew of three.

EARL FAUCONBERG.—S.; 331; bt. Wy. 1765; Owner, Henry W. Yeoman; sq. st.; three masts; 100 by 28; Capt. in 1791, Francis Agar. A Whaler. Sold to Grimsby about 1801.

EARL OF DERBY.—Owner in 1773, Jn. Harbinson.

Earl of Pembroke, 1764.

EARL OF PEMBROKE.—S.; 370; bt. Wy. 1764; Bd., Thos. Fishburn; Owner, Mr. Thos. Milner, of Whitby. Purchased by Government of Mr. Thos. Milner for Capt. Cook's first voyage to South Seas, and re-named "Endeavour." He sailed in July, 1768. The vessel had a crew of 84 seamen, and was armed with 10 carriage guns and 12 swivels.

ECONOMY.—Bn.; 108; bt. Wy. 1788; Owner, 1826, Richard Tindale; Reg. W., 1826, from Aldbro'; Reg. Sndld., 1830.

ECHO.—Bt. Wy. 1788; three masts; 74 by 24.

EDMOND.—Owner, Mrs. Pressick, Lythe, 1747-9.

ELIZABETH.—Owner, Miles Breckon, 1747-9; Capt., Martin Kildill. Lost, Oct. 6th, 1756, at Orfordness.

ELIZABETH.—Small; Capt., Francis Emlington, 1747-9.

ELIZABETH.—Small; Capt., Jn. Newton, 1747-9.

ELIZABETH.—Capt., Matthew Shipton, 1748-9. Sold, 1750.

ELIZABETH.—Owner, Benj. Ward, 1750; Transport, 1757.

ELIZABETH.—Capt., Thos. Shafto, 1756-7. Lost, 1762-3.

ELIZABETH.—New, 1765; Owner, Thos. Holt.

ELIZABETH.—S.; 321; bt. Wy. 1763-5; Owner, —. Egginton, 1814.

ELIZABETH.—Bk.; 300; bt. Wy. 1769; Owner, Chris. Pressick; Owners, 1787, Chris. Pressick, Sam. Pressick, and Robt. Swales; sq. st. Lost.

ELIZABETH.—Slp.; 51; bt. Wy. 1783; Owner, A. Hall. Lost after 1804.

ELIZABETH.—Slp.; 35; bt. Wy. 1786; Owners, Lord Mulgrave and Jn. Addison. Sailed April, 1786. Lost.

ELIZABETH.—Slp.; 37; bt. Stcktn. 1774; Owner, Wm. Douthwaite; Reg. Wy., 1786; Owner, 1790, Robt. Stephenson, Brotton. Lost after 1801.

ELIZABETH AND MARY.—Capt., Robt. Hutchinson, 1758-61.

ELIZABETH AND ANN.—S.; 292; bt. Wy. 1783; Owner, Michael Cockerill; sq. st.; three masts; two quarter windows; 96¾ by 27; Reg. Nwcstl., 1801.

ELIZA.—Thos. Hall, 1775-9.

ELIZA.—S.; 377; bt. Wy. 1782; Owner, Wm. Skinner; Capt., 1787, Roger Galilee. Sold 1798 to Commissioners for Transport Service.

ELEANORA.—Owner, Thos. Scarth, 1782. Lost.

EMPLOYMENT.—S.; bt. Wy. 1750; Owner, Isaac Scarth; 88 by 26.

EMMA.—Slp.; 63; bt. Wy. 1784; Owners, Messrs. Jackson, Danby and J. Ridley, of Stowe Brow. Launched May 18th, 1784. Lost, 1794.

ENDEAVOUR.—See "Earl of Pembroke."

ENDEAVOUR.—Capt., Robt. Harrison, 1747-9. Sold, 1749.

ENDEAVOUR.—Capt., Jos. Sleightholm, 1747-9. Sold, 1750.

ENDEAVOUR.—Capt., Jn. Moorsom, R.H.Bay. Sold, 1752.

ENDEAVOUR.—Owner, Mrs. Woodhouse. Sold, 1756.

ENDEAVOUR.—Capt., Wm. Blackburn, 1749-51. Sold, Sept., 1752.

ENDEAVOUR.—Bn.; 46; bt. Wy. 1773; Owner, Hy. Bennison; Reg. Sndld., 1795.

ENDEAVOUR.—Slp.; 52; bt. N. Shlds. 1776; Owner, Jn. Jackson; Owner, 1809, Isaac Salton, R.H.Bay. Lost.

ENDEAVOUR.—Slp.; 60; bt. Wy. 1784; Owners, Richard Gillson, R.H.Bay, Ed. Windle, and Thos. Strother, merchants, Pickering. Lost.

ENDEAVOUR.—Slp.; 58; bt. Stcktn. 1772; Owner, Lawson Hesk; Reg. Scrbr., 1787.

ENDEAVOUR.—Bn.; 47; bt. Wy. 1782; Owner, Hy. Boynton. Captured by the French, 1795.

ENCOURAGEMENT.—Bn.; 75; bt. Wy. 1787; Owners, Jn. and Anthony Twistleton, ropemakers. Sold.

EOLUS.—Capt., Thos. Milner, 1768-72.

ESK.—Owner, Mrs. Linskill, 1747-9; Owner later, Robt. Linskill. Voy. Dantzick.

ESK.—Owner, Wm. Coates, 1765-7; Capt., Jn. Thompson. To Greenland.

ESK.—S.; 629; bt. Wy. 1781; Bds., Fishburn and Brodrick; Owner, Wm. Leighton, Lndn.; 127 by 33; 44 guns, 9 and 6 pounders.

ESTHER.—Owner, Capt. H. Walker, 1747-9. Lost, 1749.

ESTHER.—S.; 1779; Owner, J. Clark.

ESSAY.—Bn.; 94; bt. Wy. 1770; Owners, Geo. Langborne and Co.; Owner, later, Wm. Rymer; later, Messrs. Dobson and Huntrods. Sold to Sndld., 1807.

EUROPEAN.—Capt., Benj. Hunter, 1749-51; Mate, J. Barry. Burned in Shields Harbour, Feb., 1764.

EXCHANGE.—Capt., Benj. Harrison, 1747-9. Lost, 1766-7.

EXCHANGE.—Owner or Capt., Thos. Jackson, R.H.B., 1747-9. Lost, 1750.

EXCHANGE.—Slp.; 65; bt. Wy. 1786; Owners, Hy. Walker Yeoman, and Co.; Pink st. Sold to Stcktn., 1790.

EXCHANGE'S INCREASE.—Capt., C. Harrison, 1758-61.

EXPERIMENT.—Slp.; 51; bt. Wy. 1767; Owner, Wm. Reed, m.m. Lost after 1790.

FAIR TRADER.—Owner, Robt. Linskill, 1751-6.

FAME.—Capt., Marshall Hill, 1751-6. Lost, 1769.

FAME.—S.; 318; bt. Scrbr. 1752; Owners, Jos. and Israel Hunter; 104 by 28. Rebuilt at Wy. in 1771. Other great repairs in 1781 and 1785. Reg. Wy. 1775-9. Lost, 1787.

FAME.—Slp.; bt. Wy. 1787.

FATHER'S GOODWILL.—Capt., Jn. Moorsom, 1756-7.

FAVOURITE.—Owner, Chris. Yeoman, 1774. Taken by the Americans when on passage from New York, Nov., 1776.

FAVOURITE.—Owner, Richard Bedlington, 1775-9.

FELL.—Owner, Chris. Richardson, 1749. Voy. to Maryland.

FIR TREE.—Owner, Richard King, 1749; Owner, 1750, Mrs. King.

FIDELITY.—Capt., Benj. Gowland, 1767-8.

FIRM.—Owner, Jn. Jackson, 1775-9.

FLY.—Slp.; Owners, Wy. Dock Co., 1756.

FLORA.—Owner, Jonas Brown, 1765. Voyages to Lisbon and America.

FLORA.—Slp.; 53; bt. Staithes, 1778; Owner, Wm. Weatherill, Staithes, 1786; bn. in 1791. Lost, 1797.

FLYING FISH.—Slp.; 58; bt. Wy. 1783; Owner, Hy. W. Yeoman; Lengthened in 1802 to Sch.; 89 tons; two boom courses; small topsails. Driven ashore near Filey, Nov., 1860. Total wreck.

FORTUNE.—Owner, Matthew Brown, 1747-9; Owner later, Jn. Webster. Sold, 1760.

FORTUNE.—Capt., C. Peacock, 1747-9.

FORTUNE.—Owner, Anthony Skinner, 1757; Owner later, Mrs. Skinner.

FOUR BROTHERS.—Owner, Jn. Galilee, 1747-9.

FOUR BROTHERS.—Owner, Thos. Dawson, Lythe, 1756-7.

FORTUNE AND PROVIDENCE.—Owner, Wm. Swales, 1758-61.

FORTITUDE.—S.; 313; bt. Wy. 1774; Owner, Wm. Benson. Lost, 1788.

FORTITUDE.—Owner, Robt. Barry; New ship May, 1779. Sold.

FOX.—Slp.; 55; bt. Stcktn. 1783; Owners, Messrs. Geo. Dodds and Co.; Reg. Wy. 1786. Lost.

FOUNTAIN.—S.; 317; bt. Wy. 1778.

FRANCIS AND JANE.—Capt., Jackson Kildill, 1747-9.

FRANCIS.—Capt., Thos. Kirk, 1756-7.

FREELOVE.—S.; 341; bt. Yrmth. 1746; Owner, Jn. Walker; Round st.; 106 by 27; Owners, 1786, Jn. Walker, N. Shlds. (ropemaker), Hy. Walker and Wakefield Simpson. August, 1792, sold to Abel Chapman and Hy. Simpson, Wy. To Greenland whale fishing and East Country voyages. Lost. In list of crew for Feb. 5th, 1747, there are ten servants or apprentices, one of whom is James Cook, age 19, of Marton, Great Ayton. His name is also in list of crew for June, 1748. The name is written "Jas. Cook." Captain, Jn. Jefferson; Mate, Robt. Watson, Horsgarth; Carpenter, Thos. Harwood, 23 years old.

FREE LOVE.—Capt., Richard Clark, 1758-61. Small.

FREE LOVE.—Capt., Jas. Morrow, R.H.Bay, 1765-7.

FREE LOVE.—S.; 329; bt. Wy. 1785; Transport in 1814.

FRIENDSHIP.—Owner, Jn. Walker; Capt., Jn. Waller. In list of crew for May, 1753, the mate is James Cook. Last entry as such, July, 1755. Lost, 1762-3.

FREEDOM.—Capt., Hy. Taylor. Lost, 1769.

FREEDOM.—Owner, Robt. Plumber, 1751-6.

FREEMASON.—Capt., Jn. Stonehouse, 1747-9.

FREE ENGLISHMAN.—Owner, Harland Wild, 1751-6. Lost, 1759.

FRIEND'S DESIRE.—Capt., Phil. Franklin, 1751-6. Lost, 1769.

FRIEND'S LOVE.—Capt., Robt. Barry, R.H.Bay, 1751-6. Lost, 1757.

FRIEND'S DESIRE.—Capt., Jn. Addison, 1751-6; Capt. later, Jn. Lotherington; afterwards Jn. Brodrick. Voy. to Virginia.

FREE BRITON.—S.; 336; bt. Wy. 1765; Owners, 1812, Messrs. Roxby and Co.

FREE BRITON.—Owner, Wakefield Simpson, 1780-1. Lost, 1787.

FRIENDSHIP.—Owner, Aaron Chapman, 1747-9.

FRIENDSHIP.—Capt., Geo. Richardson, R.H.Bay, 1747-9; Small. Parish boy from Randell. Sold 1769.

FRIENDSHIP.—Capt., Isaac Lovejoy, 1751-6. Lost, 1759.

FRIENDSHIP.—Capt., David Drummond, Sandsend, 1758-60. Lost, 1760.

FRIENDSHIP.—Owners, Greenland Co., 1776.

FRIENDSHIP.—Slp.; 55; bt. Wy. 1768; Owner, Matthew Allan, 1786. Lost.

FRIENDSHIP.—S.; 399; bt. Scrbr. 1758; Owners, Messrs. Wm. Swales, James Atty and Jonathan Saunders, 1787; Round st.; Reg. Wy., 1787. Lost, 1790.

FRIENDSHIP.—Bn.; 230; bt. Scrbr. 1783; Owners, Jn. Dale and Jn. Chapman; Reg. Lndn., 1807.

FRIENDSHIP.—Bn.; 131; bt. Fishlake 1762; Owner, Wm. White, 1787. Sold to Nwcstl., 1789.

FRIENDSHIP.—Lug.; 45; bt. Scrbr. 1770; Owner, W. Bedlington, 1787. Later a slp. with launching bowsprit. Owner, March, 1824, Wm. Tyreman. Lost after 1825.

FRIENDSHIP.—Bg.; 111; bt. Wy. 1784.

FRIENDSHIP.—Owner, Wm. Addison, Staithes, 1780.

FRIENDSHIP.—Owners, Messrs. Langborne and Co., 1789.

FRIEND'S LOVE.—Owner, Ingram Chapman, 1747-9.

FRIEND'S LOVE.—Robt. Barry, R.H.Bay, 1749-51. Lost, 1758.

FRIEND'S GLORY.—Owner and Capt., Thos. Milner; Transport in 1748. Taken by the enemy.

FRIEND'S ASSISTANCE.—Owner, Robt. Thompson, 1747-9.

FRIEND'S INCREASE.—Capt., Wm. Walker; New ship, 1747-9. Lost, 1750.

FRIEND'S ADVENTURE.—Owner and Capt., Solomon Chapman, 1747-9; Transport, 1748-9.

FRIEND'S ADVICE.—Charles Gray, R.H.Bay, 1765-7.

FRIEND'S GOODWILL.—Open boat; 37; bt. Scrbr. 1769; Owners, Peter Merry, Lythe, and Richard Scarth, Stanghowe; Reg. Wy., 1787.

FRIEND'S GOODWILL.—Bn.; 137; bt. New England 1759; Owner, 1780, Valentine Kitchingman; Later, Mary, widow of V. K.; Reg. Nwcstl., 1790.

FRIEND'S GOODWILL.—Bg.; 174; bt. Wy. 1786.

FRIEND'S GLORY.—Lug.; 45; bt. Staithes 1777; Owner, Geo. Marshall, 1788; Owner, 1796, Jn. Holdforth, Lofthouse; Owner, 1829, Chris. Harland, carpenter. Lost, 1836.

FRIENDS.—Bk.; 217; bt. Hull 1764; Owners, Benjamin Gowland and Co., 1775; Later, T. Jones; Reg. Nwcstl., 1787.

GARLAND.—Owners, Dock Company; Capt., James Blackhurn.

GENEROUS FRIEND.—Capt., Thos. Stephenson; New ship 1749. Sold, 1752.

GENEROUS FRIEND.—Owner, Jos. Marshall, R.H.Bay, 1751-6; Fishing boat.

GENEROUS FRIENDS.—Owner, Hy. Simpson, 1757.

GEORGE.—Owner and Capt., Geo. Skinner, 1761-5.

GEORGE.—Owner, Geo. Treuman, 1765-7.

GEORGE.—Owners, Messrs. Atty, 1780-1. Lost.

GEORGE.—Bk.; 252; bt. Scrbr. 1786; Owner, Richard Moorsom; sq. st. Lost, November, 1796.

GEORGE AND MARY.—Capt., Geo. Jackson, 1758-61.

GENERAL CARLETON.—Owner, Nat. Campion. Sailed 12th March, 1777.

GOOD INTENT.—Owner, James Reynolds, 1747-9.

GOOD INTENT.—Owner, Thos. Cropton, R.H.Bay, 1747-9.

GOOD INTENT.—Owner, Wm. Jackson, 1747-9. Sold, 1761.

GOOD INTENT.—Capt., Adam Parkinson, 1747-9. Lost, 1756.

GOOD INTENT.—Bg.; 160; bt. Wy. 1763; Owner, Robt. Cropton, m.m., R.H.Bay, and Jas. Atty; Reg. Sndld., 1794.

GOOD INTENT.—Owner, Mrs. Swales, 1747-9. Voy. to Rotterdam.

GOOD INTENT.—Capt., Richard Andrew, 1747-9.

GOOD INTENT.—Slp.; 56; bt. Wy. 1768; Owner, Wm. Calvert, Hinderwell; Lute st. In 1788 Bn., 77 tons. Lost, 1823.

GOOD INTENT.—Bn.; 69; bt. Wy. 1785; Owners, J. Rudd Cooper, J. Burdon and Co. Sold.

GOOD INTENT.—Capt., Ed. Adamson, 1751-6.

GOOD INTENT.—Capt., Jos. Grimshaw, 1751-6. Sold, 1752.

GOOD INTENT.—Owner, Benjamin Coates, 1756. Lost, 1756.

GOODWILL.—Owner, Newark Walker, 1747-9; Later, Mrs. Walker. Lost, 1757.

GOODWILL.—Owner, Thos. Knaggs, 1747-9.

GOODWILL.—Owner, Ingram Chapman, 1758-61.

GOOD AGREEMENT.—Owner, Harland Wild, 1756-7. Sold apparently to Dock Company.

GOOD DESIGN.—Slp.; 57; bt. Ipswich, 1736; Owner, W. Bedlington, 1786; Lute st. Sold to another port after 1787.

GOOD DESIGN.—Slp.; 64; bt. Wy. 1746; Owner, Richard Gillson, R.H.Bay, 1786; Owners, 1793, Jn. Thorne, Inn holder, and Thos. Coverdale, farmer. Lost, 1798.

GRACE.—Bk.; 258; bt. Wy. 1780; Owner, Robt. Burbank; Owners, 1787, Richard Burbank, Robt. Swales and Ch. Pressick. Captured by the French in Holland.

GREYHOUND.—Owner, Mrs. Allely, 1747; Transport in 1748. Lost, 1770.

HARWOOD.—Owner and Capt., Hy. Thompson, 1747-9; Later owner, Jos. Gibson.

HASGARTH.—Capt., Wm. Skinner, 1747-9.

HANNAH.—S.; 314; bt. Wy. 1751; Owner, Jn. Chapman; Owners, 1787, Jn. C. and Is. Stockton and I. Chapman; Cat built; Pink st. Lost.

HANNAH.—Owner, Jn. Galilee, 1751-6.

HANNAH.—S.; 279; bt. Wy. 1765; Owner, Jn. Seaton; sq. st.; Bk. later; Owners later, executors of late Hy. Linskill, of Shlds., 1786; Reg. Nwcstl. after 1806.

HANNAH.—Capt. and Owner, James Harrison, 1772-6. Lost, 1780, about.

HANNAH.—S.; 341; bt. Wy. 1760; Owner, Thos. Middleton; three masts; 102 by 28; Owners, 1786, T. Middleton, Jos. Barker, and Robt. Clark; Pink st.; raised quarter deck, poop and forecastle; Reg. Nwcstl., 1801.

HARPOONER.—S.; 341; bt. Wy. 1769; Owner, Chris. Richardson, Jos. and Thos. Holt in 1787; three masts; 104 by 27; Capt. in 1814, —. Simpson; Transport in 1814. Lost.

HARMONY.—Owner, Jn. Addison, 1760.

HARMONY.—S.; 270; bt. Wy. 1785; Owner, And. Easterby; three masts; 94 by 27; Quarter deck and poop; Reg. Lndn., 1802.

HAZARD.—Bn.; 63; bt. Lynn 1758; Owner, Ed. Huntrods, R.H.Bay, 1789. Lost, 1793.

HAPPY RETURN.—Bn.; 53; bt. Wy., 1765; Owners, 1787, Jn. Ayre and Alex. Bogue. Lost.

HAPPY RETURN.—W. Clark, Runswick, 1747-9.

HAPPY RETURN.—Jn. Hill, R.H.Bay. Lost, 1758.

HAPPY RETURN.—Jn. Kirton, 1756-7. Lost, 1759.

HAPPY RETURN.—Open boat; 49; Staithes, 1772; Reg. Wy. 1787; Owners, Wm. Ripley, Robt. Booth and Wm. Weatherill. Sold.

HAPPY RETURN'S INCREASE.—Owner, Geo. Hill, 1780-1.

HAPPY ENTRANCE.—Owner, Ed. Wood, Rnswck., 1765-7.

HECKINGTON.—Slp.; 49; bt. Fishlake 1765; Owner, Jn. Ridley, Stow Brow, 1786. Lost after 1832.

HENRIETTA.—S.; 251; bt. Wy. 1764; Owner, Nicholas Piper, Pickering, 1787; Capt., 1793, Will. Scoresby; in 1797, J. Kearsley. To Greenland. Reg. Aberdeen, Feb., 1820.

HENRY AND MARY.—Owner, Capt. H. Walker, 1747-9; Capt., Richard Woodhouse. To Greenland, 1753. Owner, 1752, Jn. Yeoman; Capt. James Todd. Lost apparently Oct., 1757.

HENRY AND ANN.—Owner, Jos. Gill, 1751-6.

HENRY AND ANN.—Owner, Dan. Yeoman; New ship, 1770-2.

HENRY AND ELIZABETH.—Bg.; 147; bt. Wy. 1788.

HENRY AND JOHN.—Jn. Williamson, 1756-7.

HENRY AND JOHN.—Owner, Jn. Yeoman; Capt., Jas. Todd; New ship, 1757-8. To Greenland, 1758. Paid muster roll Nov. 13th, 1758, to July 12th.

HENRY AND ESTHER.—Owner, Jn. Yeoman, 1765-7; Capt., Robt. Walker.

HENRY.—Will. Doughty, 1747-9.

HENRY.—Owner, Jn. Yeoman, 1756-7; Capt., Geo. Brodrick.

HENRY.—Owner, Wm. Linskill, 1756-7. Lost, 1778.

HENRY.—Owner, Wm. Linskill; New, 1766.

HENRY.—Bk.; 289; bt. Wy. 1776; Owner, James Yeoman. Sailed 17th Sept., 1776. 95 by 27; Owners, 1787, Wm. Jackson, Ann, widow of late James Yeoman, and Hen. Walker Yeoman. "Aug. 15th, 1776, launched at Whitby a vessel of 450 tons burthen, named the 'Henry,' the property of Mr. Jas. Yeoman of Whitby."—Old History re-told, "Yorkshire Gazette," 1886. Owners, 1797, Michael Cockerill and Chris. Pressick; Reg. Nwcstl., Jan., 1799.

HENRY.—Owner, Will. Jackson, 1789.

HENRY.—Owners, Messrs. Cook and Strother, 1789.

HEBE.—S.; 261; bt. Wy. 1788. Sold to Lndn., Nov., 1788.

HEBE.—Bn.; 129; bt. Wy. 1789; Owners, Thos. Clarkson and James Atty; Reg. Lndn., 1794.

HERO.—Capt., Geo. Burton, Staithes, 1758. Lndn. to Virginia, 1759. Transport, 1758-9.

HERMIONE.—Jonas Brown, 1765-7. Two voyages to America.

HERCULES.—Owners, Greenland Co., 1772-6.

HEARTS OF OAK.—Owner, Michael Potts, 1775-9.

HILDA.—Bn.; 121; bt. Wy. 1787; Owners, Will. Rymer and Co.; Owners, James Watt, m.m., Geo. and Nat. Langborne. Lengthened in 1802-3 to 157 tons. Owner, 1798, Wilson Bedlington; in 1834, William Wilkinson, junr., 32, and Thos. Andrew, 32. Lost, Oct., 1843.

HOPEWELL.—Owner, Hen. Cockerill, 1747; Transport, 1748.

HOPEWELL.—Capt., Robt. Easton, 1747-9. Sold, 1752.

HOPEWELL.—Capt., Isaac Marwood, 1747-9.

HOPEWELL.—Capt., Jacob Hudson, 1751-6. Lost, 1765-6.

HOPEWELL.—Owner, Mark Noble, 1751-6.

HOPEWELL.—Owner or Capt., Francis Hall, 1751-6.

HOPEWELL.—Owner, Jon. Porritt, 1756-7; Capt., Robt. Stockton.

HOPEWELL.—Bt. Wy. about 1775; Bd., Robt. Barry. Sold.

HOPEWELL'S INCREASE.—Isaac Marwood, 1753-6.

HOPEWELL SUCCESS.—Open boat; 44; bt. Wy. 1773; Owners in 1787, Geo. Pyman, m.m., and Geo. Richardson. Sch. in 1802 of 50 tons. Owners, 1845, Eustace Cass, tailor, 32, and Geo. Bell, 32. Lost near Hrtpl., March, 1853.

HOPE.—Owner, Benj. Lotherington, 1747-9. To Virginia. Lost, 1756.

HOPE.—S.; 318; bt. Wy. 1768; Owner, W. Clark.

HOPE.—Bn.; 102; bt. Wy. 1783; Bds., Fishburn and Brodrick. Taken by the French.

HOPE.—Bt. Wy. 1784; Bd., Robt. Barry. Sold.

HOPE.—S.; 291; bt. Hull 1749; Owners, Thos. Scarth and Co. To Greenland. Lost, 1790.

HOPE.—Bn.; 84; bt. Wy. 1786; Bd. and Owner, Hen. Barrick, shipwright. Sold.

HOPE.—Bn.; 151; bt. Wy. 1788; Owner and Bd., Hen. Barrick, shipwright, and Geo. Barrick, m.m.; Reg. Ipswich, May, 1789.

HOUND.—Slp.; 50; bt. Wy. 1766; Owners, Robt. Clark and Co., 1768; Owner, 1786, Ed. Windle, Peak Alumworks; Lute st. Sold to Lynn, 1794.

HUNTER.—Capt., Will Hunter, 1758-61.

HUMILITY.—Capt., Percy Walker, 1765-7.

HUSBANDMAN.—Slp.; 37; bt. Sndld. 1755; Owners, R. Ware and Co.; Owners, 1786, Will. Pinder, m.m., and James Brownfield. Lost.

IBETSON.—Bg.; bt. Wy. 1786.

INDUSTRY.—Bn.; 72; bt. Sole 1742; Owner, 1786, W. Frank; Reg. Sndld. after 1798.

INDUSTRY.—Capt., Robt. Barry. Sold to Scrbr., 1747.

INDUSTRY.—Capt., Ch. Grey, R.H.B.

INDUSTRY.—Owner, Will. Blackburn, 1747-9. Voyage to S. Carolina. Lost.

INDUSTRY.—Richd. Boyes. Sold, 1778.

INTEGRITY.—Owner, Cuthbert Brodrick, 1777.

INDUSTRIOUS FARMER.—Boat; 46; Staithes 1768; Reg. Wy., 1787; Owner, Thos. Trowsdale, Ellerby, farmer.

ISABELLA AND MARY.—Capt., Will. Hall, 1747-9.

ISABELLA.—Owner, Jas. Atty; Capt., Ingram Hogg, 1749-50. Voyage to Malaga. Lost, 1756-7.

ISABELLA.—Capt., Will. Bennison, 1758-9. Lost, 1760.

ISABELLA.—S.; 211; bt. Wy. 1764; Owner, Thos. Willis; Owner later, Geo. Willis; sq. st. and forecastle; 84 by 24.6. Lost, Sept., 1792.

ISABELLA.—Bn.; 156; bt. Sndld., 1786; Owner, Geo. Clark, Runswick. Sold to Sndld., May, 1789.

ISABELLA.—Isaac Dobson, 1772-6.

ISABELLA.—Bn.; 78; bt. Wy. 1788; Owners, John Peacock and Co. Lost, 1802.

JAMES.—S.; 362; bt. Wy. 1779; Owners, James and Will. Atty, and Richd. Moorsom; Transport in 1814; Reg. Lndn., May, 1800; 104 by 29.

JAMES AND MARY.—S.; 285; bt. Yrmth. 1726; Owner, Jn. Yeoman, 1761-5; Cat built; Pink st.; Owner, 1786, Hen. Walker Yeoman. To Greenland.

JAMES AND WILLIAM.—187 tons; Owner, Geo. Atty. Launched 23rd March, 1773. Sold.

JAMES AND JOHN.—Owners, Messrs. Atty, 1778.

JANE.—Bn.; 83; Isle of Wight 1761; Owner, Dan. Cole, Staithes. Sold Sndld., 1792.

JANE.—Owner, Jn. Heath; Transport, 1748. Lost, 1756.

JANE.—Owner, Robt. Stephenson, 1747-9.

JANE.—Capt., Jn. Wright, 1747-9. Voyage to Finland.

JANE.—Owner, Matthew Wilson, 1749; Later, Marmaduke Wilson.

JANE.—Owner, Jn. Stonehouse, 1751-6. Sold, 1756.

JANE.—Owner, Hen. Clark, 1766.

JANE.—Bn.; 72; bt. Leith 1770; Owner, 1787, Robt. Bedlington, R.H.B. Lost, 1793.

JANE.—Owner, Israel Hunter. A new ship, 1776. Lost, 1778.

JANE.—Owner, Will. Rowntree. A new ship, 1776.

JANE.—Bk.; 319; bt. Wy. 1778; Owners, Will. and Robt. Swales. Captured by the enemy, 1796.

JANE.—S.; 346; bt. Wy. 1779; Owners, John Chapman, Isaac Stockton; Jn. Walker, of N. Shlds. in 1786; Pink st. Lost about 1799.

JANE.—Owner, Jn. Campion, jun. Launched 11th Oct., 1779.

JANE AND ANN.—Owner, Geo. Hill, 1747-9. Lost, 1757.

JANE AND SARAH.—Owner, Geo. Dickinson. Sold, 1750.

JANE AND ELIZABETH.—Nicholas Jackson, 1758-61.

JASON.—Bk.; 386; bt. Wy. 1779; Owners, Jos. and Thos. Holt and John Mellar; 107 by 30; 10 guns. Lost, 1790.

JANUS.—Bk.; 308; bt. Wy. 1782; Owners, James Harrison and Jos. Gill, m.m. Taken by the enemy.

JENNINGS.—Capt., Jn. Wilkinson, 1749-51. Large ship.

JENNY.—Thos. Scarth; 1st mention 1756-7. To Greenland, 1767.

JENNY.—Robt. Boulby, 1761-5. Lost.

JENNY.—237; bt. Wy. 1776.

JENNY.—Owners, Messrs. Swales and Atty. Sailed 2nd March, 1780.

JENNY'S ADVENTURE.—Owner, Will. Swales. To Greenland. Sold, 1786.

JOHN.—Bn.; 157; bt. Wy. 1745; Owner, 1787, Robt. Cropton, m.m., and Co., R.H.B.; Reg. Sndld., 1789.

JOHN.—Bn.; 94; Stcktn. 1764; Reg. Wy. 1786; Owner, Robt. Wilson, Runswick; Reg. Sndld., 1791.

JOHN.—Owner, Abel Chapman, 1747-9.

JOHN.—Owner, Jn. Holt and Co., 1747-9. Later, Moorsom Holt.

JOHN.—Owner, Jn. Truby, 1747-9. Lost, 1751.

JOHN.—Capt., Richd. Clark, 1765-7.

JOHN.—S.; 331; bt. Wy. 1783; Owners, Robt. and Will. Swales. Taken by the enemy.

JOHN.—Owner, Robt. Willson, Rnswck., 1785-9.

JOHN.—Boat; 44; Scrbr. 1774; Reg. W., 1787; Owner, Jn. Richardson, R.H.B. Lost, 1804.

JOHN AND MARY.—Owner, Jos. Gaskin, 1747-9; Capt., Geo. Galilee. Lost, 1762.

JOHN AND MARY.—Owner, Thos. Linskill, 1749; Transport, 1757-8.

JOHN AND MARY.—Isaac Newton, 1756-7. Sold, 1759.

JOHN AND MARY.—Will Backas, 1765-7. Small vessel.

JOHN AND MARY.—S.; 233; bt. Wy. 1770.

JOHN AND MARY.—Slp.; 52; S. Shields 1784; Reg. W., 1786; Owner, Jn. Granger, R.H.B.; Reg. Hull, 1794.

JOHN AND MARY.—Owner, Jn. Granger, Oct., 1784.

JOHN AND MARY.—Lug.; 41; Scrbr. 1769; Owner, Jn. Storm, R.H.B. Sold to Scrbr.

JOHN AND MARY.—Owner, Charles Noddings, 1782-5.

JOHN AND MARY.—S.; 303; bt. Wy. 1788.

JOHN AND MARY.—Lug.; 49; bt. Wy. 1788; Owner, Thos. Clark, Runswick. Lost, 1798, or after.

JOHN AND DOROTHY.—S.; 253; bt. Wy. 1728; Owner, J. Moxom, 1747-9; Owners, 1786, W. Brown, m.m., Thos. Clark, ropemaker, and James Benson, Aislaby, gent.; Cat built; 99 by 25; three masts. Sold to Nwcstl., 1795.

JOHN AND DOROTHY.—Owner, Will. Brown, 1785-9.

JOHN AND DOROTHY.—Owner, Will. Frank, Staithes, 1785-9.

JOHN AND ANN.—Owner, Richd. Hill, 1747-9. Lost, 1763.

JOHN AND ANN.—Owner, Jn. Yeoman, 1756; Capt., Will. Gaskin; later, Geo. Brodrick. To Greenland, 1757. Voyage to Carolina.

JOHN AND ESTHER.—Owner, Capt. Hen. Walker; Owner later, Jn. Yeoman. Lost.

JOHN AND ELIZABETH.—Capt., Jos. Lawson, 1747-9. Sold, 1758.

JOHN AND ELIZABETH.—Apparently a new ship; Capt., Thos. Holt, 1749-51. Lost, 1762.

JOHN AND ELIZABETH.—Capt., Richd. Knaggs, 1756-7.

JOHN AND ELIZABETH.—Boat; 43; Staithes 1786; Reg. Wy. 1787; Owners, T. Trowsdale and Co.

JOHN AND JOHANNA.—Capt., Arnold Jackson, 1747-9.

JOHN AND JANE.—Owner, Newark Ingram, 1747. Voyages to Jamaica and Carolina, 1748.

JOHN AND JANE.—Capt., Jn. Moorsom, R.H.B., 1751-6.

JOHN AND JANE.—S.; bt. Wy. 1770; Owner, Abel Chapman.

JOHN AND HENRY.—Owner, Isaac Scarth; Capt., Jn. Jackson. Voyage to Virginia, 1749. Lost, 1762.

JOHN AND ROBERT.—Clark, 1749-51.

JOHN AND MARGARET.—Johnson, R.H.Town, 1751-6. Lost, 1762-4.

JOHN AND MARGARET.—Capt., Geo. Close; Voy. to Carolina.

JOHN AND HANNAH.—1756-7.

JOHN AND BETTY.—Linsley, R.H.Town, 1758-61.

JOHN AND MARTHA.—Owner, Geo. Robinson. Lost, 1762.

JOHN AND SARAH.—Jn. Gill. Lost, 1762.

JOHN AND ISABELLA.—Ed. Storm, R.H.Town, 1761-5.

JOHN AND GEORGE.—Will Allely, 1765-7.

JOHN AND CHRISTOPHER.—Owner, Christopher Richardson, 1765-7.

JOHN AND RACHEL.—Christ. Marshall. Lost, 1771.

JOHN AND REBECCA.—Owner, Jn. Jackson, 1775-9.

JOHN AND CATHERINE.—Owner, Geo. Watson, 1782-5.

JOHN'S GOODWILL.—Steward. Lost, 1758.

JOHN'S ENDEAVOUR.—Jn. Ware. Lost, 1760.

JONATHAN AND CATHERINE.—Jon. Parritt. Sold, Oct., 1754.

JOLLY BACHELOR.—113; bt. Wy. 1767.

JOSEPH.—S.; 214; bt. Wy. 1755; Owner, Will Pressick. Lost, 1757.

JOSEPH.—Capt., Benj. Chapman, 1756-7. Sold.

JOSEPH'S INCREASE.—Capt., Christ. Pressick, 1749-51.

JOSEPH AND JOAN.—Owner, Will. Hill; Capt., Jn. English. Lost, 1756. Transport, 1748-9.

JOSEPH AND ANN.—Owner, Jn. Newton, 1749.

JOSEPH AND MARY.—Tindall, R.H.Town, 1758.

JOSEPH AND HANNAH.—Owner, Jn. Anderson, 1765-7.

JOSEPH AND HANNAH.—S.; 253; bt. Wy. 1760; Owner, Jn. Emblinton, m.m.; Robt. Clark and Mary Middleton, 1787. Lost after 1803.

JUDITH.—Capt., Leonard Dale, 1747-9.

JUPITER.—Jos. Gibson. Launched 9th March, 1773.

KENT.—Owner, Geo. Skinner, 1747-9.

KENDRICK AND MARY.—Cap., Jackson Kildill. Sold, 1750.

KING GEORGE.—Capt., Will Skinner, 1760. Sold.

KING OF PRUSSIA.—Capt., Matt. Mennell. Sold to Jas. Morrow, R.H.Town, 1765.

LARK.—S.; 245; bt. Wy. 1729; Owner, 1747, Robt. Middleton; Owners, 1786, Thos. Middleton, Jos. Barker and Robt. Clark; Pink st.; three decks, three masts; Cap., 1786, Jn. Bedlington; 1787, J. Mellanby; Transport, 1748; Reg. Nwcstle., 1794.

LARK.—Slp.; 34; bt. Stcktn. 1762; Owner, 1787, Francis Watson. Lost, 1793.

LARK.—Bn.; 62; bt. Wy. 1783; Owner, Geo. Jefferson, Staithes, m.m.; Owner, 1789, Will. Weatherill, Staithes.

LARK.—Slp.; 59; bt. Sndld., 1786; Owners, Jas. Clark and Co.; Owner, 1827, Francis Watkins, 64. Sold by him in April, 1827, to John Clark, grocer, Jn. Langbourne, shipbuilder, Will Morley, shipchandler, Hen. Barrick, shipbuilder, Jn. Lawson, junr., draper, James Green, grocer, Will Cooper, draper, and Knaggs Yeoman, grocer, trustees for the Whitby New Shipping Co. Lost. Reg. cancelled Jan. 17th, 1834.

LAUREL.—Owner, Will Barker; Transport, 1748.

LAUREL.—Owner, Geo. Skinner. Lost, 1760.

LAUREL.—Slp.; 50; bt. Stcktn. 1780; Owner, Bartholomew Rudd, Guisbro'; Reg. Stcktn., Feb., 1813; Owner then Rd. Hudson, Wilton.

LATONA.—S.; 300; bt. Wy. 1789; Owners, Jn. Barry, shipwright, and Francis Barry, m.m.; Transport in 1814. Sold to Lndn., 1790.

LADY JULIANA.—S.; 379; bt. Wy. 1778.

LEVIATHAN.—Owner, Jn. Yeoman; Capt., Thos. Pyman; Capt. later, Christ. Yeoman. To Greenland, 1757.

LEPEL.—Capt., Geo. Brodrick, 1765-7.

LIBERTY AND PROPERTY.—Bt. Wy. 1750; Capt. Benj. Harrison. Sold, 1760.

LIBERTY AND PROPERTY.—S.; 249; bt. Wy. 1752; James Benson.

S. "Liberty and Property."

From a painting by Geo. Weatherill, after Geo. Chambers.

In 1786 the owners were James Benson, Aislaby, John Mellar, and Hen. Clark, the two latter being rope-makers. Later, Jn. Moss, of Trave Hall, in County of York, skinner, and John Reed, of N. Shields, in county of Northumberland, ropemaker. Sept. 21st, 1799, the executors of Jn. Mellar sold and transferred all his right, interest, etc., in the said vessel unto Will Read, of Dockwray Square, in the county of Northumberland, ropemaker. Hen. Clark also sold the same day all his right and interest to the said Will Read. February 3rd, 1809, John Moss sold and transferred all his right and interest unto Will. Hask Nichols, of Whitby, surgeon. Captains of Liberty and Property:—1786 Matt. Corner. 4th Nov., 1800, Geo. Brown, of Nwcstl. Continued in Whitby Register till 1840, when transferred to Nwcstl. Still ship rigged in 1825. Owner in 1823 John Benson, of Aislaby. "A letter dated September 26th, 1856, has been received by the underwriters of the barque 'Liberty and Property' from Mr. Hen. English, their agent sent out to Xatthammarswick, Island of Gottland, stating that the wreck would be sold for the benefit of all concerned. This ends the oldest merchant ship of Shields, and perhaps of England, being built at Whitby in 1752, and when lost was therefore 104 years old. She has always been employed in the coal and Baltic trades, and no ship was more generally known along the east coast among the sea-faring population; her antique build attracted attention wherever she went, both in British and foreign ports. When lost she belonged to Mr. Jas. Blumer, of S. Shields."—"Whitby Gazette," 1856.

LIBERTY.—S.; 400; bt. Wy. 1745; Owner, Abel Chapman; Capt., Isaac Salmon; Pink st.; 113 by 29; Owner in 1787, Jn. Chapman, senr. and junr. and Co. Sold to Nwcstl., 1799. "The 'Liberty,' of Whitby, was brought into Shields Harbour in March, 1775, after having been almost a quarter of a year on Amble sands, where to save the crew's lives she was put ashore in a violent gale of wind. It is very remarkable, and greatly to the honour of the neighbourhood, that although she had been so long ashore there was not one article of her stores missing, but everything was found in the same and as good order as they would have been in the safest harbour." — "Yorkshire Gazette," 1886.

LIDDELL.—Owner, Jn. Mellar, 1747-9.

LIVELY.—S.; 251; bt. Wy. 1765; Owner, Richd. Moorsom; Capt., Geo. Porritt; sq. st.; 87 by 26; Owners, 1824, Will. Skinner, 24, Jn. Holt, jun., 12, Geo. Ouston, 12, Robt. Kirby, 8 and Geo. Pearson, Kirkeaton, 8. The "Lively" whaler was overwhelmed by the Arctic ice, and all the crew perished in April, 1826. The news of this disaster reached Whitby early in September.

LIVELY.—Slp.; 40; bt. Wy. 1786; Owners, Geo. Dodds and Co., Boulby; Owners in 1886, Robt. Gibson and Isabel Kerr. Wrecked on Bacton Beach, May 29th, 1888.

LINGBERRY.—Owner, Will. King, 1768. Lost, 1768.

LOYALTY.—Capt., Witham Boynton, 1747-9.

LOYALTY.—Capt., Jn. Williamson. New vessel 1765-7.

LOYALTY.—Geo. Jackson. New. Sold May, 1775.

LOYALTY.—Thos. Hall. Launched Nov., 1775.

LOYAL CLUB.—Owners, Swales and Co., 1774. To Greenland.

LOVE AND UNITY.—Francis Easterby, 1756-7.

LOVE AND UNITY.—Benj. Gowland, 1765.

LOVE AND UNITY'S INCREASE.—Owner, Benj. Gowland. Taken by the enemy.

LOTTERY.—Jn. Addison. New 1775.

LOVING FRIENDS.—Capt., Geo. Addison, 1756-7. Large ship. Sold, 1763.

LORD HOWE.—Owner, Francis Gibson, 1777.

LOVELY ANN.—Owner, Jn. Pearson, 1780-1. Lost, Jan., 1786.

LORD MULGRAVE.—Owner, Jn. Addison, 1780-1. Taken by the enemy.

LORD HOOD.—S.; 356; bt. Wy. 1781.

LONDON AND BERWICK PACKET.—Bg.; 155; bt. Wy. 1784; Owners, 1817, Robt. Kirby and Jn. Langborn, shipbuilder; Owner, 1816, Gid. Smales; Reg. Lndn., June, 1819.

LONDON.—S.; 321; bt. Wy. 1788.

LONSDALE.—Bg.; 185; bt. Wy. 1788.

LYNX.—S.; 325; bt. Wy. 1776; Owners, 1787, Jos. Barker, Thos. Middleton and James Atty; Capt., Elisha Preston; 99 by 28. Launched 26th Nov., 1776; Reg. Hull, 1798.

LYON.—Owner, Adam Boulby, 1747-9; Capt., Hen. Gofferton. Lost at ye Havana, 1762.

LYDE.—S.; 359; bt. Hull 1748; Owner, Benj. Lotherington; Capt., Thos. Lotherington. Lost, 1801.

LUCK AND ANN.—Capt., Ingram Estill, 1761-5.

MARY.—Owner, Jn. Anderson, 1772-6.

MARY.—Capt., Robt. Easterby, 1747-9. Sold, 1751.

MARY.—Capt., Will Burton, 1747-9.

MARY.—Owner, Jn. Wilkinson, 1747-9; Capts., Jn. Coverdale and Martin Kildill. Lost, 1762-3. James Cook seaman on board this vessel in 1750; Capt., Gaskin.

MARY.—Capt., Matt. Mennell, R.H.B., 1747-9; Capt. later, Isaac Hornby. Sold, 1753.

MARY—Owner, Jacob Linskill, 1747-9; Capt., Thos. Linskill; Transport, 1748.

MARY.—Owner, Paul Harrison, Staithes, 1756-7.

MARY.—Bg.; 164; bt. N. Amrca., 1765; Owner, Philip Gatenby. Sold to Sndld., May, 1792.

MARY.—Bk.; 275; bt. Wy. 1780; Owner, Robt. Rickarby; Owners, 1787, R. R. and Cornelius Clark and Will. Chapman, sailmaker. Sold to Lndn., 1794.

MARY.—Slp.; 59; bt. Wy. 1784; Owner, Thos. Readshaw, m.m.; 53.10 by 17.1. Lost, 1793.

MARY PANE.—Will. Todd, R.H.B., 1772-6. Lost.

MARY AND JANE.—Owner, Robt. Campion, Staithes, 1747-9; Fishing boat. Lost, 1772-3.

MARY AND ELIZABETH.—Owner, Matt. Mennell, R.H.B., 1751-6.

MARY AND REBECCA.—Robson Richardson, 1751-6.

MARY AND SARAH.—Owner, Jn. Dale, 1751-6. Sold to Jn. Blackburn.

MARY AND ANN.—J. Stephenson.

MARY ANN.—S.; 313; bt. Wy. 1789; Owner, Robt. Clark, junr.; 100 by 27.5½. Lost, 1797.

MARY ANNE.—Slp.; 78; Owner, Hen. W. Yeoman; Owner, 1801, Thos. Callender. Lost after 1814.

MAYFLOWER.—Owner, Will. Barker, 1747; Capt., Ed. Carlen; Transport, 1748. Lost, 1760.

MAYFLOWER.—Capt., Jn. Cockerill, R.H.B., 1747-9. Lost, 1755.

MAYFLOWER.—Owner, Robt. Truefitt, Staithes. Lost, 1749-50.

MAYFLOWER.—Owner, Thos. Fishburn, 1772-6.

MAYFLOWER.—Owner, Jn. Weatherill, 1782-5.

MARLBOROUGH.—Owner and Capt., Jonas Brown, 1747.

MARLBOROUGH.—S.; 223; bt. Wy. 1761; Owner, Hen. W. Yeoman; 92.2 by 24.6. To Greenland. Lost, 1791. "The 'Marlborough' of Whitby, Thos. Walker, captain, arrived at Whitby from Savannah in Georgia, May 27th, 1776, having left on the 31st March. In Savannah river 114 barrels of rice were thrown overboard in order to lighten her. This was effected by the assistance of Capt. Barclay, of the "Scarbro'" man-of-war. Many shots were fired by the Provincials at the Marlborough, which she returned very briskly. The Provincials disguised themselves as Indians in order to surprise any boats that might come to shore from the ships for wood; a boat belonging to the Whitby transport guarded by seven soldiers being so unfortunate as to fall in their way, was fired upon, and one soldier who had been shot through the head was scalped, and another shot through the body had one leg cut off by the rebels with the woodaxe he had with him."—"Yorkshire Gazette," 1886.

MASQUERADE.—Capt., Robt. Story, 1747; Transport, 1748. Lost, 1762-3.

MATTHEW.—Owner, Isaac Storm, R.B.H., 1749-51.

MATTHEW AND ELIZABETH.—Marmaduke Wilson, 1761-5. Sold.

MARQUIS OF GRANBY.—Owner, Robt. Hunter, 1765.

MACKEREL.—S.; 363; bt. Wy. 1766; Owner, Robt. Clark; Round st; Owners, 1787, Robt., Cornelius and Rd. Clark; 106 by 29. Lost, 1797.

MARS.—S.; 286; bt. Wy. 1782.

MARIA.—280 tons; Owner, Chapman. Went into Mr. Fishburn's dock Feb. 16th, 1798, came out May 16th. Was pulled to pieces and rebuilt.

MARTHA.—Bk.; 315; bt. Wy. 1774; Owner, Will. Holt; Owners, 1787, Will., Thos. and Jos. Holt. Lost.

MARTHA.—Bn.; 133; bt. Wy. 1785; Owners, Jn. Peacock and James Watt, m.m.; 72 by 21. Sold to Nwcstl., 1800.

MARGARET AND MARTHA.—Owner, Robt. Boulby, 1775-9.

MERMAID.—Owner, Jn. Yeoman, 1747-9. Lost, 1753.

MERMAID.—Owner, Jn. Yeoman, 1756-7. A new ship. Transport, 1757-8. "Brought three Frenchmen home, which took out of prison."

MERMAID.—Owner, Thos. Hodgson, 9th April, 1785.

MENTOR.—S.; 343; bt. Scrbr. 1783; Owner, Dan. Stephenson. Captured in Holland by the French.

MERCURY.—Bn.; 93; bt. Wy. 1787; Owners, J. Atty and Jon. Lacy. Lost, 1795.

MIDSUMMER.—Owner, Ant. Jefferson, Staithes, 1747-9.

MIDSUMMER.—Slp.; 51; bt. Wy. 1769; Owner, 1788, Christ. Brown. Lost, 1801, or after.

MIDSUMMER.—Open boat; 45; bt. Staithes 1761; Owner, 1787, Jn. Crow. Lost, 1809, or after.

MIDSUMMER BLOSSOM.—Bk.; 384; bt. Wy. 1766; Owners, J. Atty, sailmaker, Will Atty, gent, and Hen. and Jon. Lacy, ropemakers—these 1787; deep waist and forecastle; 10 guns; Reg. Lndn., 1799.

MINERVA.—Capt., Blackburn, 1747-9. Lost, 1753.

MINERVA.—Owner, Francis Easterby; later owner, Jn. Addison. Lad. 24th March, 1773.

MINERVA.—Bn.; 63; bt. Gt. Yrmth. 1772; Owner, 1824, Jn. Barnard, R.H.B. Lost, April, 1840.

MINERVA.—S.; 282; bt. Dysart, N.B., 1775; Owners, 1787, Will. Hill, Jn. Coulson and James Watson; Reg. Hull, 1799.

MIRIAM.—Bk.; 263; bt. Wy. 1781; Owner, Will. Slater, gent, Jn. Chapman, merchant, and Will Chapman, sailmaker, the two latter being people called Quakers. Lost, 1798.

MIDDLETON.—Bk.; 227; bt. Rawcliff 1756; Owner, 1786, Will. Watson, Pickering. Sold to Sndld., 1795.

MIDDLETON.—S.; 353; bt. Wy. 1789; bd., Th. Fishburn; Owners, Peter Middleton, Israel Hunter, and Jos. Barker; Owner, 1814, Chilton. Lost Gulf of St. Lawrence, 1828.

MULGRAVE.—Slp.; 51; bt. Wy. 1768; Owner, Lord Mulgrave, and John Addison in 1786. Lost.

MUSLEY.—Capt., Adam Parkinson, 1758.

MYRTLE.—Jos. Barker, 1765-7.

MYRTLE.—Bk.; 297; bt. Wy. 1781; Owners, Jos. Barker and Thos. Middleton; three masts; 100 by 27. Lost, 1798.

NANCY.—Sq. st. boat; 43; bt. Staithes 1754; Owner, Jn. Sanderson, Staithes. Lost, 1793.

NANCY.—Bn.; 254; bt. Wy. 1767; Owner, Will. Jackson; two masts; 96 by 25; Reg. Hull, Jan., 1796.

NANCY.—Thos. Bredrick, 1767-8.

NAUTILUS.—S.; 399; bt. Wy. 1778; Owner, Richd. Moorsom; Owners, 1787, R. M., sen. and jun., S. Pressick, Jn. Addison, Will. Ward, Lndn., coal factor, and Will Linskill, N. Shlds.; 113 by 29; Round st. The "Nautilus" when nearly ready for sea in 1795 was burnt, according to Dr. Young on the 28th Feb. She was laid in Whitby Harbour just above the bridge on the east side. It is said that a large reward was offered to any persons who would scuttle the vessel, there being gunpowder in the hold, but none would venture. Fortunately, the fire scuttled the vessel before reaching the gunpowder. It is stated in the Whitby Magazine of 1827 that the remains of the Nautilus were utilised in building the ship "Wakefield" at Whitby in 1797-8.

NAVIGATOR.—Bt. Wy. 1785; Owner, Hammond.

NEPTUNE.—Thos. Milner and Co., 1749-51.

NEPTUNE.—Thos. Harrison, 1749-51.

NEW RANGER.—Thos. Hunter and Co., 1747-9.

NEPTUNE.—Bg.; 153; bt. Wy. 1785; bought from Berwick in 1814; Owners, Gideon Smales and Christopher Richardson, banker; Owners, 1824, Christ. Richardson and Robt. Kirby, each 32. Sold to Lndn., 1826. Bought to Wy. 1833; Owner, Geo. Barrick. Sold to Sndld., 1866.

NEPTUNE.—S.; 268; bt. Wy. 1787; Owners, Jn. and Francis Barry, shipbuilders, and Robt. Barry, gent; Transport, 1814. Sold.

NEWARK.—Jn. Stonehouse, 1749-51. Sold, 1752.

NELLY.—James Marshall, Staithes, 1758-61.

NELLY'S INCREASE.—James Marshall, 1758-61.

NEREUS.—Owner, Richd. Anderson, Staithes, 1775-9.

NEREUS.—S.; 382; bt. Wy. 1789; Owners, Hen. Barrick, shipbuilder, and Geo. Barrick, m.m. Sold to Lvpl.

NIGHTINGALE.—Owner, Adam Boulby, 1747-9. Lost, 1763.

NOBLE HOPE.—Owner, Matt. Noble, 1747-9.

NORTH SEATON.—Nathan Pickering, 1749-51.

NOTUS.—Bn.; 133; bt. Wy. 1788; Owner, J. Barry, shipwright, and Co. Sold.

NORMAN.—Capt., Will Benson, 1767. Lost, 1773.

OAK.—Owner, Hen. Walker; New ship 1748-9; Capt., Jn. Ellerington.

OAK.—Owner, Jn. Yeoman. Sold, 1760.

OAK.—Owner, Thos. Fishburn, 1767-8.

OAK.—Bn.; 76; bt. Wy. 1764; Owner, Isaac Gales. Sold to Arundel.

OAK.—Owner, Robt. Barry, 1782-5.

OCEAN.—Owner, Will. Blackburn, 1751-5.

OCEAN.—Bg.; 226; bt. Wy. 1764; Owners, 1787, Jacob Blackburn and Robt. Clark; 88½ by 25½; Reg. Lndn., 1795.

OLIVE BRANCH.—Bn.; 187; bt. Wy. 1721; Owner, 1747, Thos. Holt; Owners, 1787, Jos. and T. Holt; 83 by 23; Transport, 1748. Lost, 1794.

ORWELL.—S.; 357; bt. Wy. 1754.

OTTERINGTON.—S.; 350; bt. Wy. 1781; Owners, Christ Richardson and Will. Holt; Forecastle; three masts; 102 by 29.

OWNER'S ENDEAVOUR.—Runswick; Milburn, 1747. Sold, 1758.

OWNER'S GOODWILL.—Owner, Martin Morland, 1751. Voyage to Carolina.

PARADISE.—Capt., Will Stainton, 1765-7. Small.

PALLAS.—S.; 333; bt. Wy. 1772; Owners, Thos. and John Holt; 101 by 28. Destroyed by fire 1795.

PATTY.—S.; 327; bt. Stockwith 1782; Owners, Benj. Harrison and Jos. Barker; 6 guns. Sold to Lvpl., 1798.

PACKET.—Bn.; 132; bt. Wy. 1787; Owner, Ing. Eskdale, shipwright; Later, Chas. Noddings. Sold to Sndld., 1793.

PEARL.—S.; 317; bt. Wy. 1750; Owner, Robt. Middleton; Owners, 1787, Margaret and Thos. Middleton and J. Atty; Pink st.; Top-gallant forecastle; Quarter deck carried before the mainmast; Capt, 1757, Sam Campion. Sold to Nwcstl., 1795.

PEACE AND PLENTY.—Owner, Will. Skinner, 1765-7.

PETER AND ANN.—Owners, Jn. and Jos. Wright, 1751-6.

PEGASUS.—Francis Leng, 1751-6.

PEGGY.—Owner, Thos. Scarth, 1761-5. To Greenland. Lost, 1771.

PEGGY.—S.; 367; bt. Hull 1760; Owner, Robt. Middleton; Owners, 1787, Mary and Thos. Middleton and Will. Barker; Reg. Hull, 1796.

PEGGY.—S.; 237; bt. Wy. 1777; Owner, John Mellar; in 1787, J. Mellar, Jn. Chapman, and Jos. Holt. Lost.

PEGGY.—Bk.; $\frac{393}{405}$; bt. Wy. 1782; Owners, Sam Campion, Thos. Holt, Christ. Richardson in 1787; 10 guns. Taken by the enemy.

PEAK.—Lute st.; slp.; 53; bt. Wy. 1788; Owners, Ed. Windle and Thos. Strother, Peak Alum Works; Owner, 1812, Francis Unthank, Staithes. Lost, 1815-16.

PEAK PACKET.—Thos. Mennell, R.H.B., 1768-72.

PERSEVERANCE.—Owners, Greenland Co., 1776. Lost, 1780.

PHŒNIX.—Owner, Will. Linskill; Capt., Thos. Brodrick, 1765-7. Lost, 1770.

PHŒNIX.—Bn.; 121; bt. Wy. 1782; Owner, Jn. Ridley, 1786; Owners, Anth. Ridley, Robt. Knaggs, and Jn. Ridley, of Stowe Brow; 145 tons in 1796; Reg. Lndn., 1814.

PHŒNIX.—Owner, Richd. Jackson, 1749-51; first mention. Sold, 1753.

PHŒBE.—Capt., Norison Baker, 1751. Sold, 1754.

PLANTER.—Owner, Jn. Holt, 1768-72.

POLLY.—Capt., Robt. Shipton, 1749-51. Sold, 1752-5.

POLLY.—Owner, Jonas Brown, 1758-61. Lost, 1763.

POLLY.—Slp.; 33; bt. Lndn. 1778; Owner, James Wilkinson, m. Sold.

POLLY.—Slp.; 42; bt. Rawcliffe 1759; Owners, Jn. and Ant. Twistleton. Lost, 1801.

PORPOISE.—Owner, Jn. Yeoman, 1758-61. Capt., Richard Woodhouse. To Greenland. Lost, 1772.

POMONA.—Slp.; 51; bt. Staithes 1775; Owner, Will. Weatherill, Staithes. Lost, Jan. 25th, 1794.

POMONA.—Owner, Lord Dundas, 1789.

PRIOR.—Bn.; 69; Sndld. 1768; Reg. Wy., 1786; Owner, Richd. Forster, Attorney-at-Law, Guisbro. Sold to Nwcstl.

PROVIDENCE.—Capt., Jn. Allison, 1747-9. Sold, March, 1752.

PROVIDENCE.—Capt., Dan. Huntrods, 1747-9, R.H.B.

PROVIDENCE.—Owner, Thos. Scarth, 1761-5. Lost, 1774.

PROVIDENCE.—Owner, Benj. Chapman, 1765; Capt., Jn. Jackson.

PROVIDENCE.—S.; 230; bt. Selby 1756; Owner, Will Skinner, 1775-9; Owner, 1787, Charles Noddings. "The 'Providence,' Capt. Carlille, of Whitby, arrived at that port in July, 1776, from Greenland, with seven whales, five of which were large. She left Whitby March 13th, and was the smallest vessel that sailed thence that season to Greenland." —"Yorkshire Gazette," 1887.

PROVIDENCE.—T. Chester, 1765-7, R.H.B.

PROVIDENCE.—Slp.; 45; Hull 1774; Owner, Robt. Shaw. Lost, 1788.

PROVIDENCE.—Slp.; 54; Leith 1761; Owner, Ch. Summerson, cordwainer, 1786; Owner, 1793, Robt. Dalton, m.m. Lost, 1793.

PROVIDENCE.—Slp.; 64; bt. Maldon; re-built at Wy. 1779; Owner, 1787, James Fletcher, R.H.B. Sold to Nwcstl., 1789.

PROVIDENCE.—Slp.; 45; bt. Wy. 1766; Owner, 1786, Geo. Campbell; Reg. Sndld., Oct., 1795.

PROVIDENCE ENDEAVOUR.—Slp.; 50; bt. Wy. 1765; Owners, 1791, Geo. Sanderson, inn keeper, Will Thompson, carrier, and Jn. Bolton, mason. Lost after 1812.

PROVIDENCE AND MARY.—Capt., Ralph Frankland, 1767-8.

PROVIDENCE AND NANCY.—Owner, Will. Frankland, 1775. To Greenland.

PROVIDENTIA.—Capt., Geo. Jackson, R.H.B., 1747-9.

PROSPEROUS.—Capt., Jn. Bailey, 1747-9. Lost, 1756.

PROSPEROUS ADVENTURE.—Capt., Simon Jackson, 1751-6, Rnswck.

PROSPECT.—S.; 373; bt. Wy. 1777; Owners, James Atty and Jon. Lacy. Sold to Nwcstl., 1795.

PRINCE WILLIAM.—Owner, Capt. W. Sympson, 1747-9; Capt., Sam Milner. Sold March, 1752.

PRINCE OF ORANGE.—Owner, Thos. Harrison, 1747-9; Capt., Will. Blackburn. Voy. to Carolina. Sold.

PRINCE OF WALES.—John Holt, 1747-9; Transport, 1757.

PRINCE FREDERICK.—Owner, Jonas Brown, 1747-9; Capt., Thos. Brown. Apparently a new ship.

PRINCE FERDINAND.—Owner, Jn. Wilkinson, 1767-8. Large ship.

PRINCE WILLIAM HENRY.—Owner, Thos. Holt, 1782-5.

PRUSSIAN HERO.—Owner, James Atty, 1758-61.

PRUDENCE.—S.; 247; bt. Wy. 1788; Owners, Geo. Barrick, m.m., and Hen. Barrick, shipwright.

QUEEN.—Bn.; 109; bt. York 1781; Owner, Geo. Smith, 1786. Lost.

RANGER.—1747-9. Sold Sept., 1750.

RANGER.—Bg.; 153; bt. Wy. 1776; Reg. Wy. Oct., 1826, from Nwcstl.; Owners, James Wood, 32, and Richd. Blakey, of Bill Quay, 32: Owners, 1831, Jos. Wood, 48, Jn. Harland, Ugglebarnby, 16, Lost, 1832, or after.

RANGER.—S.; 307; Owner, Thos. Hunter, 1758-61. Lost.

RACHEL.—Owner, Will. Webster, 1747-9; Capt., Jacob Remington. Voy. to Carolina.

RACHEL.—Owner, Jn. Yeoman, 1749-51.

RACHEL.—Bk.; 303; bt. Wy. 1783; Owners, Jn. Coulson, Will. Holt and Jonath. Lacy; Quarter barges; 100 by 27. "Rachel," of Wy., belonging to Mr. Walter Carr, and commanded by Capt. Trueman, drifted ashore derelict on the coast of Ireland, 1817.

RACHEL AND MARY.—Owner, Benj. Ward, 1766.

RAKES.—S.; bt. W. 1780; Owner, Hammond, of Hull.

RESTORATION.—Capt., Will. Richardson, R.H.Town, 1747-9.

RESTORATION.—Owner, Christ. Richardson, 1747-9; Capt., Jn. Pearson.

RESTORATION.—Capt., Robt. Constable, 1747-9. Sold, 1753.

REBECCA.—Owner and Capt., Benj. Stephenson, 1747-9.

REBECCA.—Owner and Capt., Philip Skinner, 1749-51. Sold, 1758.

REBECCA AND ELIZABETH.—Owner, Peter Bedlington, 1777.

RECOVERY.—Bk.; 332; bt. Wy. 1779; Owners, Sam and Jn. Campion and Jn. Holt; Forecastle; 10 guns; 103 by 28.

REWARD.—Bn.; 69; bt. Wy. 1788; Owner, Hen. Barrick, shipwright; 105 tons in 1792; Owner, 1792, Paul Cook. Taken by the enemy, 1797.

RESOLUTION.—Owner and Capt., James Benson. Sold, 1749.

RESOLUTION.—S.; 379; bt. Wy. 1766; Owners, Jn. Walker and Simpson, 1787; Owners, Jn. Walker, of N. Shlds., ropemaker, Hen. Walker, and Wakefield Simpson, of Wy.; Later, Robt. Walker; three masts; 103 by 29; Capt., Jn. Steward, 1787; in 1790, Jn. Featherston. Lost, 1792.

RESOLUTION.—Owner, Jonas Brown, 1768.

RESOLUTION.—Slp.; 54; bt. Wy. 1768; Owner, Will. Reed; Owner, 1824, Thos. Walker, 64; last Capt. given, T. Walker, Jan., 1826. Lost.

RIDLEY.—Owner, Will. Webster, 1747-9; Transport, 1748. Lost, 1756.

RICHMOND.—Capt., Thos. Richmond, 1747-9.

RICHARD.—S.; 305; bt. Wy. 1765; Transport, 1814.

RICHARD AND MARY.—Capt., Richd. Tindall. Sold, 1749.

RICHARD AND MARY.—Owner, Thos. Simpson.

RICHARD AND MARY.—Capt., Richd. Andrew, 1751-6. Lost, 1754.

RICHARD AND JANE.—Owner, Will. Simpson, 1751-6.

RICHARD AND THOMAS.—S.; 203; bt. Wy. 1762; Owner, Richard Knaggs; Owners, 1786, Thos. Knaggs, m.m., and John Mellar and Co.; sq. st.; three masts; Reg. Nwcstl. after 1792.

ROSE.—Owner, Jas. Yeoman, 1747-9. Lost, 1752.

ROSE.—81; bt. Wy. 1744; Owner, Watson, 1812.

ROSE.—S.; 330; a French prize taken by H.M.S. "Ruby" in the West Indies; condemned Feb., 1779, and named "Lucia"; Reg. Wy., 1786; Owners, Will. Holt, Will. Hustler and Christ. Hodgson; sq. st. and poop; 89 by 25. Sold to Nwcstl., 1789.

ROSE.— Owner, Robt. Clark, 1767-8. Lost about 1777.

ROSE.—Bn.; 57; bt. Wy. 1784; Owner, Thos. Willis; 54 by 16; Owner, 1787, Geo. Willis; Owner, 1804, Will. Stoneham, Staithes; Reg. Sndld.

ROSE IN JUNE.—Owner, Will. Barker, 1747-8; Transport, 1748-9. Lost, 1752.

ROSEBUD.—Owner, Geo. Dodds, 1785-9.

ROBERT.—Owner, Mrs. Linskill, 1747-9. Lost, 1762.

ROBERT.—Bg.; 76; bt. Wy. 1768; Owners, 1786, Jn. Porritt, m.m., and Margaret, wife of Will. Brown, Rnswck; Bn. later; Reg. Sndld., 1810.

ROBERT.—Owner, Will. Linskill. Apparently a new ship 1766.

ROBERT.—Slp.; 48; bt. Sndld. 1773; Owner, Jn. Emlington, house carpenter, and Geo. Trowsdale, cordwainer, in 1786. Burnt, 1788.

ROBERT.—Owner, Robt. Bedlington, R.H.B., 1767-8.

ROBERT.—Owner, Will. Barker, 1780-1.

ROBERT AND ANN.—Capt., Robt. Burbank, 1751-6.

ROBERT AND ANN.—Bk.; 322; bt. Wy. 1789; Transport, 1814; Owner, 1840, Richmond, of N. Shlds.

ROBERT AND MARY.—Owner, Benj. Hunter, 1761-5.

ROBERT AND HANNAH.—Owner, Will. Ward, 1766.

ROBERT AND ELIZABETH.—Owner, Robt. Westill, 1767-8.

ROBIN HOOD.—Owner, T. Mennell, R.H.B., 1761-5.

RODNEY.—S.; 309; bt. Wy. 1781; Owners, Israel, Jos. and Robt. Hunter, sailmakers. Lost, 1816, or after.

ROYAL GEORGE.—Owner, Will. Ward, 1761-5.

ROYAL GEORGE.—Owner, Sam. Campion, 1761-5. Lost, 1778-9.

ROYAL BRITON.—Capt., Jn. Holt, 1761-5.

RUNSWICK.—Simon Jackson, 1748. Lost, 1752.

RUBY.—Owner, Robt. Middleton, 1747-9; Voy. to Riga; Capt., Philip Salmon.

RUSSIAN MERCHANT.—Owner, Jn. Wilkinson. Lost, 1762.

RUSWARP.—Capt., Geo. Close, 1756-7.

SALLY.—Owner, Anth. Jefferson, 1749-51.

SALLY.—Owner, Jn. Cropton, R.H.B., 1761-5.

SALLY.—Owner, Chas. Craven, 1761-5. Lost.

SALLY.—Bn.; 62; bt. Wy. 1770; Owner, Ed. Brown, Staithes; Reg. Sndld., March, 1799.

SALLY.—Slp.; 64; bt. Wy. 1776; Owner, Thos. Fishburn, shipwright. Lost, 1799.

SALLY.—S.; 340; bt. Wy. 1783; Transport, 1814.

SALLY.—Bk.; 240; bt. Wy. 1785; Owners, Robt. Galilee, m.m., and Margaret, widow of Nat. Campion; poop; 90 by 25. Margaret Campion transferred $\frac{1}{8}$ part to Robt. Galilee and $\frac{1}{8}$ part to James Weatherill, of Barnes, farmer, in 1798. Lost, 1799.

SALLY.—Lug.; 57; bt. Wy. 1787; Owner, Matt. Trattles, Staithes; Reg. Aldbro., Jan., 1810.

SALLY'S INCREASE.—Bn.; 85; bt. Wy. 1782; Owner, Ed. Brown, Staithes. Lost, 1793.

SARAH.—S.; 364; bt. Wy. 1748; Owner, Solomon Chapman; Later, Ingram Chapman, Jn. Mellar and Hen. Clark. Lost, 1796.

SARAH.—Owner, Anth. Jefferson, 1749-51.

SATISFACTION.—Owner, Geo. Ware; Capt., Benj. Gowland, 1765-7.

SATISFACTION.—1772-6. Lost, 1777-8.

SALTWICK.—And. Coates, 1765-7.

SAVILL.—Owner, Hen. Clark. New 1769.

SAMUEL AND JOHN.—Jn. Addison, 1749-51. Lost, 1759.

SAMUEL AND JANE.—S.; 407; bt. Wy. 1782; Owners, Sam and Jn. Campion and Jn. Lacy; Lad. March.; Forecastle; 10 guns; Transport, 1814.

SAINT GEORGE.—Capt., Jn. Lawson, 1758-61.

SEA ADVENTURE.—S.; 248; bt. Wy. 1724; Owner, 1747, Cornelius Clark; Owners, 1786, Corn., Richd. and Thos. Clark; Cat built; Pink st.; 94 by 25.10. "Sea Adventure, of Whitby, was lost in 1810, on the coast of Lincolnshire. She was carried up by the violence of the wind and of the tide into the midst of a field, where she was left high and dry, a good distance from the sea."—"Dr. Young's Hist. of Wy."

SEA FLOWER.—S.; 354; bt. Wy. 1740; Owner, Israel Preston; Owners, 1787, Ann Preston, Carr Hall, widow, and Jos. Hunter and James Atty; Cat built. Lost, 1797.

SEA NYMPH.—Owner, Will. Reynolds, 1747-9; Voys. to Maryland and Gibraltar. To Greenland, 1753; Capt., James Wilson, of Sndld. Lost, 1758, or after.

SEA NYMPH.—S.; bt. Wy. 1768; Owner, Will. Lacy; 76 by 25. Lost, 1777-8.

SEA NYMPH.—S.; 270; bt. Wy. 1786; Transport in 1814.

SEA HORSE.—Owner, Jn. Dale, 1751-6. Sold.

SEA LUCK.—Mrs. Jackson, 1782-5.

SHOREHAM.—Slp.; 42; bt. Shoreham 1781; Owners, Jn. Addison and Richd. Moorsom; Lute st.; Owner, 1799, Will Swales; Reg. Inverness, 1801.

SIBELLA.—Owner, Abel Chapman, 1775-9.

SIX SISTERS.—Dickinson Ward, 1749-51.

SISTERS.—S.; 328; bt. Wy. 1778; Voy. Lvpl. to Boston, 1814.

SISTERS.—S.; 335; bt. Wy. 1783; Owners, Benj. Gowland, Mich. Cockerill and Robt. Hunter, sailmakers; 100 by 28. Taken by the enemy. Last Capt. named is in 1792.

SILVER EEL.—S.; 374; bt. Wy. 1763; Owners, Jn. Addison and Richd. Moorsom; Owners, 1787, R. Moorsom and Elizabeth, widow of J. Addison; Round st. Lost after 1801.

SKINNINGROVE.—Capt., Will. Seagrave, 1749-51.

SKELTON CASTLE.—Slp.; 61; bt. Wy. 1764; Owners, 1786, Jn. Holt and Co. Lost, 1797.

SOPHIA ANN.—Slp.; 56; bt. Staithes 1787; Owner, Jn. Sanderson, 1785-9; 52 by 16. Sold to Scrbr.

SPEEDWELL.—Capt., Marshall Hill, Barnby, 1747-9. Sold, 1751.

SPEEDWELL.—Owner, Thos. Holt, 1758-61. To Greenland. Lost, 1782.

SPEEDWELL.—S.; 181; bt. Wy. 1772; Owner, 1786, Lawson Fleck, Redcar; three masts; 84 by 23. Taken by the enemy.

SPEEDWELL.—Sq. st.; open boat; bt. Scrbr. 1769; Reg. Wy. 1787; Owner, Thos. Harrison, fisherman, R.H.B.; 41 tons; Owners, 1804, Ed. Ormston Co. Lost after 1807.

SPEEDWELL.—Slp.; 55, bt. Wy. 1789; Owner, Thos. Harrison; Owner, 1819, Will. Watson, Sandsend, alum maker; Reg. Scrbr., 1823; Reg. Wy. from Scarbr., April, 1826; Owner, Will. Greenwood; Owners, 1828, T. Turnbull, 32, Will Hunton, 32; Reg. at Bridlington, May, 1829; Reg at Wy., 1830, from Bridlington; Owner, 1830, Jos. Lines Wodham, March; Owner, May, 1830, Thos. Bolton, 32, Geo. Simpson, 32; in 1832, Hen. Atley, m.m., 64. Lost, 1837, or after.

SPRING.—S.; 360; bt. Wy. 1763; Owner, Will. Barker; three masts; Owners, 1787, Jos. and W. Barker and Thos. Middleton; Cat built; deep waist; Pink st.; Quarter deck and forecastle; 105 by 29. Lost, 1798.

SPENCER.—Owner, Jacob Hudson, 1767-8. New.

SQUIRREL.—Capt., James Blackburn. Lost, 1748.

STREATHAM CASTLE.—Owner, Jn. Linskill, 1747; Transport, 1748. Lost, 1762.

STAINSACRE.—Capt., Jn. Ward, 1751-6. Sold, 1757.

STAGG.—Capt., Jn. Blackburn, 1767-8.

STAKESBY.—Owner, Jos. Barker, 1775-9. Lost, 1785.

SUCCESS.—Owner, Mrs. Fotherly, 1747-9. Sold, March, 1751.

SUCCESS.—Owner, Will. Addison, 1747-9; Owner later, Jn. Stephenson. Sold, 1750.

SUCCESS.—Owner, Jn. Rickinson, and Capt., 1747-9.

SUCCESS.—Owner, Thos. Campion, 1747-9.

SUCCESS.—Bn.; 64; bt. Wy. 1764; Owner, 1786, Peter Brown, m.m. Taken by the enemy, 1799.

SUCCESS.—Owner, Alex. Atkinson, 1765-7.

SUCCESS'S INCREASE.—Capt., Michael Cockerill, 1772-6.

SUSANNAH.—S.; 283; bt. Wy. 1762; Transport, 1814.

SUSANNAH.—Owner or Capt., Richd. Pinkney, 1749-51.

SUBMISSION.—Capt., Jn. Walker, 1761-5. Lost, 1769-70.

SUMMER.—Bn.; 89; bt. Wy. 1785; Owner, James Atty. Sold.

SUDIS.—Bg.; 312; bt. Wy. 1788; Owner, Jn. Chapman; two masts. Lost, 1793.

SWALLOW.—Will. Wood, R.H.Town, 1751-6.

SWALLOW.—Owners, Dock Company, 1751-6.

SWAN.—Capt., Will Kitchingman, 1749-51. Burnt about 1752.

SWAN.—Owner, Will Ward, 1765-7.

SWAN.—Owners, Ed. Windle and Co., 1780-1. Lost.

SYMMETRY.—

TANFIELD MOOR.—Owner, Mrs. Clark, 1747-9. Lost, 1763.

TERRIER.—Owner, Jn. Sanderson, Sept., 1785.

THAMES.—Bg.; 270; bt. Wy. 1782.

THETIS.—S.; 366; bt. Wy. 1776; Owner, Cornelius Clark; Owners, 1787, C. Clark, Richd. Watkins and Sam Pressick; Pink st.; 104 by 29. Lost at Sndld., 1796.

THREE SISTERS.—Owner, Capt. H. Walker, 1747-9; later Owner, Jn. Yeoman; Capt., 1766, Sam. Milner.

THREE SISTERS.—Owner, Robt. Noble, 1758-61.

THREE SISTERS.—Bn.; 250; bt. Wy. 1761; Owner, Jn. Galilee; Owners, 1786, Geo. Galilee, Geo. Willis and James Atty. Lost.

THREE BROTHERS.—Owner, Jn. Walker, 1747-8; Capt., Jn. Jefferson; Transport, 1748. Lost, 1753. In list of crew for 1748, first voyage, James Cook, servant; in 1749, Sept., James Cook, Ayton, seaman.

THREE BROTHERS.—Bn.; 65; bt. Wy. 1775; Owner, 1786, Matt. Stephenson, Ellerby, farmer. Lost about 1800-1.

THREE BROTHERS.—S.; 355; bt. Wy. 1776; Owners, Christ., Benj. and Will Harrison; Sq. st.; Quarter deck carried before the mainmast, and a rise before the windlass. Lost, 1792.

THREE BROTHERS.—58: bt. Wy. 1788; Owner, Ed. Wood, Runswick; slp., 1808; Sch., 1817; 63 tons 1821; Owner, 1824, Thos. Hunter, Wy. Lost, 1824.

THREE BROTHERS.—Lug.; 47; Scrbr., 1774; Owner, Matt. Storm, R.H.B., 1787.

THOMAS.—Owner, Christ. Richardson, 1747-9. Lost, 1758.

THEMIS.—Bg.; 269; bt. Wy. 1785.

THOMAS AND RICHARD.—Owner, Jn. Jefferson, 1749-51.

THOMAS AND ANN.—Bn.; 81; bt. Stcktn. 1779; Owned at Staithes; Reg. Sndld., 1795.

THOMAS AND ANN.—Thos. Leadill, Fylingdales, 1756-7.

THOMAS AND JOHN.—Thos. Harrison, Staithes, 1758. Lost, 1758.

THOMAS AND ALICE.—S.; 315; bt. Wy. 1782; Owners, Thos. Headlam, Benj. Gowland and Co.; Owner, 1800, Hen. Simpson, merchant. Lost, February, 1802.

THOMAS AND ALICE.—1780-1. Lost, March, 1782.

THOMAS AND ANN'S INCREASE.—Owner, Jn. Burnikell, 1782-5.

TRUE BRITON.—Owner, Jn. Major, 1747-9.

TRUE BRITON.—Dickinson Ward, 1747-9. Lost, 1750.

TRUE BRITON.—Will Jackson. New 1768-72.

TRUE INDUSTRY.—Francis Wilson, 1747-9.

TRUE LOVE.—Will Clark, 1747-9.

TRUE LOVE.—Slp.; 45; bt. Wy. 1765; Owners, Ed. Windle and Thos. Strother, of Peak; Owner, 1798, Gid. Smales, block and mast maker, and Thos. Littlefair; Reg. Scrbr., March, 1800.

TRIAL.—Slp.; 52; bt. Wy. 1760; Owners, Jn. Bolton, m.m., and Co.

TRIAL.—Lug.; 49; bt. Wy. 1784; Owner, Will. Brown, Runswick.

TRIAL.—Slp.; 52; bt. Stcktn.; Owner, James Dixon; later, Chris. Barker, Marske; later, Jn. Peacock; re-built Yarmouth, 1777; Re-built Wy., 1783. Lost.

TRUE FRIENDSHIP.—Owner, Thos. Willis, 1759-61.

TRAVELLER.—Owner, Jn. Anderson, 1782-5.

TRIO.—Owners, Thos. Hall and Co.; Lad. May, 1783.

TRIDENT.—Owner, Robt. Galilee, 1782-5.

TRITON.—Owner, Ant. Jefferson, 1747-9; Voy. to Carolina; Capt., Sam Galilee.

TRITON.—Bn.; 115; bt. Wy. 1787; Owner, James Atty, sailmaker. Sold.

TURBOT.—Owner, Jon. Lacy, 1747-9; Voy. to Carolina.

TWO BROTHERS.—Owner, Jn. Moorsom, 1747-9; Repaired in dock, 1760.

TWO BROTHERS.—Lug.; 47; bt. Staithes 1773; Jn. Clark, Runswick. Lost, 1811.

TWO BROTHERS.—Bg.; 224; bt. Wy. 1776; Owned at Shields, 1840.

TWO BROTHERS.—47; bt. Wy. 1779; Owners, J. Cooper, Mark and Matt. Jackson, Guisbro., 1786. Lost after 1802.

TWO BROTHERS.—Owner, Jn. Cockerill, 1758-61. Lost, 1763.

TWO BROTHERS.—Bk.; 280; bt. Wy. 1785; Owner, Jn. and Sam Pressick; three masts; 92 by 27. Sold to Nwcstl., 1796.

TWO SISTERS.—Bn.; 108; bt. Wy. 1754; Owner, 1786, Marmaduke Wilson. Lost, 1799.

TWO SISTERS.—S.; 399; bt. Yrmth. 1742; Owned at Wy. 1768-1772, Hen. Walker Yeoman. To Greenland. Lost, 1794. Round stern with two quarter windows.

TWO SISTERS.—Owner, Hen. Barrick, 1783-5.

TWO FRIENDS.—56; bt. Scrbr. 1787; Owners, Geo. Frank and Oliver Bedlington, R.H.B. Lost, 1801.

ULYSSES.—Owner, Thos. Milner, 1782-5. Taken by the enemy.

UNITY.—S.; 324; bt. Wy. 1739; Owner, Christ. Richardson; Capt., Jos. Gibson, in 1748; Voy. to Maryland; Transport, 1748.

UNITY.—Capt., Richd. Sleightholm, 1751-6.

UNITY.—Owner, Christ. Harrison, 1751-6.

UNITY.—S.; 253; Scrbr. 1768; Reg. W., 1787; Owners, N. Piper, Pickering, and R. Strong, Wy.; Reg. Nwcstl., 1795.

UNANIMOUS.—Capt, Jos. Harrison, 1756-7.

UNANIMITY.—Owners, Thos. Hall and Co. Lad. 2nd May, 1783.

UNION.—Capt., Mich. Hornby. Sold and lost, 1750

UNION.—Owners, Wy. Dock Co., 1758-61.

UNION.—Jn. Jackson, R.H.Town, 1765-7.

UNION.—Bk.; 289; bt. Wy. 1764; Owner, Jn. Chapman; Builder, Thos. Fishburn; Owners, 1786, J. C., gent., and Hannah, widow of late Abel Chapman; Sq. st. Lost after 1791.

UNION.—Bk.; 281; bt. Wy. 1779; Owners, Geo. Porritt, m.m., Will. Medd, mariner, and Robt. Hunter, sailmaker, 1786. Sold to Thos. Holt, Transport, 1814; Owner, 1827, Ann Barker. Lost, 1828, or after.

VALENTINE.—Owner, Will. Wood, 1747-9.

VALIANT.—Bt. Wy. 1763; Owner, Nath. Campion; Capt., Will Herbert, of Scrbr.

VENUS.—S.; 302; bt. Wy. 1762; Owners, Matthew Storm, of Thornton, and Jn. Chapman, Wy.; Poop and forecastle; Reg. Nwcstl., 1796.

VIOLET.—Owner, Will. Suggitt, 1749-51, Lost, 1758.

VIOLET.—Slp.; 53; bt. Wy. 1774; Owner, 1786, Francis Easterby; Lute st.; Owner, 1787, Jn. Easterby, of Skinningrove; in 1794, a round st., sch. 77 tons; Owner, Paul Cook. Taken by the enemy, 1801.

VIOLET.—Ralph Jackson and Co.

VINE.—Owner, Will. Hornby, R.H.B., 1761-5.

VINE.—Owner, Jn. Walker; Capt., Hen. Walker, 1765-7.

VINE.—Bn.; 129; bt. Wy. 1787. Sold.

VIGILANCE.—Bg.; bt. Wy. 1776.

VIGILANT.—Bn.; 200; bt. Wy. 1788; Owners, Jn. and F. Barry. Sold.

VOLUNTEER.—S.; 302; bt. Wy. 1756; Owners, Richd. Moorsom and Sam. Pressick; Round st.; 97 by 27; Owners, 1825, Richd. Moorsom, senr., R. Moorsom, jun., Margaret Pressick, and Robt. Ward, Coal Exch., Lndn.; Ship rigged in 1825;

Reg. at Hull, March, 1829; Owners, 1840, Oliver and Co., Hull. This old ship sailed from Hull for Sierra Leone in the autumn of 1841, being 85 years old.

WARD.—Owner, Will. Ward, 1756-7.

WARD.—Owner, Dan. Chilton, 1765-7. Run down 1780 by a vessel belonging to Messrs. Everard, Brown and Co., Lynn.

WATSON.—Jn. Marshall, Staithes, 1761-5.

WELCOME MESSENGER.—Bg.; 206; bt. Wy. 1768; Owner, Jn. Stephenson; Owners, 1787, Ann, widow of Jn. S., and James Atty, sailmaker; two masts; 85 by 24. Lost, 1790.

WHITBY.—S.; 376; bt. Wy. 1748; Capt., Jn. Mellar, 1747-9; Voy. to Riga; Owners, 1787, Jn. M., Is. Stockton and Hen. Clark; Round st. Lost, 1793.

WHITBY.—S.; 302; bt. Wy. 1770; Owners, Jn. and Will. Barker and P. Middleton; three masts; 95 by 27; Whaler in 1786. Sold to Nwcstl., 1790. Lost Petereat Point, entrance of Gaspé Bay, St. Lawrence, May, 1827.

WHITBY PACKET.—Bn.; 91; bt. Wy. 1757; Owner, Paul Cook, baker. Taken by enemy.

WHITBY MERCHANT.—Capt., Jn. Pearson, 1772-6.

WILLIAM.—Owner, Will. Richardson, R.H.B., 1749-51.

WILLIAM.—Bg.; 227; bt. Hull 1762; Owners, Thos. Willis and Co. Taken by the French, 1795.

WILLIAM AND JANE.—S.; 237; bt. Wy. 1717; Owner, Hen. Clark, 1750; Cat built; Owners, 1787, Hen. Clark, Thos. Milner, and Isabella, widow of late Isaac Richardson; Reg. Nwcstl., 1789.

WILLIAM AND SARAH.—Capt., Jacob Hudson, 1747-9.

WILLIAM AND JANE.—Owner, Jn. Hill, 1747-9.

WILLIAM AND MARY.—Owner, Will. Coulson, 1747-9. Sold, 1759.

WILLIAM AND MARY.—Bk.; $\frac{376}{400}$; bt. Wy. 1762; Owner, Abel Chapman; Owners, 1786, Jn. Chapman and Isaac Stockton; Sq. st.; 110 by 29; in 1799, Robt. Chapman, gent., Ed. and Aaron Chapman, ship builders; Capt., 1791, Constable Dunning. Sold to Nwcstl., April, 1800.

WILLIAM AND JANE.—Will Croft, 1775-79.

WILLIAM AND ANN.—Bk.; $\frac{344}{369}$; bt. Wy. 1781; Owners, Will Skinner and Francis Skinner and Will. Reynolds; 101 by 29. To Greenland; Capt., Will. Bridekirk. Lost, 1830.

WILLING MIND.—Capt., Thos. Gale, 1758-61.

WISK.—S.; 254; bt. Wy. 1777; Owners, Jn. and Thos. Holt and T. Milner; Poop and forecastle; 92 by 26. Condemned at Lndn., 1811.

WYLAM.—Capt., Fergus Foster, 1758-61.

YOUNG JOHN.—S.; 337; bt. Wy. 1776; Owner, Hen. Walker Yeoman; Pink st.; Forecastle. Captured by enemy, 1796. Reg. Lndn., 1801; Wy. Register.

YOUNG WILLIAM.—S.; 431; bt. Wy. 1779; Owner, Geo. Atty; Owners, 1814, Hall and Co.

YORK.—Owner, Christ. Richardson, 1765-7. A large ship.

YORK.—Bg.; 126; bt. York 1775; Owners, Jn. Peacock and Richd. Pressick, of Newholm, 1787; Reg. Nwcstl., 1805. Lost at sea.

YORKSHIRE.—S.; bt. Wy. 1776. "August 15th, 1776, launched at Whitby a fine ship named 'Yorkshire,' burthen 650 tons, and pierced for only 16 guns, though large enough to mount 24. She is the largest ship yet built at that port, and is the property of Mr. Hammond, of Hull, being the seventh ship of large tonnage this gentleman has had built at Whitby within the last few years."

ZEPHYR.—Bk.; 388; bt. Wy. 1780-1; Owner, Thos. Middleton. Sailed 8th May, 1781. Sold to Hull. Owners, 1840, Nicol and Co., Nwcstl.

ZEPHYR.—Bn.; 98; bt. Scrbr. 1786; Owner, Will. Addison, Staithes. Sold to Sndld., 1794.

SECOND SECTION.

Containing the sailing vessels built at Whitby and their builders, both for local owners and for other ports, from 1790 to 1871, both inclusive. Chronologically arranged, with alphabetical index at the end.

See abbreviations and explanations before first section.

1790 SWIFT.—Bn.; 133; bd., Geo. and Nat Langborne. Sold. Reg. Lndn., 1792.

BARZILLAI.—S.; 281; bd., Hen. Barrick; Reg. Lndn., 1792.

AMPHITRITE.—S.; 286; bd., Jn. and Francis Barry; two stern windows; Reg. Grnsy., 1791.

SALUS.—S.; 292; bd., Reynolds and Co.; Owners, Jn. Knaggs, m.m., and Jn. Mead, Newholm; Reg. Lndn., 1792.

EDWARD.—Bn.; 165; bd., Hen. Barrick, jun.; Owners, Jn. Steward, m.m., J. Wakefield Simpson, and J. Atty. Sold, 1807, or after; Reg. Nwcstl.

CHOICE.—Bn.; 202; bd., J. and F. Barry; Owners, Anth. Buck, m.m., Will Chapman, sail-maker, and Gid. Smales, block and mast maker; Reg. Sndld., July, 1795.

ADEONA.—S.; 283; bd., Thos. Fishburn; Owners, J. Atty and Will. White, m.m.; Quarter barges. Sold, 1792.

FAVOURITE.—S.; 312; bd., Thos. Fishburn; Owners, T. Brodrick, Wy., and Will. Brodrick, Newington Butts, Lndn. Sold.

ACALUS.—Bn.; 142; bd., J. and F. Barry; Reg. Lndn., 1792.

ANN.—S.; 369; bd., Thos. Fishburn; Owners, Jos. and Will Barker and Robt. Middleton; Transport in 1814; Reg. Lndn., 1815.

HOPE.—Bn.; 107; bd., Hen. Barrick; Owners, James Dixon, m.m., and John Routh, schoolmaster. No record, but last Capt. 1799.

TYRO.—Bn.; 193; bd., Thos. Fishburn; Reg. Nwcstl., 1792.

BROTHERS.—Bn.; 163; bd., Ing. Eskdale; Reg. Dbln., 1792.

AMITY.—S.; 364; bd., Thos. Fishburn; Owners, Ed Chapman, m.m., and Jn. and Will. Chapman; Late Owners, Abel Chapman, of Parish of St. Giles, Lndn., and Jonath. C., of Lloyd's Coffee House; Reg. Wy., Jan., 1791; 102 by 29. Lost, 1796.

ESK.—S.; 305; bd., Thos. Fishburn; Owners, Jn. and Will Chapman; Reg. Wy., Feb., 1791; Reg. Nwcstl., 1822; Capt., 1814, J. Coates.

STREONSHALH.—S.; 281; bd., Ing. Eskdale; Owners, Hen. and Wakefield Simpson and Will. Chapman. Sold, 1801.

HENRY.—Slp.; 68; bd., Ing. Eskdale; Owner, Thos. Strother, Peak; sch. 1840; Owner, 1825, Sam Ireland, Peak; Owner, 1854, T. Turnbull; Owner, 1876, S Wishart, W. Hartlepool. Lost near Seaham Harbour, Oct. 31st, 1881.

AUTUMN.—Bg.; 195; Owner, 1840, Lambert, Sndld.

WELLINGTON.—Bg.; 344; Owner, 1840, Anderson, S. Shlds.

ELIZABETH.—Sch.; 84.

MERMAID.—Bg.; 77; Owner, 1814, Bridges.

REBECCA.—200; in Reg. of 1814.

ECLIPSE.—Slp.; 72; bd., Ing. Eskdale; Owner, Jn. Sanderson; Reg. Boston, 1798.

1791 BARRICK.—S.; 261; bd., H. and T. Barrick; Owners, H. B. and Robt. Gill, m.m.; 91 by 26; Capt., 1814, Braithwaite. Sold.

WILLIAM.—S.; 319; bd., T. Fishburn; Owners, Jn. Boulby, m.m., Israel Hunter, and Thos. Holt. Lost, 1797.

LEVIATHAN.—S.; 326; bd., J. and F. Barry; three masts; 99 by 28. Sold.

MELANTHO.—S.; 262; bd., T. Fishburn; Owners, Hen. Wilkinson, m.m., and Jn. Bennett, Runswick, and J. Wilkinson, Wy.; Transport in 1814. Sold to Lndn., 1793.

SYLPH.—S.; 320; bd., Reynolds and Co.; Owners, W. Reynolds, Will. Holt, and Nath. Langborne, shipbuilder, the latter in trust for Geo. Langborne, a minor; Reg. Lndn., 1791-2.

ATTY.—S.; 379; bd., T. Fishburn; Owners, Will. White, m.m., and J. Atty; Quarter barges. Lost.

FIDES.—S.; 353; bd., H. and T. Barrick; Owners, H. Barrick and Geo. B., m.m.; Transport, 1814; Reg. Hull, March, 1820.

CANADA.—S.; 319; bd., T. Fishburn; Owner, Abel Chapman; Reg. Lndn., 1793. Lost at Miramichi, Sept., 1819.

HANNAH.—S.; 294; bd., T. Fishburn; Owners, Ingram Chapman, sen. and jun., m.m., and W. Chapman, being people called Quakers. Lost, 1798.

ADRIATIC.—S.; 184; bd., Ing. Eskdale; Owner, James Atty.

VALIANT.—S.; 340; bd., G. and N. Langborne; Owners, Robt. Campion, m.m., and Lacy Lotherington, gent.; Transport, 1814. Lost, 1822.

HYGEIA.—S.; 232; bd., H. Barrick; Owners, J. Atty and Christ. Yeoman. Sold to Lndn., 1792.

EXPEDITION.—Bg.; 83; Owners, Robt. Medd, m.m., and Thos. Nettleship, baker; Reg. Wy., 1794, from Stcktn.; Reg. Stcktn., 1796.

DAEDALUS.—S.; 317; Transport, 1814; In Reg., 1822.

NANCY.—Bg.; 237.

PALLAS.—Bg., 219.

ABRAHAM AND MOSES.—Bg.; 111.

AVON.—S.; 367; Owner, Harford, 1813.

1792 HORTA.—Bn.; 123; bd., J. Barry. Sold to Sthmptn., 1793.

IRIS.—S.; 251; bd., T. Fishburn. Sold to Lndn., 1793.

VIGILANT.—S.; 321; bd., H. and T. Barrick; Owners, Jn. and Thos. Holt and Christ. Richardson. Lost, 1797.

PALLADIUM.—Bn.; 154; bd., G. and N. Langborne. Sold to Wtrfd., 1794.

MAY.—Bn.; 116; bd., T. Fishburn. Sold to Lndn., 1794.

ALBION.—S.; 400; bd., T. Fishburn; Owners, Christ. and Benj. Harrison.

HANNAH.—Bg.; 183; bd., H. and T. Barrick; Owner, Robt. Hodgson, m.m. Sold to Lynn, 1794.

TRAVELLER.—S.; 393; bd., G. and N. Langborne; Owners, Jos. Holt and Jn. Mellar. Lost, 1807.

ORIENT.—S.; 286; bd., Ing. Eskdale; Owners, J. Atty and Christ. Yeoman; Quarter window; 92.10 by 27. Sold to Lndn., 1793.

CYGNET.—S.; 319; bd., T. Fishburn; Owners, Jos. and Will Barker. Sold.

URANIA.—S.; 218; bd., T. Fishburn; Owners, Will Oxley, m.m., Robt. Burbank, and H. Barrick; Reg. Nwcstl., after 1797.

DAPHNE.—Bg.; 119; bd., Will. Reynolds and Will. Holt; Reg. Sndld., 1805.

MARINER.—S.; 371; bd., T. Fishburn. Sold to Lndn., 1793.

RAMBLER.—S.; 346; bd., Ing. Eskdale; 103.10 by 28.7; Reg. Lndn., 1797.

SOVEREIGN.—S.; 314; bd., H. and T. Barrick; Owners, Robt. Gill, m.m., Hen. Barrick, and Jn. Watson, grocer. Captured by the French, 1796.

ARK.—S.; 316; bd., G. and N. Langborne; Owners, Geo. Willis, m.m., Hen. Simpson, banker, and W. Chapman, sailmaker.

DOLPHIN.—S.; 336; bd., T. Fishburn; Owner, Thos. Clarke, m.m. Captured by the enemy, 1797.

DANAE.—S.; 342; bd., J. Barry; Owner, Will. Middleton; last Capt named is in 1796.

PROGRESS—S.; 280; bd., T. Fishburn. Sold to Lndn., 1794. Owner, Will. Usherwood, in 1810; three masts; Transport in 1814. Lost on the Saltees, near Ballyteige Castle, coast of Wexford, Ireland, at 1 a.m., Aug. 2nd, 1826.

CRESCENT.—S.; 309; bd., T. Fishburn; Owners, Sam and Will. Pressick and Co. Sold to Lndn., 1799. Captured by the enemy.

THOMAS AND MARTHA.—Bn.; 60; Owners in 1848, T. Trowsdale, W. Fenwick, W. Prodham, Wy., postillions; previously owned by T. Theaker, Staithes; bg. in 1825; bn., 1848. Lost near Grimsby, 1855.

1793 WILLIAM.—S.; $\frac{264}{239}$; bd., T. Fishburn; Owner, Will. Usherwood; Capt., Robt. Usherwood; three masts; 90.4 by 26.6. Lost in Baltic Sea, Oct. 28th, 1852.

NYMPH.—S.; 265; bd., H. and T. Barrick; Owners, James Calvert, Stokesley, and James Atty. Sold to Lndn., 1796.

EOLUS.—S.; 325; bd., T. Fishburn; Owners, Jn. Mead and Co. Lost, 1796.

ELIZABETH.—S.; 313; bd., G. and N. Langborne; Owners, Jos. Holt and Jn. Campion. Lost, 1807 or after.

FIDELITY.—S.; 310; bd., T. Fishburn; Owners, Jn. Knaggs, Jn. Miller, and Will. Chapman. Captured by enemy, 1795.

HANNAH.—Bn.; 147; bd., H. and T. Barrick; Owner, Robt. Hodgson; Reg. Lndn., 1796.

THALIA.—S.; 247; bd., H. and T. Barrick; Owners, Robt. Burbank and Will. Reed, of N. Shlds. Lost, 1803.

BELLONA.—S.; 366; bd., J. Barry. Captured by enemy.

VESTA.—S.; 328; bd., T. Fishburn; Owners, Thos. Willis and Will. Hustler. Captured by French, 1793.

VENTURER.—S.; 233; bd., Ing. Eskdale; Reg. Sndld., 1794 or after.

ALBION.—Bn.; 148; bd., G. and N. Langborne; Owners also.

LAUREL.—S.; 396; bd., T. Fishburn; Owners, Jos. and Will. Barker. Lost.

CERES.—Bn.; 148; bd., J. Barry. Sold to Sndld., 1795.

JOHN.—S.; 409; bd., T. Fishburn; Owners, Aaron, John, and Will Chapman. Captured by enemy.

GALATEA.—S.

MAJOR.—283; Owner, 1822, — Major.

1794 HARBINGER.—S.; 365; bd., T. Fishburn; Owners, Wakefield and Hen. Simpson and Abel Chapman. Wrecked and broken up at Miramichi, 1832.

BRITON.—S.; 323; bd., H. and G. Barrick; Owner, Will. Hill, Wy.; 102 by 27. Lost.

FORTRESS.—S.; 299; bd., Ing. Eskdale. Lost, 1796.

DEFENCE.—S.; 430; bd., T. Fishburn. Lost, 1794.

MARINA.—S.; 250; bd., Jn. Barry; Owners, Jn. Featherstone, m.m., Thos. Waite, and J. Barry. Sold to Grnck.

PATRIOT.—S.; 372; bd., Ing. Eskdale; Reg. Lndn., 1795.

ARETHUSA.—S.; 466; Transport, 1814.

JOHN CLARK.—S.; 408; Owner, Sedgwick, in 1814.

MAYFLOWER.—S.; 286; Owner, Hansell, 1814.

BOA VENTURA.—S.; 336; Owner, Simpson, 1822.

RANGER.—S.; 201; Owner, J. Harper, 1822.

SOVEN ZOGLE.—S.; 300; a London Transport, 1814.

FARMER'S INCREASE.—Slp.; 52; Owner, T. Napper, Brotton, 1825; Owner, 1794, Thos. Trowsdale; Reg. Stcktn., Dec., 1830.

WEAR.—Bg.

VIOLET.—

1795 ZEALOUS.—Bn.; 145; bd., T. Fishburn. Sold to Lndn., 1796.

BATTALION.—S.; 211; bd., Jn. Barry. Sold to Lvrpl., 1796.

DESIRE.—S.; 349; bd., T. Fishburn; Owners, Geo. Brodrick, m.m., and T. Brodrick; Last Capt., 1805. Lost.

BENSON.—S.; 330; bd., T. Fishburn; Owners, T. Willis and Will. Chapman, sailmaker; Capt., 1814, T. Willis; later, Rutherford; Transport, 1814; Reg. Lndn., 1818.

ENTERPRISE.—S.; 320; bd., T. Fishburn; Owner, Ed. Lister; Capt., Isaac Chapman; Reg. Lndn., 1802.

SCIPIO.—S.; 294; bd., H. and T. Barrick; Owners, Will. Hustler, T. Willis, and Rev. James Brownfield. Sold to Government and Reg. Lndn., 1818.

NEREID.—S.; 332; bd., Fishburn and Brodrick; Owners, Geo. Yeoman, m.m., Will. Chapman, and Rachel, widow of John Yeoman. Lost, 1799.

ARIADNE.—S.; 418; bd., G. and N. Langborne. Owner, Lacy Lotherington; Reg. Lndn., 1796.

PURSUIT.—S.; 408; bd., Ing. Eskdale; Reg. Lndn., 1799.

RENEWAL.—S.; 328; bd., H. and T. Barrick; Owners, Will. Middleton, gent., and Martha Middleton, spinster; Reg. Lndn., 1799.

CAMILLA.—S.; 218; bd., G. and N. Langborne. Sold foreign.

NIMBLE.—Bn.; 115; bd., Fishburn and Brodrick. Captured by the enemy.

LONDON.—S.; 337; bd., H. Barrick; Reg. Lndn., 1810; Owners, Will, Thos., and Ed. Chapman; Reg. Wy., July, 1816, and rebuilt; Transport, 1814; Reg. Lndn., 1825.

FAIRFIELD.—S.; 351; Owner, 1840, Westlake, Scrbr.; Transport, 1814.

ELBE.—S.; 312; In Reg. of 1814.

EQUESTRIS.—S.; 370; In Reg. of 1814.

MARY.—Bg.; 139; Owners, 1814, Wright and Co.

COMMERCE.—Bg.; 74.

COVERDALE.—S.; 579; bd., Fishburn and Brodrick; Owner, Norrison Coverdale, Lndn.

1796 CYGNET.—Bn.; 103; bd., Will. Reynolds and W. Holt; lengthened to 145 tons in 1802. Lost.

ACTEON.—S.; 262; bd., Fishburn and Brodrick. Sold to Lndn., 1796.

TRIDENT.—S.; 236; bd., Fishburn and Brodrick. Sold to Lvrpl., 1796.

GEORGE.—S.; 366; bd., G. and N. Langborne; 104 by 29; Transport, 1814; Owners, 1827, T. Chilton 12, Harrison Chilton 12, W. Jameson 12, Geo. Langborne 12, and Robt. Consitt 16; Owners, 1829, Harr. Chilton 16, Geo. Langborne 16, Th. Chilton 32; Reg. Lvrpl., 1838; Reg. Wy., 1841; Owner, T. Chilton 64; Reg. Lndn., 1852; Capt., 1822, Robt. Consitt; Owner, 1873, Elizabeth Smurthwaite, Nwcstl.

NAVIGATOR.—Bn.; 159; bd., John Barry; Owners, J. Barry, Th. Waite, and James Wake, lighterman. Sold to Dundee, 1799.

AIMWELL.—S.; 263; bd., Fishburn and Brodrick; Owner, Francis Agar. Lost, Aug., 1824.

SWIFT.—Bn.; 79; bd., Fishburn and Brodrick. Captured by enemy.

ARDENT.—Bg.; 175; bd., G. and N. Langborne. Sold to Lndn., 1797.

SUCCESS.—Bg.; 204; Owner, 1814, Will. Richardson; Capt., Addison Brown.

SURF.—Owner, J. Atty.

HATFORD.—S.; 312; Owner, Chapman; Transport, 1814.

HADDOCK.—Bg.; 256; In Reg. of 1814.

DALRYMPLE.—Bg.; 233; Owned at N. Shlds. in 1837.

AUGUSTA.—S.; 368; Owner, 1814, W. Clark.

ECONOMY.—Bg.; 190; In Reg. of 1814.

ARCADIA.—S.; Owner, Chapman.

MARY AND CLARA.—Bg.

1797 HOPE.—Bg.; 274; Owned at N. Shlds. in 1840; Transport in 1814.

ADROIT.—S.; 299; bd., Fishburn and Brodrick; Reg. Lvrpl., 1798.

PACIFIC.—S.; 365; bd., Fishburn and Brodrick; Owners, Will. Benson, m.m., Thos. Willis, and Will Hustler; 105 by 28. Lost.

HAZARD.—S.; 178; bd., Chapman and Campion; three masts; 80 by 23; Reg. Lndn., 1807 or after.

OLIVE BRANCH.—Bn.; 113; bd., Jn. Barry; Reg. Hull, 1797 or after.

ENTERPRISE.—Bg.; 184; bd., Ing. Eskdale. Sold to Lndn.

ALERT.—Slp.; 60; bd., Falkingbridge.

AID.—Bg.; 160; Owners, 1814, Capt. Brown and Co.

ISABELLA.—S.; 266; Owner, 1814, G. Robson.

OCEAN.—Bk.; 271; Owned at Lndn., 1840.

CAMBRIDGE.—S.; 351; Owners, 1814, Fletcher and Co.

WILL.—S.; 259; Owner, 1814, Metcalf.

1798 POLLY.—S.; 389; Owner, 1814, Henkey.

WAKEFIELD.—S.; 330; Transport, 1814.

COLUMBUS.—S.; 352; bd., Chapman and Co.; Owners, 1814, Gordon and Co.

AMATHEA.—Bn.; 144; bd., Ing. Eskdale; Reg. Lndn., 1802.

THREE BROTHERS.—Bn.; 146; bd., T. Barrick; Owners, Steph. Burn, m.m., and Jn. and James Burn, Sneaton. Sold about 1808.

MARY.—Bn.; 116; bd., Fishburn and Brodrick; Owner, J. Noddings; Reg. Lndn., 1807.

JOHN.—S.; 357; bd., Fishburn and Brodrick. Owners, Robt. Chapman, gent., Will. Chapman, sailmaker, and Ed. Chapman, shipbuilder; 102 by 28. Lost.

MARY.—Bn.; 194; bd., G. and N. Langborne; Reg. Grnck., June, 1798.

ALBION.—Bn.; 74; bd., G. and N. Langborne; Owners, N. and G. Langborne, the latter too ill to register; Owners, 1801, Jn. Watson, Thos. Marwood, merchant, and Robt. Anderson, mariner; Owners, 1825, Thos. Marwood, Richd. Ripley, surgeon, and Richd. Willis; Owner, 1837, Thos. Mills, Wy., m.m., 64. Lost, Dec., 1848.

ROVER.—Bn.; 120; bd., Fishburn and Brodrick. Sold.

EMERALD.—Bn.; 314; bd., Fishburn and Brodrick; Owners, Ing. Chapman and Jn. and Will. Chapman; 97.8 by 27.9; two masts; Transport, 1814; Reg. Lndn., 1820.

CAMPERDOWN.—S.; 351; Owner, Richd. Hutchinson; 102.5 by 28.7; Reg. Lndn., 1799; Reg. Wy., Feb., 1803; Reg. Hull, June, 1816.

ANDROMEDA.—S.; 301; Transport in 1814.

CORNWALL.—S.; 380; Owners, 1822, Gladstone and Co., Lvrpl.

COVE.—S.; 374; Owners, 1837, Messrs. Spivey and Cooper, Hull; Reg. at Quebec, 1854.

ELIZA.—S.; 350; Transport in 1814.

GRANT.—S.; 386; Transport in 1814.

1799 COMMERCE.—Bk., 188; Owners in 1822, Brown and Co.

CHARLOTTE.—S.; 331; bd., G. and N. Langborne; Owners, Christ. and Will. Richardson; 101 by 28; Reg. Lndn., 1799.

STRANGER.—S.; 185; bd., Fishburn and Brodrick; Owner, Elisha James Bell, N. Shlds.; 80 by 23; three masts; Reg. Jamaica, 1804.

ALERT.—S.; 380; bd., Fishburn and Brodrick; 107 by 29; Reg. Lndn., March, 1800; Transport, 1814.

ANN.—S.; 311; bd., Fishburn and Brodrick; Owners, Will. Hustler, Will Hill, and Rev. James Brownfield. Lost.

LIBERTY.—Bn.; 231; bd., Chapman and Co.; Owners, Jn. Chapman, Wak. Simpson, banker, and Will. Chapman; two masts. Lost, 1801 or after.

HERALD.—S.; 338; bd., J. Barry; Owners, Robt. Waite, m.m., and J. Barry. Sold to Government and Reg. Lndn., 1816.

AMITY.—S.; 323; bd., Chapman and Co.; Owners, Ed., Will., and Robt. Chapman; three masts; 100 by 27.10; Transport, 1814; Reg. Lndn., 1818.

REFUGE.—S.; 191; bd., Fishburn and Brodrick; 82.4 by 23.6. Sold to Hull, 1800.

INDEFATIGABLE.—S.; 549; bd., Ing. Eskdale; three masts; 127 by 31.8; Transport, 1814. Burnt at Batavia, Oct. 23, 1815.

SPRIGHTLY.—Bn.; 153; bd., Chapman and Co.; Owners, Ed., Aaron, and Robt. Chapman; Sold Jan. 14, 1800, for £2,460, and Reg. Scrbr., March, 1800; Reg. Wy. from Scrbr., July, 1803, and Owner, Will. Hill; 190 tons in 1807. Taken by the enemy.

EFFORT.—Bn.; 214; bd., J. Barry. Sold to Nwcstl., 1800.

REQUEST.—S.; 248; bd., T. Barrick; Owners, T. Barrick, Robt. Gill, mariner, and Jn. Watson, merchant; Reg. Nwcstl., July, 1815.

CONCORD.—Bn.; 74; bd., Th. Coates; Owner, James Wake; Reg. Sndld., 1800 or after.

AIMWELL.—S.; 380; Owners, 1814, Anderson and Co.

HUGH JONES.—Bk.; 190; in 1814 Reg.

MARY ANN.—S.; 387; Owner, 1814, Bone; Transport in 1814.

1800 WILLIAM.—Bg.; $\frac{185}{223}$; Owner, 1840, Thompson, S. Shlds.

WESTMORELAND.—S.; 366; Owners, 1814, Gladstone and Co., Lvrpl.

LORD MELVILLE.—Bg., 177; Owner, 1814, T. Wilson.

OAK.—Slp.; 78; bd., Thos. Fishburn, jun., and T. Brodrick, and Owners; lengthened in 1803 from 61.11 by 17.5 to 78 by 22 into Bg. 160 tons; Reg. Scrbr., 1829.

SUPPLY.—Bn.; 95; bd., J. Barry, and Owner; Reg. Sndld., Feb., 1811.

THAIS.—Bn.; 117; bd., Ing. Eskdale; Owner, Christ. Pearson, m.m.

BRITANNIA.—S.; 362; bd., Chapman and Campion; Owners, Aaron, Ed., and Will Chapman; 104 by 28.9; Transport, 1814. Burnt at Hudson's Bay, Jan., 1819.

GARLAND.—S.; 353; bd., Fishburn and Brodrick; Owner, Jos. Barker; Capt., Peter Barker. Sold to Government, 1818.

BRITISH QUEEN.—S.; 360; bd., G. and N. Langborne, and Owners with Geo. Langborne, m.m.; 106 by 28; Reg. Lndn., Oct., 1800.

DOLPHIN.—Bn.; 88; bd., Will. Webster; Owners, Will. and Jn. Oxley, and Jn. Ridley, R.H.B.; Reg. Scrbr., 1803.

MENTOR.—S.; 204; bd., Fisbhurn and Brodrick, and Owners; 85.5 by 23.11; Reg. Lndn., 1802.

SPRING.—S.; 397; bd., Fishburn and Brodrick; Owners, Jos. and Will. Barker; Capt., Constable Dunning; 110 by 29.2. Sold to Government and Reg. Lndn.

SWAN.—Bn.; 121; bd., G. and N. Langborne, and Owners; Capt., Jn. Scholefield. Sold.

MELANTHO.—S.; 289; bd., Ing. Eskdale; Owners, Christ., Will., and Jn. Richardson; Transport, 1814; Reg. Beaumaris, Jan., 1826.

MONARCH.—S.; 333; bd., Jn. Barry; Owners, Jn. Barry and Mary, wife of Rev. Geo. Robertson, and Elizabeth Barry, widow. Sold to Government, 1818.

GRATITUDE.—Bn.; 146; bd., T. Barrick; Owners, H. Barrick, Robt. Gill, and Jn. Watson. Reg. Lndn.

DASH.—Bg.; 61; bd., Chapman and Campion; Owners, Christ. Richardson, banker, and Will. Holt, merchant. Sold to Sndld., 1803 or after.

DIADEM.—Bk.; 367; bd., Chapman and Campion; Owners, Ed. Aaron and Robt. Chapman. Sold to Government, 1818.

SOPHIA.—Slp.; 66; bd., Fishburn and Brodrick; Owner, Right Honourable Henry, Lord Mulgrave, Baron Mulgrave of Mulgrave; Lute stern; Quarter deck and cockpit; afterwards a sch.; Owner, 1876, Jane Purvis. Sold to W. N. Jackson, Hrtlpl., and Walter Jn. Hocking, Trimdon. Broken up, March, 1885.

ALLIANCE.—Bg.; 291; bd., Fishburn and Brodrick; Owners, Will. Usherwood, merchant, and Robt. U., m.m.; 96 by 26.10. Proceeding in ballast to London in 1814, on transport service, was lost on Hasebro' sand. Capt. J. Usherwood and some of the crew drowned.

ESK.—Bn.; 69; bd., Jonath. Lacy, being one of the people called Quakers. Sold to Hull.

LORD NELSON.—S.; 177; bd., Ing. Eskdale; Owners, Jn. Wilson, m.m., and Jn. Earnshaw, surgeon; three masts; 78 by 23.5; Reg. Dominica, 1808.

OAK.—Bn.; 158; bd., Chapman and Campion; Owner, Atty. To Whale fishing, 1803-4-5-6. Taken by the enemy.

SIMPSON.—Bk.; 354; bd., Fishburn and Brodrick; Owners, Hen. Simpson, banker, and Matt. Akenhead, Gateshead; 105 by 28.2; Transport, 1814. Lost, 1818. First cost and outfit, including stores, £6,542. 1st voy., Wy. to Lndn., thence Portsmouth, Madeira, Demerara, Martinique, Portsmouth and London. Jan., 1801, to Sept. 7. Nett Profit, £190 6s. 2nd voy., Government service, Gibraltar. Oct., 1801, to June, 1802. Nett Profit, £816 18s. 8d. 3rd voy., Petersburg. June to Oct., 1802. Profit, £12 19s. 2d. 4th Dantzic. Oct. to Dec., 1802. Profit, £281 17s. In the "coppered" service from Oct., 1804, to Jan., 1815. Nett Profit for that period, £15,030 9s. 1d. Repaired at Wy., 1816. Cost, £1,491 9s. 11d. Capt. in 1818, J. Bowes.

CONCORD.—Bg.; 70.

BEATRIX.—Bn.; 174; In 1811 Owners, Jn. Usherwood, m.m., and Will Usherwood, junr. Bought from London, 1811. Lost on Yarmouth beach, Nov. 12, 1877.

ELIZABETH.—Sch.; 79.

SPRIGHTLY.—S.; 395; In a Register of 1814 as Transport.

JAMES.—S.; 346; Owners, Richd. Moorsom and Jn. Addison; Capt., 1814, Smith; three masts; 106 by 28. A whaler. Brought in 24 whales in 1824. Reg. Abrdn., 1828.

Dec. 6, 1826, Mr. J. Smith, aged 64, many years Capt. of "James" in the whale fishery.

1801 ACTIVE.—S.; 346; Owners, Hall and Co., Lndn.

ROSS.—S.; 383; Owner, Brodrick, Hull.

SUSSEX.—S.; 371; Owner, 1814, Fletcher.

HARLEQUIN.—Bg.; 220; Transport in 1814.

LITTLE HENRY.—Slp.; 64; bd., Fishburn and Brodrick; Owner, Lord Mulgrave. Lost, 1843. Owner, Will. Watson, Lythe. When the landslip happened at Kettleness in 1829 this sloop was "laid on," and the houseless people took refuge on board.

UNION.—Bn.; 190; bd., Fishburn and Brodrick; Owners, Jn. and Will Steward, m.m. Lost, 1828.

MAJESTIC.—S.; 406; bd., Chapman and Campion; Owners, Ed., Aaron, and Robt. Chapman; 110 by 29.9½; Transport, 1814. Sold to Government and Reg. Lndn., 1810.

RESOLUTION.—Bn.; 117; bd., Jonath. Lacy. Lost.

LATONA.—S.; 348; bd., Fishburn and Brodrick; Owners, Jn. Campion Coates, Jos. Holt, and T. Hall, m.m.; 103 by 28; Transport, 1814; Reg. Hull, March, 1835.

RETRIEVE.—Bg.; 175; bd., Chapman and Campion. Lost, 1806.

ALEXANDER.—Bk.; 313; bd., G. and N. Langborne; Capt., 1801, Geo. Langborne, m.m.; Capt., 1806, Robt. Ross, Lndn.; 99.10 by 27.8; Transport, 1814. Taken by the enemy.

STANDARD.—Bn.; 335; bd., Fishburn and Brodrick; Owners, Ingram, John, and Will Chapman; two masts; 101.8 by 27.11. Lost, 1803.

DOROTHY.—Bk.; 202; bd., Fishburn and Brodrick; Owners, Thos. Willis, W. Benson, Thos. Benson, and Will. Willis, m.m.; 83 by 24; Bg. 1804, 193 tons; Transport, 1814; Reg. Hull, 1806.

ELIZABETH.—Bn.; 117; bd., W. Webster; Owners, W. and Jn. Webster; Reg. Scrbr., 1805; Reg. Wy., 1810; Reg. Scrbr., June, 1810.

LAVINIA.—Bn.; 173; bd., Chapman and Campion; Owners, Ed., Aaron, and Robt. Chapman; Reg. Lndn., 1802.

CROWN.—S.; 383; bd., Jn. Barry, and Owner. 105.10 by 29.3. Lost, 1833 or after. "The 'Crown,' London towards Whitby, Sunday, Jan. 13, 1828. Strong breeze from S.E., with dark, cloudy weather; weighed and made sail down the river. 9 a.m. abreast of the Nore, weather clearer and moderate, made all sail possible down the Swin. 5 p.m. crossed the Stamford with a fresh breeze from W. by N. and brought up in Yarmouth Roads, where we remained till Wednesday. At daylight a fresh breeze sprang up from S.E. with a heavy rolling swell. We tried to get the anchor, but having broken the windlass, we were obliged to slip, and make sail. We proceeded out of the Roads, and across the Deeps during the day, with a strong breeze from the S.E. At 9 o'clock the watch thought they saw Flambro' light about W. We then close reefed the top sails, reefed the foresail and stood to the

Eastward, it blowing a heavy gale. Soon after we found a great quantity of water in the hold, which increased rapidly. We endeavoured to wear about 11 p.m., but could not get her round—cut away the mizzen mast, hove to; and the pumps being choked we bailed with buckets till about 5 a.m. on Thursday, when Capt. Wray, supposing that we were near the land, wore the ship to the Eastward. At daylight the ship, having a strong list, was nearly gunwale under to leeward. We tried to get the vessel before the wind, and had to cut away the main top mast, but this not being sufficient, we cut away the mainmast and succeeded. We decided to put the ship ashore, having seven feet of water in the hold. Shortly after we fell in with the brig 'Earl of Strathmore,' of Sunderland, Jn. Melville, commander, and we hoisted a signal of distress. He immediately hove his brig to; and we with great difficulty got the boats out, but the long boat filled and sank. Six hands, with a woman and child, passengers, got into the skiff and safely reached the brig. Four hands returned to the 'Crown' in the skiff, and got some more of the crew. Just then the weather cleared, and land was seen, Boulby, near Staithes. We were obliged to wear the brig off the land. Seeing this, the rest of the crew of the 'Crown' lowered the jolly-boat from the stern and got safely into it. We now wore again and stood for the boat, and about 11 a.m. on Thursday we were all safe on board the brig, and received every attention. We bore away for Sunderland, where we arrived about 3 p.m."

"During the violent gale of Jan. 17, 1828, a large ship came on shore at Skinningrove, with the main and mizen masts gone, and abandoned. It was found to be the 'Crown,' of Whitby, owned by Mr. Jn. Barry, which left London Jan. 13. The vessel has been refloated, with the aid of a tug-boat, and brought into the harbour."—Wy. Repository.

The "Crown" left Whitby for Quebec with 30 passengers, May 15, 1828.

AUTUMN.—Bn.; 106; bd. T. Barrick; Owners, H. and G. Barrick; Owners, 1805, Brodricks', Wy.; 127 by 32. Lost, Nov., 1810, at Harwich.

CULLAND'S GROVE.—S.; 599; bd., Fishburn and Brodrick; Owners, Messrs. Atty and Co.

1802 FORTUNE.—Bg.; 138; Owner, 1814, Moorsom.

JOHN AND ROBERT.—Bg.; 303; bd., Chapman and Co.; Owner, Chapman; Transport, 1814. Lost at Plymouth, Jan., 1828; Capt., Swinton. Crew saved.

HODGKINSON.—Bg.; 128; Owner, Brodrick.

ADVENTURE.—Bg.; 173; Owner, 1814, Larkin.

DIADEM.—S.; 455; bd., Chapman and Campion; Owners, Ed. and Aaron Chapman and Robt. Campion; Transport, 1814; Capt., 1814, Jn. Buck.

"The skeleton of a curious animal has been landed at Portsmouth from the 'Diadem' transport of this town. It was shot by Lieut. Emery, near the island of Mombassa, East Africa. When first seen it had a striking resemblance to the human form. The sailors judged it to be a mermaid—the existence of which has been so much disputed. There were two others in company. Lieut. Emery ate some of the flesh, which he thought very good. The bones are preserved entire." — "Wy. Magazine," 1827.

ALERT.—Bn.; 132; bd., John Barry. Sold to Lndn., 1802.

HAPPY RETURN.—Lug.; 57; bd., Robt. Marshall; Owned at Rnswck. Lost with all hands.

MARGARET.—S.; 272; bd., Fishburn and Brodrick; Owners, Benj. Hunter, m.m., Robt. Hunter, sailmaker, and Israel Hunter, gent. Captured by the enemy.

AMITY.—Slp.; 63; bd., Peter Cato; Owners, James Nailor and Jn. Fewster; Reg. Stcktn., 1812; Reg. Wy. from Stcktn., Jan., 1819; Owner, Richd. Barnard. Lost. Reg. cancelled, Sept. 15, 1837.

NEPTUNE.—S.; $\frac{237}{267}$; bd., Fishburn and Brodrick, and Owners; three masts; 90.9 by 24.8. Taken by enemy.

AGRICULTURE.—Slp.; 63; bd., Fishburn and Brodrick; Owner, Matt. Stephenson, Ellerby; Owner, 1812, Christ. Richardson. Lost, 1823.

FLY.—Bn.; 107; bd., G. and N. Langborne, and Owners; Reg. Lndn., 1809.

NYMPH.—Bn.; 117; bd., T. Barrick, and Owner. Sold to Lndn., 1802.

CHILTON.—S.; 276; bd., Fishburn and Brodrick; Owners, Thos. and Harrison Chilton and Thos. Pierson; Transport, 1814; Capt., 1822, Sam. Galilee; Owners, 1825, Harrison Chilton, sen. and jun.; Jan., 1832, H. Chilton, jun., sold 32/64 to Thos. Chilton, Hull; Sept., 1837, Harr. Chilton sold 32/64 to Th. Chilton, Lvrpl.; Reg. Lvrpl., Nov., 1837.

ALERT.—Slp.; $\frac{48}{84}$; bd., G. and N. Langborne; Owner, Robt. Ward, Ruswrp.; enlarged in 1806; Owner, 1854, Will. Simpson, m.m., 64; Reg. Nwcstl., Oct. 8, 1856; Reg. Wy. from Nwcstl., March 16, 1863. "1860, May 25, the 'Alert,' sch., reg. at Newcastle, and owned by Will Jarvis, residing at Cley, Norfolk, left Lynn for Hartlepool, Capt. Jarvis and two men. On the 28th, off Runswick, distant two miles, the wind suddenly changed to N.E. and blew a gale. Took in the sails, but the vessel became unmanageable, and ran ashore near Sandsend. Expected to be got off little damaged." Owner, 1863, Dav. Gray Gibson, 64; Owners, 1869, Ant. Jackson, 32, Ed. Barker, 32; Owner, 1896, Jn. Danby. Sold to Hull, 1902.

BEE.—Sch.; 74; bd., T. Barrick. Captured by enemy.

GALILEE.—Bn.; 196; bd., Fishburn and Brodrick; Owners, Robt. Galilee, Staithes, John Campion Coates, and Harrison Chilton. Taken by the enemy.

SNEATON.—Slp.; 52; bd., P. Cato; Owner, Jn. Miles, Sneaton; later, Sam Flintoft and W. Lister. Lost, 1840.

FLORA.—Slp.; 62; bd., Ing. Eskdale; Reg. Bridlington, 1805 or after.

LONDON PACKET.—Sch.; 72; bd., Jonath. Lacy; Owner, Robt. Dickinson, grocer; lengthened 1803 to Bn., 107; Reg. Lndn., 1807.

BETSY.—Lug.; 57; bd., Marshall Copley; Owner, Jacob Brown, Staithes; Owners, 1825, Ellis and Margt. Brown and Diana Sanderson. Lost, 1851.

PEACE.—Slp.; 59; bd., James Wake and Co. Lost.

ELEANOR AND ANN.—Lug.; 55; bd., Will Webster; Owners, T. Clark and Co., Runswick; Owner, 1825, Will. Tyerman. Lost, 1831 or after.

ZEPHYR.—Slp.; 61; bd., James Wake; Reg. Bstn., 1802.

BROTHERLY LOVE.—Lug.; 61; bd., Jn. Skelton; Reg. Scrbr., Sept., 1809.

TRIAL.—Lug.; 59; bd., Marshall Copley; Owner, Addison Brown, Staithes; Reg. Nwcstl., 1829.

ELIZABETH AND SALLY.—Lug.; 56; bd., Robt. Marshall; Owner, Matt. Heselton. Lost.

BRUNTON.—Slp.; 60; Owner, Lord Mulgrave.

1803 ROBERT AND ANN.—108; bd., Eskdale, Cato and Co.; Owner, R. Henderson, Sndld.

RESOLUTION.—S.; 291; bd., Fishburn and Brodrick; Owners, T. Fishburn, junr., Thos. Brodrick, and Will. Scoresby, m.m.; 100.3 by 26.2; Lad., Feb. 21; Capt., 1803, Will. Scoresby, sen.; Owner, 1826, Thos. Brodrick, sen. Sold, Nov., 1829, to James Hogg, of Peterhead, by Jn. Todd, of Hull, Jn. Brodrick, of Hull, Thos. Simpson, of Ruswarp, banker, and Thos. Brodrick, of Wy., all executors of Thos. Brodrick, sen., of Ruswarp; Reg. Abrdn., Dec., 1829. A Peterhead whaler in 1846.

BETSY AND SALLY.—Bg.; 81; bd., Eskdale, Cato and Co.; Owner, Matt. Stephenson, of Ellerby, farmer. Sold to Ed. Wood, Rnswck. Owners, 1815, Francis Spencelayh and Isaac Mills, R.H.B. Lost at Cley, 1821.

VISITOR.—Bn.; 75; bd., Richd. Wake. Sold to Lndn., May, 1803.

SOVEREIGN.—S.; 369; bd., Jn. Barry, and Owner; Transport, 1814. Lost, October, 1814.

WHITBY.—S.; 336; bd., Chapman and Campion. Transport, 1814; Capt., 1814, Jn. Bowes. Burnt, 1814.

HEBE.—Bg.; 133; bd., Fishburn and Brodrick, and Owners; Owner, 1813, Geo. Lawson, Wy.; Capt., Ralph Horne; Reg. Sndld., March, 1824; Reg. Wy. from Sndld., Aug., 1828; Owner, Sarah Letbe, R.H.B. Lost.

DUKE OF BRONTE.—Bg.; 195; bd., T. Barrick; Owners, Jn. Wilson and Geo. and Matt. Marwood and Marmaduke Marwood; Transport, 1814; Reg. Lndn., March, 1815. Left Shlds. for Lndn., Dec. 13, 1825. A missing ship.

NEWBEGIN.—Slp.; 67; bd., Eskdale, Cato and Co.; Owners, Jn. Young and Co.; Owner, 1832, Andrew Smales, Wy., 64. Lost.

LORD NELSON.—Slp.; 67; bd., Eskdale and Cato; Owners, Will and Thos. Clarkson, ironmongers; Reg. Scrbr., Feb., 1821.

RUSWARP.—Slp.; 57; bd., Eskdale, Cato and Co.; Owner, Dymoke Wells; Reg. Lndn., 1805, to Miles and Wells.

SCEPTRE.—S.; 369; bd., Chapman and Campion, and Owners; 105.10 by 29; Capt., 1814, Fearon; Transport, 1814. Lost, Oct., 1814.

EGTON.—Slp.; 57; bd., Eskdale, Cato and Co.; Owner, Dymoke Wells, Wy.; Reg. Rochester, 1805.

BOUNTIFUL.—Bn.; 165; bd., Richd. Boyes Wake; Owner, James Wake; Reg. Lndn.

SUSANNA.—Bn.; 171; bd., Fishburn and Brodrick; Owners, Francis Agar and Co.

DUKE OF BRIDGEWATER.—Slp.; 71; bd., Thos. Newbitt; Owner, Jn. Boanson. Lost.

BETTER LUCK STILL.—S.; 215; bd., Lacy, Eskdale and Cato; Owner, Dymoke Wells; Reg. Lndn.

BETSY.—Bn.; 91; bd., Wm. Jackson; Owner, James Naylor; Bg., 1824; Owners, 1849, Isaac Mills, and Robt. Davidson, of Broughton, farmer; Reg. Ipswich, 1849.

HARMONY.—Bn.; 135; bd., Richd. Wake; Owner, James Wake. Sold to Government and Reg. Lndn., 1812.

ADSTON.—Sch.; 68; bd., Jonth. Lacy; Owners, Dymoke Wells and Robt. Adston, m.m.; Reg. Bstn., 1810.

ALDBRO.—S.; 249; bd., Eskdale, Cato and Co.; Owners, Thos. Hall and Sons, Hull.

ESSEX.—S.; 276.

GEORGE.—S.; 360; Owner, 1814, Fenwick; Transport, 1814.

HANNAH.—S.; 277; Transport, 1814.

HOPE.—Bg.; 142.

INGRIA.—Bk.; 317; Owners, 1814, Cooper and Co., Hull. Hull to Davis Straits.

NEREUS.—S.; 433.

CHATHAM.—S.; 256.

WOLGA.—S.; 352; Owner, 1840, W. Ward, Hull; Transport, 1814.

SAMUELS.—S.; 399; Owner, 1814, Hewitson. Hull to Davis Straits.

ANN.—Lug.; 56; bd., Thos. Gale; Owner, Verrill, Staithes; 28 tons in 1836. Lost, 1836 or after.

1804 BALTIC MERCHANT.—S.; 250; bd., Eskdale, Cato and Co.; Owners, Robinson and Co., Hull; Owner, 1840, Wright, Nwcstl.; Lad., Nov. 23, 1804; Transport, 1814.

MARMION.—Bg.; 160; Owner, 1814, Clark. Transport, 1814.

LORD WHITWORTH.—S.; 294; Owner, 1814 Cummings.

LORD ST. HELENS.—S.; 297; bd., Eskdale, Cato and Co.; Owner, Jn. Cummings, of Lndn.; Capt., Turnbull; Owner, 1814, Woodcock; Transport, 1814; Owned at Nwcstl. Wrecked at Miramichi, Feb., 1833.

DALE.—Bk.; 458; Owners, 1837, Roydon and Co., Lvrpl.

LINCOLN.—S.; 372; bd., Fishburn and Brodrick; 107 by 28.8; Reg. Leith, 1808.

ACTIVE.—Slp.; 59; bd., T. Barrick; Owner, 1820, Jn. Gill, R.H.B. Lost.

MAJESTIC.—S.; 377; bd., Holt and Richardson; Owners, Ed. and Aaron Chapman and Robt. Campion. Burnt, 1808.

THOMAS AND SALLY.—Slp.; 70; bd., Thos. Coates. Lost.

IDAS.—S.; 243; bd., Fishburn and Brodrick; Owners, Jn. Linton, East Row, m.m., and Co.; Bn. in 1825. Lost at the Mumbles, Quebec to Cardiff, Dec., 1829; Capt. Ramsden.

ACORN.—Sch.; 80; bd., Holt and Richardson; Owner, 1824, Jacob Huntrods, Ruswarp. Lost, 1824.

KINGSTON.—S.; 341; bd., Eskdale, Cato and Co.; Owner, 1841, Chapman, Lvrpl.

LAVINIA.—Bn.; 171; bd., Eskdale, Cato and Co.; 1st reg. Owners, Gideon Smales and Co.; Reg. Scrbr., no date. Sold to W. Moorsom, of London.

ANN AND SUSANNA.—Slp.; 60; bd., Val. Pinkney; Owner, 1818, Will. Race; Reg. Faversham.

HERALD.—S.; 336; bd., Jn. Barry; Owners, R. Barry and Robt. Waite, m.m.; Transport, 1814. Lost at Honduras, 1820.

GRATITUDE.—Bn.; 124; bd., Richd. Wake; Owner, James Wake; Reg. at Flmth.

OXFORD.—S.; 401; bd., Fishburn and Brodrick; Owners, Ed. and Aaron Chapman and Robt. Campion; 108 by 29; Transport, 1814; Reg. Grangemouth, April, 1818.

EXPEDITION.—Bn.; 80; bd., Mark Dring; Owner, Robt. Dickinson; Reg. Hull, Nov., 1809.

AURORA.—Bn.; 163; bd., Eskdale, Cato and Co.; Owners, Gideon Smales and Co. Sold to Geo. Langtry, Belfast, 1804.

DORIS.—S.; 375; bd., Holt and Richardson; Owner, Christ. Richardson; Transport, 1814.

ALBION.—S.; 343; bd., Fishburn and Brodrick; Owners, Will., Ed., and Aaron Chapman. Lost.

SNIPE.—Slp.; 72; bd., Jn. Barry, and Owner; Reg. Bstn., 1805.

ORION.—Bg.; 198; bd., Holt and Richardson, and Owners; Transport, 1814. Sold to Lndn.

DUBLIN.—S.; 262; bd., James Wake; Owners, Peter Grantham and Co., Wy.; Reg. Dbln., May, 1806.

EDGAR.—Bg.; 218; bd., G. and N. Langborne, and Owners; Transport, 1814; Reg. Nwcstl., 1818.

THOMAS AND ELEANOR.—Lug.; 58; Owner, Matt. Heseltine, Rnswck.

HARMONY.—Bg.; 184; Transport, 1814.

1805 MINERVA.—Bg.; 170; Reg. Gottenberg, 1814.

JOHN.—S.; 387; In a Reg. of 1822.

RESOURCE.—S.; 296; bd., Holt and Richardson; Owners, Mich. and Ja. Harrison; three masts; 97.3 by 27.2½.

VINE.—Bn.; 110; bd., Fishburn and Brodrick, and Owners; Reg. Sndld., July, 1810.

KING GEORGE.—S.; 365; bd., Fishburn and Brodrick; Owners, W. Skinner, T. Fishburn, jun., T. Brodrick, and Will. Harrison, of Field House; 104.3 by 23.10. Lost.

BETSY.—Bn.; 77; bd., Eskdale, Cato and Co.; Owners, David Wood, Rnswck., and Will. Legg, Roxby; 57.5 by 18.2; Reg. at Sndld., Aug., 1810; Reg. Wy. from Scrbr., Feb., 1839; Owners, Jn. Milburn, 32, Jn. Hogarth, m.m., 32; Owners, 1850, Jn. Hoggarth, 32, and Jane Sedman, widow, 32; Owners, 1854, Charles Mason, 32, of York, railway manager, and Matt. Snowdon and others not of Wy.; Owner, March, 1855, Thos. Gibson; Owners, April, 1855, Geo. Park and Geo. T. Knaggs, Matt. Snowdon and others, co-partners, trading together at and near Wy., under the firm of the "Eskdale Iron, Stone and Steam Sawmill Co."; Owner, 1858, Jn. Harding, 64. Lost, April 2, 1859.

CURLEW.—Bn.; 127; bd., Jn. Barry. Lost.

BRILLIANT.—S.; 242; bd., James Wake; three masts; 86.4 by 25.10. Sold to London.

SPRIGHTLY.—Bn.; 194; bd., Fishburn and Brodrick. Sold to Government and Reg. Lndn., 1816.

HALCYON.—Bn.; 160; bd., James Wake, and Owner. Sold to Whthvn.

NAUTILUS.—Bn.; 182; bd., Holt and Richardson. Sold to Lndn.

CYRUS.—Bn.; 126; bd., Thos. Barrick; Owners, 1853, T. Turnbull and Benj. Garminsway; a Bg., 149 tons, in 1853. Lost, 1862.

AID.—S.; 399; Owners, 1814, Moore and Co.

LARKINS.—S.; 418; bd., Eskdale, Cato and Co.; Lad., April 14. Sold to Geo. Haworth, jun., Hull. Shlds. to Greenland whale fishery.

CHARLES.—Bk.; 334; Owners, 1837, Douglas and Co., Lndn.

SHIPLEY.—S.; 388; a Transport in 1814.

MARY.—Bg.; 149; bd., Eskdale, Cato and Co.

CICERO.—S.; 482; bd., Eskdale, Cato and Co.; Owner, Robt. Dale, Lndn.; Lad., Nov. 22.

1806 RICHARD AND SARAH.—Bn.; 178; bd., Thos. Coates; Owner, Richd. Unthank of Staithes; Reg. Scrbr., March, 1817.

HERALD.—Bn.; 79; bd., James Wake; Owners, Jn. and Anth. Twistleton; Reg. Bstn. later.

RUBY.—Bn.; 136; bd., Fishburn and Brodrick, and Owners with Robt. Campion. Lost, March, 1814.

OCEAN.—Bg.; 210; bd., Eskdale, Cato and Co.; Owners, Gideon Smales and P. Cato. Sold to Messrs. Conway and Davidson, Lvrpl., Oct., 1806.

ARK.—Bn.; 120; bd., Holt and Richardson, and Owners. Sold to Sndld., May, 1808.

THETIS.—Bg.; 183; bd., Eskdale, Cato and Co., and Owners. Sold to Lvrpl., Feb., 1807.

VIGILANT.—Slp.; 81; bd., Jn. Barry, and Owner. Sold to Stcktn.

ROBUST.—S.; 297; bd., Fishburn and Brodrick; 96.4 by 26.10½. Sold to Glsgw., 1807.

ACTIVE.—Bn.; 78; bd., Holt and Richardson; Owners, Jn. Anderson, R. Campion, and T. Hunter. Captured, 1812.

ANN GRANT.—Bk.; 378; Owned at Sligo.

COMMERCE.—Bg.; 93; In Reg., 1814.

FLEETWOOD.—S.; 417; Owner in 1822 Reg. Urquhart.

IRWIN.—S.; 388; Owner, 1814, Lawrence.

ISABELLA.—S.; 384; Owner, 1814, A. Fleming.

RICHARD.—S.; 345; Owner, 1814, Gladstone, Lvrpl.

SIBELLA.—Bg.; 82; bd., Eskdale, Cato and Co.; Owners, Barrett and Co., Stcktn.; Lad., Oct. 11.

1807 MARIA.—Bg.; 119; Owner, 1814, Heseltine; Reg. Stcktn., 1835.

ADONIS.—Bg.; 140.

STOCKTON.—Sch.; 67; bd., Eskdale, Cato and Co.; Owners, Capt. Gresham and Co., Stcktn.; Owner, 1863, John Millburn; drove ashore near Filey during a gale, April 30; Owners, 1866, Jn. Bedlington Ayre, 32, Jn. Lennard and Jos. Brown, 32 jointly. Lost at Deal, Jan. 7, 1867.

SPRING.—Bn.; 90; bd., Jn. Barry, and Owner. Lost near Dunkirk.

POMONA.—Bn.; 97; bd., Smales and Co., and Owners. Sold to Whthvn., 1807.

LORD MULGRAVE.—S.; 414; bd., T. Barrick; Owners, Ed., Will., and Hen. Chapman; 112.2 by 29.7½; Reg. Lndn., 1817.

VIGILANT.—Bg.; 193; bd., Eskdale and Co.; Owners, Ward and Brown, Bridlington; Lad., Aug. 16.

LEDA.—S.; 399; bd., Holt and Richardson; Owners, Christ. Barker and John Richardson, shipbuilder; 108.9 by 29.5; Transport, 1814; last Capt. given is in 1817.

MARINER.—S.; 446; bd., Fishburn and Brodrick; Owners, Jos. Barker, Wy., and Chapman; 113.6 by 30.3½; Transport, 1814; Reg. Lndn., 1807.

DOLPHIN.—Lug.; 63; bd., Robt. Marshall; Slp. later; Owners, T. Garbutt, Jn. Copley, and Jn. Gibson, Rnswck. Broken up at Bridlington, 1824.

PLANTER.—S.; 259; bd., Fishburn and Brodrick; 91.9 by 25.8; Reg. Brstl., 1809.

BRITON.—S.; 386; bd., Jn. Barry, and Owner; Owners, 1825, J. Campion and J. Barry; 108 by 29.2½; Transport, 1814. Lost, 1828 or after.

ARGO.—S.; 484; bd., Eskdale, Cato and Co.; Owner, Robt. Dale, Lndn.; Lad., Sept. 17.

1808 BRAGANZA.—S.; 286; bd., Smales and Cato.

AURORA.—S.; 471; bd., Fishburn and Brodrick; Owner, Brodrick, Hull; 115.6 by 30.8; Transport, 1814; Capt. at one time, Joshua Cherry; Reg. Hull, 1830.

HERO.—Bn.; 79; bd., Smales and Cato; Owner, 1811, Thos. Clark, Rnswck. Lost, Feb. 20, 1817, off the Farne Islands.

ROYAL BRITON.—Bg.; 237; bd., Holt and Richardson; Owners, Jn. Campion Coates and Will. Holt, shipbuilders. Lost, 1820.

HERO.—S.; 415; bd., Holt and Richardson, and Owners; Transport, 1814. Lost, 1840 or after.

OCEAN.—S.; 437; bd., Thos. Barrick; 116 by 29.9; Reg. Lndn., 1828.

PATRIOT.—Bn.; 148; bd., Fishburn and Brodrick and Owners; Bg. later; Transport, 1814. Sold to Bridlington, 1809.

ZEPHYR.—Sch.; 116; bd., Holt and Richardson; Owner, Will. Holt; Owner, 1819, Jos. Holt. Sold to Nwcstl., 1825.

DOMINICA.—S.; 402; bd., Eskdale, Cato and Co.; Owners, 1822, Urquhart and Hope.

MARY AND ANN.—S.; 329; Owners, 1814, Mitchell and Co.

MEDCALF.—S.; 230; Owner, 1814, Medcalf, Lndn.

Bow of "Leda."

LEDA.—Slp.; 91; bd., Fishburn and Brodrick, and Owners; Bn., 1834; 61 by 19.2. Broken up, Dec., 1869; Owner then, Robt. Cuthbert.

1809 DAPHNE.—Bn.; 108; bd., Smales; Owners, G. Smales and Cato. Sold to Hull, 1810.

PERSEVERANCE.—Bn.; 167; bd., Jn. Barry, and Owner. Sold to Lvrpl., 1810.

DOVE.—Slp.; 61; bd., Smales and Co.; Owners, Smales and Cato; Owner, 1810, Jn. Ditchburn. "The 'Dove,' Pearson, of Whitby, coal laden from Stockton, went ashore near the mouth of the Tees, Oct. 13, 1827, and has become a total wreck."

HARMONY.—S.; 364; bd., Holt and Richardson; Owners, John Holt, Will. Skinner, and Jn. Campion Coates; 99.6 by 29.9; Owners, 1825, Will. Skinner, Wy., 32, Richd. Walker, 8, Will. Braithwaite, 8, Will. Skinner, jun., 8, Thos. Walker, 2, Jn. Holt. Skinner, 2, Richd. Walker, jun., 2, and Geo. Skinner, 2, the last seven all of Stcktn.; Reg. Hull, Dec., 1827.

MOUNTAINEER.—S.; 487; bd., Smales and Co.; 114.5 by 31; Transport, 1814. Sold to Glsgw., 1810.

ATLAS.—S.; 361; Owners, 1814, Leitch and Co. A West Indiaman.

FORTITUDE.—Bg.; 184; Owner, 1814, Barrick.

METCALF.—S.; 423.

MINERVA.—Bg.; 168.

STAR.—S.; 488.

TRELAWNEY.—S.; 455; Owner, 1814, Gordon.

PEKIN.—S.; 330; Owner, 1822, A. Belcher.

1810 MONARCH.—S.; 309; bd., Holt and Richardson; Owners, Jn. Holt and Will. Skinner. Sold to Montrose, 1813.

ORIENT.—Bn.; 118; bd., Jn. Barry, and Owner. Sold to Lndn., 1813.

THREE BROTHERS.—Bn.; 114; bd., Fishburn and Brodrick; Owner, Jn. Clark, Rnswck. Taken by the enemy.

MINERVA.—S.; 488; bd., Smales and Cato; 113.3 by 31.6½; Transport, 1814; Capt., And. Smales; Reg. Lndn., March, 1811.

HYPERION.—S.; 468; bd., Jn. Barry; 116.5 by 30.9. Sailed from Wy. to the East Indies direct, Jan. 3, 1817. Lost about 1821.

GOTHEBORGS WALGANG.—Bg.; 316; Owned at Gothenburg.

ANN GREEN.—S.; 330; bd., Smales and Cato; Owners, Grove, Watson and Co., Grnck.

JAMES.—S.; 419.

NESTOR.—S.; 345; Owners, 1837, Smith and Co., Glsgw.

NEPTUNE.—S.; 483; Owners, Roberts and Co.

SCIPIO.—Bg.; 158; Reg. Grnck., 1810.

HALCYON.—S.; 382; Owners, Reed and Co.

JOHN HAMILTON.—S.; 532.

PERCIVAL.—Bg.; 325; bd., Smales and Cato; Reg. Nwcstl., 1835.

1811 WILLIAM.—S.; 197; bd., Fishburn and Brodrick; Owner, Will. Martin; three masts; 84.1 by 23.5½; Bn., 1815; Owners, 1825, Robt. Braithwaite, 32, and Robt. Jackson, of Goldsbro', 32; Capt., 1825, Thos. Weatherill; Capt., 1831, Jos. Hill. Lost, 1831 or after.

BROTHERS.—Lug.; 49; bd., Marshall Copley; Owner, Anth. Causton of Rnswck.; later, Will. Langster; Reg. Sndld., March, 1837.

JUNO.—Bn.; 106; bd., Smales and Co.; Owners, Will Storm and Co., R.H.B.; Owner, 1831, M. Waugh; Reg. Scrbr., July, 1832; Reg. Wy. from Scrbr., 1833; Owner, Robt. Hill, 64; Owners, 1836, R. Hill, 48, and Ed. Corner, 16; Reg. Scrbr., April 27, 1844.

REGENT.—S.; 392; bd., Holt and Richardson; Owner, Jn. Holt, jun.; 106.4 by 29.7. Lost, 1823.

CENTURION.—S.; 536; bd., Fishburn and Brodrick, and Owners; 123.6 by 31.7; Capt., Will. Kelly. Lost, Dec., 1811.

NEPTUNE.—Bg.; 215; bd., Thos. Barrick, and Owner; Transport, 1814; Capt., Oxley; Reg. Nwcstl., 1823.

LORD WELLINGTON.—S.; 410; bd., J. Langborne and Co.; Owners, Jos. Holt, Jn. Campion Coates, and Jn. Richardson; Transport, 1814; Last Capt. named, 1822.

THETIS.—S.; 252; bd., Jn. Barry, and Owner; Transport, 1814; Reg. Nwcstl., 1820.

SPECTATOR.—S.; 421; bd., Smales and Co.; Reg. Lndn., March, 1812.

CYRUS.—S.; 408; bd., Holt and Richardson; Owners, Holt and Skinner; Transport, 1814; Reg. Nwcstl., 1823; Owner, 1837, Crawford, Nwcstl.

DEXTERITY.—S.; 397. A Leith whaler in 1814.

CYGNET.—Bk.; 408; Reg. Nwcstl., 1828.

1812 ISABELLA.—Bn.; 117; bd., Smales and Co.; Owner, Emmanuel Parkinson. Lost, 1817.

EAGLET.—Bn.; 138; bd., Holt and Co., and Owners; Reg. Sndld., 1824.

ATLANTIC.—Bg.; 204; bd., Jn. Barry, and Owner. Sold to Lndn., Jan., 1813.

BELLONA.—S.; 465; bd., Fishburn and Brodrick, and Owners. Lost, Nov., 1813, according to Wy. Custom House Register. Tombstone in Wy. Churchyard, "Cap. Jn. Foxton, who was drowned in the 'Bellona' near Brest, coast of France, Jan. 4, 181-" (last figure worn away).

NAUTILUS.—S.; 335; bd., Smales and Cato, and Owners. Sold to Lndn., Oct., 1812.

POMONA.—Bn.; 116; bd., Fishburn and Brodrick; Owner, T. Brodrick. Lost, 1822.

ATLAS.—S.; 501; bd., T. Barrick, and Owner; 115.6 by 32.2; Transport, 1814. Lost after 1815.

STATELY.—S.; 474; bd., Jn. Barry, and Owner; 116.11 by 30.11; Transport, 1814; Reg. Lndn., 1815.

COMPETITOR.—S.; 423; bd., Smales and Co., and Owners; 113.6 by 29.5; Capt., 1814, Anth. Buck; cost £10,396 19s. 4d.; Reg. Lndn., 1820.

DUNCOMBE.—S.; 393; bd., Holt and Richardson, and Owners with Will. Skinner; 109 by 29.1; Transport, 1814. Lost at Sydney, port of Cape Breton, as per certificate from Collector, dated June 12, 1824; Owner, Jn. Holt, Ruswarp, 64.

ESK.—S.; 354; bd., Fishburn and Brodrick, and Owners; 106.6 by 27.11; Capt., Will. Scoresby; Reg. at Wy., Feb. 25th, 1813. This vessel in 1826, owned by Mr. Thos. Brodrick, and commanded by Dunbar, when returning to Whitby from the whale fishing, having experienced light winds since leaving Shetland, and the captain endeavouring to make use of the tides near the land to reach home, was caught by a sudden N.E. gale, and driven ashore at 11 p.m., Sept. 6, on the rocks adjoining to Marske, near Redcar, with the loss of the captain and all the crew, except three men, one other having been landed at Shields. One of the three men saved was lame, and had to use a crutch, which washed ashore close to the man. The vessel was a total wreck. Leach, Boyes, and Pearson saved. Jn. Skinner landed at Shields. When the Esk first went to sea in 1813, the owners put on board six silver tea-spoons. The first year one of them was lost. In 1826 the other five were left ashore when the ship sailed. After the vessel was lost the missing spoon was found on Redcar sand, and was returned to the owner, then Mr. Thos. Brodrick.

COSSACK.—Bg.; 72.

MAGNET.—S.; 228; bd., Smales and Cato; Owner, Moorsom, Seaham.

NEW DARLINGTON.—Bg.; 123; Owners, 1840, Stcktn. Shipping Co.

REGULUS.—S.; 368; Owner, 1840, Fenwick, Lndn.; Transport, 1814; Owners, 1854, Evans and Co., Lvrpl.; Plymouth to Sydney.

NYMPH.—Bg.; 121; bd., Smales and Cato; Owners, Saunders and Co., Aberdeen.

1813 CLIO.—Slp.; 82; bd., Jn. Barry, and Owner; Reg. Scrbr., 1815. A brig in 1847. Reg. Wy., March 5, 1847, from Scrbr.; Owner, Will Estill, 64; Reg. Shlds., Feb. 18, 1851.

EMMA.—S.; 399; Owners, Robt. Clark and Geo. Brodrick; 110 by 29.1½. Lost. Certificate delivered at Quebec, 1816.

MINSTREL.—Bn.; 123; Owners, Messrs. Simpson and Chapman. Lost.

ASIA.—S.; 458; Owner, Ed. Chapman; 118.8 by 29.9; Transport, 1814; Reg. Lndn., 1825.

MEDUSA.—Bg.; 217; bd., Thos. Barrrick; Owners, Thos. Hutchinson and Thos. B. Lost, 1830, or after.

REGALIA.—S.; 358; Owners, Jn. Holt Richardson and Robt. Campion; 103.8 by 28.8; Reg. Lndn., 1818; Transport, 1814.

THALIA.—Bg.; 247; bd., G. and N. Langborne and W. Jameson, and Owners; Reg. Lndn., Nov., 1814; Reg. Wy., Jan., 1820; Owner, Thos. Garbutt, Sandsend. Lost, 1823.

NESTOR.—S.; 387; bd., Jn. Barry, and Owner; Capt., Jn. Theaker; 107.10 by 29.1; Transport, 1814; Reg. Lndn., Aug., 1817.

VITTORIA.—S.; 403; bd., W. S. Chapman and Co.; Owners, Hen. Simpson and W. S. Chapman; 107.7 by 29.10; Transport, 1814; Reg. Lndn., Dec., 1817.

FLORA.—Bn.; 84; bd., Fishburn and Brodrick; Owner, T. Barrick; bg., 1825; bn., 1834; Owner, 1825, Lord Mulgrave. Lost, 1834, and Owner, Jn. Langborne.

SAPPHO.—S.; 360; bd., Holt and Richardson; Owners, Christ. Richardson and Co.; 104.1 by 28.9; Reg. Lndn., 1814.

MINERVA.—S.; 356; bd., Fishburn and Brodrick, and Owners; Bk., 1825; Owners, 1830, T. Simpson, banker, 32, Dorothy Akenhead, 16, and Isabella Willis, 16; Owner, 1838, Mr. Thos. Simpson, 64. The "Minerva," belonging to Mr. Simpson, came into Whitby to dry dock, March, 1838. Reg. Glasgow, 1844.

BRILLIANT.—Bg.; 237; bd., Jn. Barry, and Owner; Capt., 1814, A. Smales. Sold to Lndn., 1814.

GRANTHAM.—S.; 229; bd., Fishburn and Brodrick; three masts; Reg. Lndn., Jan., 1815.

CAMDEN.—S.; 399; bd., W. S. Chapman and Co.; Owner, Hen. Simpson, Wy., Ed. Chapman, Wy., and Aaron Chapman, Lndn.; 107.3 by 29.3. Went to America about March 28, 1838. A whaler 1833 to 1837. Reg. Lndn., 1824.

CHANCE.—Bg.; 140; bd., T. Brodrick, and Owner; Reg. Lndn., 1814.

LEVANT.—S.; 231; Owners, 1814, Cook and Co.

VIOLET.—Bg.; 84; bd., Fishburn and Brodrick, and Owners.

MESSINA.—S.; 353; Owner, 1822, Fishburn; Capt., 1839, Jn. Pierson.

1814 MONARCH.—Bg.; 210; bd., Holt and Richardson; Owner, James Dixon. Foundered June, 1828, 90 miles north of the Shetlands; six drowned. Master (C. Harrison) and three others picked up by a brig.

VICTORY.—S.; 420; bd., Fishburn and Brodrick, and Owners; 115.8 by 28.10; Owner, 1839, T. Fishburn as executor; Owners, 1846, James Terry, Ugthorpe, 32, and Jn. Mews,

Rotherhithe, 32; Reg. Lndn., April 3, 1847. The ship "Victory" was commanded by John Braithwaite. She was an East Indiaman for some years. Capt. Braithwaite died July 21, 1826, aged 38 years, at Stanchio, an island in the Archipelago, formerly called Cos or Coos. It is near that part of Asia Minor known as Anatolia, and almost opposite Bodroun, the ancient Hallicarnassus.

LILY.—Bn.; 100; bd., Fishburn and Brodrick, and Owners; Owner, 1837, Jn. Barritt, m.m., 64; Owner, 1838, Thos. Johnson, Wy., 64. Lost, 1840.

STANDARD.—S.; 367; bd., Robt. Campion; Owners, 1814, Hen. and Edmund Lotherington; Capt., 1814, Thos. Lotherington; Reg. Lndn., 1814; 111.9 by 30.0½; Reg. Wy. from Lndn., April, 1826; Owners, 1826, Edmund Lotherington, 32, Hen. Lotherington, 32; Owner, 1829, Robt. Campion. Lost. Reg. cancelled Jan. 12, 1832.

STAKESBY.—S.; 437; Owners, Hen. Simpson, Ed. and W. S. Chapman; Owners, 1825, Ed. and W. Chapman; Reg. Lndn., May, 1829.

JOHN BARRY.—S.; 520; bd., John Barry, and Owner; Reg. Lndn., 1825; 120.5 by 31.10½; Reg. Wy., Jan. 27, 1834; Owner, Jn. Barry, 64; Owners, Sept. 27, 1838, Robt. Barry, Rev. Will Barry, of Longstow, Cambridge, and Seaton Trattles, executors of late Jn. Barry. The vessel sold to Stephen Ellerby, of Bow Road; Reg. Lndn., Oct. 12, 1838.

The "John Barry," Capt. Roach, for Rotterdam, put back to Batavia, Jan. 15, 1827, with loss of rudder, but discharged to repair.

The "John Barry" passed by an American ship on Friday, Oct. 30, 1835, North of the equator, bound to Sydney, Australia, with 260 convicts.

The "John Barry," an opium hulk at Hong Kong, after being dismasted in a typhoon about 1841, in charge of Hugh McGregor, afterwards chief of the first Whitby police in 1856.

BRITISH TAR.—Bn.; 266; Owners, Matt. Akenhead and Hen. Simpson. Lost. Reg. cancelled 1841.

REGRET.—S.; 356; bd., T. Barrick; Owners, John Watson, Hen. Barrick, and Geo. Barrick, jun. Burnt in 1824.

ARCTURUS.—S.; 372; bd., Holt and Richardson, and Owners with Christ. Richardson. Lost, 1815.

FORTITUDE.—S.; 361; bd., Fishburn and Brodrick, and Owners; 106.4 by 28. Sold to Lndn., April, 1815.

1815 CONCORD.—S.; 384; bd., R. Barry; Owners, Jos. Addison and Robt. Campion in 1824; 109.6 by 28. Burnt at Miramichi, Oct., 1824.

ENDYMION.—S.; 352; bd., W. S. Chapman; Owners, Thos. Simpson and Jn. Chapman, bankers, and W. S. Chapman; Owners, 1824, Thos. Garbutt, Sandsend, 22, Zachariah Garbutt, 21, Zachariah Garbutt, sen., 21; Reg. Hull, Jan. 7, 1840; Owner, 1854, Brodrick, of Hull.

SALUS.—Bn.; 105; bd., Fishburn and Brodrick, and Owners; Reg. Lndn., 1816.

BROTHERS.—S.; 431; bd., W. S. Chapman and Co.; Owners, W. and E. Chapman. Reg. Lndn., 1817.

TRITON.—S.; 405; bd., Fishburn and Brodrick, and Owners; 113.9 by 28.9; Reg. Greenock, 1822.

MACKAREL.—Bn.; 135; bd., Robt. Barry; Owner, Jn. Barry; Reg. Lndn., 1818.

ARGO.—Bn.; 113; bd., W. S. Chapman; Owner, Ed. Dale, Wy. Lengthened 1821 to 143 tons. A brig in 1866, and Owner, W. Todd Anderson, R.H.Bay. Wrecked on Saltfleet Sands, April 13, 1876.

HOLDERNESS.—Bg.; 231; bd., Robt. Barry, and Owner; Reg. Lndn., May, 1823.

AUTUMN.—Slp.; 77; bd., Gid. Smales, and Owner; Capt. in 1823, W. Moorsom. Lost.

WOODFORD.—S.; 378; Owner, 1817, Chapman; Owner, 1834, Jn. Lawson, Wy. Lost, 1838.

NAIAD.—Bg.; 112; Owner, 1840, Mitchell and Co., Leith.

INTEGRITY.—Bg.; 177; Owner, 1840, Wishart, Leith.

BETSY.—Bg.; 128; Owned at Wy. in 1837.

HORSLEY HILL.—Bg.; 239; Owner, John Lotherington; Capt., T. Buck.

INDIA.—S.; 522; Owners, Gibbons and Co.

RICHARD AND SARAH.—Lug.; 49; Owners, Robt. and Richd. Verrill, Staithes. Lost, with all hands, April, 1815.

1816 MELANTHO.—Bn.; 165; bd., T. and H. Barrick; Owners, J. Ward, Wy., and John and Robt. Porritt, Runswick; Lad. March 1; Reg. Lndn., 1821.

PHŒNIX.—S.; 324; bd., W. S. Chapman and Co.; Owners, Will., Thomas and Ed. Chapman; 103 by 27.5; Lad. Jan. 15, 1816; Owners, 1826, Will Chapman, Ed. Chapman, Robt. Chapman, of Parish of St. Andrew's, Holborn, Jonathan Chapman, Tooting, Aaron

Chapman, of Highbury Park, and Thos. Chapman, late of Whitby, now British agent at Elsinore, 1826.

The "Phœnix," whaler, according to Dr. Young, brought into Whitby in the year 1832, being the only ship that year, 234 tons of oil (195 Imperial measure), the largest quantity ever imported here in one vessel. In the ship's log, it is stated that on arrival she anchored in Sandsend roads to lighten, and that three small vessels, "Lark," "Henry," and "Industrious Farmer," were loaded from her.

In 1837 this vessel, being towed out of Whitby Harbour by the steamboat "Streonshalh," broke adrift from the steamer, which was too light to tow her, and drove ashore on the Scar behind the East Pier, April 6. Crew saved. On April 20 she was refloated and brought into the harbour. She was repaired in dry dock. Sold to Scrbr. and Reg. there Oct. 17, 1837. She was in the timber trade for some years after this.

MARS.—S.; 343; bd., Fishburn and Brodrick, and Owners; Lad. Feb. 14; 101.7 by 29.6; Owner, 1826, Robt. Clark, Wy., 64; Bk. in 1825. Lost, 1828.

OSBALDESTON.—Bn.; 245; bd., John Holt; Owners, Robt. Clark and Will. Darley; Lad. March 13; Reg. Nwcstl., 1823.

HANNAHS.—Bn.; 116; bd., Holt and Richardson; Owners, Thos. Hay, m.m., Francis Spencelayh; Lad. March 29. Enlarged 1817 to 146 tons. Owner, 1824, Thos. Hay, m.m., 64; Lost end of 1824.

STAR.—Bg.; 113; bd., Fishburn and Brodrick, and Owners. Sold to W. Burdon, Stcktn., Sept., 1817.

CRISIS.—Bn.; 131; bd., R. Barry; Owner, Geo. Clark, Wy.; Lad. July 10; 73 by 20.8. Brig 1825; 131 tons. Owners, 1825, Will Martin, Wy., 11, and Geo. Clark, 53; Capt., 1816, Geo. Clark; 1817, Aug., Robt. Braithwaite; 1820, Geo. Clark; 1820, Aug., Ja. Spink; 1821, G. Clark; later, Chas. Barker; 1822, Feb., W. Martin; Reg. Scrbr., 1830, April 26, to Will Smith.

EQUITY.—Bg.; 195; bd., W. S. Chapman and Co.; Owners J. Storr and Peacock; Owners, 1824, W. Chapman, Wy., 8, Ed. Chapman, 8, Aaron Chapman, Highbury, 8, John Storr, Wy., 32, and Robt. Chapman, of Parish of St. Andrew's, Holborn, 8; Owner, 1854, Hewson, N. Shields; Reg. Nwcstl., 1827, Nov.

Geo. Chambers, sen. (artist), was bound apprentice for seven years to Capt. Storr, of the "Equity." G.C. was born 1803. He was in a small coaster for about two years before being bound to Capt. Storr.

WILLIAM HARRIS.—S.; 342; bd., Robt. Barry; Owner, Jn. Barry; bk. 1834; Lad. Oct. 22; 101.2 by 28.2; Owners, 1837, Robt. Barry, 40, Thos. Barry, 16, W. Brodrick, Bow Church Yard, 8. Lost, 1843.

MIRABLES.—Bg.; 215; bd., Gid. Smales, and Owner with John Rutherford. Lad., Dec. 19; Reg. Lndn., 1817.

WILLIAM PENN.—S.; 253; Owner, 1817, Chapman.

CLIO.—Slp.; 86; bd., Robt. Barry, and Owner; Sch. in 1824; Capt., 1816, Jos. Wray.; Reg. Scrbr., March 7, 1835.

1817 ORION.—Bg.; 233; bd., Holt and Richardson; Owners, Jn. Holt and Chrst. Richardson; Reg. Lvrpl, Sept., 1817.

LAUREL.—Bn.; 105; bd., Holt and Richardson, and Owners; Reg. Hull, June 29, 1819.

ECONOMY.—Bn.; 145; bd., W. S. Chapman and Co.; Owner, Geo. Willis, m.m.; Owners, 1827, Richd. Willis, Ed. Corney and Geo. Willis. Lost, 1834.

FRIENDS.—Bn.; 113; bd., Fishburn and Brodrick; Owner, Stephenson Lawson, m.m.; Reg. Lndn., June, 1820.

CLEOPATRA.—Bg.; 267; bd., Robt. Barry; Owners, Geo. and And. Brodrick; Reg. Lndn., Nov., 1825.

FAIRY.—Bn.; 77; bd., W. S. Chapman and Co.; Owners, Hen. Simpson and Ed. W. S. Chapman; Reg. Hull, Oct., 1817. Lost in the Texel, Dec., 1846. Owner, Tyerman.

WHITBY.—Slp.; 44; bd., Robt. Barry; Owner, Jn. Barry; Reg. Kingston, Jamaica, Feb., 1819.

SULTAN.—Bg.; 191; Reg. Wy. from Lndn., 1828; Owners, Jn. Lawson and Will. Cooper. Lost at Prince Edward Island, 1832.

LOYAL BRITON.—Bg.; 300; Reg. Lndn.; Reg. Wy. from Lndn., April, 1832; Owners, R. and T. Clark; Reg. Lndn., March, 1843.

EMULOUS.—Bg.; 225; Reg. Lndn., 1831, Owner, Chapman.

HESSLE.—S.; 351; In Reg. of 1822.

TRANSIT.—S.; 250; Owner, 1822, Fisher. To West Indies and South Seas.

1818 RIBEY GROVE.—Bg.; 243; Owners, 1831, Torr and Co , Hull.

MARY.—Bk.; 298; Owner, 1838, Chadwick, Lndn.

LUNA.—Bg.; 203; Owner, 1840, W. Reed, Scrbr.

DELIGHT.—Bg.; bd., Holt and Richardson, and Owners.

PROVIDENCE.—Bg.; 162; bd., Fishburn and Brodrick. Owners, Geo. Smith and Ed. Nettleship; In Feb., 1839, during a N.E. gale and heavy sea, the Providence came ashore leaky, on Whitby sands, and broke up a few days later; Owner, 1839, Ed. Nettleship, 48, and Jn. Pearson, 16.

MARY.—Bn.; 118; bd., Fishburn and Brodrick; Owner, Jn. Martin Ayre, Wy. Lost, 1828.

ANN.—Bg.; 209; bd., Robt. Barry; Owners, Robt. Appleton, Benj. Gowland and Jos. Addison.

SKELTON.—S.; 260; bd., Holt and Richardson; Owners, James, sen. and jun., and Will Dixon; three masts; Owners, 1825, Will Dixon, of Skelton, 16, James Dixon, 32, and Mich. Trowsdale, of Northallerton, 16.

July 30, 1828, the "Skelton," Capt. Percy, of Wy., Trinidad for London, struck on a rock 13ft. under water, Anguilla Island bearing East, distant 10 miles, and foundered. Crew saved.

MULGRAVE.—Lug.; 28; bd., Christ. Gale; Owner, R. Verrill, Staithes; afterwards a sch.; Owner, 1859, John Cross, Rswrp.; Owner, 1890, Alexander Hobson. Broken up, 1891.

HIBBERTS.—S.; 439; bd., Robt. Barry; Owner, Jn. Barry; Lad. Oct. 1; 112.4 by 30.5½; Reg. Lndn., Oct., 1820.

AMITY.—S.; 369; bd., T. Barrick; Owners, Ed., Abel, Will. and Aaron Chapman; Lad., Oct. 30; 105 by 28.3; Reg. Lvrpl., May 27, 1842.

ADVENTURE.—Bn.; 108; bd., Robt. Barry, and Owner; Lad. Jan. 12, 1819; Reg. Jersey, May, 1819.

LABURNUM.—S.; 261; bd., Holt and Richardson; Owner, John Holt; Lad. Oct. 30, 1818; altered rig., 1822, to Bn.; Reg. Lndn., March, 1825.

MARGARET.—S.; 375; Owners, 1822, Fairlie and Co.

SURREY.—S.; 400; Owners, 1822, Welbank and Co.

1819 HARVEY.—Bg.; bd., Langborne.

WILLIAM.—S.; 362; Owners, 1822, Moore and Co. To Jamaica.

COUNTESS OF MULGRAVE.—Lug.; 62; bd., Falkingbridge; Owners, Matt. Dobson and Jos. Tose, Rnswck. Lost, with all hands, about 1819.

WILLIAM PITT.—263; bd., Robt. Barry; Owners, Geo. Brodrick, sen. and jun.; Owners, 1824, And. Brodrick, 28, Geo. Brodrick, 28, and Will Brodrick, Bow Church Yard, 8. Lost, 1833, or after.

PLEIADES.—Bn.; 183; bd., Holt and Richardson; Owner, Jn. Holt, jun.; Lad. Feb. 10, 1819; Reg. Lvrpl., 1823; Reg. Wy. from Lvrpl., May 30, 1837; Owners, Jn. Kirby, 16, Thos. Horsley, 16, Geo. Young Kirby, 16, and Mary Thompson, 16. A brig in 1837. Lost. Reg. cancelled at Limerick, Dec. 26, 1840.

MITTEN HILL.—Slp.; 65; bd., John Spencelayh; Owner, Thos. Sawdon, Wy., farmer; Reg. Sndld., June, 1823.

HARMONY.—Slp.; 14; bd., Peter Ayres; 30.10 by 10; Owners, P. Ayres and Jos. Britain; Reg. Sndld., 1822.

SMALES.—Bg.; 161; bd., F. Spencelayh; Owner, Gid. Smales; Capt., T. Parkinson; Lad. June 10. Lost, 1834.

SOVEREIGN.—S.; 433; bd., Fishburn and Brodrick, and Owners; Lad. June 8; 114.7 by 29.3½; Bk. 1834; Owner, 1838, Harrison Chilton, jun., 64; Capt. in 1842, Will Galilee; March, 1852, Harr. Chilton, late of Wy., now of Hull, sold 64/64 to Jn. Armstrong, Harley Goodall and Harrison Chilton, of Tokenhouse Yard, London, partners in firm "Armstrong, Goodall and Chilton"; May, 1852, Harrison Chilton, of Hull, assigned 64/64 to Harr. Chilton, jun., of Tokenhouse Yard, Lndn.; Reg. Lndn., Feb., 1853; Bk.; Reg. Hull, 1860.

HINDOSTAN.—S.; 425; bd., Holt and Richardson; Owners, Christ. Richardson and Co.; 109.10 by 29.10; in 1836, 544 tons; Owners, 1850, Jn. Richardson, 32, and Christ. Richardson, 32. Lost, Aug. 27, 1851.

OSWY.—Bn.; 126; bd., Fishburn and Brodrick, and Owners; Sold to Will Irving, of Hull, 1825, and Reg. Hull; Owner, 1825, Thos. Brodrick, 32, and Thos. Fishburn, 32.

VIGILANT.—Bg.; 244; bd., Robt. Barry, and Owner; Reg. Lndn., April, 1821.

AMOS.—Bn.; 70; bd., Jn. Spencelayh; Owner, Jas. Atkins Cook, m.m.; Reg. Scrbr., 1820; Reg. Wy. from Scrbr., April, 1836; Owner, Francis Wilson. Lost, 1838, or after.

HYPERION.—Bg.; bd., Fishburn and Brodrick; Owner, 1822, Brodrick.

CANE GROVE.—Bg.; 182; bd., Fishburn and Brodrick, and Owners; Owner, 1830, Alex. Robinson, 64. Lost, 1842.

1820 INO.—Bn.; 120; bd., Robt. Barry, and Owner; Lad. March 30; Reg. Bridlington, Jan., 1821; Owner, 1840, Judd and Co., Prtsmth.

SIMPSON.—S.; 336; bd., Fishburn and Brodrick; Owners, Hen. Simpson, jun., and Thos. and Hen. Simpson, bankers; Lad. May 12; Reg. Lndn., 1824. In the outfit for her voyage to Bombay in 1825 a bill of £46 paid to Orton, butcher, the Tichborne Claimant's father.

MUTA.—Bn.; 162; bd., Robt. Campion; Lad. June 8; Owners, Robt. Appleton and Seaton Trattles; Owners, 1848, S. Trattles, 32, Jos. Addison, 16, and Ann Appleton, 16; Reg. Ipswich, May, 1848; Reg. Wy., Nov. 1, 1861; Owner, Marshall Granger, of Rochester, 64. On June 18, 1840, came into Wy. dismasted, laden with coals. July, 1862, the "Muta," Granger, of Wy., Narva for Hartlepool, timber, having grounded on leaving Narva, filled, put into Lilles to discharge and repair. Lost on the Sunk Sand, 1865.

HALLFIELD.—Bg.; 128; Owned in Lndn., 1837.

IONIA.—Bg.; 232.

ARMY.—Bg.; 224; bd., T. Barrick; Owners. Gee and Co., Hull; Owner, 1854, F. Storry, Hartlepool.

1821 DAVID.—Slp.; 50; bd., Cato and Co.; Owner, David Hunton, Lofthouse; Owner, 1836, Addison Brown, 43, Jos. Brown, 21; Owner, 1839, Addison Brown, 64; Reg. Stcktn., 1849.

MARY ANN.—Slp.; 48; bd., Cato and Co.; Owner, David Hunton; Owner 1824, Robt. Usherwood; Owner 1828, Will. Lorrains, m.m.; Owner, 1834, Robt. Usherwood. Wrecked at Staithes, 1834.

IRIS.—Bn.; 130; bd., Robt. Barry; Reg. Lndn., 1821; Bg. later.

ELIZABETH.—Lug.; 62; bd., Falkingbridge; Owner, Matt. Heseltine, Rnswck.; Owner, 1826, Francis Roberts, of Wy.; Reg. Stcktn., May, 1826.

SNEATON CASTLE.—S.; 285; bd., Robt. Campion; Owners, R. Campion and Richd. Brown; Capt., 1827, Edmund Lotherington; 1832, Zachariah Garbutt, of Lvrpl. Lost.

COLUMBUS.—S.; 309; bd., Robt. Barry, and Owner; Reg. Lndn., 1825.

WOODHOUSE.—Bk.; 284; Owners, 1838, Terry and Co., Hull.

ROYAL GEORGE.—S.; 432; Owner, Robt. Barry, Lndn. Licensed Indiaman.

CHRISTIAN.—Bg.; 260; Reg. Copenhagen, 1840.

FILEY.—Bg.; 188; Owned at Shields, 1840.

ELIZA.—Bg.; 244; bd., Langborne; Owners, 1837, Anderson and Co., Lvrpl.

GRATITUDE.—Bg.; 129.

TERRYS.—Bk.; 244; Owner, 1837, Coulson, Scrbr.

THOMPSON.—Bg.; 276; Owner, 1822, Hobbs.

1822 LIVONIA.—Bn.; 136; bd., R. Campion; Owners, R. Campion and Will. Carr, m.m.; Reg. Scrbr., April 26, 1824.

TIMANDRA.—S.; 370; bd., T. Barrick; Lad. March 21; Owners, Hen. Barrick, m.m., Jn. Langborne, farmer, and T. Barrick; Reg. Lndn., Nov., 1822.

VINE.—Bn.; 131; bd., Fishburn and Brodrick; Owners, 1824, Richd. Brown, 43, and Jos. Gill, 21; Owner, 1829, John Martin Ayre, 64; Reg. Bristol, July 24, 1834.

Jan., 1850, the brig "Vine," of Bristol, laden with oats, came for the harbour just flood. She struck outside the pier end, but was driven in (wind at E. or E.S.E.), and in a short time she filled.

The masts went and the cargo floated up the harbour, many cobles engaged securing some of it. She drove up towards the Scotch Head. The master remained by the vessel till about 5 p.m., having been knocked down by the sea several times. The crew had left long before, but the master, being intoxicated, was obstinate and would not leave with them. He was induced to leave by a stratagem. The vessel received much damage by some men getting on board and letting go the anchor, over which she beat. It was reported that the vessel was built by Mr. Brodrick, of Whitby.

HERCULES.—S.; 482; bd., Fishburn and Brodrick; Owner, Ed. Chapman; 119.8 by 30.5; Lad. June 20; Reg. Lndn., April, 1823.

GEORGE.—Bg.; 188; bd., R. Campion; Owners, Geo. and Richd. Lawson.

ANN.—Bg.; 204; bd., T. Barrick; Owners, Geo. and Robt. Porritt, Rnswck. Lost. Reg. cancelled Feb. 9, 1835.

ARETHUSA.—Bn.; 209; bd., R. Barry; Owner, Robt. Clark, Wy.; Reg. Lndn., Aug., 1838.

BETHEL.—Sch.; $\frac{78}{90}$; Owners, James and John Wood, Wy.; Reg. Wy., June, 1836, from Hull. In June, 1851, a strong breeze sprang up, and the "Bethel" "laid on" at Peak, became a wreck.

NAVY.—Bg.; 193; Owners, Gee and Co., Hull.

TWIST.—Bg.; 188; Owner, 1840, Coulson, of Hull.

CYNTHIA.—Bn.; 120; bd., Robt. Barry, and Owner; Reg. Lndn., April, 1822.

1823 VALIANT.—S.; 224; bd., R. Campion; Owners, R. and J. Campion, bankers; Lad. Jan. 29th. "On the 8th Dec., 1827, Capt. Francis Agar, jun., of the ship 'Valiant,' died on board when nearing the English Channel, homeward bound from Quebec. The mate had the body put into a coffin in hope of it being interred on land, but it had to be cast into the sea.

On Saturday last, Dec. 22, 1827, a coffin containing a body came on shore at Chisel Cove. An inquest was held, and the body interred in Portland Churchyard."—Extract from "John Bull" of Dec. 24, 1827.

"Mr. Robt. Campion, Owner of the 'Valiant,' has written to the minister of Portland Church to inform him of the name and station of the deceased. Capt. Agar was 33 years of age."—"Wy. Panorama." Owner, 1826, Robt. Campion, 48, John Campion, 16; Capt., 1828, Thos. Willis. The "Valiant," transport of Whitby, Capt., Thos. Willis, totally lost on the coast of Portugal, March, 1828. Crew saved. Reg. cancelled at Lndn., April, 1828.

ACCESSION.—Bg.; 207; bd., J. Jackson and Co.; Owners, John Boyes, Wy., and John Linton, East Row. Lost. Reg. cancelled at Kirkwall, March 27, 1834.

HECTOR.—Bn.; 113; bd., T. Barrick; Owner, T. Barrick; Owners, 1824, Will. Darley, Wy., 32, and Peter Cammish, of Filey, 16, and Co.; Lad. April 14. Reg. Scrbr., March, 1832.

ACTIVE.—Slp.; 53; bd., Robt. Barry, and Owner. Lost.

MARMION.—Bg.; 249; bd., J. Langborne; Owners, Langborne and Jameson. Lost, 1829, or after.

CICERO.—Bn.; 172; bd., T. Brodrick; Owners, Geo. Stephens and Richd. Wilson. "Cicero," Stephens, arrived at Wy. from Pictou, with timber, Jan. 19, 1828. Lost, 1829, or after.

DOVE.—Bn.; 132; bd., R. Barry; Reg. Lndn., Nov., 1823.

ELFLEDA.—Bg.; 136; bd., T. Brodrick; Reg. Lndn., Feb., 1825.

DON.—Bg.; 196; Owners, 1838, Harris and Co., Waterford.

CYRUS.—Slp.

ELIZABETH.—Bg.

1824 DEPENDENT.—S.; 257; bd., R. Campion; Owners, R. Campion, Richd. Willis and Will Carr; Reg. Lvrpl., 1836; Reg. Wy. from Lvrpl., Aug., 1837; Owner, 1837, Geo. Clark, 64; Reg. Bridgewater, March, 1838.

LINNET.—Sch.; 79; bd., T. Barrick, and Owner; lengthened 1826 to 95 tons. Missing since Aug. 19, 1845.

DIANA.—S.; 320; bd., T. Brodrick; Owners, Robt. and John Braithwaite and J. Frankland; Reg Lndn., 1832; Reg. Hull, 1851.

ACASTA.—Bg.; 238; bd., R. Barry; Owner, Robt. Clark, Wy. Lost, 1831, or after.

FRIEND.—Bg.; 146; bd., Spencelayh; Owners, Robt. Preston, attorney, and J. and R. Spencelayh; Owners, 1832, Seaton Trattles, 32, and Ann Appleton, widow, 16, and Geo. Trattles Knaggs, 16. Lost in the Thames Aug. 25, 1852.

EDGAR.—Bg.; 213; bd., Cato and Co.; Owner, Edgar Richardson, Wy., m.m. Lost. Reg. cancelled Feb., 1825.

LINGBERRY.—Slp.; 66; bd., W. Holkirk; Owners, Will Hunton and T. Turnbull; Capt., Whitwell Theaker. Lost, Jan., 1825.

EUPHROSYNE.—S.; 285; bd., T. Barrick; Owners, Thos. Hutchinson, of Brotton, and H. Barrick, jun., Shields; Owners, 1838, John Summerson, 32, Hen. Barrick, 24, and G. T. Knaggs, 8. Wrecked Oct. 31, 1842. Reg. cancelled at Quebec.

Capt., Jn. Summerson, who died at Malta, Jan. 11, 1851, aged 53 years.

ARK.—Bg.; 158; bd., T. Brodrick, and Owner; Owner, 1840, W. Estill, Wy.; Owners, 1853, Mat. Todd, m.m., Sampson Estill Clark, R.H.B., Rev. Geo. Dickson, Egton and Elizabeth Goddon, R.H.Bay., each 16 shares; Owners, 1864, James Steele and Hezekiah Godden. Sold to Hrtlpl., April, 1864.

GEO. CANNING.—Bk.; 393. "On Wednesday, Jan. 30, 1828, when this vessel, homeward bound from Alexandria to Liverpool, was about three days sail from Holyhead and during a heavy gale, Mr. Benjamin Yorke, aged 17, an active and promising youth, eldest son of Mr. Joseph Yorke, schoolmaster of this town, fell in the execution of his duty from the lee main top gallant yard arm into the sea. It being nearly dark and a high sea running, no assistance could be rendered, and he was drowned." Owner, 1835, Fenwick, Nwcstl.

MULGRAVE.—S.; 362; Owners, 1840, Coulson and Co., Scrbr.

HANKINSON.—Bg.; 229; Owner, 1831, J. Straker, Nwcstl.

MARYS.—Bg.; 219.

BENJAMIN.—Bg.; 238; Owner, 1837, B. Sedman, Bridlington.

1825 HELEN.—Bg.; 143; Owner, 1831, Yeoman.

HAMBURG.—Bg.; 106; Owners, 1831, Eglon and Co.

LOUNDES.—Bg.; 115; Owner, 1837, J. Eglon, Hull.

UNANIMITY.—Bg.; 166; Owner, 1837, Herbert, Scrbr.

JUDITH.—S.; 243; Owner, 1840, T. W. Torr, Hull.

URANIA.—Bk.; 286; Owners, 1854, Wright and Co., Cork.

VALLYFIELD.—S.; 343; Owner, Chapman, Lndn. Lndn. to Hobart Town, 1840.

CERES.—Slp.; 53; bd., R. Barry, and Owner. Nov. 23, 1871, the "Ceres," slp., late the property of Mr. Robt. Barry, deceased (died Sept. 30, 1871, aged 78), was sold by auction by Mr. Jos. Thompson to Mr. T. Mennell for £138.

Oct., 1872, the "Ceres," owned by Mr. T. Mennell, John Hind, master, and one hand, being "laid on" at Sandsend with lime, strong weather came on. The vessel began to leak, and the lime took fire and burnt it.

COMET.—Slp.; 63; bd., Falkingbridge; Owners, Ed. Ormston, jun., Jos. Harland, and J. Gibson. Total wreck near Filey, April 25, 1854.

MARIA.—S.; 300; bd., T. Barrick; 98.1 by 26.9; Owners, Gid. Smales, Geo. Hen. Wakefield, farmer, Robt. Simpson Wakefield. Lost, 1833.

STREONSHALH.—Bg.; 245; bd., J. Langborne; Owners, Geo. and Jn. Langborne and Will. Jameson. Missing ship, Capt. Constable Dunning. Left Mauritius for Lndn. Feb., 1829, and supposed to have been lost during a hurricane which occurred four days after the vessel sailed.

ORION.—Sch.; 69; bd., Thos. Hutton Scrafton; Owner, Thos. Beaumont; Reg. Dunbar, March, 1826.

SISTERS.—Slp.; 65; bd., R. Campion; Owners, W. Hunton and R. Campion. Lost, April, 1834.

ARCTURUS.—S.; 269; bd., J. Spencelayh; Owners, Jn. Martin Ayre and Jn. Holt, jun.; Reg. Lndn., April, 1831; Reg. Wy. from Lndn., Feb., 1839; Owner, Jn. Holt, Wy., 64. Lost at Coatham, May, 1840. Owner, Geo. Ouston.

CLEVELAND.—S.; 385; bd., R. Barry; 106.5 by 29.1; Owners, R. and J. Barry; Capt., Geo. Willis; Owners, 1847, Marwood and Pickernell. Broken up April, 1849.

FRIENDS.—Bg.; 145; bd., Thos. Barrick; Owners, Thos. Brown, 32, Addison Brown, 16, and J. Smith, Stockton, 16; Reg. Lndn., June, 1840.

MARWOOD.—Bg.; 206; bd., R. Campion; Owners, Richd. Willis, T. Marwood, and Richd. Ripley; Reg. Lvrpl., Jan. 30, 1840.

LARPOOL.—Bg.; 202; bd., Spencelayh; Owners, J. F. and Phil Spencelayh; Owners, 1855, Geo. Calvert, tailor, Jn. Hardcastle, m.m., and Francis Dobson, tailor. Lost at Rousham, East coast of Russia, Sept. 23, 1857.

July 31, 1839, Wednesday afternoon a heavy rain and N.E. wind, about 1 o'clock some timber broke adrift from the brig "Larpool," and broke a yawl adrift and then a Dutchman. Both came nearly under the bridge, the yawl a wreck and a man drowned. The Dutchman got clear about 5 o'clock, not much damaged. A little laden schooner sunk close to the Custom House.

1826 FOSTER.—Bk.; $\frac{342}{448}$; Owner, 1838, Brodrick, Hull. Lengthened 1851 to 555 tons; Owner, 1854, Hankey, Lndn.

ASTREA.—Bg.; 111; bd., J. Spencelayh; 64.2 by 20.7; Owners, J. Fenwick, T. Tate, and Jn. Miller. This vessel, it was said, was partly built from the timber of the brig "Matthews" wrecked on Whitby sand in 1825.

On Thursday evening, Dec. 13, 1828, the crew of the "Astrea," Capt. Barritt, then in London, retired to rest while a fire was left in the forecastle, the hatch being on to keep out the cold. Early next morning the master's wife, then on board, was awakened by a stifling vapour, and the mate being called up to see what was the matter, found four of the crew, two laid on the floor and two in their berths in a state of insensibility. One of them soon recovered and the other three were taken to a hospital, where one of them, Will. Garbutt, of Whitby, died the next day, and another, Jn. Jackson, a Whitby youth, died soon after.

Mr. Will. Coulson Summerson, aged 21, mate of the "Astrea," of Whitby, at Goole, was swept off the deck by being accidentally entangled in the cable, Dec. 13, 1827.

The "Astrea" made voyage to Riga in the summer of 1827.

The "Astrea" went ashore near Filey in a strong gale Nov. 12, 1856, having a valuable cargo, which was discharged. Vessel refloated.

The "Astrea" was blown off the land on Sunday, Oct. 19, 1862, and was not seen until she entered the harbour on Wednesday, the 22nd, having lost her fore yard port stanchions and the bulwarks. Owners, 1876, T. Turnbull, Jn. Weighill, and Ed. Outhard. Later, Robt. Johnson, 64. Broken up Dec., 1889.

NORTHFIELD.—Slp.; 68; bd., Jn. Spencelayh. Owners, Will Brown and Paul Coverdale, of Ellerby. Came ashore Dec. 12, 1830, near Upgang, having been with oil for the North.

FOWLER.—Slp.; 63; bd., W. Falkingbridge; Owners, Jn. Cooper and Ed. Knaggs, of Sandsend. Stranded and totally wrecked at Sandsend Jan. 7, 1876; Owners, 1876, Jn. Lennard, 32, and Jn. Danby, 32.

GEORGE AND MARY.—Bg.; 262; bd., R. Barry; Owners, Geo. and And. Brodrick. Lost, 1838, or after.

BRIDGEHOLME.—Bg.; 159; bd., Spencelayh; Owners, J. F. and R. Spencelayh; Owner, 1840, Francis Watkins. Lost on the Gunfleet sand Dec., 1847.

SWALLOW.—Slp.; 70; bd., Robt. Holmes; Owner, Jos. L. Wodhams; Owner, 1828, Will. Greenwood, R.H.Bay.; Reg. at Hull, Feb., 1829.

CAPTAIN COOK.—S.; 451; bd., Robt. Campion; 116 by 29.9½; Owner, 1828, R. Campion, 48, Geo. Willis, sen., 8, and Geo. Willis, jun., 8; Reg. Lndn., 1833; Owner, 1837, Gordon and Co., Lndn.

LADY FEVERSHAM.—S.; 430; bd., R. Barry; Owners, 1837, R. Barry, 16, and Stephenson, Ellerby; Parish of Stepney, Lndn., 48; Reg. Lndn., 1837.

LOTUS.—S.; 397; bd., T. Barrick; Owners, 1837, Thos. Hutchinson, Brotton, 32, Hen. Barrick, 16, and Jos. Sampson, Bridgewater, 16. Lost about 1837.

JANE.—Bg.; 93; bd., Cato and Co., and Owners; Reg. Lndn., May 30, 1827.

GALE.—Sch.; 88; bd., Christ. Gale, and Owner with company; built in Church Street; Owner, 1849, Will. Gale, 64. Sold to Ramsgate, 1856.

NEW CLIO.—Sch.; 125; bd., R. Barry; Owner, J. Barry. This schooner at the time of launching, Sept. 30, 1826, had her sails all bent, her stores on board, and but for the want of ballast, which was taken in the same day, was ready for sea. She was registered and cleared at the Custom House and sailed the following day for Dantzic. Lost. Reg. cancelled Dec. 27, 1830.

BARJONA.—Sch.; 88; bd., P. Cato; Owners, Geo. Laverick, Staithes, 32, and Jn. Linton, East Row, 32; Owner, 1837, Geo. Laverick, 64. Lost, 1837, or after.

AVON.—Bk.; 263; bd., T. Brodrick; Lad. Nov. 1; Owner, Richard W. Haden, m.m.; Reg. Lndn., 1827.

ROMANOFF.—Bk.; 314; Owner, 1840, Anderson, Nwcstl.

DWINA.—Bg.; 130; Owner, 1837, John Thain, Dundee.

1827 JOHN.—Bg.; $\frac{143}{154}$; bd., John Spencelayh and Co.; Owners, W. F. and Phil. Spencelayh; Owner, 1840, Jn. Holt, banker, 64; Reg. Stcktn., 1840; Reg. Wy. from Stcktn., Sept., 1847, and Owners, Thos. Wright, Stcktn., 43, and James Mutter, 21; Reg. Stcktn., Aug. 24, 1848.

LIVELY'S INCREASE.—Bg.; 116; bd., Cato; Owners, J. Frankland and Abraham Cole, Staithes, and Jos. Hodgson. Lost, Aug., 1833.

K

STAR.—Bg.; 201; bd., Cato; Owner, Jas. Wood; Owner, 1841, Will Cavillier, 48, and Chas. Fisher, 16. Lost. Last Capt., Stephen Lincoln, 1842.

IVY.—Sch.; 104; bd., T. Brodrick; Reg. Hull, Aug. 16, 1828; Owners, 1838, W. Stephens and Co., St. Ives.

CLARENCE.—Bg.; 177; bd., R. Campion. Sold Oct., 1827, to James Harding, of Workington, and Reg. at Whitehaven Oct. 29, 1827.

SALACIA.—Bg.; 296; bd., R. Barry; Owners, J. and R. Barry and Jos. Addison; Owners, 1841, Richd. Barry, 48, and Will Addison, 16; Reg. at Dartmouth, March, 1852.

OAK.—Sch.; 72; bd., Hen. Dring, and Owner; built on Boyes Staith; Owner, 1831, Will Taylor, Littlebeck, m.m.; Owner, 1853, Geo. Cook, m.m., and Co.; Owners, 1859, Geo. and Will Ebblewhite, Will Cuthbert, and Will Hutton.

"Oak," schooner, John Hinds, master, and two hands, owned by Messrs. Geo. Ebblewhite and Co., Whitby, left Newcastle the 24th July, 1862, for Pettycur, Fifeshire. On Friday, 25th, at 6 a.m., wind W. by N. blowing a gale, the vessel riding at anchor in Skate Roads near the Farn Islands with both anchors down, drove to sea, with both anchors at the bows. Set the mainsail to try to get the anchors in, but could not succeed. The ship still driving slipped both chains and wore to the south, leaking badly. Kept the pumps going. At 1 p.m. saw a smack and hoisted signal of distress, but they took no notice. At 2 a.m. saw a vessel to windward, which bore down upon us and asked if we wanted assistance. Replied yes, our vessel just sinking. Attempted to launch our boat but failed, the mate getting disabled in the attempt. A boat was launched from the vessel and took us on board. The "Oak" sank 25 minutes later. The vessel, "The Elsie," of Findhorn, Capt. Storm, landed us at that port.

When the Bk. "Judith" was in dock at Whitby she was altered to a Bg., and the mizen lower mast was sold for a new main lower mast for the schooner "Oak" in 1858.

GREEN END.—Sch.; 68; bd., J. Spencelayh; Owners, J. Peckett, J. Copley, and J. Sly; Reg. at Jersey, June, 1829; Reg. Wy. from St. Helier, Jersey, Aug., 1842, and Owner, J. T. Smith, Robin Hood's Bay. Foundered in Boston Deeps, May 16, 1854.

HEBE.—Bg.; 162; bd., R. Barry; Reg. Lndn., 1829; Capt., 1828, Ed. Theaker.

ADMIRAL MOORSOM.—S.; 391; bd., J. Langborne; Owners, 1827, John, Nath. and Geo. Langborne, and Will Jameson, who sold the vessel April, 1828, to David Hall, Charles McGarel, and Alexander Hall, of Austin Friars, Lndn. (Hall, McGarel and Co.), for £5,288 10s. 6d.

ARETHUSA.—Bg.; 141; bd., Cato and Co.; Owned, 1828, at Hull.

ABBOTSFORD.—Bg.; 169; bd., T. Brodrick; Lad. Sept. 22, 1827; Owner, 1875, Will. Storm. Sold a wreck at Yrmth., Jan., 1883.

BRANKEN MOOR.—Bg.; 257; bd., Langborne; Lengthened 1837 to Bk. $\frac{321}{372}$.

CADIZ PACKET.—Bg.; 165; bd., T. and H. Barrick; Owners, Chas. Barry and Co., Lndn.

ISABELLA.—Bk.; 323; bd., T. Barrick; Lad. June 26; Owner, 1840, H. Nelson, Lndn.

MARIA.—Bg.; 160; bd., T. Brodrick; Owner, Hall, Scrbr.

ARGO.—Bg.; 141; bd., Cato; Owner, 1853, Geo. Barrick, Wy.

CLAREMONT.—Bg.; 177.

1828 ROBIN HOOD.—Bg.; 105; bd., R. and N. Campion; Owners, Will. Greenwood, of R.H.Bay, and Richd. Scott, of Wy.; Reg. at Hull, May 12, 1832.

JOHN.—Bg.; 227; bd., H. and Geo. Barrick; Owners, Gid. G. H. Wakefield and J. W. Smales, and R. S. Wakefield. "The 'John,' brig, Wakefield, of Whitby, Petersburg for London, totally lost on Island of Bornholm, Nov. 10, 1829."—"Whitby Magazine." Lost. Reg. cancelled Nov. 17, 1830, Wy. Custom House.

HELEN MARR.—Bg.; 255; bd., Cato and Co., Owner, Will. Benson, Wy.; Owners, 1829, Will Benson, 48, Thos. Benson and Robt. Hunter, of Shadwell, Lndn., 16, jointly (firm of Benson and Co.); Reg. Lndn., July, 1839.

SYLPH.—Bg.; 148; bd., Robt. Barry; Reg. Lndn., March 12, 1831, as belonging to the port of Wy.; Reg. Wy. from Lndn., April, 1837; Owner, 1837, James Pierson, Egton, 64; Owners, 1839, Will Pennock, 48, and John Larkin, 16. Foundered in the North Sea, Oct. 13, 1855.

BELLONA.—Bg.; 200; bd., Cato and Co.; Reg. Lndn., Dec., 1828; Owner, Jos. Burrill.

SARAH.—Bg.; 233; bd., H. and Geo. Barrick; Owner, Jos. Mellanby, Wy.; Owners, 1830, Jos. Mellanby, draper, 32, and Co.; Owners, 1838, J. Mellanby, 16, Richd. Willis, 32, Chas. Barrett, Darlington, 16. Lost. Reg. cancelled Oct., 1839.

ELLEN.—Bg.; 165; bd., T. Barrick; Lad. July, 1829; Reg. Lndn., April 4, 1829; Owner, Mr. Johnson, of Lndn.

MEG MERRILEES.—Bg.; 228; bd., Campion; Bust head and quarter barges.

HOPEWELL.—Bk.; 268; Bd., Langborne and Co.; Owner, G. White, Lndn.; Owners, 1840, Leslie and Co., N. Shields.

MICHAEL.—Bk.; 243; bd., H. Barrick; Owner, Mr. Stewart, Lndn.; Lad. July 28. This new vessel, which had been put into the dry dock, belonging to the builder, to be fitted for sea, fell over with all her masts and rigging standing, Aug., 1828. No lives lost, and no material injury.

CLAUD.—Bk.; 371; bd., Brodrick; Owner, 1840, Bucknell, Shoreham.

EDWARD LOMBE.—Bk.; 347; bd., Brodrick.

1829 HEYWORTH.—Bg.; 221; bd., R. and N. Campion; Owners, Richd. Willis, Richd. Wilson, and Richd. Ripley; Lad. Jan., 1829; Reg. Lvrpl., April 23, 1836.

SYKES.—S.; 258; bd., T. Brodrick; Owners, Robt. Braithwaite, sen. and jun., and Jn. Frankland. Lost on the Virgin Rocks, near Wyborg, Sept., 1857. Owner when lost, Robt. Braithwaite.

VIRGINIA.—Bk.; 275; bd., P. Cato; Reg. Lvrpl., 1830; Reg. Wy. from Lvrpl, Dec., 1837; Owner, Geo. Clark, Wy. Lost in Tangier Bay. Reg. cancelled Jan. 18, 1840.

FANCY.—Slp.; 70; bd., P. Cato; Owner, Geo. Noble, Wy. Lost, 1837, or after.

IONA.—Bg.; 218; bd., R. and N. Campion; Owner, Thos. Parkin; Reg. Lndn., March 12, 1832.

CANTON.—Bg.; 273; bd., R. and N. Campion; Owners, 1830, J. Lawson and Son. Lost on Brian Island, St. Lawrence, Oct., 1837. "Capt. Will Garbutt, his wife Elizabeth Lawson, and their infant drowned."

SYMMETRY.—Bg.; 250; bd., R. Barry; Reg. Lndn., Oct. 15, 1830.

ROYAL SOVEREIGN.—S.; 336; bd., H. and G. Barrick; Reg. Lndn., 1838.

RUTLAND.—S.; 376; bd., Hen. Barrick; Owner, J. H. Coulson, Scrbr.

BRANKEN MOOR.—Bg.; 273; bd., Langborne; Owner, J. White, Lndn., as stated in Wy. Repository.

CYRUS.—Sch.; 105; bd., T. Brodrick; Reg. Sndld., 1840; Lad. May 20.

............—Bg.; 240; bd., T. Brodrick; Lad. Nov. 12; not named.

INTREPID.—S.; 401; bd., T. Brodrick; Reg. Hull, 1830, to Messrs. Chilton and Brodrick; Capt., T. Robson. Owners, 1832, John Beadle and John Eggington, both of Sculcoates, and of the firm of J. Beadle and Co., and Thos. Holderness, of Hull, 4 shares jointly, and Jos. Smith Eggington, of the above firm, and of Kirkella, Hull, 60 shares. Sailed from Wy. to Quebec (emigrants), 1830. Lost in 1835.

JACKSON.—Bk.; 251; bd., T. Brodrick; Owner, Thos. Jackson, Wy.; Reg. at Dundee, March, 1839. Took emigrants to Quebec, 1830.

1830 CATO. — Bg.; 213; bd., Cato and Jackson; Owners, P. Cato, Estill Cato, m.m., and Robt. Harrison, m.m.; Reg. Sndld., 1839; Owner then, R. Harrison.

EARL OF ELDON.—S.; 513; bd., R. Barry; 119.3 by 31.6; Sq. stern; Carvel built; Quarter galleries, bust.

This fine full-rigged ship, Whitby owned, but registered in London, was burnt in the Indian Ocean on Sept. 27, 1834. Mr. Henry Simpson, afterwards of the firm of Simpson and Chapman, bankers, of Whitby, was second mate of the ship at the time. The following account of this disaster is by a passenger, T. T. Ashton, of the Madras Artillery: — "On the 24th August, 1834, I embarked on board the ship 'Earl of Eldon,' of London, 600 tons, Capt. Theaker, at Bombay. She was the finest and strongest ship in the trade, and was cotton loaded. On Sept. 26 we got into lat. 9°27′ South and between 70° and 80° E. Longitude, and began to anticipate our arrival at the Cape.

Ship "Earl of Eldon."

On the morning of the 27th I arose early and went on deck, finding one of my fellow passengers there; we perceived steam rising from the fore hatchway. I went down to dress, and about half-past six the captain told me that the cotton was on fire. At 8 o'clock the smoke became thicker, and before nine we discovered that that part of the deck had caught fire. The captain ordered the boats to be got out and stocked in case of necessity, and about half-past one the three ladies, two sick passengers, an infant four months old, and a female servant were put into the long boat. At 3 o'clock we all got into the boats, the captain being the last, just as the flames were bursting through the quarter deck. When we were about a mile from the ship she was in one blaze, and her masts began to fall in. The sight was grand, though awful. Between 8 and 9 o'clock her masts had fallen, and she had burned to the water's edge. Suddenly there was a flash and a dull heavy explosion. Her powder had caught. A few seconds and all was dark, and the waters had closed over the 'Earl of Eldon.' Sad was the prospect now before us. There were in the long boat, 23ft. by 7ft., 25 persons, and in each of the other two boats 10 individuals. We were, by rough calculation, about 1,000 miles from Rodrigue. About 11 o'clock, having humbly committed ourselves to Providence, we rigged the boats and got under sail. On the third day it began to blow fresh, with rain. We were totally without shelter, and the discomfort and misery of our situation may be imagined. There was a large water cask in the boat, on the top of which I slept, whilst we were in the boats. The next day the weather grew worse, and one of the small boats, in which were Mr. Simpson, the second mate, and nine others, was split by the sea. We took in her crew and abandoned her. We were now stowed as thick as we could hold, wet, crushed, and miserable; the night passed away. I again felt that hope which had never entirely deserted me. We had three small meals of biscuits and some jam, etc., and three half-pints of water per day. The ladies were wretched, yet they never uttered a repining word. On the 13th evening we began to look out for Rodrigue. The captain told us not to be too sanguine as his chronometer was not to be depended upon. The night fell and I went to sleep. About midnight I was awoke by the cry that land was right ahead. I attempted to compose myself, and sat down and smoked with a sensation I had long been a stranger to. With the first light of dawn Rodrigue appeared right ahead, distant about six miles, and by 8 o'clock we were all safely landed."

Custom House, Port Louis, Mauritius.

"Received from Capt. Theaker, late of the ship 'Earl of Eldon,' of Whitby, the Register granted at that port, No. 13, of April 23, 1830, for that ship, which is delivered for the purpose of transmission to the Registrar General of Shipping, London, Nov. 8, 1834."—Geo. C. Cunningham, Collector of Customs.

GULNARE.—S.; 338; bd., Hen. Barrick. Sold, 1831, to Lowrie, Stringer and Co., Lvrpl., for £4,570. "Gulnare," Capt., Will. Summerson, sailed for Quebec in 1830 with 230 emigrants.

LABOURER'S INCREASE.—Lug.; 65; bd., W. Falkingbridge.

DAHLIA.—Bg.; 163; bd., R. and N. Campion; Owners, Campion and Taylor; Owner, 1833, Will. Taylor, 64. Lost, 1836.

ROYAL WILLIAM.—S.; 451; bd., H. and Geo. Barrick; 114.2 by 30.2; Quarter barges; Bust head; Reg. Lndn., Nov. 18, 1831.

EARL STANHOPE.—Bk.; 295; bd., John Langborne; Owners, Langborne and Jameson. Sailed for Quebec with 70 emigrants June, 1830. Sold to Sydney, N.S. Wales, Oct., 1830. Reg. Lndn., 1838.

NAUTA.—Bg.; 119; bd., R. and N. Campion; Owner, N. Campion; Reg. at Lynn, Sept., 1831.

NYMPH.—Bg.; 159; bd., Barry. Last vessel built by Mr. Robt. Barry. Sold to East Teignmouth, Jan., 1836. Reg. Lndn., Feb., 1836.

1831 FRIENDS.—Lug.; $\frac{32}{62}$; bd., Falkingbridge; Owner, Matt. Simpson, m.m.; Sch., 1849; Owner, 1854, Pat. Frank; Owners, 1876, Alex. Hobson and Nessfield Hodgson. Broken up May, 1879.

KING WILLIAM.—S.; 380; bd., Robt. and N. Campion; Owners, Campion and Carr.

Capt., Will. Carr, aged 32, died on his passage in the "King William" from Bombay to Lvrpl. Sept. 28, 1833. Buried in the Lvrpl. Necropolis, Oct. 15. Reg. Bristol, Sept., 1836.

OCEAN QUEEN.—S.; 267; bd., J. Langborne and Co.; Capt., Will. Jameson; Owners, 1836, Jane Langborne, 16, Geo. Brown, Greenwich, 16, Will. Jameson, 16 in his own right, and also 16 as surviving executor under the will of the late Will. Jameson, shipbuilder; Reg. Lndn., Jan. 3, 1840.

IDA.—Bg.; 239; bd., Hen. Barrick. Sailed for Quebec with passengers, March, 1831. Sold, 1833, to Sir John Tobin, Lvrpl., for £2,630. Reg. Greenock, 1840.

VICTORIA.—Bg.; 220; bd., R. and N. Campion; Owners, J. Campion and Richd. Wilson and Richd. Willis; Reg. Lvrpl., June 29, 1835.

MARCH.—Sch.; 106; bd., Hen. Barrick; Owners, T. Turnbull, Isaac Pennock and James March; Reg. Lndn., 1833.

MAGNET.—Bg.; 186; bd., H. and G. Barrick; Owner, Gid. Smales; Capt., W. B. Smith; Lengthened, 1845, to Bk. $\frac{226}{253}$; Reg. Nwcstl., 1846; Owner, 1854, Humble, of Shields.

1832 NIGHTINGALE.—Bg.; 263; bd., R. and N. Campion; Owners, Campion and Jn. Nightingale, of Saltholm, Will N., of Tunstall, James N., of Tafford Hill, and Richd. N., of Aislaby Grange; Reg. Lvrpl., 1838.

REGINA.—Bg.; 228; bd., Robt. and N. Campion; Female head; Capt., Jn. Leng. Sold to Barbadoes, April 17, 1833.

COLUMBUS.—S.; 467; bd., H. and G. Barrick; 115.9 by 30.3½; Billet head; Capt., H. Barrick, jun. Sailed from Whitby for Quebec with passengers, April, 1832. Owner, 1873, Bk., Edmund Handcock, Falmouth.

FOR
QUEBEC
and the Canadas,
with goods and passengers,
and carries a surgeon,
The fine New Ship
"COLUMBUS,"
burthen 750 tons,
H. Barrick, Commander,
will sail from Whitby about the first week in
April, 1832.

This ship having a poop and forecastle and 7ft. 6in. between decks, affords superior accommodation for passengers desirous to embark for America. For terms of passage (the ship finding water and fuel) and freight of goods, apply to Messrs. H. and G. Barrick, shipbuilders, Whitby, who will give letters of recommendation to their agent at Quebec; also ample information respecting the employment of labourers and small capitalists for the sale of land in Upper Canada.

Early applications are requested, as the ship is expected soon to be filled up.

R. ROGERS, Printer, Whitby.

"Columbus." Capt. Chas. McGregor relates: — About 1876, when he was chief mate of the barque "Hesse Darmstadt," of Whitby, Capt. Ramsdale, bound for the St. Lawrence, the vessel made a long passage, and when near the Banks of Newfoundland, the crew had been on short allowance of food for some time, as Capt. McGregor puts it, "nine days on a biscuit a day." A vessel appearing to leeward, he was sent with a boat's crew to obtain provisions. The vessel turned out to be the old "Columbus," then owned at Falmouth, but he was unaware that she was built at Whitby. He describes her as a fine specimen of her day. Sold to Norwegians, July 3, 1883.

CORSAIR.—264; bd., H. Barrick. Sold to Messrs. James Ewing and Will. Mathewson, of Glasgow, Sept., 1832, for £3,050.

ATLANTIC.—Bg.; 200; Owned, 1840, at South Shields.

1833 MEDORA.—S.; 299; Capt., H. Barrick; Reg. Lvrpl., 1834; Owners, Messrs. Isburn and Higgins.

PALINURUS.—Bk.; 300; bd., Campion, and Owner, with Nightingale; Reg. Lndn., 1833.

EMMA EUGENIA.—Bk.; 383; bd., H. and G. Barrick; first named "Colonist." Sold to J. Somes, Lndn. In 1840, voyage Lndn. to N.S. Wales.

ROSSENDALE.—Bk.; 298; Owner, 1838, Heyworth, Lvrpl.

JOHN AND JAMES.—Bk.; 288; Owned, 1838, at Grimsby. Coppered, 1837.

1834 HINDOO.—Bk.; 310; bd., H. Barrick. Sailed from Whitby for Quebec with 100 passengers, March 7, 1834; Reg. Lvrpl., Oct., 1834.

CAPTAIN ROSS.—Bk.; 310; bd., R. and N. Campion; Owners, Campion, Kneeshaw and Nightingale; Reg, Lvrpl., July, 1836.

PUELLA.—Bn.; 146; bd., Robt. Campion; Reg. at Lvrpl., Sept., 1835.

ROCHDALE.—Bg.; 191; Owner, 1838, T. Chilton, Hull.

MARCH.—Sch.; 140; bd.. H. Barrick; Owners, Turnbull, Pennock and March; Lad. Jan. 10, 1834. Lost near Archangel, Dec. 29, 1846.

1835 HEBER.—S.; 441; bd., Campion; Lad. March 13; Reg. Bristol, 1838.

DELHI.—S.; 357; bd., H. Barrick; Lad. March 14; 101.10 by 28.5; Reg. Lvrpl., Feb., 1836.

MAJESTIC.—S.; 504; bd., H. and G. Barrick.

Capt. Hen. Barrick, jun., who commanded the ship 'Columbus,' of Whitby, in 1832, as before stated, was also commander of the 'Majestic' on her first voyage. She sailed from Whitby in 1835 for Quebec, carrying mules, etc., and was totally lost on the passage up the St. Lawrence at Brandy Pots, Hare Island. Capt. H. Barrick was born in Sept., 1810, was son of Mr. Hen. Barrick, of Church Street, Whitby, head of the firm of H. and G. Barrick, shipbuilders. He retired from sea at an early age, and went to reside at Limehouse. He became the owner of a fleet of sailing ships in the East and West India and Black Sea trades. At one time he and the late Mr. Will. Rose were in partnership at Wapping, London, as Barrick and Rose, anchor smiths, etc. Later he obtained the appointment of shipping master at the Board of Trade Office in the Minories, from which he in due course retired, and went to reside with some of his family at Gravesend, where he died in August, 1905, within a month of 95 years of age."—From a letter of Mr. W. Mead Corner ("Whitby Gazette," Sept. 1, 1905), with whose father, Mr. W. Elgie Corner, Mr. Barrick was at one time in partnership. Vessel lost July, 1835.

DART.—Lug.; 61; bd., Falkingbridge; Afterwards a sch.; Owner, 1855, W. Pinkney.

The "Dart," schooner, owned by Elizabeth Pinkney, Capt., Val. Pinkney, and one hand, left Hartlepool for Sandsend with coals, sprung a leak and sank in Runswick Bay, 11th Feb., 1872.

SMALES.—Bg.; 235; bd., H. and G. Barrick; Owner, Gid. Smales; Off. No. 23781; cost £2,614. Sold to W. Hrtlpl., 1861.

RAJAH.—Bk.; 352; bd., J. Langborne. Sold by Executors of Jn. Langborne, 18th April, 1837, to John Smith, of Leith, Scotland. Reg. Lndn., May 15, 1837.

FLORA.—Bn.; 121; bd., J. Langborne, and Owner, with W. Jameson; Owner, 1839, John Pond, R.H.Bay. Reported lost Dec., 1843. Reg. cancelled April, 1844.

HIRONDELLE.—Sch.; 135; bd., H. Barrick; Reg. Dundee, 1836.

ESK.—Bg.; 226; bd., R. Campion; Owner, Gid. Smales. Cost £2,358.

Owners, 1860, James Pearson, Will Dotchon, J. K. Hill, Thos. Clegg, Ed. Laws, John Barry, J. B. Nicholson, and Jos. Thompson, each 8 shares.

The "Esk," Capt. Myers, from London, in ballast, was making for Sunderland Harbour, 18th Dec., 1871, when she ran ashore south of the pier. She struck twice or thrice before finally grounding on the rocks, where she now lies holed in several places and full of water. The crew landed. The vessel has been stripped and sold as a wreck.

PATRIOT.—Bk.; 333; bd., R. Campion; Owners, R. W. and J. Campion; Reg. Lndn., 1836.

FRISK.—Bg.; 181; bd., H. Barrick; Owner, Chapman, Lvrpl., 1835.

PEAK.—Slp.; 58; bd., R. Campion; Lad. March, 1835. Supposed to have been lost in the great storm of 25th Sept., 1851.

FRIEND'S ADVENTURE.—Lug.; 64; bd., Robt. Marshall, of Wy.; Owners, Sanderson, Theaker and Co. Sold to Hartlepool, 1860.

1836 WILLIAM BRODRICK.—Bk.; 288; bd., R. Campion; Owner, Geo. Smith; Reg. Lndn., 1838.

MARY.—Bg.; 308; bd., H. and G. Barrick; Owner, Robt. Usherwood. Lost on Kent's Group, Bass's Strait, 1852.

HAIDEE.—Bk.; 288; bd., Hen. Barrick. Sold at Lvrpl. to Mr. Walter Cockburn, and Reg. at Leith, Dec., 1836. Voy. Maryport to West Indies, 1854.

THOMAS AND MARY.—Lug.; 32; bd., W. Falkingbridge.

STREONSHALH.—Paddle Steamer; bd., H. and Geo. Barrick; Lad. Jan. 19; Reg. Shields, 1858. Said to be a coal hulk for tugs on the Tyne, 1904.

MEDUSA.—S.; 453; bd., H. Barrick; Owners, 1838, Gray and Co., Lndn.; Poop and forecastle; Female head.

WHITBY.—Bg.; 164; bd., Robt. Campion; Owners, Will. Wilkinson, S. Storm, and W. Weatherill, cabinet maker; Lad. Aug. 1; Owner, 1844, Thos. Foxton, 64; Owners, 1848, Thos. Foxton, 48, John Ponsonby, Pickering, 16; Reg. Shields, 1853.

EMMA.—Bg.; 146; bd., R. Campion; Owners, Richd. Wilson, T. Rickinson, and J. Leng; Lad. Sept. 27; Reg. Wisbech, 1839.

THOMAS MARGARET.—Sch.; 27; Re-bought to Wy. 1859; Owner, Thos. Snaby, York, fisherman.

VERNON.—Bg.; 172; bd., R. Campion; Owner, J. Park, Lndn., 1840; Lad. July 28.

1837 CYGNET.—Bg.; 191; bd., H. Barrick; Owners, Geo. Westgarth, Thos. Strutt, and Robt. Garbutt. Lost, Oct., 1844.

GRAHAM.—Bk.; $\frac{319}{402}$; bd., R. Campion and Co.; Owner, John Irving; Lad. April 2; £3,756; Reg. Bristol, Oct. 27, 1837; Reg. Lndn., 1838.

SULTANA.—S.; 374; bd., Hen. Barrick. Sold to Lvrpl., Dec., 1837.

LADY HILDA.—S.; $\frac{396}{489}$; bd., Geo. Barrick, jun.; Owners, Robt. Barry, T. Simpson, banker, W. Jameson, Nath. Langborne, executors of Jn. Langborne; Reg. Lndn., Jan., 1838. Last vessel built by Messrs. Langborne.

FIDES.—Bg.; 276; bd., H. and G. Barrick; Owners, Will Steward and Co.; Reg. Scrbr., Feb., 1839.

YOUNG QUEEN.—Bk.; 328; bd., R. Campion; Owner, Hen. Boyes; Lad. July 4th; Reg. Greenock, 1837.

WANDERER.—Bg.; 315; bd., H. and G. Barrick, Sold to Lndn., Feb., 1838.

AID.—Bg.; 259; bd., Robt. Campion; Owner, Gid. Smales; £1,929. Lost off Hartlepool, Dec. 17, 1854.

ENDEAVOUR.—Slp.; 58; bd., R. Campion; Owners, Laverick and Co.; Owners, 1848, Jn. Danby, Sandsend, 32, Bryan Wood, Saltburn, 32; £560.

WHITBY.—S.; $\frac{347}{437}$; Owner, Chapman, Lndn.

"Evening Post," Aug. 6, 1894.

"Our Exchanges notify the death within the last few days of several old colonists. Marlborough mourns the loss of Mr. Geo. McDonald, one of the pioneers of Nelson, who came out in the ship 'Whitby' in 1841, and for some time was attached to a survey party in various parts of the Nelson district. After the New Zealand Co. stopped operations he bought land at Wakapuaka, where he resided till 1852, when he went to the Wairau to manage a run for Mr. Wold, driving the first cattle into Marlborough from Nelson on foot, horses being very scarce in those days. He has lived at Wairau Valley over 40 years."

OCEAN.—Sch.; $\frac{105}{114}$; bd., R. Campion; Lad. Nov. 27; Owners, 1838, Wright and Co., Boston. £1,050.

1838 SARAH.—Bg.; 168; bd., H. and G. Barrick; Owners, 1866, James Ward, of Wy., sailmaker, 22; Matt. Peacock, m.m., 21, and Will. Perry, Grosmont, innkeeper, 21; Owner, 1875, James Ward, 64.

"Sarah," brig, Owner, James Ward, Capt., John Jameson, and 7 hands, Portsmouth for Sunderland. Tuesday, 2nd March, 1886, at 4 p.m., passed Whitby High Lights. Weather thick, with snow, blowing a gale. At 5 p.m. the wind shifted from E.N.E. to N.E. About 5.30 sighted Kettleness point, and found that the ship could not weather the point. Decided to run the vessel ashore to save life. Headed for Sandsend Beach, where she stranded about 5.55 p.m., and will become a total wreck.

AYTON.—Bn.; 132; bd., H. Barrick; Owners, W. Moss and H. Robinson, of Ayton; Owner, 1844, Phil. Poad, R.H.Bay. Lost off Hasebro' light 25th April, 1853.

CONRAD.—S.; 406; bd., H. Barrick. Sold to Lndn., 1839.

SATELLITE.—Sch.; 90; bd., Hen. Barrick; Owner, Hen. Simpson. Lost on Colebrook Beach 13th Oct., 1860.

ELIZA.—Bk.; 321; bd., J. and W. Campion; Owner, J. Campion; Reg. Bristol, Jan. 31, 1843; Voy. to Quebec.

SEINE.—Sch.; 80; bd., W. Lister; Owners, Lister and Flintoft; Owners, 1841, Jn. Milburn, 16, Miles Hall, 16, Thos. Lanchester, Stockton, 16, Thos. Dixon, Norton, 16.

The "Seine," Stephen Hodgson, master, owned by Miles Hall and Thos. Lanchester, of Stockton, left Newcastle 29th Oct., 1861, coal laden for London. Fine weather, with light N.E. breeze. Saturday, Nov. 2, weather thick with N.W. by W. gale, with snow. The vessel at anchor in S.W. reach parted from her anchors, made sail to get over to the weather shore, set topsail, foresail and foretopmast staysail and mainsail all close reefed. The gale increasing, carried away all sail except the topsail. Let go two anchors and kedge, but the vessel being so far to leeward and the tide falling, she came to the ground and became a total wreck on the East Barrow. At 11 p.m. took to the boat and remained by the wreck till midnight. They were then driven before the sea till 8 a.m., when they were picked up by the S.S. "Tubal Cain." N.E. spit buoy on Margate sand bearing N.W. by W., distant 1½ mile, and landed at London on Monday, 4th Nov., at 10 a.m., all well. Master and three hands. Insured for £400.

WILBERFORCE.—Bg.; 165; bd., W. Hobkirk; Owner, J. Craven, Scrbr.; Reg. at Wy. March, 1866, from Sndld.; Owner, Benj. H. Tindale, R.H.Bay. Lost with all the crew on the Kentish Knock, Nov. 14th, 1866. First vessel built by Mr. Wm. Hobkirk.

WILLIAM RANDFIELD.—Bg.; 177; bd., W. Hobkirk; Owners, Isaac Mills and W. Randfield. Lost.

ELEANOR.—Sch.; 165; bd., J. and W. Campion; Owners, Campion and T. Wilson; Owners, 1864, Bedlington, Mills and Co., R.H.Bay. Lost off the Humber, 4th Dec., 1869.

MARMION.—Bg.; 169; bd., W. Hobkirk; Owners, Will Jameson and Jane Langnorne; Owners, 1857, Will. Thompson, 11, Will Dotchon, 10, M. Hart, 11, J. Park, 11, Ann Farndale, 10, W. H. Park, 5, Emma E. Park, 6; Owner, 1858, W. Thompson, railway manager, 64. Lost on Island of Oesel, gulf of Riga.

W. AND M. BROWN.—Bg.; 297; bd., Hen. Barrick; Owner, W. Brown. Lost, 23rd Aug., 1853, on rocks in Bass's Strait, near Hobart Town.

T. AND R. JACKSON.—Bg.; 141; bd., H. and G. Barrick; Owners, T. Watson and J. Jackson, Lythe; Capt., 1842, Benj. Gales. Lost.

DEWDROP.—Bg.; 262; bd., J. and W. Campion; Owners, Jas. Storm and T. Coggin, R.H. Bay. Lost near Arbroath, 6th Jan., 1854.

PROVIDENCE.—Sch.; 37; bd., R. Marshall; Owner, Geo. Thurlbeck, Staithes. Foundered July 31st, 1864.

WAVERLEY.—Bk.; 365; bd., H. and Geo. Barrick; Owner, Chapman, Lndn.

SALUS.—Sch.; 76; Owned, 1873, in Dublin.

1839 WRIGHT.—Bg.; 178; bd., Thos. Wright; Owners, 1839, Thos. Wright, 21, Richd. Wright, m.m., 21, Jas. Mutter, baker, 8, Will. Marsingale Wilkinson, of Manchester, 14; Owners, 1861, Richd. Wright, 21, W. W. Wilkinson, 35, Hen. Robinson and Ed.

Corner, 8 jointly; Owners, 1866, Geo. Ebblewhite, 12, Will. Ebblewhite, 12, Will Lewis, 8, H. Robinson and E. Corner, 8 jointly, John Cummins, 12, and J. White, 12; Owners, 1876, J. Cummins, 12, Christ. Marwood, 12, Jn. Wright, 8, David Richardson, 8, Emily Sabina Matilda Peat, 16, and Innocent Caroline Peat, 8; Owners, 1877, J. Cummins, Christ. Marwood, J. Weighill and Co.; Capt., 1840, St. Crosby; 1842, J. Mutter; 1844, Robt. Pinkney; 1845, Jn. Spence; 1848, Richd. Rippon; 1849, Jn. Burnett. Lost, with all the crew, Tyne to Dunkirk, Feb., 1877.

HARRISON CHILTON.—Bk.; 451; bd., W. Hobkirk; Owner, H. Chilton; Reg. Lvrpl., May, 1845.

EGLANTINE.—Bg.; 185; bd., Campion; Owners, Campion and Addison; Capt., Richd. Weatherill, March, 1840. Supposed to have been lost in the North Sea on or about the 12th Dec., 1883, then owned at Seaham.

SALSETTE.—Bk.; 422; bd., Hen. Barrick; Owner, T. O. Harrison, Sndld.; Reg. Lndn., 18th Oct., 1842.

SIR ROBERT PEEL.—Bn.; 158; bd., W. Hobkirk; Owners, 1839, Ralph Hayes, grocer, 8, Ed. Corner, 8, Jn. Corner, 8, Thos. Stewart, tailor, 8, Jn. Miller, 8, Ant. King, sailmaker, 8, Jn. Chilton, 8, Thos. Tate, furniture broker, 8. Lost, 1842.

SUNBEAM.—Bg.; 192; bd., H. and G. Barrick; Owners, Jn. and Sarah Schofield and Christ. Walker. Lost on island of Oesel, gulf of Riga, 6th Aug., 1860.

SOVEREIGN.—Bg.; 214; bd., H. Barrick; Owners, H. Barrick and Jos. Tindale; Owner, 1872, Will. Russell, R.H.Bay, later of H'pool, chandler. Lost off Yarmouth, 17th Feb., 1884.

MANFRED.—Bg.; 278; bd., W. Hobkirk; Owners, Marwood and Pickernell. Lost. Reg. cancelled Dec., 1845.

INDUSTRY.—Sch.; 59; bd., J. and W. Campion; Owners, 1839, Geo. Allen, 32, Geo. Gaskin, 16, And. Joures, of South Shields, tailor, 16. Lost in the Cockle Gat, 19th Dec., 1846.

WAVE.—Slp.; 55; bd., H. Barrick; Owners, Turnbull and Hunton; Sch., 1840.

Capt. Thos. Benson Page suffered with all hands on this coast in the schooner "Wave," belonging to this port, Sept. 25th, 1851.

HEART OF OAK.—Bk.; 339; bd., J. and W. Campion; Owners, Campion and Mills; Reg. at Swansea, 1842. Run down in the Channel by the screw steamer "Lady Jocelyn," 1866, and ten lives lost. Capt., T. Puckrin.

THEMIS.—Bg.; 219; bd., H. and G. Barrick; Owner, Will Steward; Owner, Dec., 1853, Robt. Parkinson, R.H.B., 64. Burnt down when lying off Eupatoria (Black Sea) on the night of 23rd Dec., 1855.

THOMAS RICKINSON.—Bg.; 239; bd., Campion; Owners, Richd. Wilson, saddler, and Thos. Rickinson; Reg. at Hull, 1840.

EAGLET.—Sch.; $\frac{54}{76}$; bd., Hobkirk; Owners, Geo. Westgarth and Geo. Laverick; Owner, 1886, Hen. Hobson. Converted into a hulk, July, 1886.

UNICORN.—Bk.; $\frac{315}{375}$; bd., Campion; Owners, 1840, Mullins and Co., Lndn.

COUNTESS OF MINTO.—Bk.; $\frac{265}{300}$; Owner, 1840, J. Wishart, Leith.

AUTUMN.—Sch.; 90; bd., H. Barrick; Owner, 1840, S. Suggitt, Scrbr.

CENTENARY.—Bk.; 303; Owners, 1840, Smith and Co., Scrbr.

MARY.—Sch.; 62; Owners, 1840, Gibson and Co., Hull.

1840 FRIENDSHIP.—Bg.; 230; bd., H. Barrick; Owners, Geo. and Robt. Wood and Co. Lost on Winterton beach, 31st Jan., 1854.

LEO.—Bg.; 295; bd., W. Hobkirk; Owner, Gid. Smales. Lost, 11th Sept., 1847, off Cape Breton, North America, on the outward passage.

ARABELLA.—Bk.; 267; bd., J. and W. Campion; Owner, Thos. Jackson. Lost in River Plate, 10th Feb., 1850.

SARAH AND ELEANOR.—Bg.; 222; bd., H. Barrick; Owners, Will Cavillier, 28, Ed. Wood, 28, Chas. Fisher, 4, Alice Close, 2, and Charlotte Close, 2; Owners, 1861, B. Granger, 36, B. T. Robinson, 14, Richd. Robinson, 14. Lost, Jan., 1862.

BROTHERS.—Sch.; 95; bd., J. and W. Campion; Owners, Harrison and Storm, R.H.Bay. Lost on Lydd Beach, Kent, 10th May, 1855.

CATO.—Bg.; 251; bd., J. and W. Campion; Owner, Robt. Harrison; Reg. Wy., Feb. 26th; Owners, 1840, Sept., Gee and Co., Hull.

XL.—Sch.; 92; bd., H. and Geo. Barrick; Owners, Corner and Bovill. Lost, 1860.

JOHN COGGIN.—Bn.; 136; bd., H. Barrick; Owners, T. and J. Coggin; Lengthened 1849 to Bg., 171. Sold by Fanny Coggin, 1882, to W. Watson, of Seaham. Foundered off Seaham, March 1st, 1889.

SEA-DRIFT.—Bg.; 276; bd., J. and W. Campion; Owners, Addison and Campion; Capt., 1840, Truefitt; 1842, Richd. Weatherill, 15th Feb.; Reg. Lndn., 3rd Feb., 1853.

SISTERS.—Bg.; 243; bd., Hobkirk; Owner, Robt. Usherwood; Owners, 1846, Mary Usherwood, widow, 32, Will Usherwood, shipowner, 32; Owner, 1860, 28th Feb., Will. Usherwood, 64.

The "Sisters," Capt. Granger, West H'pool for Rochester, with coals, lost on the Patch Sands 28th Feb., 1862. Crew saved by the Caistor life-boat with great difficulty, being a heavy sea and a dark night.

Reg. cancelled March 22, 1862.

BRITON.—Bg.; 262; bd., H. and G. Barrick; Capt., Jn. Barrick; Figure-head of Nelson and his famous signal, "England expects that every man this day will do his duty," on the head boards; Reg. Newcstl., 1846; Owner, Dec., 1862, T. Coggin. Lost on the Scaw Reef, Nov., 1864.

NIMROD.—Sch.; 129; bd., J. and W. Campion; Owner, Hen. Simpson; Capt., Jn. Bennett. Newcastle to Dordt with coals, drove ashore and became a wreck on the coast of Holland, 23rd Aug., 1864.

WILLIAM AND THOMAS.—Bg.; 239; bd., Hobkirk; Owners, Wilkinson, Andrew and T. Page, m.m. Lost at Malta, 31st Aug., 1851.

ALCHYMIST.—Bg.; 251; bd., J. and W. Campion; Owners, Marwood and Pickernell; Reg. at Stcktn., 1851.

JOHNS.—Sch.; 127; bd., Hobkirk; Owners, Jn. Parry and Co.; Reg. Lndn., 1842.

SCHOFIELD.—Bg.; 214; bd., J. and W. Campion; Owners, Jn. Schofield and Jn. Walker; Owner, 1855, J. Walker; Reg. Hartlepool, 1855.

When the "Schofield" was being launched she fell over and laid till next day. No accident, Aug., 1840.

VIXEN.—Bg.; 158; bd., H. Barrick; Reg. Poole, 1841.

STAR.—Sch.; 77; bd., H. Barrick; Owner, Robt. Barry. Sold to Lowestoft, Dec., 1867.

ESK.—Bg.; 249; bd., H. Barrick; Owner, Gid. Smales. Lost near Aldbro', Oct., 1852.

ALPHA.—Bg.; 262; bd., T. Turnbull; Lad. Oct. 12. Lost Gulf of Finland, 1850. First vessel built by Mr. Turnbull.

GEO. ARMSTRONG.—S.; 423; Owner, 1843; Bold and Co., Lvrpl.

HEROINE.—Bk.; 266; Owners, 1843, Trail and Co., Lndn.

DIADEM.—Bk.; 398; bd., H. Barrick; Owner, Chapman, Lndn.

AMITY.—Bg.; 209; Owners, 1840, Estill and Co., Hull.

1841 SAMUEL BODDINGTON.—S.; $\frac{523}{660}$; Owner, Boddington, Lndn. Lndn. to Australia, 1851.

GANYMEDE.—Bn.; 107; bd., Hobkirk; Owner, Wm. Henry Cramp; Reg. Ipswich, 1846.

GOOD INTENT.—Sch.; 33; Owners, Cole and Co., Staithes. Sold to Scrbr., 1863.

ROSEBUD.—Bg.; 139; bd., H. Barrick. Lndn. to Algoa Bay.

DOWLAH.—Bk.; 336; bd., Hobkirk.

RICHARD.—Sch.; 92; bd., Hobkirk

GUIDE.—Bg.; 177; bd., Hobkirk; Owners, Eglon and Co., Hull.

PALATINE.—S.; 507; Owners, 1854, Worrall and Co., Lvrpl.; Lengthened to 615 tons in 1851.

WILLIAM AND JOHN.—Lug.; 34; Altered to Sch., 1855; Owners, 1855, Jn. Robinson, 32, and Jn. Adamson, 32. Lost at Staithes, July, 1863.

GEORGE CLARK.—Bg.; 262; Owner, Geo. Clark. Sold, Aug., 1854, to Robt. Usherwood; Owners, 1845, Mary Usherwood, 48, and Will Usherwood, 16; Reg. at Shields, 1850.

WHITBY.—Sch.; 106; bd., H. and G. Barrick; Owners, W. P. and L. S. Co. Sold 29th July, 1870, to Robt. Butcher, of Orford, Suffolk, by Will Jameson, Gid. Smales, Hen. Simpson, and G. T. Knaggs. Wrecked on the Norfolk coast Nov., 1875. The stern with name on washed ashore.

PICKERING.—Sch.; 106; bd., H. and G. Barrick; Owners, W. P. and L. S. Co.

The "Pickering," Capt., James Girdwood, and 3 hands, run down and sunk in the Thames by the schooner "Cornwall," of Plymouth, May 31st, 1865.

EMMA.—Bg.; 174; Owner, Richd. Wilson; Owners, 1853, Jos. Tindale, 48, Benj. Tindale, 16; Reg. at Hartlepool, 16th Sept., 1854; Reg. Wy., July, 1857; Owner, B. Granger; Owners, 1866, Jos. Avitt, 16, Benj. Granger, 16, Tindale Avery, 16, and Jane Storm, 16. Sold a wreck in 1876.

TARTAR.—Bn.; 153; bd., Hen. Barrick, and Owner; Reg. Hull, 7th March, 1843.

LONDON.—Sch.; 106; bd., Hobkirk; Owners, W. P. and L. S. Co.; Owner, 1870, Benj. Andrew, 64; Reg. at Hull, 1873.

DUKE.—Sch.; 89; bd., T. Turnbull; Owners, Turnbull and Hunton. Foundered at sea.

ENDEAVOUR.—Bn.; $\frac{80}{69}$; bd., Campion; Owners, R. and G. Wright; Owner, April, 1860, Ripley.

The "Endeavour," Ripley, whilst lying at the dock gates of Mr. Hen. Barrick, west side, was observed to be on fire about 6.30 a.m., the 21st Jan., 1868. Efforts were at once made, and the fire soon got put out without much damage being done. The previous night the captain left a fire in the cabin to dry a mat which he had been washing, and whether this caught fire or not is a matter of doubt. The vessel was insured against fire. Made a hulk, Nov., 1887

BRITISH OAK.—Bg.; 204; bd., T. Turnbull; Owners, Turnbull and Pennock.

This vessel was sent a new ship to London for sale. Thos. Wright, master. She laid there a year unsold, and then Mr. Thos. Smales took her to sea (his first command), having been mate of the "Concord" previously. Lost near Holyhead, Nov., 1849.

LEVISHAM.—Bg.; $\frac{170}{184}$. Apparently unsold until 1843. Owners, Francis Thompson and Will. Stead Lost near Yarmouth, Jan., 1847.

SARAH AND ANN.—Sch.; 51; Owners, Trattles and Co., Staithes. Sold to W. H'pool, 1863.

SEA-DRIFT.—Lug.; 67; bd., W. Falkingbridge; Reg. at Scrbr., 1847.

HIMALAYA.—S.; 507; bd., H. Barrick; Owners, Messrs. Wilson and Cook, Lndn.

BERMONDSEY.—S.; $\frac{445}{508}$; Owners, Messrs. Wilson and Cook, 1842.

ZIPPORAH.—Lug.; 64; bd., Chris. Gale; Owner, Richd. Verrill; Reg. at Scrbr., 1864.

On the 30th Aug., 1881, the "Zipporah," owned by Mr. W. Featherstone, Snaith, master, and one hand, with 28 tons of coal, after discharging at Runswick, was anchored in the bay. Bad weather came on, and she drove ashore and became a total wreck.

BROTHERS.—Lug.; 34; Owners, Trattles and Co.; Owned at Scrbr., 1860.

1842 CHINA.—S.; $\frac{601}{730}$; bd., H. and G. Barrick. Sold to Lndn. and renamed "Radcliffe"; 124 by 29; June, 1842, two large ships and a large brig belonging to Messrs. Barrick sent to Lndn. for sale, and a ship belonging to Mr. H. Barrick, West Side.

MANDARIN.—S.; $\frac{532}{629}$; bd., H. Barrick; Lad. June 25th. Sold to Jos. Somes, Lndn., and renamed "Lord Petrie."

GUARDIAN.—S.; $\frac{336}{400}$; Owners, Chadwick, Lndn.; Lndn. to Sydney, 1851.

HIBBERT.—Bg.; $\frac{230}{250}$; Owned at Lvrpl., 1854; Lvrpl. to River Plate.

NYMPH.—Bg.; 242; Owner, Barrick.

LYDIA.—Sch.; 151; bd., W. Hobkirk; Owners in 1853, J. and W. Wood; Reg. Portsmouth, Nov., 1857; Reg. Dundee, 1873.

LAUREL.—Sch; 134; bd., Hobkirk; Owners, Geo. Chapman and Robinson Gales; Owners, 1852, W. Hobkirk, 32, Sam Flintoft, 32. Lost on Tynemouth rocks, 25th April, 1859.

SPRAY.—Sch.; 164; bd., Turnbull; Owners, Turnbull and Co.; in 1849, bg. 141 tons. Sunk in the Thames; Raised and Reg. Lndn., 1853.

BETSY.—Bn.; 158; bd., W. Hobkirk; Owners, Mark Weighill, John Ireland, and W. Hobkirk. Lost off Shields, 1851.

SEAFLOWER.—Lug.; 35; bd., W. Falkingbridge; Owners, W. Smith, Wy., flaxdresser, and George and Jn. Hutton, fishermen. Sold away south. In May, 1880, lying in Blakeney Harbour a wreck.

GENOA PACKET.—Sch.; 151; bd., H. Barrick; Lad. March 3rd, 1843.

1843 ERA.—Bg.; 247; bd., H. Barrick; Owner, Gid. Smales. Lost at Hartlepool, Oct., 1859.

MORA.—Bg.; 258; bd., H. Barrick; Owner, Gid. Smales. Lost, 31st March, 1863, on island of Borkum, Frisian Islands, North Sea.

IRIS.—Bg.; 179; bd., Turnbull; Owners, Turnbull, Pennock and C. Leng. Lost, 1st July, 1845.

EDWARD.—Bn.; 146; Owner, Edward Turner; Capt., J. Carling; Reg. Colchester, 17th Feb., 1855.

GOVERNOR.—Bn.; 151; Owner, Boulcott, Lndn.; Lndn. to New Zealand, 1844.

PROVIDENCE.—Sch.; 79.

STANLEY.—Bg.; 210; bd., Hobkirk; Owner, W. Jameson; Owners in 1862, Jn. Danby, 48, Jn. Spence, 16. Lost off Hartlepool, Feb., 1871.

EBENEZER.—Sch.; $\frac{71}{86}$; bd., Campion, per M. Clough; Owner, Thos. Douglas, pilot; Reg. Maldon, 1846.

ESTHER.—Bk.; $\frac{242}{273}$; Reg. Lndn., 1846.

PROSPEROUS.—Sch.; bd., Hobkirk.

HARRISONS.—Bn.; 131; bd., H. and G. Barrick; Owners, T. J., T. and W. Harrison, R.H. Bay; Owned at Hartlepool, 1869. Totally lost at Hartlepool, Feb., 1880.

1844 GWALIOR.—S.; $\frac{600}{523}$; bd., H. Barrick. Sold to Messrs. Chapman, Lndn., and renamed "Mariner." Lad. May, 1844.

NO. 6.—Bd., Turnbull.

TITANIA.—Bn.; 139; bd., H. Barrick; Owner, H. B.; Reg. Lndn., 1845.

ORB.—Bg.; 185; bd., H. Barrick; Owner, Gid. Smales; Owners, 1879, Will. Bedlington, 32, Matt. Storm, 32. Lost at Bridlington, 8th Dec., 1886.

ROBERT.—Bg.; 253; bd., W. Hobkirk; Owners, W. and R. Usherwood; Reg. Lvrpl., 1849.

GEM.—Bg.; 186; bd., Hobkirk; Owner, Gid. Smales; Owners in 1861, Matt. Storm, 13, Thos. Storm, 13, Will Steel, 12, Will Bedlington, 13, and Will Storm, 13. Missing since 2nd Dec., 1863, Hartlepool to Lndn.

DANBY.—Bn.; $\frac{149}{161}$; bd., Hobkirk; Owners, W. Thompson and Sarah Nesfield. Missing since 28th March, 1850, bound to Dantzic.

1845 ZEPHYRUS.—Bg.; 238; bd., W. Hobkirk; Owners, Geo. Smith, 32, Wy., and Thos. Thistle, 16, and S. Griffiths, 16, both of Lvrpl.; Capt., Robt. Smith; Owner, 1857, Robt. Harrowing, 64. Lost near Three Island Point, White Sea, 21st June, 1857.

LUCK'S ALL.—Lug.; 36; bd., Falkingbridge; Owned at Sndld., 1865.

IVY.—Bg.; 150; bd., Hobkirk; Owner, Gid. Smales. Sold to Sndld., 1861.

SUCCESS.—Lug.; 34; bd., Falkingbridge; Owner, 1870, Ed. Peacock, R.H.B. Foundered 30th Jan., 1894, 10 miles off Staithes.

LIVERPOOL.—Bk.; 307; bd., H. Barrick; Lad. 16th Sept. Sold, 1845, to Jos. Brooks, Gates and Co., Lvrpl; Voy. to Jamaica, 1854.

CHAPMANS.—Bk.; 280; Owners in 1854, Philpots and Co., Lndn.; Voy. Lndn. to China.

1846 BONA FIDE.—Bg.; 259; bd., Hobkirk; Owner, Geo. Smith; Owners, April, 1859, W. B. Smith, 42, Thos. Thistle, 14, Thos. Harwood Woodwark, 8. Lost on the Wolf Rock, Cornwall, Jan., 1862.

HEBE.—Bg.; 197; bd., W. Hobkirk; Owners, Jas. Arthur, m.m., and Tomlinson.

Capt., W. Storm, of brig "Hebe," of Whitby, reports 19th Oct., 1862 :—Left London and encountered heavy gales till 29th Oct., when Flambro' Head bearing W. ½ N., distant 157 miles, fell in with the abandoned schooner "Eliza Jane," of Exeter. With great difficulty got a rope on board and towed her till Friday, 31st Oct., when Capt. Bully, of the smack, "Miranda and Fanny," took her in tow per agreement.

Owners, 1870, Matt. Bedlington, jun., 32, Will Harrison, 32. Wrecked 6 miles North of Spurn, 28th Oct., 1880.

DORIS.—Bg.; 197; bd., H. Barrick; Owner, Gid. Smales. Sold to W. Hartlepool, 1861.

HILDA.—Yacht; 20; bd., Falkingbridge; Owner, Thos. Richardson; Reg. Lndn., May, 1851; Reg. Aberystwyth, 1873.

NIO.—Bg.; 195; bd., W. Hobkirk; Owner, Gid. Smales. Lost on Middle Sand, off Essex, Jan., 1852.

FLY.—Bg.; 160; bd., W. Hobkirk; Owner, Gid. Smales. Missing since 7th Nov., 1849.

1847 MARIA.—Bg.; 207; bd., Will. Hobkirk; Owner, Gid. Smales; Owners in 1874, Matt. Storm, 32, Will. Bedlington, 32. Lost with all the crew in the great gale of March 19th and 20th, 1874, in the North Sea.

ETHEL.—Bg.; 209; bd., H. Barrick; Owner, Gid. Smales; Capt., Geo. S. Willis; Owners, 1866, Will Steel, 56, Jn. Nellist, 8.

The "Ethel," Capt., J. Nellist, and six hands, left Aarhuus for London, barley, 17th Jan., 1868. On 23rd a heavy gale from E.N.E., with snow and decks all ice; could not handle the sails, and the ship being unmanageable, bore away. At 4.30 a.m., 24th Jan., sighted Hessle light, S.E. by S. ½ E. Kept ship away, and five minutes later she struck, and remained beating heavily on the reef, running out from Hessle Island. Left the vessel settling down with about eight feet of water in her, and landed on island of Hessle.

REGINA.—Bg.; 258; bd., H. and G. Barrick; Owners, Rickinson and Cowart; Reg. Lndn., 1855.

MARY BULL.—Bg.; 214; bd., Hobkirk; Owners, Sarah Nesfield and Co. Lost in the Gulf of Finland, 25th Nov., 1847.

JET.—Bg.; 174; bd., Hobkirk; Owners, S. Flintoft and W. Lister; 10 weeks building; Capt., J. E. Lund. Lost on coast of Denmark, 18th Nov., 1849.

HER MAJESTY.—Bg.; 221; bd., Hobkirk; Owner, Rickinson.

A tragedy occurred on board of this brig on the 28th June, 1855, when homeward bound from Salonika, maize, to Cork or Falmouth, for orders. In the Bay of Biscay one of the crew stabbed the Capt., Will. Wright, and killed him. The mate, hearing something wrong on deck and coming up from the cabin, was also killed. The man then attacked and fatally wounded the steward. He then attempted to scuttle the vessel, and finally hung or strangled himself. The vessel was fallen in with by the brig "Isabel," of Bristol, and the mate of her navigated the "Her Majesty" to Queenstown. The "Brazilian Packet" also came up shortly after the "Isabel." Capt. W. Gray Newton apprentice on board at the time.

Lost 23rd Oct., 1857, Cronstadt for Lndn., tallow, Capt., Benj. Osborne, near Yarmouth, all crew drowned.

1848 ELLEN.—Bg.; 222; bd., Hen. Barrick; Owners, 1848, H. Barrick, 32, T. W. Langborne, 16, Geo. Ebblewhite, 16; Owners in 1878, R. Harrowing, 24, H. Hobson, Will Simpson, Jos. Simpson, Jn. Brand, Will James, and Jn. Harland. Abandoned in a sinking state 40 miles N.N.E. of the Texel, 24th Aug., 1882.

OAK.—Bg.; 180; bd., W. Hobkirk; Owners, W. and T. Hobkirk; Owner in 1864, Isabel Granger. Lost coast of Denmark, Sept., 1864.

SEDULOUS.—Bg.; 226; bd., H. and Geo. Barrick; Owners, Robt. Harrison, 56, and Matt. Marsay, 8; Reg. Lndn., 1851.

MAGNET.—Bg.; 178; bd., W. Hobkirk; Owner, Gid. Smales. Lost, April, 1856.

LEO.—Bg.; 207; bd., Hobkirk; Owner, Gid. Smales. When off the Texel drove ashore and became a wreck, 17th Nov., 1860.

ARGO.—Bn.; 164; bd., W. Hobkirk; Owned at Selby, 1854.

RELIANCE.—Bg.; 265; bd., H. Barrick; Owner, Rickinson; Lad. Sept. 15. Sold to Will. Steward, Wisbech, April, 1849.

1849 BOUNTY.—Bg.; 168; bd., H. Barrick; Owner, Gid. Smales; Owner in 1882, Reuben Storm, 64. Lost, 1888, Hartlepool to Gluckstadt. Capt., R. Storm.

STANDARD.—Bg.; 162; bd., Hobkirk; Owner, Will. Thompson. Lost in the White Sea, 17th Aug., 1852.

OSWY.—Bg.; 172; bd., H. Barrick; Owner, Gid. Smales; Owned at Hartlepool, 1880; At Gravesend later. Wrecked at Cleethorpes, 18th Nov., 1893.

BARRICK.—Bk.; 304; bd., H. and G. Barrick; Owner, Barrick, Lndn., 1854.

ALICE GILL.—Bk.; 255; bd., Hobkirk; Owners, Thistle and Co.; Capt. in 1854, Chas. Wright.

1850 ROBERT STEPHENSON.—Bg.; 203; bd., W. Hobkirk; Owners, Hobkirk and J. and E. Corner; Reg. Shields, 1854.

ANT.—Bg.; 232; bd., Thos. Hobkirk; Owner, Gid. Smales. Sold to Stcktn., 1861.

BEE.—Bg.; 229; bd., H. Barrick; Owner, Gid. Smales. Sold to foreigners, 1873.

FLY.—Bg.; 153; bd., Thos. Hobkirk; Owner, Gid. Smales. Sold to Sndld., 1861.

AFFIANCE.—Bk.; 349; bd., H. and G. Barrick; Owners, Barrick and Co., Lndn.

1851 HILDA.—Bg.; 212; bd., Thos. Hobkirk; Owners, Jn. Leng, 32, Jn. Weighill, 16, Christ. Harrison, 16. Lost in Russia, 23rd Nov., 1857.

EVA.—Bg.; 185; bd., Thos. Hobkirk; Owners, Christ. Harrison and Jn. Weighill. Lost, 20th Nov., 1858.

SPRING.—Bg.; 221; bd., Thos. Hobkirk; Owner, Gid. Smales.

Nov. 23-4, 1851, off Hartlepool, the night being very dark, a large barque ran down a laden brig, supposed to belong to Mr. Gideon Smales, of Whitby, on her first voyage. All the crew drowned.

Missing since Nov., 1851.

PET.—Bg.; 238; bd., H. and G. Barrick; Owners, Riley and Co., Dundee, 1851.

Launched from Messrs. Cato's old yard, the last till Messrs. Smales Brothers built there in 1866.

1852 EMILY.—Bg.; 233; bd., H. Barrick; Owners, Coggin and Co.; Owners in 1874, Will. Steel, 56, Jn. Speedy, 8. Missing, supposed to have foundered in the North Sea about 25th Jan., 1883.

QUEEN OF ENGLAND.—S.; $\frac{481}{588}$; bd., H. and Geo. Barrick; Lad. May 5; Owner, H. Barrick, Lndn., 1854; Figurehead of Queen; Voy. Lndn. to Sydney, 1860.

When this ship went to sea, the bridge rails had to be removed to allow room for her to pass through, owing to her large guard boards.

WILLIAM AND CHARLES.—Bg.; 214; bd., H. Barrick; Owner, Gid. Smales. Sold to Hartlepool, 1861.

SWAINSON.—Bg.; 222; bd., T. Hobkirk; Owner, Gid. Smales. Sold to W. H'pool, 1861. Reg. Wy., April, 1882; Owners, 1882, Christ. Marwood, 32, Jn. Rowland, 32. Abandoned 60 miles E. off Spurn, 20th Jan., 1884.

HINDA.—Bg.; 177; bd., H. Barrick; Owners, C. Harrison and J. Weighill and Co. Wrecked at Tralleborg, Baltic, Dec., 1863; foggy weather.

LYRA.—Bg.; 186; bd., T. Hobkirk; Owners, J. and J. H. Barry; Owners, Feb. 1858, Jn. Barry, 40, J. H. Barry, 16, Will Storm, 8. Burnt, Nov., 1859, Soderhamn to Spalding, deals.

IRIS.—Sch.; 60; bd., T. Turnbull; Owners, Turnbull and Hunton; Owner in 1866, Geo. Welland, Clift, S. Shields, 32, D. G. Gibson, 32. Pilot shelter on Tees, Dec., 1900.

1853 CHOLMLEY.—Bg.; 228; bd., H. Barrick; Owner, Gid. Smales. Sold to Hartlepool, 1861. In collision, and sold a wreck at Boulogne, Dec., 1876.

LAVINIA.—Bk.; 323; bd., H. and G. Barrick; Owners in 1863, Jn. Rickinson and W. B. Smith, 64 jointly. Lost in the Bosphorus, Dec., 1866.

JULIA.—Bg.; 193; bd., Hobkirk; Owner, Gid. Smales. Sold to Sndld., 1861.

ROBINSON.—Bg.; 256; bd., H. and G. Barrick; Owners in 1853, Hen. Robinson, m.m., and Ann Robinson, widow, 64, as executors of late Richd. Atkinson Robinson. Lost, 1862.

NIO.—Bg.; 171; bd., H. Barrick; Owner, Gid. Smales; Owners, 1890, Isaac Mills and Jos. Avitt. Total wreck at Saltfleet, 14th Oct., 1892.

UNIVERSE.—Bk.; 283; bd., Hobkirk; Owners, Thistle and Co.; Owners, June, 1874, Will. Thompson, Will Ryder, of Staithes, Thos. Petch, Liverton, and Jn. Seymour, of Staithes. Lost island of Gothland, 14th Oct., 1880.

JOHN LAWSON.—Bk.; 308; bd., Turnbull. Owners, J. and John N. Lawson; Reg. Lvrpl., 1855; Reg. Grnck., 1864; Reg. Wy. from Grnck., April, 1865; Owner, Sanderson Brown, of Staithes. Sold to Hull, 1869.

1854 WATERSPRITE.—Bk.; 345; bd., Turnbull; Capt., T. Smailes; Owners, 1875, Jn. Lennard, Geo. Milburn, Will. Milburn, Will. Walker, Jn. Wallis, and Jn. Milburn. Supposed to have foundered in the North Sea on or about Dec. 7th, 1879.

NORMA.—Bg.; 215; bd., H. Barrick; Owners, Christ. Harrison and Co.

Capt. Lawson Wright was lost with all the crew in the brig "Norma" on his passage from Ystad, S. Sweden, to London, 2nd Dec., 1857.

ACORN.—Bg.; 187; bd., Turnbull; Owners, T. Wilson and Co.; Owners, 1872, T. Wilson, 48, James Houghton, 16; Reg. Lndn., July, 1875.

MINORCA.—Bg.; 214; bd., Hobkirk; Owners, W. Tose and Son; Owners, 1864, Will Tose, 42, Francis Britain, 22.

The "Minorca," Capt. Jn. Tose and 7 hands, left Nicholaieff, 2nd Aug., 1870, with 355 tons of rye for orders. Friday, 9th Sept., at 1.35 a.m., weather hazy, with a gale from N.W. by N., the land being just visible and supposed distance about 6 miles, the ship struck heavily upon a coral reef about 7 miles S.E. from Cape Bon. Every effort was made to float her. The long boat was got out and provisioned, and seeing that nothing more could be done to save the ship, abandoned her and pulled to the shore. The vessel then full of water and the sea washing over her. The following day got a spar and a sail from the ship, and proceeded in the boat to Pantellaria, where we got assistance, and returned with a schooner and got 25 tons of cargo and most of the ship's materials above decks, which were taken to Tunis and there sold.

STAR OF HOPE.—Bg.; 240; bd., Turnbull; Owners, Sarah Nesfield and Co.

The "Star of Hope," owned by Mr. James Knott, of Newcastle, Jn. Robt. Walker, master, and five hands, left Dieppe for Shields, 26th Nov., 1882. On the 4th Dec. a strong gale at W.N.W.; at 6 a.m. on the 5th the wind veered to E.N.E. with a heavy gale, and increasing sea; Spurn light W.S.W. distant 50 miles. At 2 a.m. 6th

Dec. passed Flambro' Head. At 8 a.m. South Cheek, R.H.Bay distant 6 miles, the wind increasing, and a very heavy sea with blinding snow squalls. At 10 a.m. Whitby Abbey bore W.N.W. distant 3 miles. Finding the vessel would not clear the land on either tack deemed it prudent to run ashore at Whitby for safety of vessel and crew. Came ashore at noon about 60 yards west of the pier. Total wreck.

YENIKALE.—Bk.; 318; bd., Hobkirk; Owners, Benj. Pearson, 43, and Chas. H. Wright, 21; Reg. at Lvrpl., 1863.

ELIZA ANN.—Bg.; 237; bd., T. Hobkirk; Owners, Dotchon and Co. Lost near Kustendje, Black Sea, 20th April, 1856.

RELIANCE.—Bg.; 185; bd., H. and G. Barrick; Owners, T. Foxton, W. Steward, Jn. Rickinson and Co.; Owners, 1866, W. T. Roberts, 8, Jn. Rickinson and W. B. Smith, 28 jointly, Middleton Cowart, 28. Reg. at Maldon, 1866.

1855 ALMA.—Bg.; 246; bd., H. Barrick; Owners, Chris. Harrison and Jn. Weighill and Co. Totally wrecked in the White Sea, July 15, 1876.

DANUBE.—Bg.; 207; bd., Hobkirk; Owner, W. Steward; Owners, 1887, Geo. Milburn, Will Harrison, and Jos. Brown. A coal hulk, 1901.

EDWARD THORNHILL.—S.; $\frac{421}{328}$; bd., H. and Geo. Barrick; Owner, Thornhill, London.

The Last *Ship* built at Whitby.

GANYMEDE.—Bg.; 184; bd., Turnbull; Owner, 1861, S. Andrew, 64. Abandoned in the North Sea, 1863, grain laden from the Baltic. Was seen several times afterwards.

SALEM.—Bg.; 215; bd., Hobkirk; Owner, Jn. Walker. Lost on Hasebro' Sand, Jan., 1865.

SCLAVONIA.—Bk.; 297; bd., Hobkirk; Owner, Marwood; Capt., Mutter. Passed Aldbro', Nov. 29, 1867. Not since heard of.

1856 AZOFF.—Bg.; 227; bd., H. and G. Barrick; Owner, Barrick; Capt., W. James; Reg. Plymth., 1861.

KIRKDALE.—Bg.; 280; bd., H. Barrick; Owner, 1857, Jn. Lougton, Lvrpl.

OLIVE BRANCH.—Bg.; 196; bd., Turnbull; Owners, J. Robinson and Isaac Bate; Reg. Scrbr., 1875. Wrecked near Wy., Feb., 1886.

WILD ROSE.—Bk.; 280; bd., Hobkirk; Owners, Thistle and Co.; Reg. May 15. Sold to Brixham, 1866. Lost at East London, in the colony of Cape Town, 25th Sept., 1872.

EUGENIE.—Bk.; 265; bd., H. and G. Barrick; Owner, Barrick; Reg. Lndn., 1860. Lost at Bahamas, 1862.

RENOWN.—Bk.; 324; bd., Hobkirk; Owners, Benj. Pearson and Anna Pyburn; Reg. at Wy., 29th Jan., therefore built in 1855; Sold to Falmouth, 1867. Owner, 1873, Edmund Handcock, Falmouth.

ROYAL ROSE.—Bk.; 295; bd., Hobkirk; Owners, S. Storm, 32, Ralph Hayes, 16, Sam. Andrew, 16; Reg. at Wy., Sept. 23; Owners, April, 1859, Sampson Storm, 40, Samuel Andrew, 24.

On Sunday afternoon, the 21st Dec., 1862, blowing hard, with a heavy sea, about one o'clock a barque hove in sight, evidently coming for the beach. She laid some time broadside to the sea. The crew, except the helmsman, in the mizzen rigging. She took the sand about high tide, and soon began to break up. A strong force of men took the old lifeboat, the "Petrel," up the Khyber Pass, and under the superintendence of Mr. Christ. Gale, smack builder, lowered it down what is called the Caulkhills, and with great difficulty brought the crew ashore. The mainyard of the barque passed right through the lifeboat whilst the crew were getting into it. Rockets had been fired, but the strong wind blew the lines back, except one which passed over the royal stay out of reach of the men. The vessel proved to be the "Royal Rose," Capt. Storm, grain laden Black Sea for Leith. She was leaky, and the grain swelling, she broke up immediately.

The "Royal Rose," Capt. Jn. Storm, crew of 12 inclusive, with wheat from Odessa for Leith, Thursday, 18th Dec., 1862, at 4 p.m., ebb tide, weather hazy, wind W.S.W., strong and squally, the vessel being on the starboard tack under close reefed topsails and leaking at the rate of two inches an hour. At 8 p.m. wore the ship to the North, the water increasing. At 2 a.m., in a squall and a heavy sea, the cargo shifted and threw the ship on her beam ends. At 5 a.m. again wore round, the water still increasing. All hands were sent to the pumps. The cargo shifted on every tack, which threw the vessel on her beam ends. This continued till Sunday, the 21st, when off Hartlepool wore the ship and bore up for Bridlington Bay. Sounded the pumps and found seven feet of water. Deemed it advisable to run the ship ashore at once to save life. Did so, and came on Whitby sand and struck at 1.15

p.m. The vessel commenced breaking up, and became a total wreck. All the assistance that could be given from the shore by means of the rocket apparatus was given, and also by the beach lifeboat, not the National Lifeboat, which saved the crew. A Russian pig was the first living thing to reach the shore, being washed overboard.

GEM OF THE OCEAN.—Dy.; 30; Reg. at Montrose, 1878; Reg. Wy., Aug., 1881; Owner, T. Mennell.

1857 PATRIOT.—Bk.; 268; bd., Turnbull; Owners, W. Dotchon and Co. Sold to foreigners, 1873.

VERBENA.—Bk.; $\frac{296}{325}$; bd., Hobkirk; Owners, Thistle and Co.; Owner, 1876, Will. Thompson. Sold to Germans, 1882.

SYLVAN.—Bk.; $\frac{306}{333}$; bd., Hobkirk; Owner, Smales; Reg. Wy., Feb., 1858.

On 13th March, 1858, the "Sylvan," leaving the Tyne on her first voyage, coal laden for Marseilles, got upon the middle ground, and remained until the following tide, when her stern broke.

The "Sylvan" was sold by Messrs. Smales Bros., June, 1881, to Mr. Isaac Whitfield, of Sunderland. She had laid two years in Whitby harbour. The "Sylvan" sailed from the Tyne, coal laden, 25th Jan., 1883, and became a missing ship.

TRUE LOVE.—Ywl.; 29; 56 by 17; Owner, J. Hodgson, baker, and Cole and Thompson, fishermen. Sold to Lynn, Dec., 1871.

1858 JAPAN.—Bk.; 307; bd., H. Barrick; Lad., 15th April. Sold to Lndn. and renamed "Sea Belle," 1860.

ANTIGUA.—Bk.; 287; bd., H. and Geo. Barrick; Owner, Jefferson, of Whitehaven. Signal letters, N.D.T.W. Wy. to West Indies, 1859.

BELLE.—Bg.; 198; bd., Turnbull; Owners, Turnbull, Garminsway and Co.; Owners, 1887, Geo. Galilee and Eliza Walker; Owner, 1888, R. Hutton. Sold to Scrbr., 1889.

ECLIPSE.—Bk.; 298; bd., Hobkirk; Owners, Rickinson and Co., West H'pool; Reg. at Hartlepool, 1859.

PRINCESS ROYAL.—Ywl.; 33. Total loss on Rosedale beach, Jan., 1895.

RACEHORSE.—Dy.; 36. Sailed from Largo, Fifeshire, for West H'pool, 21st Jan., 1897. Was last seen in the Firth of Forth on the 24th, and has not since been heard of. Owners, Jn. Theaker and Co., Staithes.

1859 FANNY.—Bg.; 209; bd., H. Barrick; Owners, T. Coggin and Co. Lost, 1862.

SIR HENRY HAVELOCK.—Bg.; 197; bd., Hobkirk; Owners, Jameson and Co.; Owners, 1888, Geo. and Will Milburn, Robt. Lennard and Will. Eves. Stranded and total wreck at Cleethorpes, near Grimsby, 18th Nov., 1893.

MAUD.—Bg.; 238; bd., Turnbull. Sold to Fleetwood, 1864.

COMPETITOR.—Bk.; 437; bd., Hobkirk; 10 months building; Owner, Smales; Reg., Jan. 10, 1860.

When bound to Cadiz from Cardiff on 27th Feb., 1862, and in latitude 46 N., longitude 10 W., this vessel took fire. The Captain, Rackley, his son, and one man were killed by an explosion. One man was drowned, and the remainder of the crew got to Gibraltar.

HERO.—Bg.; 188; bd., Hobkirk; Owners, Granger and Robinson. Lost in the North Sea and all the crew, 16th Oct., 1862.

1860 CHASE.—Bg.; 245; bd., Hobkirk; Owners, T. Wilson and Will Whidby, of Sunderland; Owner, 1865, T. Walker, Blyth, 64. Lost in the Gulf of Finland, 12th July, 1865.

CHANCE.—Bg.; 193; bd., H. and G. Barrick; Reg. at Lndn., 1865.

MARY.—Bg.; 169; bd., Turnbull. Sold to foreigners, March, 1864, for £1,650.

COSGROVE.—Bg.; 213; bd., H. Barrick. Sold to H'pool, 1861.

1861 JENNY.—Bg.; 221; bd., Hobkirk; Owners, Harrowing and Fletcher; Owners, 1862, Robt. Harrowing, 48, Richd. Gibson, 16; Owner, 1865, Robt. Harrowing, 64; Reg. in Lndn., 1867.

ENID.—Bg.; 271; bd., Turnbull; Owners, 1867, T. Turnbull, 16, Jn. Pearson, 48.

The "Enid," Capt. Jn. Pearson, Enos for Plymouth, orders, 2,160 qrs. of wheat, Feb., 1869. Arrived Plymouth 29th April, ordered to Leith. Run down by the Screw Steamer "Pilot," of London, 8th May, 1869, Flambro' Head bearing N.N.W. distant 28 miles.

LILY.—Bg.; 247; bd., T. Hobkirk; Reg. Grnck., Feb., 1862. Sunk in collision off Flambro', Oct., 1897.

1862 RESCUE.—Bg.; 204; bd., H. Barrick; Owner, T. Vasey, of London.

SHARON'S ROSE.—Bg.; 205; bd., Hobkirk; Owners, B. Granger, Richd. Robinson, and Benj. Tindale; Owners, 1880, J. B. B. Mead, 21, Thos. Mennell, 21, and Moorsom Mennell, 21. Lost on Holkam beach, Oct., 1880, Norfolk.

THOMAS TURNBULL.—Bk.; 369; bd., T. Turnbull. Sold to Thos. Dobson Woodhead, Hull, Dec., 1879. Lost near Lowestoft, 18th Jan., 1880.

MERRIE ENGLAND.—Bk.; 444; bd., Hobkirk; Owner, Smales.

Two of the crew, Thos. Easton, carpenter, and Frederick Norman, A.B., washed off the jibboom and drowned, Sept., 1871.

Lost on the coast of Florida, 13th Dec., 1877.

The last vessel built by Mr. Thos. Hobkirk.

RESULT.—Bk.; 242; bd., H. and G. Barrick; Lad., April 2. Sold to Bristol, 1863.

REFUGE.—Dy.; 36; Owners, 1880, J. Trattles, 32, Hannah Brown, 16, Ann Brown, 16. Sold to Lowestoft, Oct., 1897.

1863 SHAMROCK.—Bk.; 365; bd., H. Barrick; Owners, Smales Bros.; Lad., April 6; 116 by 26.

"Shamrock," Capt. Jn. Storm and 11 hands, left Ardrossan 12th Feb., 1872, for St. Jago, Cuba, 552 tons of coal. Proceeded, wind S.E. to S.S.E. strong and increasing, and thick with rain. About 7 p.m. the island of Ailsa Craig was sighted, bearing N.N.E. distant ½ to ¾ of a mile. The ship was then kept about W.N.W. until 10 p.m. and going at the rate of 4½ knots, and then N.W. until 1 a.m., and nothing being seen she was hauled by the wind and tacked two or three times. On Tuesday, 13th, at 2.45 a.m., thick with rain, wind S.S.E. strong, being then under whole topsails courses and square mainsail and steering by the wind on the port tack head S.W., land was seen nearly right ahead and apparently close to. Sounded and found about 6 fathoms. The helm was at once put hard down, but the ship missed stays. The helm was then put hard up to wear round, and just as she was got round she struck heavily aft, and passed over what was supposed to be a rock, and in about five minutes she struck again, and remained fixed on the rocks. The sea being heavy, she rolled and struck heavily, and heeled over with her decks to the sea, so that the boats and everything were washed off the decks. All hands were obliged to take to the rigging, where they remained until daylight, at which time the decks were starting and the ship breaking up. The place where the ship was stranded was about 2 miles North from the village of Cushendun, Ireland, in Red Bay. About 7 a.m. some coastguardmen and others got on the rock about 40 or 50 yards from the ship, when a line was thrown to them from the jibboom, by which they hauled a hawser ashore, along which the crew passed from the end of the jibboom to the rocks, and were afterwards taken to the village of Cushendun, about 2 miles south from the ship. Two days afterwards, when the weather moderated, some sails and spars were saved. The ship became a total wreck.

ROYAL DANE.—Bk.; 344; bd., H. and G. Barrick; Owner, Rickinson, Hartlepool; Lad., July 30th.

WARRIOR.—Bk.; 445; bd., T. Turnbull; Owners, Turnbull and Sons, 56, John W. Turnbull, 8; Square stern; Male figurehead; 132 by 26.

William Henry Clark, mate of the "Warrior," Capt. Jn. Turnbull, of Wy., outward bound to Bombay, whilst furling jib fell overboard. The ship was put about and all possible aid rendered, but he sank almost immediately. On the Agulhas Bank, S. Africa, 1868.

Owners, Feb., 1874, T. Turnbull, 48, West Hodgson, 16. Sold to foreigners at Buenos Ayres, Nov. 1878.

1864 CONFLICT.—Bg.; 227; bd., H. Barrick; square stern; demi-female head. Sold, 1864, and Reg. at Shoreham, 1865.

MARY.—Bk.; 308; bd., Thos. Turnbull; Owners, T. Turnbull, jun., 56, R. M. Hunton, 8; Elliptic stern; Head a shield. Sold foreign, Oct., 1872.

1865 MAUD.—Bk.; 276; bd., Turnbull; Owners, Turnbull and Hunton; Elliptic stern; Figurehead, a shield. Sold to Belfast, Aug., 1872.

VICTORY.—Bk.; 399; bd., H. and G. Barrick; 7 months building; Owners, 1866, Jn. Simpson, 18, Chas. Jn. Brightman and Wm. Hy. Turner, 16 jointly, and Will Brown, 30, all of London.

The last vessel built by Messrs. H. and G. Barrick.

1866 PRINCESS ELFLEDA.—Bk.; 476; bd., Smales Bros., and Owners. Lost near the Dudgeon light, 21st April, 1872.

REVENGE.—Bk.; 354; bd., H. Barrick. Sold, May, 1867, to Messrs. Hen. Else and Son, of Lndn., and renamed "Constantia."

The last vessel built by Mr. Henry Barrick.

1867 WILLIAM HUNTON.—Bk.; 414; bd., Turnbull and Sons, and Owners; Elliptic stern; Lad., Feb.; 136 by 27. Sold to Thos. Dobson Woodhead, Hull, and Reg. transferred to Hull, Feb., 1880.

MARYS.—Ywl.; 38; Owner, Jn. Miller. Lost at Souter Point, April, 1876.

1868 GAUNTLET.—Bk.; 388; bd., Turnbull; Owners, Turnbull, Hunton, and J. Dinsdale. Lost at Kilia, Nov., 1868.

MARIA WAKEFIELD.—Bk.; 361; bd., Smales Bros., and Owners; Composite; 121 by 26; Figurehead; Lad., April 7. Sold to Reynolds, of Lvrpl., Aug., 1879.

When being towed went ashore, taking the tug with her, and became a wreck near Swansea.

1869 No ocean going vessels launched in 1869.

1870 KING ARTHUR.—Bk.; 399; bd., Turnbull and Sons, and Owners. Iron beams; Two decks. Sold to Lvrpl., and renamed "Hazelholme," 1873.

The last sailing vessel built by Messrs. Turnbull.

1871 MONKSHAVEN.—Bk.; 371; bd., Messrs. Smales Bros., and Owners; Composite; 128 by 27; Class 16 years; Lad., Feb. 20th.

The last wooden sailing vessel built at Whitby.

The "Monkshaven," laden with 657 tons of coal, from Swansea for Valparaiso, took fire in the South Atlantic. The crew were rescued by Lord Brassey in the yacht "Sunbeam," 28th Sept., 1876.

See abbreviations, etc., previous to First Section.

ALPHABETICAL INDEX

of the Vessels in the foregoing Section, all built at Whitby, and the date when each Vessel was built.

Abraham and Moses	1791	Aimwell	1796
Abbotsford ...	1827	Aimwell	1799
Acalus	1790	Albion	1792
Acasta	1824	Albion	1793
Accession	1823	Albion	1798
Acorn	1804	Albion	1804
Acorn	1854	Aldbro	1803
Acteon	1796	Alchemyst	1840
Active	1801	Alert	1797
Active	1804	Alert	1799
Active	1806	Alert	1802
Active	1823	Alert	1802
Adroit	1797	Alexander	1801
Adston	1803	Alice Gill	1849
Adeona	1790	Alliance	1800
Adriatic	1791	Alma	1855
Adonis	1807	Alpha	1840
Admiral Moorsom ...	1827	Amphitrite ...	1790
Adventure	1802	Amity	1790
Adventure	1818	Amity	1799
Ælfleda	1823	Amity	1802
Affiance	1850	Amity	1818
Agriculture	1802	Amity	1840
Aid	1797	Amathea	1798
Aid	1805	Amos	1819
Aid	1837	Andromeda ...	1798

Name	Year
Ann	1790
Ann	1799
Ann	1803
Ann	1818
Ann	1822
Ann and Susannah	1804
Ann Grant	1806
Ann Green	1810
Ant	1850
Antigua	1858
Ardent	1796
Arcadia	1796
Arcturus	1814
Arcturus	1825
Arethusa	1794
Arethusa	1822
Arethusa	1827
Ariadne	1795
Arabella	1840
Army	1820
Ark	1792
Ark	1806
Ark	1824
Argo	1807
Argo	1815
Argo	1827
Argo	1848
Asia	1813
Astrea	1826
Atty	1791
Atlas	1809
Atlas	1812
Atlantic	1812
Atlantic	1832
Autumn	1790
Autumn	1801
Autumn	1815
Autumn	1839
Augusta	1796
Aurora	1804
Aurora	1808
Avon	1791
Avon	1826
Ayton	1838
Azoff	1856
Baltic Merchant	1804
Barrick	1791
Barrick	1849
Barjona	1826
Barzillai	1790
Battalion	1795
Beatrix	1800
Bee	1802
Bee	1850
Bellona	1793
Bellona	1812
Bellona	1828
Benson	1795
Benjamin	1824
Bethell	1822
Bermondsey	1841
Belle	1858
Better Luck Still	1803
Betsy	1802
Betsy	1803
Betsy	1805
Betsy	1815
Betsy	1842
Betsy and Sally	1803
Boa Ventura	1794
Bountiful	1803
Bona Fide	1846
Bounty	1849
Brothers	1790

Name	Year
Brothers ...	1811
Brothers ...	1815
Brothers ...	1840
Brothers ...	1841
Briton ...	1794
Briton ...	1807
Briton ...	1840
Britannia ...	1800
British Queen	1800
Brotherly Love	1802
Brunton ...	1802
Braganza ...	1808
Brilliant ...	1805
Brilliant ...	1813
Bridgeholm ...	1826
British Tar ...	1814
British Oak...	1841
Branken Moor	1827
Branken Moor	1829
A Bg., no name	1829
Canada ...	1791
Camilla ...	1795
Cambridge ...	1797
Camperdown	1798
Camden ...	1813
Cane Grove ...	1819
Captain Cook	1826
Cadiz Packet	1827
Canton ...	1829
Cato ...	1830
Cato ...	1840
Captain Ross	1834
Ceres ...	1793
Ceres ...	1825
Centurion ...	1811
Centenary ...	1839
Choice ...	1790
Charlotte ...	1799
Chilton ...	1802
Chatham ...	1803
Charles ...	1805
Chance ...	1813
Chance ...	1860
Christian ...	1821
China ...	1842
Chapmans ...	1845
Cholmley ...	1853
Chase ...	1860
Cicero ...	1805
Cicero ...	1823
Clio ...	1813
Clio ...	1816
Cleopatra ...	1817
Cleveland ...	1825
Clarence ...	1827
Claremont ...	1827
Claud ...	1828
Commerce ...	1795
Commerce ...	1799
Commerce ...	1806
Coverdale ...	1795
Columbus ...	1798
Columbus ...	1821
Columbus ...	1832
Cornwall ...	1798
Cove ...	1798
Cossack ...	1812
Concord ...	1799
Concord ...	1800
Concord ...	1815
Competitor ...	1812
Competitor ...	1859
Countess of Mulgrave	1819
Comet ...	1825

Corsair	1832	Dewdrop	1838
Conrad	1838	Diadem	1800
Countess of Minto...	1839	Diadem	1802
Cosgrove	1860	Diadem	1840
Conflict	1864	Diana	1824
Crescent	1792	Dolphin	1792
Crown	1801	Dolphin	1800
Crisis	1816	Dolphin	1807
Cullands Grove ...	1801	Dorothy	1801
Curlew	1805	Doris	1804
Cygnet	1792	Doris	1846
Cygnet	1796	Dominica	1808
Cygnet	1811	Dove	1809
Cygnet	1837	Dove	1823
Cyrus	1805	Don	1823
Cyrus	1811	Dowlah	1841
Cyrus	1823	Duke of Brontë ...	1803
Cyrus	1829	Duke of Bridgewater	1803
Cynthia	1822	Dublin	1804
Daphne	1792	Duncombe	1812
Daphne	1809	Duke	1841
Dalrymple	1796	Dwina	1826
Dash	1800	Eaglet	1812
Dale	1804	Eaglet	1839
Danae	1792	Earl of Eldon ...	1830
David	1821	Earl Stanhope ...	1830
Dahlia	1830	Ebenezer	1843
Danby	1844	Eclipse	1790
Danube	1855	Eclipse	1858
Dart	1835	Economy	1796
Dædalus	1791	Economy	1817
Defence	1794	Edward	1790
Desire	1795	Edward	1843
Dexterity	1811	Edgar	1804
Delight	1818	Edgar	1824
Dependent	1824	Edward Lombe ...	1828
Delhi	1835	Edward Thornhill ...	1855

N 2

Effort	1799
Egton	1803
Eglantine	1839
Elizabeth	1790
Elizabeth	1793
Elizabeth	1800
Elizabeth	1801
Elizabeth	1821
Elizabeth	1823
Elizabeth and Sally...	1802
Elbe	1795
Eleanor and Ann ...	1802
Eleanor	1838
Eliza	1798
Eliza	1821
Eliza	1838
Eliza Ann	1854
Ellen	1828
Ellen	1848
Emma	1813
Emma	1836
Emma	1841
Emma Eugenia ...	1833
Emerald	1798
Emulous	1817
Emily	1852
Enterprise	1795
Enterprise	1797
Endymion	1815
Endeavour	1837
Endeavour	1841
Enid	1861
Eolus	1793
Equestris	1795
Equity	1816
Era	1843
Esk	1790
Esk	1800
Esk	1812
Esk	1835
Esk	1840
Essex	1803
Esther	1843
Ethel	1847
Euphrosyne ...	1824
Eugenie	1856
Eva	1851
Expedition	1791
Expedition	1804
Favourite	1790
Farmer's Increase ...	1794
Fairfield	1795
Fairy	1817
Fancy	1829
Fanny	1859
Fides	1791
Fides	1837
Fidelity	1793
Filey	1821
Fly	1802
Fly	1846
Fly	1850
Flora	1802
Flora	1813
Flora	1835
Fleetwood	1806
Fortress	1794
Fortune	1802
Fortitude	1809
Fortitude	1814
Fowler	1826
Foster	1826
Friends	1817
Friends	1824

Friends	1825	Hannah	1792
Friends	1831	Hannah	1793
Friend's Adventure...	1835	Hannah	1803
Friendship ...	1840	Hannahs	1816
Frisk	1835	Harbinger	1794
Galatea	1793	Hatford	1796
Garland	1800	Haddock	1796
Galilee	1802	Hazard	1797
Gale	1826	Happy Return ...	1802
Ganymede	1841	Harmony	1803
Ganymede	1855	Harmony	1804
Gauntlet	1868	Harmony	1809
George	1796	Harmony	1819
George	1803	Halcyon	1805
George	1822	Halcyon	1810
George Canning ...	1824	Harvey	1819
George Armstrong...	1840	Harlequin	1801
George and Mary ...	1826	Hallfield	1820
George Clark ...	1841	Hankinson	1824
Genoa Packet ...	1842	Hamburg	1825
Gem	1844	Haidee	1836
Gem of the Ocean ...	1856	Harrison Chilton ...	1839
Gotheborgs Walgang	1810	Harrisons	1843
Good Intent ...	1841	Henry	1790
Governor	1843	Herald	1799
Grant	1798	Herald	1804
Gratitude	1800	Herald	1806
Gratitude	1804	Hebe	1803
Gratitude	1821	Hebe	1827
Grantham	1813	Hebe	1846
Green End	1827	Hero	1808
Graham	1837	Hero	1808
Gulnare	1830	Hero	1859
Guide	1841	Hessle	1817
Guardian	1842	Hercules	1822
Gwalior	1844	Hector	1823
Hannah	1791	Helen	1825

Helen Mar 1828
Heyworth 1829
Heber 1835
Heart of Oak ... 1839
Heroine 1840
Her Majesty ... 1847
Hibberts 1818
Hibbert 1842
Hindustan 1819
Hindoo 1834
Hirondelle 1835
Himalaya 1841
Hilda 1846
Hilda 1851
Hinda 1852
Hope 1790
Hope 1797
Hope 1803
Horta 1792
Hodgkinson ... 1802
Holderness 1815
Horsley Hill ... 1815
Hopewell 1828
Hugh Jones ... 1799
Hygeia 1791
Hyperion 1810
Hyperion 1819
Idas 1804
Ida 1831
Indefatigable ... 1799
Ingria 1803
Integrity 1815
Indian 1815
Ino 1820
Intrepid 1829
Industry 1839
Ionia 1820

Iona 1829
Iris 1792
Iris 1821
Iris 1843
Iris 1852
Irwin 1806
Isabella 1797
Isabella 1806
Isabella 1812
Isabella 1827
Ivy 1827
Ivy 1845
James 1800
James 1810
Jane 1826
Jackson 1829
Japan 1858
Jet 1847
Jennie 1861
John 1793
John 1798
John 1805
John 1827
John 1828
Johns 1840
John Clark 1794
John Hamilton ... 1810
John Barry 1814
John Coggin ... 1840
John Lawson ... 1853
John and Robert ... 1802
John and James ... 1833
Juno 1811
Judith 1825
Julia 1853
Kingston 1804
Kirkdale 1856

King George ... 1805
King William ... 1831
King Arthur ... 1870
Laurel 1793
Laurel 1817
Laurel 1842
Latona 1801
Lavinia 1801
Lavinia 1804
Lavinia 1853
Larkins 1805
Laburnum 1818
Larpool 1825
Lady Feversham ... 1826
Lady Hilda ... 1837
Labourer's Increase 1830
Leviathan 1791
Leda 1807
Leda 1808
Levant 1813
Leo 1840
Leo 1848
Levisham 1841
Liberty 1799
Lincoln 1804
Little Henry ... 1801
Lily 1814
Lily 1861
Livonia 1822
Linnet 1824
Lingberry 1824
Lively's Increase .. 1827
Liverpool 1845
London 1795
London 1841
London Packet ... 1802
Lord Melville ... 1800
Lord Nelson ... 1800
Lord Nelson ... 1803
Lord Whitworth ... 1804
Lord St. Helens ... 1804
Lord Mulgrave ... 1807
Lord Wellington ... 1811
Loyal Briton ... 1817
Lowndes 1825
Lotus 1826
Luna 1818
Luck's All 1845
Lydia 1842
Lyra 1852
May 1792
Mayflower 1794
Mary 1795
Mary 1798
Mary 1798
Mary 1805
Mary 1818
Mary 1818
Mary 1836
Mary 1839
Mary 1860
Mary 1864
Marys 1824
Marys 1867
Mary Ann 1799
Mary Ann 1821
Mary and Ann ... 1808
Mary and Clara ... 1796
Mary Bull 1847
Mariner 1792
Mariner 1807
Major 1793
Marina 1794
Margaret 1802

Margaret	1818	Minerva	1805
Marmion	1804	Minerva	1809
Marmion	1823	Minerva	1810
Marmion	1838	Minerva	1813
Magnet	1812	Minstrel	1813
Magnet	1831	Mirables	1816
Magnet	1848	Mitten Hill ...	1819
Majestic	1801	Michael	1828
Majestic	1804	Minorca	1854
Majestic	1835	Monarch	1800
Maria	1807	Monarch	1810
Maria	1825	Monarch	1814
Maria	1827	Mountaineer ...	1809
Maria	1847	Mora	1843
Mackarel	1815	Monkshaven ...	1871
Mars	1816	Mulgrave	1818
Marwood	1825	Mulgrave	1824
March	1831	Muta	1820
March	1834	Nancy	1791
Manfred	1839	Navigator	1796
Mandarin	1842	Nautilus	1805
Maud	1859	Nautilus	1812
Maud	1865	Naiad	1815
Maria Wakefield ...	1868	Navy	1822
Mermaid	1790	Nauta	1830
Melantho	1791	Nereid	1795
Melantho	1800	Neptune	1802
Melantho	1816	Neptune	1810
Mentor	1800	Neptune	1811
Medcalf	1808	Newbegin	1803
Metcalf	1809	Nereus	1803
Medusa	1813	Nestor	1810
Medusa	1836	Nestor	1813
Messina	1813	New Darlington ...	1812
Meg Merrilees ...	1828	New Clio	1826
Medora	1833	Nimble	1795
Merrie England ...	1862	Nightingale ...	1832

Name	Year
Nimrod	1840
Nio	1846
Nio	1853
Northfield	1826
No. 6	1844
Norma	1854
Nymph	1793
Nymph	1802
Nymph	1812
Nymph	1830
Nymph	1842
Oak	1800
Oak	1800
Oak	1827
Oak	1848
Ocean	1797
Ocean	1806
Ocean	1808
Ocean	1837
Ocean Queen	1831
Olive Branch	1797
Olive Branch	1856
Orient	1792
Orient	1810
Orion	1804
Orion	1817
Orion	1825
Orb	1844
Osbaldeston	1816
Oswy	1819
Oswy	1849
Oxford	1804
Pallas	1791
Palladium	1792
Patriot	1794
Patriot	1808
Patriot	1835
Patriot	1857
Pacific	1797
Palinurus	1833
Palatine	1841
Peace	1802
Perseverance	1809
Pekin	1809
Percival	1810
Peak	1835
Pet	1851
Phœnix	1816
Pickering	1841
Planter	1807
Pleiades	1819
Pomona	1807
Pomona	1812
Polly	1798
Progress	1792
Providence	1818
Providence	1838
Providence	1843
Prosperous	1843
Princess Royal	1858
Princess Ælfleda	1866
Pursuit	1795
Puella	1834
Queen of England	1852
Rambler	1792
Ranger	1794
Rajah	1835
Racehorse	1858
Rebecca	1790
Renewal	1795
Refuge	1799
Refuge	1862
Request	1799
Resolution	1801

Resolution 1803
Retrieve 1801
Resource 1805
Regent 1811
Regulus 1812
Regalia 1813
Regret 1814
Regina 1832
Regina 1847
Reliance 1848
Reliance 1854
Renown 1856
Rescue 1862
Result 1862
Revenge 1866
Richard and Sarah... 1806
Richard and Sarah... 1815
Richard 1806
Richard 1841
Riby Grove ... 1818
Rover 1798
Robert and Ann ... 1803
Ross 1801
Robust 1806
Royal Briton ... 1808
Royal George ... 1821
Royal Sovereign ... 1829
Royal William ... 1830
Royal Rose 1856
Royal Dane... ... 1863
Romanoff 1826
Robin Hood... ... 1828
Rossendale 1833
Rochdale 1834
Rosebud 1841
Robert 1844
Robert Stephenson... 1850

Robinson 1853
Ruswarp 1803
Ruby 1806
Rutland 1829
Salus 1790
Salus 1815
Salus 1838
Samuels 1803
Sappho 1813
Salacia 1827
Sarah 1828
Sarah 1838
Sarah and Eleanor... 1840
Sarah and Ann ... 1841
Satellite 1838
Salsette 1839
Samuel Boddington 1841
Salem 1855
Scipio 1795
Scipio 1810
Sceptre 1803
Schofield 1840
Sclavonia 1855
Seine 1838
Sea Drift 1840
Sea Drift 1841
Sea Flower 1842
Sedulous 1848
Shipley 1805
Sharon's Rose ... 1862
Shamrock 1863
Simpson 1800
Simpson 1820
Sisters 1825
Sisters 1840
Sibella 1806
Sir Robert Peel ... 1839

Sir Henry Havelock 1859
Skelton 1818
Smales 1819
Smales 1835
Sneaton 1802
Sneaton Castle ... 1821
Snipe 1804
Sovereign 1792
Sovereign 1803
Sovereign 1819
Sovereign 1839
Sophia 1800
Soven Zogle ... 1794
Sprightly 1799
Sprightly 1800
Sprightly 1805
Spring 1800
Spring 1807
Spring 1851
Spectator 1811
Spray 1842
Streonshalh ... 1790
Streonshalh ... 1825
Streonshalh ... 1836
Stranger 1799
Standard 1801
Standard 1814
Standard 1849
Star 1809
Star 1816
Star 1827
Star 1840
Star of Hope ... 1854
Stockton 1807
Stately 1812
Stakesby 1814
Stanley 1843
Success 1796
Success 1845
Supply 1800
Sussex 1801
Susanna 1803
Sultan 1817
Surrey 1818
Sultana 1837
Sunbeam 1839
Surf 1796
Swift 1790
Swift 1796
Swan 1800
Swallow 1826
Swainson 1852
Sylph 1791
Sylph 1828
Sykes 1829
Symmetry 1829
Sylvan 1857
Tartar 1841
Terrys 1821
Thomas and Martha 1792
Thomas and Eleanor 1804
Thomas and Sally... 1804
Thomas and Mary... 1836
Thomas and Margaret 1836
Thomas Rickinson... 1839
Thomas Turnbull .. 1862
Thalia 1793
Thalia 1813
Three Brothers ... 1798
Three Brothers ... 1810
Thais 1800
Thetis 1806
Thetis 1811
Thompson 1821

T. and R. Jackson ... 1838
Themis 1839
Timandra 1822
Titania 1844
Trial 1802
Traveller 1792
Trident 1796
Trelawney 1809
Triton 1815
Transit 1817
True Love 1857
Twist 1822
Tyro 1790
Union 1801
Unanimity 1825
Unicorn 1839
Universe 1853
Urania 1792
Urania 1825
Valiant 1791
Valiant 1823
Valleyfield 1825
Vesta 1793
Venturer 1793
Vernon 1836
Verbena 1857
Vigilant 1792
Vigilant 1806
Vigilant 1807
Vigilant 1819
Visitor 1803
Vine 1805
Vine 1822
Vittoria 1813
Victory 1814
Victory 1865
Virginia 1829
Victoria . .. 1831
Vixen 1840
Violet 1794
Violet 1813
Wakefield 1798
Wanderer 1837
Waverley 1838
Wave 1839
Water Sprite ... 1854
Warrior 1863
Wellington 1790
Wear 1794
Westmoreland ... 1800
Whitby 1803
Whitby 1817
Whitby 1836
Whitby 1837
Whitby 1841
Will 1797
William 1791
William 1793
William 1800
William 1811
William 1819
William Harris ... 1816
William Penn ... 1816
William Pitt ... 1819
William Brodrick ... 1836
William Randfield... 1838
W. and M. Brown... 1838
William and Thomas 1840
William and John ... 1841
William and Charles 1852
William Hunton ... 1867
Wilberforce ... 1838
Wild Rose 1856
Wolga 1803

Woodford ...	... 1815	Zealous ...	... 1795
Woodhouse	... 1821	Zephyr ...	... 1802
Wright ...	... 1839	Zephyr ...	... 1808
XL	... 1840	Zephyrus ...	... 1845
Yenikale ...	... 1854	Zipporah ...	... 1841
Young Queen	... 1837		

Some vessels said to have been built at Whitby, but date unknown :—

AMELIA.—S.; 379; Owner, Jn. Mellar; Capt., M. Simpson, before 1817.

AMELIA AND HANNAH.—Sch.; 102.

ANTONIO TERESA.—Owned at Bilbao, 1817.

BELISARIUS.—Bg.; 165; In Reg. of 1817.

CAROLINE.—Bg.; 182; In Reg. of 1817.

CAROLUS.—S.; 317; In Reg. of 1817.

INDUS.—S.; 290; Before 1831

MECKLENBERG.—S.; 405; In Reg. of 1817.

ORLANDO.—S.; 361; In Reg. of 1817.

PARAGON.—S.; 391; In Reg. of 1817.

THEODOSIA.—Bg.; 200; Repaired in 1818.

WARRIOR.—S.; 392; In Reg. of 1817.

—Whitby Abbey—

"A large and noble ruin placed most happily, as if to impart dignity and interest to a coast tract not otherwise rich in stately edifices. A landmark for the seamen."

THIRD SECTION.

Containing the Sailing Vessels owned, but none of them built at Whitby, from 1790 to 1900, both inclusive, alphabetically arranged to first two letters.

See Abbreviations and Explanations previous to First Section.

ABBOT.—Bk.; 248; Arbroath, 1851; Reg. at Wy., 1867; Owners, 1867, B. T. Robinson, 16, Benj. Granger, 16, Robt. Sample, 16, Richd. Robinson, 16. Sold foreign, 1874.

ABYSSINIAN.—Bk.; 331; Sndld., 1853; Reg. June, 1862; Owners, J. Beal, Geo. Manson, and Robt. Harding; Owners, 1880, John Beal, R. H. Harding, Pickering, and John Stainsby, Wy., m.m. Sold to be broken up, 1880.

ABEONA.—Bk.; 212; Wear, 1826; Reg. Wy., Feb. 9, 1826; Capt., Raw; Owners, Thos. Watson and James Watt; Owners, 1833, T. Watson, 16, James Watt, grocer, 16, Will Raw, silversmith, 16, and Richd. Willis, late of Wy., but now of Lvrpl., 16; Reg. Nwcstl., July 2, 1836.

ABEONA.—Bg.; 186; Arbroath, 1850; Reg. Lndn., not Wy.; Owners, Pritchard and Wood; Reg. Seaham later.

ABERDEENSHIRE.—Bg.; 240; Aberdeen, 1825; Reg. Wy., 1837; Owners, J. T. and Jos. Wood; Owners, 1863, Mary, Thomas and James Wood, jun., and John Thistle, 64 jointly; Reg. Shields, 1863.

ABDIEL.—Bg.; 104; Sndld., 1827; Reg. Wy., 1830; Owner, T. Dobson, Mickleby; Reg. at Cley or Wells, Norfolk, on death of T. Dobson, m m.

ACTIVE.—Bg.; 148; Tyne, 1838; Reg. Wy., 1849; Owner, T. Douglas, pilot. Wrecked on Whitby sand, Oct. 9, 1865. Hull sold for £71. Materials extra.

ACTIVE.—Bg.; 200; Peterhead, 1834; Reg Wy., 1854; Owners, 1854, J. Carling and Will. Sherwood; 1870, Geo. S. Willis, 64. Lost on Island of Aland, Gulf of Bothnia, 19th Oct., 1872.

ACTIVE.—Bg.; 140; Stockton, 1840; Reg. Sept., 1854; Owners, M. Robinson and R. Seymour and Co. Lost at Sndld., March, 1876.

ACASTA.—Bg.; 143; Sndld., 1818; Reg. Wy., Oct., 1829; Owner, J. Storer. Lost, 24th May, 1830.

ACHILLES.—Bg.; 195; Thames, 1826; Reg. Wy., 1846; Owners, Harrisons and Storms, of R.H.B. Total wreck at Staithes, 29th Jan., 1849.

ACHILLES.—Bg.; 275; Sndld., 1840; Reg. Wy., 1850; Owners, Flintoft and Lister; Owner, 1852, S. Flintoft, 64. Lost on the coast of Maine, U.S.A., 14th July, 1852.

ADA BELLA.—Bg.; 161; Sndld., 1827; Reg. Wy., 1829; Owner, Seaton Trattles. Lost, 1831.

ADA.—Bg.; 180; Tyne, 1845; Reg. Wy., 1856; Owner, Robt. Harrowing; Owners, Nov., 1889, The Tyne Wherry Co. Foundered off Hartlepool, 7th July, 1893.

ADAM SMITH.—Bg.; 220; Greenock, 1844; Reg. Wy., 1853; Owners, J. Schofield, 32, Richd. Weatherill, 32; Man figure head; Reg. Lndn., 1855.

ADDISON.—Bg.; 233; Sndld., 1824; Reg. Wy., Jan., 1824; Owner, Addison Brown, of Staithes. Sailed from Wy., April, 1830, for Quebec, with 80 emigrants. Lost, 1837.

ADDISON BROWN.—Bg.; 289; Wear, 1837; Reg. Wy., 1837; Owner, Addison Brown, Staithes. Lost on the Outer Dowsing.

ADONIS.—Bn.; 132; Sutton, Yorks., 1805; Reg. Wy., 1820; Owner, Dan. Brown, Staithes, later Alice Brown. Lost, 1843.

ADVENTURE.—S.; 379; French Prize, 1793; Reg. Wy., 1803; Owner, Will. Benson; 100.5 by 30. Lost, 1815.

ADVENTURE.—Bg.; 163; Stcktn., 1817; Reg. Wy., 1833; Owner, Geo. Willis; Lengthened in 1833 in Messrs. H. and G. Barrick's dock to 202 tons, and nearly rebuilt. Run down and sunk by the brig "Alabama," of Tralee, 3rd Nov., 1853; Owner, Geo. Willis.

ADVICE.—Sch.; 55; Sndld., 1840; Reg. Wy., 1840; Owned by Thos. Garbutt, Sandsend; Reg. Sndld., 1844.

ADVENTURE.—Slp.; 72; Lincolnshire, 1802; Reg. Wy., 1819; Owner, Will Yates, Lofthouse, m.m.

ADOLF.—Bg.; Owned at Wy., 1837.

AËRIEL.—Bg.; 256; Wear, 1839; Reg. Wy., 1839; Owner, Richd. Atkinson Robinson; Reg. Shields, Oct., 1857; Owner, 1874, Will Baxter; in 1886, Will. Baxter, 16, Ch. Harrison, 16, M. Storm, 16, James Waller, 8, and Will. Milburn, 8. Total wreck on Bacton beach, 29th Dec., 1886.

AGENORIA.—Bn.; 156; Sndld., 1818; Reg. Wy., 1819; Owner, J. Barker, Wy. Lost in the Baltic, 1826.

AGENORIA.—Lug.; 63; Scrbr., 1820; Reg. Wy., 1820; Owner; Zeb. Wood, Runswick; Reg. Berwick, Aug., 1841.

AGENORIA.—Sch.; 24; Lowestoft, 1838; Reg. Wy., 1861; Owner, Will Adamson; Owner, 1873, Will. Featherstone. Total wreck on Wy. sand, 10th Jan., 1877.

The lifeboat, when going to the rescue of the crew, capsized, and of the lifeboat's crew, Sam Lacy, Richd. Gatenby, and Jn. Thompson were drowned.

AGNO.—Sch.; 139; Reg. Hartlepool; Owners, 1853, Peter Lattimore, Wy., and Co.

Early in the morning of 17th Dec., 1854, the schooner, "Agno," Lattimore, with a fair wind, ran into the sledway and struck. Broke up the same day.

AID.—Bg.; 181; Sndld., 1855; Reg. Wy., Feb., 1856; Owner, Gid. Smales, and in 1873. Supposed to have foundered with all hands, 19th Nov., 1875, on passage from Shields to London.

ALACRITY.—Bg.; 176; Sndld., 1844; Reg. Wy., 1874; Owners, Hansell Gibson and Harrison Allison. Lost on the Gunfleet Sand, May, 1875.

ALBION.—Bg.; 93; Sndld., 1820; Reg. Wy., 1834; Owner, Will Blackburn; Owners, 1804, T. Simpson, banker, Hen. Simpson, ropemaker, James Walker, and James Estill, m.m. Lost near the Humber, 7th Oct., 1849.

ALBION.—Sch.; 84; Boston, Lincolnshire, 1826; Reg. Wy., 1845; Owner, Geo. Lennard, Middlesbro'; Reg. Stcktn., 1847.

ALBION.—Bg.; 248; Wear, 1836; Reg. Wy., 1863; Owners, Benj. Granger, B. T. Robinson, and Richd. Robinson. Lost, Revelstone, 1st June, 1863, as per letter from Revel.

ALBION.—Bg.; 273; Aberdeen, 1826; Reg. Wy., 1863; Owners, Mary and Thos. Harrison, R.H.B. Abandoned in the North Sea, Nov., 1863.

ALBION.—Sch.; 60; Wells, Norfolk, 1807; Reg. Wy., 1875; Owner, Benj. Andrew. Foundered 6 miles off Staithes, 29th Jan., 1879.

ALEXANDER.—Bg.; 212; Sndld., 1841; Reg. Wy., 1849; Owner, Isaac Mills; Owners, 1861, Isaac Mills, 32, Jn. Mills, 16, and Will. Levitt, m.m., 16. Lost near Heligoland, 2nd April, 1870.

ALEXANDER.—Bg.; 137; Montrose, 1828; Reg. Wy., 1856; Owners, David Slater, sen. and jun.; Owners, 1870, Will. Slater, Will. Ramsdale, and Hen. Roberts, 64 jointly; Reg. Middlesbro', Aug., 1870.

ALEXANDRA.—Sch.; Capt., J. Stephenson. In Boghall Dock, 1894.

ALEXANDRINA.—Bg.; 165; Nova Scotia, 1839; Reg. Wy., 1843; Owners, Isaac Wood Sinclair and Francis Banks. Lost near Harwich, 1855.

ALERT.—Bg.; 81; A prize to H.M.S. "Woodlark," May, 1811; Formerly called "Emilie and Louisa"; Reg. Wy., 1812; Owners, Jn. English, m.m., Thos. Bedlington, and Will. Mills, a fisherman, R.H.B.; Reg. Sndld., 1820.

ALERT.—Bn.; 88; Stcktn., 1807; Reg. Wy., 1838; Owners, Geo. Rowland, joiner, James Sayer, and Thos. Horseman; Owner, 1854, Will. Robinson, Egton, 64; Reg. Stcktn., 1855.

ALERT.—Sch.; 104; Berwick, 1813; Reg. Wy., 1845; Owners, Thos. Pressick and Jn. Eskdale. Stranded at and sold to Ipswich, 1847.

ALLIANCE.—Bn.; 205; Sndld., 1855; Reg. Wy., 1865; Owners, Jn. Hesp and Co.; Owners, 1867, T. Hesp, 22, Thos. Wood, 21, and Robt. Robinson, W. H'pool, 21. Abandoned 100 miles east of May Island, 1867.

ALLISON.—Bg.; 197; Sndld., 1838; Reg. Wy., 1876; Owner, Thos. Mills, R.H.B. Lost on Dungeness beach, Jan., 1879.

ALICE.—Bn.; 153; Prince Ed. Island, 1849; Reg. Wy., 1850; Owners, Francis Dobson and Geo. Calvert. Lost on the Oester Bank, Schouwen, Holland, July, 1870.

ALPHA.—Sch.; 73; East Howden, Northumberland, 1849; Reg. Wy., 1865; Round st.; Owner, Will Tyerman; Owner, 1885, Richd. Gray, Bridlington Quay. Broken up in 1889.

AMELIA.—Bg.; 237; Stcktn., 1833; Reg. Wy., 1833; Owners, Will Brown and Robt. Porritt, Hinderwell. Lost near Runswick with all hands in the great gale of Jan., 1857.

Was at Calcutta, 1847. July, 1863, Capt. McLean, of the "Little Henry," picked up 140 fathoms of chain cable in Runswick Bay supposed from wreck of "Amelia," which had washed round into the bay.

AMELIA.—Bg.; 135; Selby, 1826; Reg. Wy., 1856; Owner, Thos. Coggin, R.H.B.; Owners, 1872, Hansell Gibson, 32, Harrison Allison, 32.

"The Amelia," Capt., Hen. Watson, East Hartlepool for Krautsende, on the Elbe, near Hamburg, foundered in the North Sea, having sprung a leak, the 1st of May, 1874. Crew saved by the Danish schooner "Laura."

AMELIA HILL.—Bg.; Dundee, 1841; Reg. Wy., 1857; Owner, Henry Dale. Lost on St. Ubes Bar, Portugal, Sept., 1860.

AMITY.—Bg.; 145; Selby, 1821; Reg. Wy., 1855; Owner, Matt Walker. Foundered in the North Sea off Dimlington, Oct., 1862. Crew saved by smacks and landed at Grimsby; Owned by Mr. Heselton and Capt. W. Walker.

AMI.—Bg.; 182; Sndld., 1844; Reg. Wy., 1845; Owners, Matt. Bedlington, Isaac Storm, and J. Barry, Sndld.; Owned at Shields in 1879. Wrecked on the coast of Holland, 14th Nov., 1880.

AMY.—Bg.; 217; New Brunswick, 1846; Reg. Wy., 1847; Owner, Moses Ligo, of Sutton Bridge; Owners, 1848, Paul Stokill, 21, Mary Nesfield, 21, Moses Ligo, Sutton, 22. Lost on the Lemon sand, North Sea, Sept., 1851.

AMY.—Bg.; 218; a prize in 1854; Foreign name "Emilie"; Reg. Wy., 1864; Owner, Constable Cassap. Sold, 1867, to Jn. Ray, of Sndld. Lost in the Swin, 1870.

AMORETTE.—Bg.; 264; P. Ed. Island, 1872; Reg. Wy., 1890; Owner, Isaac Mills. Sunk by a collision one mile S.W. of the South Sand Light, Goodwins, July, 1891.

AMPHITRITE.—Bg.; 147; Peterhead, 1815; Reg. Wy., June, 1836; Owners, Will and S. Butterwick and Mary Godden. Lost, 1840.

AMIGOS.—Bg.; $\frac{333}{381}$; Sndld., 1846; Reg. Lndn.; Owner, Hen. Barrick, 1853.

ANDALUSIA.—Bg.; Prize, 1805; Reg. Wy., 1807; Owners, Will Raine, Sandsend, and Co.; Owner, 1811, Jos. Gowland, 64; Reg. Lndn., 1817.

ANDERSONS.—S.; 273; Poole, 1798; Reg. Wy., 1810; 3 masts; 98 by 25.7; Owners, Mich. Teasdale and Co. Lost, 1825.

ANN.—Bn.; 125; Chester, 1784; Reg. Wy., 1806; Owners, Will Todd, m.m., and Hezekiah Godden, both of R.H.B. Lost, Jan., 1825.

ANN.—Slp.; 31; Stcktn., 1761; Reg. Wy., 1811, in March; Owner, Paul Cook; Reg. Sndld., June, 1811; Reg. Wy., 1815; Owner, 1815, Jn. Ball, Wy.; Sch. in 1823; Owner, 1825, Laurence Hebron, m.m., Wy., 64; Reg. Nwcstl., June, 1831.

ANN.—Bn.; 129; Thorne, Yorks, 1801; Reg. Wy., 1816; Owners, Todd and Co., R.H.B. Lost at Harwich, Nov., 1820.

ANN.—Bg.; 175; Sndld., 1818; Reg. Wy., 1827; Owner, David Hunton, Skinningrove; Reg. at Scrbr., May, 1836.

ANN.—Bg.; 127; Sndld., 1799; Reg. Wy., 1831; Owner, Z. Granger, R.H.B.; Owner, 1847, Jos. Bovill, 64; Capt., 1849, Snowdon Mackuen. Lost near the Galloper Light Vessel, April, 1852.

ANN.—Sch.; 132; Aberdeen, 1827; Reg. Wy., 1833; Owner, John Storer, Wy., grocer; Owner, 1862, Geo. Cook, 64; Reg. W. H'pool., Dec., 1865.

ANN.—Bg.; 266; Stcktn., 1833; Reg. Wy., 1836; Owners, Will Brown and Robt. Porritt; Capt., Stonehouse. Lost on the Goodwin Sands, 1853.

ANN.—Sch.; 114; Sndld., 1842; Reg. Wy., 1843; Owner, Jn. Chambers; Owners, 1852, Jn. Chambers, 32, Jn. Liles, of Lndn., 32; Reg. at Ipswich, March, 1857.

ANN.—Sch.; 98; Wallsend, 1825; Reg. at Wy., 1846; Owner, Isaac Gale. Lost on the coast of Denmark, 1848.

ANN.—Slp.; 19; Newburgh, Fife., 1841; Reg. Wy., 1851; Owners, Will Laverick, of Staithes, Will Adamson, cordwainer, and H. Frank; Owner, 1853, Will Maffin, mariner, and Jas. Miller, Eskdaleside, farmer. Lost, 1862.

ANN.—Bg.; 178; Gateshead, 1815; Reg. Wy., 1852; Owners, Jn. Harland, sen. and jun. Lost at Flambro', 1853.

ANN.—Bg.; 164; Sndld., 1845; Reg. Wy., 1854; Owner, Harrison Allison, R.H.B.; Capt., Edward Bedlington. Sold to Lndn., Oct, 1871. Sold a wreck at Hartlepool, 5th Aug., 1877.

ANNA.—Gall.; 49; Toure, 1846; Reg. at Wy., 1860; Owners, F. Anderson, Jas. Andrew, R. J. Milestone, and T. Smales. Sold to Lndn., 1868. Lost near Southwold, 1869.

ANNA.—Bg.; 211; Sndld., 1845; Reg. W. H'pool; Owner, James Gray; In Whitehall Dock, March, 1869.

ANNS.—Sch.; 95; Sndld., 1826; Reg. Wy., 1841; Owner, Geo. Hopper and Ed. Clark. Lost at Yarmouth, 1847.

ANNE.—S.; 235; Quebec, 1825; Reg. at Wy., 1828; Owners, Robt. Allan, surgeon, and Ann Bolton. Lost, June, 1829.

ANNE.—Bg.; 234; Sndld., 1832; Reg. Wy., 1843; Owner, Richd. Watkins. Lost, 1846.

ANN MACKAY.—Sch.; 47; Inverness, 1840; Reg. Wy., 1848; Owners, Jn. Storey, carpenter, and Matt. Harland, m.m. Lost on Theddlethorpe Beach, Lincolnshire, 22nd Sept., 1858.

ANN McLISTER.—Bk.; 375; Quebec, 1845; Reg. Wy., 1863; Owners, James Gray, 26, Thomas Bird, 22, and Will. Bird Gray, H'pool, 16. Wreck at Calais, 1867.

ANN CLARK.—Bg.; 213; N. Scotia, 1848; Reg. Wy., 1850; Owner, T. Wilson. Capt., Frank Barry; Owners, 1868, Simon Tose and Co. Totally wrecked off Broadstairs, 29th Oct., 1882; owned at Hartlepool.

ANN ELIZA.—Bg.; 158; Sndld., 1851; Reg. Wy., 1851; Owner, Robt. Sleightholm. Lost on the isle of Majorca, 1854.

ANN AND MARY.—Sch.; 61; Sndld., 1842; Reg. Wy. from Nwcstl., 1852; Owner, Will Wood. Sold, 14th Oct., 1856, to Matt. Trattles, shipowner, 32, and Thos. Rodham, boat builder, both of Staithes, 32. Left Skinningrove with ironstone, 8th Nov., 1861, and was never heard of. Capt., Thos. Lyth; Capt., 1852, Geo. Barnett.

ANN AND JANE.—Sch.; 45; Yarmouth, 1837; Reg. Wy., 1856; Owners, Thos. Caygill and Thos. Rayment. Sold to Nwcstl., 1863.

ANNE ISABELLA.—Bg.; 178; Montrose, 1854; Reg. Wy., 1866; Owner, Will Steel. Sold to W. H'pool, Jan., 1887, by Christ. Marwood.

ANNIE WILLIAMS.—Bk.; 583; New Brunswick, 1863; Reg. Glstr.; Owner, Francis Pearson. In Wy., 1874.

ANTIAS.—Bg.; 178; Sndld., 1855; Reg. Wy., 1856; Owners, W. R. Smales and Thos. Chapman Smales, of Nwcstl.; Reg. at H'pool, 1874.

ANN AND SARAH.—Bg.; 288; Stcktn., 1846; Owner, Will Todd, jun.; Reg. H'pool, 1873.

APOLLO.—Bn.; 131; Hull, 1799; Reg. Wy., 1800; Owner, James Atty; Owners, 1818, Will. Watt, m.m., James Watt, grocer, and Thos. Nettleship, baker. Lost, March, 1820.

APOLLO.—Bg.; 167; Littlehampton, 1790; Reg. Wy., 1817; Owner, James Bell, Wy. Lost, 1823.

AQUILA.—Sch.; 100; Sndld., 1827; Reg. Wy., 1829; Owners, Jn. Barry, shipwright, and Matt. Ord; Owner, 1840, Will Todd, Wy. Reg. at Scrbr., 1844.

ARAB.—Bg.; 155; Sndld., 1837; Reg. Wy., 1838; Owners, Jn. Ripley, printer, and Rippon Falkingbridge; Owners, 1860, David Baxter and J. Kell, Seaton Carew. Lost near Dundee, March, 1872.

ARCANA.—Lug.; 19; St. Ives, 1869; Reg. Wy., 1876; Owners, J. and W. Thompson, Staithes. Wrecked at Seaham, April, 1877.

ARDENT.—Bn.; 74; Stockton, 1840; Reg. Wy., 1845; Owner, Zachariah Fletcher, Sandsend: Reg. Lvrpl., 1847.

ARIADNE.—Bg.; 121; Nwcstl., 1790; Reg. Wy., 1809; Owner, James Naylor; Capt., Jos. Gowland; Reg. Nwcstl., 1833.

ARIADNE.—Bn.; 134; Sndld., 1819; Reg. Wy., 1832; Owners, Thos. Coggin and James Storm, R.H.B.; Owners, 1879, Matt. Storm, 22, Will Steel, 21, and Will Bedlington, 21. Sold to Nwcstl., 1879.

ARETA.—Bg.; 210; Sndld., 1840; Reg. Wy., 1850; Owners, J. Baxter and J. Skerry, R.H.B.; Re-registered at Wy., 1876; Owners, 1876, J. Skerry, J. H. Storm, Christ. Harrison, and Jn. Weighill; Owners, 1878, J. H. Storm, 24, Christ. Harrison, 16, Jn. Brand, 8, and Robt. Wellburn, 16.

"'Areta,' Capt. James Baxter, Riga to London, wood, laid at anchor off the Black Tail Oct. 30, 1864, at 4.30 p.m., with lights burning brightly;

was run into by the barque 'Jane Gandie,' of London, doing much damage."

Lost with all the crew on the coast of Holland, 1878.

ARIEL.—Bg.; 190; Arbroath, 1839; Reg. Wy., March, 1854; Owners, James and David G. Pinkney; Reg. at Plymth., 1859.

ARIEL.—Bg.; 187; Hartlepool, 1850; Reg. Wy., 1855; Owners, Benj. Granger and Co.; Reg. Sndld., 1860.

ARICA.—Bg.; 184; Lvrpl., 1831; Reg. Wy., 1855; Owner, J. Harrison; Owner, 1881, Will. Harrison. Stranded at Whitley, Northumberland, and sold a wreck, Dec., 1881.

ARION.—Bg.; 236; Gothenburg, 1830; Reg. Wy., 1864; Owners, Greenwell Robinson, Mickleby, and Clarke, Verrill, and Addison; Off. No. 45737; Signal letters U.F.N.C. Lost off Gefle, July, 1867.

ARGUS.—Bk.; 633; Amsterdam, 1841; Reg. Wy., Feb., 1862; Owners, Christ. Harrison, Jn. Weighill, Will Clark, and Jn. and Richd. Leng. Lost, 1866.

ARGUS.—Bg.; 249; Hull, 1802; Reg. Wy., 1862; Owner, Estill Frank. Lost, Oct., 1868.

ARK.—Bg.; 198; Sndld., 1839; Reg. Wy., 1839; Owners, Geo. Laverick, Mark Hall, and Richd. Verrill; Reg. Stcktn., 1848; Reg. Wy. from Mbro., May, 1863; Owners, 1863, P. G. Raine and David Gray Gibson. Wrecked about 40 miles from Reval, June, 1877.

ASSISTANCE.—S.; 232; Scrbr., 1793; Reg. Wy., Nov., 1793; Owner, James Atty. Captured by the enemy, 1795.

ASTREA.—S.; 205; New England, 1762; Reg. Wy., Jan., 1790; Rebuilt on Tyne, 1777; Owners, 1790, Jn. Pressick and Jn. Ridley, R.H.B. Lost after 1799.

ATALANTA.—Bg.; 184; Whitehaven, 1822; Reg. Wy., 1857; Owners, Ed. Corner and R. Kilvington; Reg. Ipswich, 1865.

ATHABASCA.—Bk.; 477; Pictou, 1836; Reg. Wy., March, 1837; Owner, Will Smales, Dorothy Wilson, of Grove Hall, St. Nesfield, m.m., and Jn. Welsh, of Lvrpl. Lost after 1837.

ATLAS.—Screw steamer; 106; Hull, 1857; Reg. Wy., Oct., 1861; Owners, "The Albert Iron and Cement Works, Leeds"; Owner, Jan., 1865, James Taylor, Mbro., wharfinger, 64; Owners, Feb., 1865, Jn. Barratt, Coniston, 32, Matt. Caine, Lvrpl., 32. Lost off the Bell Rock, March, 1865.

ATTALIA.—Bg.; 177; Sndld., 1827; Reg. Wy., 1834; Owners, Jn. and J. Skerry, R.H.B.; Owner, 1877, B. T. Robinson. Broken up, 1878.

AUTUMN.—Bg.; 133; Sndld., 1822; Reg. Wy., 1842; Owners, David Douthwaite, Ann Hardcastle, and Barbara Miller. Lost, Nov., 1844.

AUTOMATIA.—Bg.; 244; Sndld., 1847; Reg. Wy., 1866; Owners, Hen. Burton, m.m., Jn. Harding, and Jackson Harding.

"'Automatia,' Capt. F. Snaith and 7 hands, left Reval for Ljusne, 18th Oct., 1870. Brought up 21st Oct. at entrance to Ljusne. The weather coming on bad, the vessel dragged her anchor and drove ashore, and became a total wreck."

AVA.—Bk.; 460; N. Brunswick, 1833; Reg. at Wy., March, 1846; Owners, Marwood and Co.; Reg. Scrbr., 1848.

BALTIC.—Bg.; 199; Sndld., 1833; Reg. Wy., 1852; Owners, Simon Tose and Robt. and Humphrey Orren. Lost on the Gunfleet sand, Dec. 26, 1868.

BALTIC.—Bg.; 196; Sndld., 1842; Reg. Wy., 1867; Owners, 1867, Will Milburn, 32, Geo. Milburn, 16, and Geo. Milburn, Jos. Brown, and Jn. Lennard, 16 jointly.

"The 'Baltic,' Capt. W. Milburn, left Dordt for Newcastle 5th Sept., 1868, with sulphur ore. Reached the Lemon light ship on the 7th at midnight. At 4 a.m. the wind freshened from the N.E. Double reefed the topsails. At 3.30 p.m. passed the Outer Dowsing, weather more favourable. About to shake out a reef when one of the crew discovered smoke issuing from the forecastle. On going down the after cabin companion found the hold in flames. Water was passed down, but made no impression, the fire increasing. Proceeded to get out the boats, but before we could launch the long boat were driven from the deck by fire and smoke. Left the vessel about 11.30 p.m. in the small boat, without being able to save clothes, etc., and at 3 a.m. on the 8th got on board the 'Gavelia,' of Gefle, having the boat nearly filled. Landed at Hull about 10 a.m. the same day."

BANK-NOTE.—Slp.; 58; Prize, 1812; Reg. Wy., 1820; Owner, Will Harrison, m.m.; Owner, 1826, Will Pearson, m.m. Lost, 1829.

BARBARA.—Bg.; 112; Southwick, 1805; Reg. Wy., 1827; Owner, Francis Roberts, m.m. Lost, 1843.

BARBARA.—Sch.; $\frac{59}{63}$; N. Shields, 1826; Reg. Wy., 1838; Owners, James Frank and T. W. Dotchon; Owners, 1862, Geo. Frank, 32, and T. Robinson, 32. Lost on Deal Beach, July, 1867.

BARONET.—Bg.; 196; Kincardine, 1831; Reg. Wy., 1843; Owner, Isaac Dobson; Reg. Stcktn., 1849.

BASILEIA.—Bg.; 248; Sndld., 1854; Reg. Wy., Sept., 1854; Owners, Jn. Rickinson and Middleton Cowart. Stranded at Port Elizabeth, S. Africa, Oct., 1859.

BATO.—Bqtn.; 188; Memel, 1871; Reg. Wy., 1902; Oak built; Owned by Chas. Smales and Son.

BEATITUDE.—Bg.; 185; Sndld., 1831; Reg. Wy., 1836; Owners, Jn. and Christ. Barnard and Geo. Falkingbridge; Reg. at Stcktn., 1839.

BEATITUDE.—208; Sndld., 1839; Reg. Wy., 1839; Owners, J. Barnard and Co. Lost, Oct., 1858.

BEAMISH.—Bn.; 105; Sndld., 1811; Reg. Wy., 1821; Owner, Edward Dale; Reg. Stockton, Jan., 1827.

BEAVER.—Bn.; 100; N. America, 1766; Reg. Wy., 1802; Owner, Will. Race. Lost after 1807.

BEDALE.—Bg.; 219; Mbro., 1839; Reg. Wy., 1843; Owner, Thos. Wright. Lost near Harwich, 1856.

In Nov., 1854, this vessel was stopped at the bridge, the owner refusing to pay the toll demanded.

BEDLINGTON.—Sch.; 91; Blyth, 1837; Reg. Wy., 1852; Owner, Will Seymour. Lost near Harwich, 1859.

BEESWING.—Bn; $\frac{113}{143}$; Sndld., 1840; Reg. Wy., 1847; Owner, Z. Granger, R.H.B.; Capt., 1847, Will Baxter; April, 1853, Jn. Storm; Nov., 1853, Will Cooper; April, 1854, Christ. Moorsom; Owner, 1864, Alfred Walker.

The "Beeswing," owned by Z. Granger, Daniel Chaston, master, and six hands, left Boulogne, 25th May, 1860, in ballast for H'pool, at 2 a.m., high water, wind S.W., moderate, fine weather. On Monday the 28th May, wind S.S.E., fresh, with rain, the vessel, when off Rosedale, distant about ¾ mile, was caught by a sudden gale from the N.E., which split the whole of her sails, and drove the vessel on the beach near Rosedale harbour. The crew, except captain and a boy, left the vessel in the ship's boat on the tide ebbing. The vessel was got off on the 30th and towed into Whitby harbour.

Beeswing, brigantine. Report of Capt. Walker, Newcastle to Honfleur, coals:—Left Newcastle June 18th, 1863. On the 21st, at 3 a.m., thick fog, passed through Hasebro' Gat. Outside the Cross Sand saw a schooner apparently abandoned. The boat was lowered, and the mate, James Page, and a seaman, James Lamb, went on board the vessel, which proved to be the "Thomas Prothero," of Fowey, with pig iron. The men ran the schooner clear of the sand, pumped the water out, and got her manageable. Proceeded through Hewitt Gateway, the schooner following, very thick fog. Succeeded in anchoring both vessels in Lowestoft roads. The schooner was soon after towed into the harbour and placed in charge of the receiver of wreck.

Lost on the Newcome sand, Lowestoft, Dec., 1865.

BEESWING.—bg.; 163; Hull, 1828; Reg. Wy., Aug., 1849; Owners, Geo. Russell and Harrison Allison. Wrecked at W. H'pool, Dec., 1874.

BEE.—Slp.; 40; Prize, 1811; Reg. Wy., 1806; Owner, Jn. Stephenson, farmer. Lost, 1820.

BEE.—Sch.; 101; Sndld.; 1836; Reg. Wy., Oct., 1856; Owners, Geo. and James Estill. Lost on Hasebro Sands, Oct., 1857.

BELLE.—Bk.; 246; N. Brunswick, 1843; Reg. Wy., Jan., 1848; Owners, Geo. Pyman, English and Co. In 1853 a brig; Owners, 1853, Benj. Garminsway, 21, R. C. Jefferson, 21, and Thos. Bell, London, 22. Lost on Roccas Island, or reef, July, 1857.

BENJAMIN SHAW.—Bk.; 283; Prize, 1807; Reg. Wy., Mch., 1824; Owner, Will. Hill, Wy.; Owner, 1835, Will. Mead, 64, Wy.; Reg. Aberystwyth, 1835.

BERDINKA.—Bg.; 250; Sndld., 1853; Reg. Wy., June, 1853; Owners, Marwood, Pickernell and Co.; Owner, 1864, Sam. Andrew, 64; Owners, 1865, S. Andrew, 32, and James Gray, 32; Owners, 1867, J. Gray, 32, and Christ. Thompson, 32. Sold to Newcastle, Oct., 1873.

BESSIE.—Slp.; 50; Sutton, near Hull, 1793; Reg. Wy., 1813; Owners, Hen. Simpson and Ed. Chapman; Owners, 1820, J. Ayton and T. Coates; Reg. at Stockton, 1820.

BESSIE.—Slp.; 49; Wisbech, 1802; Reg. Wy., 1813; Owner, John Holt, Wy., shipbuilder. Lost, 1817.

BETSY.—Slp.; 51; Hull, 1807; Reg. Wy., 1821; Owner, Thos. Newton, Barnby; Owner, 1831, J. Terry, 64. Lost April, 1831.

BETSY.—Slp.; 70; Kincardine, 1796; Reg. Wy., 1837; Owner, Jos. Tate. Lost, March, 1838.

BETSY.—Bn.; 99; Looe, Cornwall, 1826; Reg. Wy., 1850; Owners, David G. Pinkney, 22, Thos. Pinkney, Whitesmith, 21, and W. Pearson, 21, who bought the vessel from London; Owner, 1852, Will Pearson, 64; Owners, 1855, Hen. Roberts, mariner, 32, Hen. Roberts, shipowner, 16, Robt. Pennock, labourer, 16. Lost, April 13, 1859. Reg. lost with vessel, as per notice of owner dated 7th Feb., 1862.

BETSY HAY.—Slp.; 62; Newburgh, Fife, 1834; Reg. Wy., 1840; Owner, Will. Tyerman. Lost, Nov., 1842.

BETSY WILLIAMS.—Bk.; 374; U.S.A., 1846; Reg. Wy., April, 1865; Owners, Matt. Snowdon and Co.; Capt., Swales; Ashore at Teesmouth, Nov., 1866; Owners, 1866, Matt Snowdon, 32, Isaac Cooper, 16, W. Leng, 8, J. Swales, 8.

The Betsy Williams, proceeding from Stockholm to load timber, struck upon a rock, filled, sank, and became a total wreck, May 31st, 1868.

BILBOA.—Bn.; 129; Hull, 1785; Reg. Wy., Jan., 1807; Owner, Geo. Hutchinson, m.m.; Reg. Nwcstl., 1811; a Brig later of 175 tons; Owner, 1873, Thos. White, Seaham.

BILLY.—Bg.; 136; Stcktn., 1811; Reg. Wy., March, 1811; Owners, Will Brown and Jn. Porritt, Runswick; Owners, 1865, Hen. Roberts, 24, Robt. Pennock, 24, and H. Roberts, jun., 16. Lost with all hands off Southwold, Jan., 1866.

BLACK BOY.—Bg.; 194; Sndld., 1835; Reg. Wy., 1853; Owner, Jn. Mennell. Lost, 1862.

BLACK PRINCE.—Bg.; $\frac{257}{272}$; Maryport, 1838; Reg. Wy., March, 1876; Owners, Richardson Dixon and Andrew Storm.

The "Black Prince," of Whitby, Capt. Huggitt, arrived at Newhaven from Cronstadt, deals, etc. Had to throw overboard the whole of the deck cargo.—"Whitby Gazette," Nov., 1880.

Owner, 1890, R. K. Smith. Foundered off Skinningrove after collision, March, 1890.

BLAKISTON.—Bg.; 157; Sndld., 1822; Reg. Wy., 1825; Owners, Will Swales, Robt. Lamb, and Matt. Hill; Reg. at Galway, April, 1831.

BLENHEIM.—S.; 381; London, 1791; Reg. Wy., 1836; Owners, Jas. Terry, Francis Wilson, Hen. Prescott, and Will Clarkson.

BLESSING.—Smk.; 35; Brixham, 1783; Reg. Wy., 1854; Owners, Brown, Frankland and Terry; Reg. at Berwick, 1859.

BLOSSOM.—Bg.; 235; Dundee, 1851; Reg. Wy., Dec., 1865; Owners, Geo. Russell, Thorpe, and Daniel Chaston, Thorpe, m.m. Lost Desart (Dazard?) Point, Cornwall, Sept., 1869.

BLUCHER.—Bg.; 183; Sutton, Yorks, 1815; Reg. Wy., Nov., 1815; Owners, Geo. and Thos. Clark; Reg. Lndn., April, 1822.

BLUCHER.—Slp.; 72; Deptford, Kent, 1815; Reg. Wy., 1834; Owner, Robt. Campion. Foundered after 1836.

BLYTH.—Slp.; 55; Blyth Nook, 1793; Reg. Wy., 1816; Owner, Will Porritt, Lofthouse; Owner, 1836, Jn. Frank, 64.

The "Blyth" drove ashore on "Filly Tail" and became a total wreck, moderate weather, 2nd Jan., 1845.

BODDINGTONS.—Bk.; 301; Limehouse, Thames, 1793; Reg. Wy., 1840; Owner, James Terry, Ugthorpe. Lost, 1841.

BONA FIDE.—Bg.; 228; Sndld., 1825; Reg. Wy., 1825; Owner, Jn. Gardiner, tailor; Owners, 1836, Thos. Galilee, 32, Robt. Gardiner, 32. Wrecked near Pakefield, Dec., 1836; Capt., Richd. Foster.

BORDEAUX.—Bg.; 174; Newcastle, 1841; Reg. Wy., 1856; Owner, Jos. Bovill. Lost on coast of Holland, 20th Oct., 1865.

BORDER CHIEFTAIN.—Bg.; 170; Sndld., 1835; Reg. Wy., Oct., 1865; Owner, P. G. Raine. Lost with all hands at Egmond, coast of Holland, 25th Oct., 1865.

BOSTON PACKET.—Slp.; 76; Hull, 1795; Reg. Wy., 1820; Owner, Jn. Anderson; a Schooner in 1823; Owner, 1829, Peter Appleton, stonemason; Reg. at Nwcstl., April, 1831.

BOYTON.—S.; 218; Ipswich, 1796; Reg. Wy., 1799; Owner, Richd. Hutchinson; Reg. at Hull, June, 1801.

BOULBY.—Slp.; 56; Stcktn., 1829; Reg. Wy., 1829; Owners, Geo. Westgarth and Geo. Laverick. Lost, 1838.

BOWEN.—Bg.; 108; Southtown, Suffolk, 1814; Reg. Wy., 1827; Owner, Isaac Bedlington. Run down off the Mouse Light, River Thames, Nov., 1848.

BONNIE LASSIE.—Bk.; 353; Dundee, 1861; Reg. at Jersey; Owners, Francis Robinson and Jn. Robinson, 1873.

BRAZILIAN PACKET.—Bg.; 185; Tyne, 1842; Reg. Wy., Jan., 1855; Man bust figurehead; Owners, J. H. Storm and Co.; Capt., Thos. Pyman. Lost, Gulf of Finland, Sept., 1865.

BRECHIN CASTLE.—Bg.; 189; Arbroath, 1826; Reg. Wy., 1862; Owners, Greenwell Robinson, Mickleby, 32, Addison Verrill, 16, and Joseph Verrill, 16. Lost in Seaford Bay, Sussex, Feb., 1864.

BRITANNIA.—Bn.; 109; Gt. Yarmouth, 1805; Reg. Wy., 1822; Owners, Geo. Willis and Jn. Bowes; Owner, 1829, Jn. Bowes, 64. Lost, 1830.

BRITANNIA.—Bg.; 145; Peterhead, 1806; Reg. Wy., 1835; Owners, Stephen Crosby, butcher, and Robt. Crosby, m.m.; Owners, 1863, James Hunter, R.H. Bay, 32, Christ. Sedman, R.H.B., 32. Lost at Flambro' Head, 1866.

BRITANNIA.—Bg.; 137; Stockton, 1787; Reg. Wy., 1838; Owners, Jn. Ripley, printer, and Rippon Falkingbridge; Managing Owner, Oct., 1875, Jn. Ripley, 42, Baxtergate; Owner, 1878, Christ. Marwood, trustee, 64. Broken up, 1878.

BRITANNIA.—Slp.; 47; Ipswich, 1821; Reg. Wy., 1841; Owner, Robt. Vipond; Owner, 1843, Will Campion. Lost at Peak Alum Works, Dec., 1849.

BRITANNIA.—Bg.; $\frac{193}{219}$; N. Scotia, 1840; Reg. Wy., 1844; Owner, Geo. Blenkhorn, Sandsend; Later, Thos. Harland.

The "Britannia," owner Thos. Harland, East Row, Capt. Robt. Hitcham and 6 hands, Rochester for West Hartlepool, Oct., 1865. Friday, 13th, 8 a.m., wind N.E. by E., fresh breeze, being off Whitby High Lights, bearing about S. distant about 8 miles, a heavy sea running, the fore-topmast went away, taking with it the main topgallant mast and cap. Bore away for Whitby harbour, seeing no chance of keeping off the land. In entering the harbour struck the pier and started sternpost, rails, etc. Succeeded in getting in at 10 a.m.

BRITANNIA.—S.; 556; Pictou, 1841; Reg. Wy., Sept., 1845; Owners, J. and T. Marwood; Capt., Jn. Willis Bowes; Reg. Gloucester, March, 1853.

BRITANNIA.—Bg.; 118; Yarmouth, 1801; Reg. March, 1850; Owner, Hen. Streeting, R.H.B., m.m. Missing since Sept., 1851.

BRITANNIA.—Smk.; 20; Dartmouth, 1815; Reg. Wy., 1854; Owners, Jas. Brown, Will Frankland, Fern Hill, and James Terry. Lost on Hornsea Beach, Dec., 1857.

BRITANNIA.—Bk.; 513; Blyth, 1855; Reg. Wy., July, 1870; Owners, James Gray, Christ. Harrison, and J. W. Andrew and Co.

Capt. Gibson, of the Steamer "Levant," of Liverpool, from Pomoron, reports:—Left Villa

Real on the 27th of Sept., 1871, and on the 29th, lat. 42° N., long. 14° W., fell in with the barque "Britannia," showing a flag of distress. She was bound to Alexandria with coal. The wind at the time was blowing a gale and the sea running very high. It was with difficulty that we managed to get within hail, those on board not understanding the use of signals. We were informed by the crew that their Captain had died of small pox two days previously, and the mate for some cause was unable to be on duty. They therefore requested that some-one should be sent on board to navigate the ship, as they understood nothing whatever of their position. After considerable difficulty I managed to get out a boat, by which, with the assistance of four of my crew, my chief officer, Mr. R. Frazer, who holds a master's certificate, was enabled to get on board the barque, which he was instructed to take to Gibraltar, or to her port of destination, and telegraph her arrival at either place. Whilst getting my boat on board again she was stove in and broken, and the men narrowly escaped being injured. The wife of the deceased captain was on board the barque, and his name was H. Edis.

Broken up, Sept., 1879. Owner, 1879, Thos. Lyons.

BRITON.—Bg.; 117; Sndld., 1819; Reg. Wy., 1840; Owners, Christ. and Jos. Thompson; Reg. at Stcktn., 1854.

BRITISH QUEEN.—Bg.; 182; N. Scotia, 1843; Reg. Wy., 1856; Owner, James Sayer, afterwards W. Ripley, Ed. Dale, J. B. Dale, and Levi P. Mead. Lost on Corton Sands, Dec., 1858.

BROTHERS.—Sch.; 58; Prize, 1811; Reg. Wy., 1812; formerly called "Prosper," a private ship of war; Owner, Thos. Verrill, Staithes; Reg. Lndn., Jan. 27, 1813.

BROTHERS.—Bg.; 126; Sndld., 1809; Reg. Wy., 1828; Owner, Will Greenwood, R.H. Bay. Lost, April, 1829.

BROTHERS.—Bg.; 183; Sndld., 1829; Reg. Wy., 1829; Owners, Paul Stokill and Moses Ligo; Owners, 1863, Will McKenzie, Ed. Moorsom, R.H. Bay, and Alice Waugh. Lost, 27th Sept., 1867, Wanquova, R. Weser.

BROTHERS.—Bg.; 234; Scarbro', 1824; Reg. Wy., 1852; Owners, Ed. Corner, spirit merchant, 16, J. B. B. Mead, 16, Matt. Gray, solicitor, 16, Will. Elgie Corner, of 18, Wapping Wall, London, provision merchant, 16. Lost on Scroby Sand, Yarmouth, Nov., 1853.

BROTHERS.—Sch.; 31; Scrbr., 1805; Owner, 1836, Nath. Gardiner, innkeeper; Owner, 1856, George Moffitt, blacksmith, Middlesbro'. Foundered, Nov., 1857.

BROTHERS.—Bg.; 85; Leith, 1814; Reg. Wy., 1859; Owner, Ant. Moody Newton, R.H.B.

The crew of the "Brothers," Middlesbro' for London, which sunk off the Newarp Light Vessel after collision with the "Colleen Bawn," landed at Falmouth by the latter vessel, May, 1863.

BROTHERS.—Bg.; 168; Kincardine, 1834; Reg. Wy., 1865; Owner, James Hall, of R.H.Bay, who died April 17, 1874; Owners, Nov., 1875, Nathan Hewson, and Thos. Phillips, minister, R.H.B.; Owner, 1881, Dixon Taylor Sharper, jun., West H'pool, 64. Supposed lost in the North Sea, about 26th Jan., 1883.

BROTHERS.—Bk.; 377; Sunderland, 1854; Reg. Wy., June, 1868; Owner, Geo. Russell; 114 by 27.6.

"The barque, 'Brothers,' Capt., J. Sayers, left Alexandria for Hull 11th Feb., 1871, cargo cotton seed. On the 17th March the vessel was becalmed off the African coast some 14 miles from Ceuta, and was drifting nearer to the land. About 4.30 p.m. three boats of a dark colour, and containing apparently about 40 or 50 men, were observed coming off from the shore. The crew of the 'Brothers,' ten all told, were greatly alarmed, as that part of the coast was noted for piracy. The captain, after consultation with his mate, Mr. George Cook, decided to leave the vessel in their own boat. The supposed pirates having quickly rowed up to about three or four cable lengths from the ship, and making strange gesticulations, halted, apparently waiting till dark to board. As the barque was not provided with means of defence, there being only two small guns but no powder, the captain and crew thought themselves justified in rowing away. One of the boats chased the crew for a considerable time. After leaving, the crew saw the supposed pirates board their vessel and hang out lights, which were answered by fires on the land. The crew reached Ceuta about 4 a.m. the next day, and some of them were put into quarantine. The 'Brothers' was afterwards given up by some Spaniards, and £333 salvage had to be paid. It was afterwards stated that the men who frightened the crew were peaceful coral fishers, who wished to make a communication. It was also reported that the Spaniards, fishermen, had found the barque abandoned and anchored. The mate did not think the men who had brought in the vessel were like those in the three boats. It was supposed that the pirates, if they were pirates, had found the ship's cargo not worth the risk of looting.

An official inquiry was held at Hull, 29th April, 1871, at which the captain was exonerated from blame for leaving his vessel, as there were no means of defence."—"Whitby Gazette."

The "Brothers," Thomas Easton, carpenter, left Alexandria 11th Feb., 1871, for Hull, with cotton seed. Proceeded all well till 17th March, wind

W.N.W. blowing fresh, the vessel being then about 18 or 20 miles S.E. of Ceuta and about 14 miles from the land at noon, when she was tacked with her head to the north, but soon after the wind died away and it became calm. The strong current then drifted the ship to about 8 miles from the land. At 4.30 p.m. a light S.S.E. wind nearly calm, the master, mate and deponent were in the cabin having tea, when a seaman on deck saw three boats coming from the land towards the ship, which he pointed out to them when they left the cabin. On looking through the telescope, and when the boats were about four miles from the ship, one large and two small ones, they were distinctly seen to be full of men and rowing direct for the ship. All hands being of opinion that they were pirates, and there being no arms on board nor any means by which they could defend themselves, the master ordered the jollyboat to be got out and hung in the tackles ready for use if required. As the boats approached the men were heard shouting and whistling to each other, and when they got within about a quarter of a mile of the ship at about 7.30 p.m., the crew hastily got together a few of their clothes, and all hands got into the boat, and left the ship, the helm being lashed nearly hard-a-port, and the yards braced forward on the starboard braces, with the wind light airs from W.N.W. The crew pulled about 50 yards away from the ship and remained to watch the proceedings of the pirates, and saw the largest boat's crew board the vessel on the starboard bow, and one of the small boat's crew board it on the port quarter; that immediately after they got on board a bright light was hung from the ship's port quarter, which was at once answered by a fire from the shore, and just then the crew saw the third boat pulling towards them, and fearing that mischief was intended, they rowed away as fast as they could in the direction of Gibraltar, and were chased by the pirates for about three hours, when they were lost sight of. Before the ship was lost sight of it was seen that the pirates had got her head round towards land. About midnight the weather became bad, which compelled the crew to bear up for Ceuta, which island they reached about 4 a.m. on the 18th and landed at daylight. On the afternoon of the same day they were taken round the island to a small harbour there, by the Spanish authorities, who placed them under quarantine till the 19th, when the captain of the port of Ceuta sent the mate with four seamen to take charge of the ship, which had been taken into Ceuta Bay on the opposite side of the island, by some Spanish fishermen, and the vessel was got into Ceuta harbour on the 20th, on which day the master, deponent, and three men were removed from quarantine to the Guard House, and kept under guard until the 23rd, when they were ordered to go on board of the ship to assist in taking care of her, but they were prevented by bad weather until the 24th, when they got on board. On the 25th the master went to Gibraltar respecting the ship's business, and returned on the 27th. On the morning of the 30th the ship sailed from Ceuta and reached Gibraltar the same day, and having provisioned, sailed from Gibraltar on the 31st March and arrived at Hull on the 18th April. A Spanish Guard was kept on board the vessel at Ceuta, until the salvage, said to be £420, was paid to the fishermen. When the crew regained the ship they found that most of the clothes left behind were taken away. It was his opinion, and that of the crew, that the three boats' crews were pirates intending to seize and plunder the ship and probably kill the crew.

The "Brothers" foundered Nov. 26, 1878, in latitude 30° 50′ North and longitude 71° 29′ W.

BRUNSWICK.—S.; 485; Howden Pans, Tyne, 1795; Reg. Wy., 1809; Owner, T. Benson, Wy.; Capt., Geo. Simpson; 114 by 31.8. Lost, 1811.

BRILLIANT.—Bg.; 181; Montrose, 1839; Owner, J. Bedlington.

BRANSTONS.—Bg.; 172; Owner, 1853, Robt. Scott, Wy.

BURDON.—"Garbutt, of Wy.; Quebec to Lndn. Abandoned at sea, waterlogged, Dec. 4, 1829."—"Whitby Magazine."

CATHARINE.—Bg.; 148; Cork, 1788; Owner, Thos. Chilton; Reg. Wy., 1803; Reg. Lndn., 1807.

CATHARINE.—Bn.; $\frac{84}{100}$; Boston, Lincoln, 1806; Owner, Thos. Thompson Granger, R.H.Bay; Reg. Wy., 1811; Reg. Scrbr., 1819; Reg. Wy., June, 1844, from Sndld.; Owner, Jn. Postgate. Lost on the coast of Lincolnshire, 1859.

CATHARINE.—Bg.; 133; Perth, 1828; Reg. Wy., June, 1845; Owners, Richd. Terry, Wy., and Geo. Simpson, Lvrpl.; Female bust. Sunk off Lowestoft, July, 1848.

CATHARINE.—Bg.; 193; Perth, 1866; Reg. Wy., 1883; Owner, Christ. Marwood. Lost near Winterton, Oct., 1888.

CAMBRIAN.—Bg.; 130; Lincolnshire, 1802; Reg. Wy., 1818; Owner, Walker Tindale, R.H.Bay; Owner, 1827, John Storer, Wy. Lost after 1828.

CALEDONIAN.—S.; 358; N. Brunswick, 1815; Reg. Wy., 1826; Owner, Thos. Jackson, Wy.; Reg. Hull, May, 1831.

CAMPO BELLO.—Bk.; 302; N. Brunswick, 1824; Reg. Wy., 1830; Owners, Will. Swales, Robt. Lamb, and Thos. Eskdale. Lost, March, 1838.

COMPTON.—Bg.; 107; Wells, Norfolk, 1800; Owner, Jn. Barnett, Wy.; Reg. Wy., 1832. Lost, 1834.

CAROLINE.—Bg.; 113; Yarmouth, 1825; Owners, Jn. Wake and Jn. Coverdale; Reg. Wy., July, 1850; Woman bust. Lost, 1862.

CAROLINE.—Bg.; 180; Dundee, 1847; Reg. Wy., 1860; Owners, Chas. and J. Wright. Lost in the Baltic, April, 1861.

CASPIAN.—Bg.; 178; Sndld., 1850; Reg. Wy., Nov., 1850; Man bust; Owners, John Gaskill, schoolmaster, 8, Will Dotchon, 32, Geo. Coulson, 16, Jn. Wadsworth, of Leeds, 8; Owners, 1857, J. H. Barry, 20, Jn. Barry, 18, James Shotton, Warkworth, 15, Jane Douglas, widow, 7, and Dav. Ditchburn, m.m., 4. Lost in Sweden, March, 1863.

CACTUS.—Bg.; 252; Sndld., 1856; Reg. S. Shields; Owner, Will Tose, of S. Shields, 1873 (Capt. Baxter, of Wy.). Wrecked on the Black Middens, Feb., 1883.

CANADA BELLE.—Bk.; 655; Quebec, 1862; Reg. Wy., Dec., 1862; 153 by 30½; Owner, Gid. Smales, jun., Hartlepool; Owners, 1877, Chas. Geo. W. Wakefield and Emily Smales; Capt., W. Tindale. Sold to foreigners, March, 1877.

CALDEW.—Bk.; $\frac{288}{300}$; Sndld., 1845; Owner, Hen. Barrick, Lndn., 1853 and 1856.

CERES.—Slp.; 1856; Staithes, 1795; Reg. Wy., 1795; Owner, Will. Weatherill. Lost.

CERES.—Slp.; $\frac{78}{82}$; Stcktn., 1817; Reg. Wy., 1830; Sch. in 1832; Owner, Will. Smallwood, jun., Hinderwell, plumber and glazier. Abandoned in the North Sea, Jan., 1854.

CELERITY.—Bg.; 155; Sndld., 1831; Reg. Wy., 1831; Owners, Thos. Galilee and Gid. Smales; Owners, 1842, Gid. Smales, 48, Mary Parkinson, 16; Owners, 1854, Mary Parkinson, 48, Will. Parkinson, 16.

On March 21st, 1857, came to the sand at Whitby waterlogged. Crew taken out. Tides bad, and the coals coming out of her, she drove higher up next tide, and became a wreck.

CELESTINE.—Ketch, 63; Caen, date unknown; Reg. Wy., 1856, from Woodbridge; Owners, Jn. Belsey, and Will. Hill, carpenter; Sch. later; Owner, 1863, Will. Hill, 64. Lost in Holland, Aug., 1868.

CEYLON.—Bk.; 399; Sndld., 1870; Reg. N. Shields, 1873; Owner, Jn. Henry Barry, Amble.

CHARLOTTE.—Sch.; 59; Goole, 1842; Reg. Wy., 1855; Owner, Geo. Westgarth; Reg. Scrbr., 1859.

CHARLES.—Slp.; 50; Prize; Formerly the "De Jone and Helena"; Reg. Wy., July, 1808; Owner, Sam. Holsey. Lost.

CHANGE.—Bk.; $\frac{364}{403}$; Sndld., 1849; Owner, Gid. Smales, jun., Hartlepool.

The "Change," Capt. Brandth, Hartlepool for Quebec, total wreck on Port Neuf shoal, St. Lawrence, Oct., 1861. Crew saved.

CHANCE.—Bn.; 56; Prize, 1809; Reg. Wy., 1809; Owner, Will. Hill, Wy.; Reg. Sndld., 1809.

CHANCE.—Sch.; 23; Foreign, where and when unknown; Reg. Wy., 1854; Owner, Alfred Walker; Reg. Wick, May, 1857.

CHASE.—Bg.; 197; Dundee, 1831; Reg. Wy., 1844; Owners, Sam. Flintoft and Co. Lost on island of Anholt, Oct., 1850.

CHASE.—Sch.; 39; Scrbr., 1818; Reg. Wy., 1849; Owners, Jn. Lennard, Sam Davison, and Geo. Bilton, tinner; Owners, 1868, W. Laverick, joiner, Staithes, 16, Robt. Brown, fisherman, Staithes, 16, and Hen. Carter Pickersgill, Mbro', 32. Lost at Hornsea, Jan., 1869.

CHASE.—Sch.; 21; Yarmouth, 1825; Reg. Wy., Jan., 1857; Owners, Francis Smallwood and Geo. Jefferson, Runswick; Owner, 1858, Will. Wedgewood, Hawsker, 64. Lost, 1859.

CHOICE.—Bg.; 151; Dundee, 1824; Reg. Wy., 1866; Owner, Thos. Hardcastle; Owners, 1866, T. Hardcastle, 32, W. Craven, 32.

Capt., T. Hardcastle, and five hands, Shields to London, 9th Dec., 1872, making for the Humber in heavy weather, struck the Spurn Bank about 1½ miles N.W. of Spurn light, came off and sank. Crew landed near Withernsea.

CHEVERELL.—Bk.; 318; Wear, 1841; Reg. Wy., Dec., 1856; Owners, Robt. Harrowing, 32, and J. H. Thomas, York, 32; Capt., Caygill. Wrecked at Southwold, 1857.

CHRISTIANA CARNALL.—Bg.; 193; Southampton, 1850; Reg. Wy., 1867; Owner, Will. Peck. Sold foreign, Feb., 1873.

CHRISTOPHER AND WILLIAM.—Slp.; 62; Scrbr., 1772; Reg. Wy., 1793; Owner, Will. Ripley; Owner, 1801, Jn. Wellburn, R.H.B.; Owner, 1808, Jn. Walker, Wy.; 1813, Will. Tose and Thos. Urwin: Owner, 1824, Thos. Urwin, 64; Reg. Nwcstl., June, 1826.

CHOICE.—Owner, 1791-5, Anth. Buck.

CLIO.—Bk.; 372; Sndld., 1845; Reg. in Lndn.; Owners, Geo. Ebblewhite, Christ. Harrison and J. Cummins.

Capt. Jn. Cummings died at sea on board this vessel and was buried at Lisbon. The vessel, in charge of the mate, Mr. Leng, was run down by a steamer off Dungeness about 1875.

CLIO.—Bk.; 267; Lancaster, 1797; Reg. Wy., 1832; Owners, Will. Clarkson, draper, and Will. Clarkson, shipowner; Owner, 1838, Elizabeth Clark, of Barnby. Lost at Prince Edward Island, Dec., 1838.

CLIO.—Bk.; 280; P. Ed. Island, 1848; Reg. Wy., April, 1865; Owners, Stephen Hall, South Shields, then Ed. Lothian and Chas. Barnard; Owners, 1869, Will. Parkinson, 48, and Geo. Grantham, 16.

"Clio," Capt., Will Parkinson, run ashore to save life, the vessel driving on to a reef near Ystad, 31st Dec., 1873.

CLARA.—Bg.; 144; Stcktn., 1839; Reg. Wy., Aug., 1859; Owner, Alfred Walker. Sold to Seaham, 1862.

Sold a wreck to foreigners, and sold again by them under the name "Maria," now "Clara."

Foundered off R.H.Bay, May, 1866.

CLARA JANE.—Bg.; 155; Sndld., 1849; Reg. Wy., 1857; Owner, Jn. Mills, R.H.Bay.

In Feb., 1868, when bound from London to Hartlepool, sprung a leak in heavy weather, and was run on shore on the island of Borkum.

CLARET.—Bg.; $\frac{146}{177}$; Sndld., 1835; Reg. Wy., July, 1854; Owner, Jn. Harrison, R.H.Bay; Owners, 1866, Geo. Ebblewhite, J. Cummins, Cuthbert Hutton, and James White.

Was towed into Whitby, July, 1862, having been in collision off R.H.B. with a Scarborough barque about 4 a.m.; considerable damage.

Lost on the west coast of Jutland, May, 1867.

CLEVELAND.—Bg.; 111; Stcktn., 1817; Reg. Wy., Sept., 1858; Owners, Jn. Wake and Isaac Bedlington; Bn. in 1860; Owners, 1860, Jn. Wake, 32, Jn. Brand, shipwright, 16, and Hannah Stephenson, widow, 16.

In April, 1862, the "Cleveland" was in collision with the French schooner "Amazon," of Dunkirk, both vessels being assisted into Yarmouth. One man missing.

On the 26th April, the brig "Spring Flower" landed in the Tyne a seaman named Eric Haggstrom, who was picked up at sea in an open boat. He was one of the crew of the schooner "Cleveland" recently in collision. He had got the boat out and was driven away. He had washed about during a stormy night, when Mr. Pritchard, master of the "Spring Flower," who heard his cries, bore down and rescued him.

When bound to France in Dec., 1863, was never heard of.

CLYMENE.—Bk.; 447; Sndld., 1846; Reg. Wy., Nov., 1855; Owners, Sam Flintoft, 12, Isaac Greenbury, 13, Ed. Dale, 13, J. B. Dale, 13, Matt. Gray, 13.

In 1859 arrived at Whitby with guano from the Kuria Muria islands.

Abandoned dismasted, and in a sinking condition, off the island of Sardinia, 23rd Feb., 1860.

COMMERCE.—S.; 223; Newnham, 1783; Reg. Wy., 1794; Owner, Harrison Chilton. Lost.

COMMERCE.—Bn.; 169; Stockton, 1800; Reg. Wy., July, 1800; Owner, Sarah, wife of Robt. Richardson; Reg. Lndn., 1803.

COMMERCE.—Bg.; 104; Sndld., 1795; Reg. Wy., June, 1819; Owner, Jos. Wood, Wy., mariner; Owners, 1836, Robt. Scott, 32, and Jos. Wood, 32.

Dec. 14, 1854, Robt. Scott, m.m., late of Wy., but now of Middlesbro', transferred 64 to James Croft, Margate.

Reg. Ramsgate, 1855.

COMMERCIAL.—Bg.; 138; Aberdeen, 1815; Reg. Wy., 1824; Owners, T. Wilson, Will Swales, and R. Lamb; Owner, 1847, T. Wilson, 64; Reg. Nwestl., April, 1847.

COLLENS.—Bg.; 118; Selby, 1791; Reg. Wy., 1825; Owners, Thos. Marwood and Robt. Usherwood; Owners, 1846, James Sayer, 16, Ralph Horne, 16, Will Dotchon, 16, Geo. Hopper, 16. Lost in Boston Deeps, Sept., 1853.

CORA.—Bg.; 116; P. Ed. Island, 1822; Reg. Wy., 1826; Owners, Thos. Frater, James Moffatt, and Jn. Fewster; Owners, 1848, Jn. Milburn, 48, and Robt. Sawdon, 16; a Bn. later.

"Cora," Bn., Capt. Will Storm and four hands, left Newcastle for London, coal laden, 13th Dec., 1859, at 10 p.m. flood tide, weather strong, wind N.N.E. strong. The ship having sprung a leak, and having two feet of water in the hold, set the pumps going and kept all hands at them. On Wednesday afternoon, 18th Dec., when off the Gunfleet, at about 2.30 p.m. the wind changed to N.N.W., blowing strong, with thick snow showers, the water in the hold increasing. At 5 p.m. came to anchor off the Maplin sand. Kept the pumps still going, but found the water had increased to 4½ feet. At 7 p.m. again sounded, and found 5½ feet. The crew got into the boats and remained by the vessel until about 9 o'clock, when she sunk. At 11 p.m. we were picked up by the "Halifax," of and from London for Middlesbro'. At 9 a.m. on Thursday morning were transferred to the "Eliza," of Whitby, Hartlepool to London, and were landed at 9 on Friday morning.

CONCORD.—Bg.; 188; Sndld., 1831; Reg. Wy., 1832; Owners, James Cowart, Matt. and Jn. Rickinson; Owners, April, 1868, T. Turnbull, Isaac Pennock, and Will Hunton. Lost on the coast of Holland on or about 30th April, 1868.

CONSERVATOR.—Bg.; 279; Sndld., 1839; Reg. Wy., 1839; Owner, Addison Brown, Staithes. Lost in the Gulf of St. Lawrence, May, 1850.

CORUNNA.—Bg.; 239; Sndld., 1843; Reg. Wy., 1844; Owner, Addison Brown, Staithes; Owners, 1858, Jn. Yeoman, Jn. Wilson, and Thos. Pressick; Owner, 1868, Jos. Will. Tinley; Owners, 1879, Christ. Marwood and Co. Totally wrecked on Yarmouth Sands, 17th Jan., 1881. All the crew drowned.

COBURG.—Bn.; 120; Yarmouth, 1816; Reg. Wy., Aug., 1846; Owner, Jn. Cassap; Owners, 1858, J. Wake, 48, Geo. Stephenson, 16. Lost near Bridlington, 1858.

COBURG.—Bg.; 197; Sndld., 1845; Reg. Wy., 1848; Owner, J. Kell, Wy., 1854. Sold to H'pool, 1859.

"Coburg," Tate, of Hartlepool, foundered off Montrose, March, 1866.

COLUMBINE.—Bk.; 199; Dumbarton, 1833; Reg. Wy., July, 1848; Owner, Richd. Gibson Gales. Lost on the Maplin Sand, Dec., 1848.

COLONY.—Bg.; 145; Southwick, Wear, 1841; Reg. Wy., 1849; Owners, James Andrew and Jn. Holiday. Lost on Tyne Bar, Feb., 1858.

CORNER.—Bk.; 299; Russian prize "Sophie Eveline"; Reg. Wy., Jan., 1854; Owners, Ed. Corner, 32, Elizabeth Wood, Hunstanton, 32; Capt., Jn. Mead; Reg. Lvrpl., 1862.

COQUETTE.—Bg.; 169; Sndld., 1839; Reg. Wy., 1859; Owner, Andrew Storm; Owners, April, 1880, Jn. Wake, 32, Will. Oliphant, 16, Geo. Hall, 16; Owners, Aug., 1880, Geo. Hall, 16, and G. M. Stephenson, Mbro., 48. Lost 50 miles E.N.E. of Spurn Point, Jan., 1883.

COMET.—Bg.; 200; Sndld., 1833; Reg. Wy., 1863; Owner, Will. Baxter. Foundered in the North Sea, Sept., 1865.

CONQUEROR.—Bg.; 192; Sndld., 1845; Reg. Wy., Nov., 1865; Owners, Will. Baxter, James Gray, Chas. Richardson, and Richd. Jackson, of Lythe; Owner, 1871, Will. Baxter, 64. Wrecked at Seaham, Dec., 1874.

CORALLINE.—Bn.; 184; Hartlepool, 1857; Reg. Wy., Jan., 1871; Owner, Alfred Walker. Broken up, 1902.

CORINNA.—Sch.; 71; Yarmouth, 1816; Reg. Wy., April, 1868; Owner, J. B. Nicholson, Wy.

The "Corinna" schooner, Capt. Jn. Gatenby, capsized by a squall when riding at anchor close to the Herring Sand, in Clay Hole. The crew took to the rigging, but for some time no one could assist on account of the violence of the weather. The crew, consisting of Capt. Gatenby, his son, the mate, and a seaman, remained many hours. At last a boat was sent, manned by Capt. Doughty, of the

"Rachel Lotinga," his mate, Frederick Barker, a seaman, and S. W. Wells, Custom House Officer, but before they could reach the "Corinna" the captain's son and the seaman had perished. The captain held his son in his arms till he died. Capt. Gatenby and his mate, John Smith, were rescued; the latter soon recovered, but the former, though quickly sent to Boston for medical help, died two days later. This catastrophe happened 30th Sept., 1871.

The "Corinna" was wrecked on Filey Beach, Nov., 1874.

CORNISH LASS.—Bg.; 111; place and time unknown; Foreign name "Fabian"; Reg. Wy., Aug., 1868; Owner, Geo. Robinson, Wy.; Reg. Lvrpl., Dec., 1868.

CORNUCOPIA.—Bg.; 210; Salcombe, 1848; Reg. Wy., 1871; Owner, Hen. Roberts, Wy.; Owners, 1882, Christ. Marwood and Jn. Rowland and Co. Stranded and totally wrecked on the Kentish Knock, 7th Nov., 1883.

COMMOT.—Bn.; 85; Llanelly, 1803; Reg. Wy., 1810; Owners, Will. Todd, Jonathan Skerry, and Will Estill, 1810; Owner, 1861, Will Simpson.

The "Commot," Capt. Will Simpson and three hands, Lowestoft for Seaham, was anchored 30th Sept., 1867, in Sandsend roads in a gale of wind at N.E. Parted from her anchor and came ashore on Whitby sand a total wreck.

COLUMBUS.—Bg.; 164; Sndld., 1815; Reg. Wy., 1816; Owner, Addison Brown, Staithes. Lost after 1831.

COMPACT.—Bg.; 147; Stockton, 1801; Reg. Wy., 1801; Owner, James Atty; Reg. at Lvrpl., Feb., 1807.

CONTEST.—S.; 966; Quebec, 1870; Reg. Lndn.; Owner, 1873, Ben. Pearson, Wy.

CORNHILL.—Bk.; 339; Sndld., 1847; Owner, Jn. Spence, 1876.

COMMERCE.—Bk.; $\frac{605}{640}$; N. Brunswick, 1838; Reg. at Lndn.; Owner, Ben. Pearson, Wy., 1853.

CROSBY.—Sch.; 110; Plymouth, 1825; Reg. Wy., 1850; Owner, Andrew Storm, R.H.B.; Reg. Sndld., March, 1860.

CRISIS.—Bk.; 345; Sndld., 1851; Reg. Wy., 1851; Owners, T. Turnbull and Co. Lost on coast of S. America. Certificate delivered at Valparaiso, Nov., 1852.

CRESSWELL.—Bg.; $\frac{183}{203}$; Sndld., 1848; Reg. Wy., 1855; Owner, Geo. Hopper; Owner, 1866, Jonathan Skerry, 64. Stranded near Havre. Sold a wreck, 1866.

CROWN.—Bg.; 212; Stromness, 1844; Reg. Wy., May, 1863; Owners, James Skerry, 48, J. Skerry Storm, 16; Lengthened, 1856. Lost near island of Odinholm, Oct., 1867.

CRESCENT.—Bn.; 150; Chepstow, 1796; Reg. Wy., 1815; Owner, Will Welch, Wy.; Owners, 1824, W. Welch, 60, Geo. Brown, 4. Lost in the Baltic, 1826.

CRESCENT.—Owner, 1791-5, Sam. Pressick.

CRAGGS.—Bg.; 200; Stcktn., 1848; Reg. Wy., May, 1875; Owners, Robt. Harrowing, 32, Will Cuthbert, 8, Jn. Brand, 8, Geo. Featherstone, 8, Snowden McKuen, 8; Reg. Guernsey, 1878.

CUBA.—Bg.; 248; Sndld., 1833; Reg. Wy., July, 1850; Owners, Robt. Farns, Runswick, and Will. Smith, grocer, Wy.; Owners, 1858, Robt. Jordison, 24, Robt. Farns, 16, Jn. Ripley, 16, and Dorothy Smith, 8. Lost off Winterton, Oct., 1859.

CYRUS.—Bn.; 126; Wear, 1806; Reg. Wy., June, 1823; Owner, Isaac Mills; Owners, 1836, Isaac Mills, 32, and Will Randfield, Harwich, 32; Reg. at Hartlepool, 6th April, 1854.

CYRUS.—Bg.; 282; Hylton, Durham, 1810; Reg. Wy., 1833; Owner, Will Hill. Lost.

CYRUS.—Bg.; 164; Capt., W. Storm, 1837; Capt. Rickinson, 1837.

CYGNET.—Owner, 1791, Jos. Barker.

CZAR.—Bg.; 297; N. Brunswick, 1825; Reg. Wy., Sept., 1872; Owner, Jn. Spence, m.m. Burnt at Gefle, Nov., 1874.

CZARINA.—Bg.; 222; Sndld., 1851; Reg. Wy., 1866; Owner, Robt. Mills. Lost near Coquet Island, Feb., 1871.

DAPHNE.—Bg.; 158; Sndld., 1807; Reg. Wy., 1813; Owners, Hen. Bennison and Will Gales, Wy. Captured by the enemy, Aug., 1813.

DAPHNE.—Bg.; 146; Sndld., 1824; Reg. Wy., 1836; Owners, Will. Foster, publican, Richd. Frankland, and Ed. Turner, furniture broker; Owners, 1842, Geo. Cummings, shoemaker, 48, and Jnt. Newton, m.m., 16, both R.H.B. Lost after 1843.

DAMPIER.—Bg.; 208; Tyne, 1833; Reg., 1840, Wy.; Owner, Will. Swales. Lost after 1841.

DANTE.—Bn.; 176; Greenck., 1851; Reg. Wy., 1881; Owner, Christ. Marwood. Foundered 7 miles from Fifeness, Oct., 1883.

DART.—Sch.; 72; P. Ed. Island, 1836; Reg. Wy., Oct., 1849; Owner, Geo. Copley Garbutt, m.m. Lost off Sndld., March, 1850.

DART.—Sch.; 63; Charlestown, Fifeshire, 1835; Reg. Wy., Dec., 1865; Owner, Robt. Abbot, 1865; Will Abbott, 1866. Lost off Dungeness, Aug., 1872.

DARING.—Bg.; 151; Cardiff, 1844; Reg. Wy., 1861; Owner, Jn. Harrison, R.H.Bay.

Leith to London, Feb., 1873, got ashore on S.W. Patch, Cross Sands, off Yarmouth. Wrecked.

DAUNTLESS.—Bg.; 228; Wear, 1839; Reg. Wy., 1846; Owner, Jn. Rose, who sold 32 in 1846 to W. E. Corner, of London, provision merchant, and Geo. Rose, m.m.; 1851, W. E. Corner sold 16 to Will Rose, Wapping.

DAHLIA.—Sch.; 99; Sndld., 1841; Reg. Wy., 1842; Owner, T. Pressick; Reg. Nwestl., 1847.

DAPPER.—Slp.; 62; Stcktn., 1812; Reg. Wy., 1834; Owner, Richd. Wright; Owner, 1838, Matt. Corner, 64; Reg. Stcktn., Dec., 1838.

DEVRON.—Bg.; 277; N. Scotia, 1826; Reg. Wy., May, 1828; Owners, Richd. Willis, Jn. Pennock, and Richd. Wilson. Sold to Hull, 1835, to Thos. Humphrey.

DEFT.—Sch.; 67; Ipswich, 1823; Reg. Wy., 1844; Owners, Jn. Andrew, Elizabeth and Jos. Harrison. Lost, Nov., 1845.

DELTA.—Bg.; 226; Sndld., 1839; Reg. Wy., 1843; Owners, Thos. Watson and Jn. Moffitt, Lythe.

"Delta," belonging to Thos. Wright, when towing from Shields to Middlesbrough, in Feb., 1846, broke adrift from the steamer, but arrived safe in the bay.

Feb. 10th, 1871, great storm at Bridlington; among others, the "Delta" was wrecked, and all the crew drowned. Four of the crew launched a boat, which was swamped, and the men drowned. The Captain, Will. Calvert, was clinging to the vessel, and to save him the lifeboat was launched, but capsized, and six of her crew, as well as the Captain, were drowned.

Owners, 1846, Thos. Wright, 16, Will. Frankland, Fern Hill, 16, Matt. Mutter, 16, James Wilkinson, 16; Owner, 1864, Thos. Forrest, 32, Hen. Robinson and Ed. Corner, 32 jointly; Owner, 1864, later, Thos. Forrest, 64.

DEPTFORD.—Bg.; 180; Sndld., 1849; Reg. Wy., 1855; Owner, Jn. Pearson; Owned at Hartlepool, 1870, by Thos. Greenwood, but still registered at Whitby. Wrecked on coast of Suffolk, 18th Jan., 1881.

DEVONIAN.—Bg.; 285; Sndld., 1846; Reg. Wy., 1858; Owners, Addison Brown, Margaret Hodgson and Ann Unthank. Lost off the Dudgeon, 1859.

DEVANHA.—Slp.; 60; Newburgh, Fifeshire, 1810; Reg. Wy., 1819; Owner, Francis Harrison, Wy., shipwright; Owner, 1825, Will. Hebden, R.H.Bay., 64. Lost, May, 1828.

DERWENT.—Bg.; 227; Sndld., 1842; Reg. Wy., June, 1850; Owner, Smith Stainthorpe.

"Derwent," Owner, S. Stainthorpe, Capt., Will Estill, Hartlepool for Erith, Tuesday, 30th June, 1865, strong gale, N.E. by E., lost topmast and could not clear away the wreckage in time to save the ship from going ashore on the Waybourne Beach, Norfolk, at 3 a.m., 1st July, and broke up. Crew saved by rocket lines.

DEODAR.—Bk.; 410; Dundee, 1858; Reg. W. Hartlepool, 1873; Owner, Isaac Bedlington, West Hartlepool.

DELTA.—S.S.; 1001; Hartlepool, 1865; Owner, Robt. Harrowing, 64. Sold to foreigners at Odessa, Jan., 1868.

DIANA.—Bg.; 182; Dundee, 1845; Reg. Wy., 1864; Owner, Richd. Robinson, R.H.B.; Benj. Granger, managing owner, Nov., 1875. Lost on the Lincolnshire Coast, Oct., 1880.

DILIGENCE.—Bn.; 69; Yarmouth, 1775; Reg. Wy., 1799; Owner, Will Swales; Bg. 1824; Owners, Matt. Peacock, 27, Christ. Jobling, 21, John Frank, 16. Lost, 21st July, 1828.

DILIGENCE.—Bg.; 111; Aberdeen, 1797; Reg. Wy., 1848; Owners, Robt. Harrison and Co., Wy.

Oct. 22nd, or early 23rd, 1850, run down off Huntcliff, near Staithes, by the brig "Argo."

DISPATCH.—Slp.; 56; Stockton, 1806; Reg. Wy., 1809; Owners, Jn. Anderson and Thos. Hunter; Owner, 1857, Geo. Westgarth, Boulby; Owner, 1869, Hen. Hobson.

The "Dispatch," owned by Geo. Westgarth, Boulby, left Staithes for Inverness, Epsom salts, Capt. Wilson and two hands, 16th Dec., 1862. In a heavy gale shifted her cargo, carried away sails, etc. Taken in tow by a smack, and in the heavy sea rolled her masts overboard. Towed into Whitby

"Dispatch," owned by H. Hobson, riding in Sandsend roads, 15th June, 1869, was driven ashore by a gale from N.E.

A ketch in 1825. Afterwards a schooner. Owned at Hartlepool later, then at Ramsgate. Broken up, Nov., 1886.

DISPATCH.—Sch.; 76; Stockton, 1799; Reg. Wy., 1835; Owner, Jn. Elwood, Wy.; Owners, 1839, T. Bird, Pickering, Will Nesfield, Wy., and James Sneaton, Wy., m.m.; Reg. Nwcstl., 1846.

DISPATCH.—Slp.; 47; Leith, 1801; Reg. Wy., 1847; Owner, Geo. Allan. Lost near Cromer, Nov., 1850.

DISPATCH.—Sch.; 69; Sndld., 1793; Reg. Wy., 1817; Owner, Jn. Cole, Staithes; Reg. Scrbr., 1823.

DILIGENCE.—Sch.; 49; Scrbr., 1817; Owners, 1854, Griffiths and Co., Wy.; Owner, 1859, Mich. Taylor, Sndld.

Capt. Charles Taylor, master, Berwick for Yarmouth, 24th Oct., 1859, with iron, left Berwick at 11.30 a.m. Tuesday, 25th Oct., when off Whitby, the wind changed to the S.S.E. and blew very strong. Tacked ship when off Whitby lighthouses, and reached off to sea until midnight, when the wind having changed to the E., laid the ship with her head to the S.S.E. 27th, 4 a.m., wore ship, but in so doing the mainsail split. At daylight the wind changed to S.W., and the vessel reached to the N. 3 p.m. wind changed to N.W. and blew very strong, accompanied with rain. Wore ship and stood to the S.S.E., 28th Oct., 2 a.m., the Humber bearing W. by N. 60 miles distant. Finding that the vessel had sprung a leak, and that there was 18 inches of water in the hold, tacked and stood towards the N., one pump kept constantly going. 29th, 8 a.m., off Whitby, wind changed to N.W. At 11 a.m. low water, strong wind at N.W., brought up in Sandsend Roads. 3 p.m. weighed anchor and ran for Whitby. On nearing the harbour mouth the tide swept the vessel, in consequence of her having no sail set aft, to the South of the East Pier. Let go anchor, and began to get towline up to be ready if a steam tug came to her assistance. The "Hilda" steam tug passed the vessel close to the mouth of the harbour, and when it was seen that deponent's vessel was being swept to the south she was hailed from the pier head to return and tow her into the harbour. No notice was, however, taken, and the "Hilda" proceeded to Sandsend roads. About 5 p.m. the chain broke, and the vessel was driven on the rock, and broke up next tide. When the tide ebbed the stores were saved, and the bottom of the vessel was sold by auction.

Oct., 1859, the schooner "Diligence," laden, in attempting the harbour struck the East Pier and went behind. She rode a short time--a coble and crew went to get a rope to assist the vessel, but the crew would not give them one, and although a rocket was afterwards fired on board they took no notice of it. She then drove up, and with some difficulty the crew of three men were got out by ropes from the cliff. The vessel soon broke up.

DON.—Bk.; 410; New Brunswick, 1839; Reg. Wy., 1840; Owners, Alexander Robinson, Wy., 27, Anth. Collier, 11, Will Collier, 10, and T. Muir, 16; Reg. Lndn., 1852.

DON.—Bg.; 150; Sndld., 1827; Reg. Wy., 1842; Owner, Isaac Wood Sinclair. Lost.

DOVE.—Slp.; 57; Stockton, 1797; Reg. Wy., 1827; Owners, Margaret Webster, widow, and Ed. Turner, cabinet maker. Lost at the Tees, 1827.

DORSET.—Bn.; 305; Howdon Pans, Northumberland, 1796; Reg. Wy., 1807; Owner, Thos. Hunter, Wy.; two masts; 99.9 by 27.6.

DOWSON.—S.; 352; Paul, Hull, 1807; Reg. Wy., March, 1824; Owner, Jn. Boyes, Wy.; three masts; 104.10 by 28.1; Owners, 1834, Hen. Boyes, 40, Elizabeth Boyes, 8, Catherine Boyes, 8, Jane Boyes, 8. Lost. Last Capt. named was Jn. Coulson, 1836.

DONINGTON.—Bg.; 118; Boston, 1803; Reg. Wy., 1825; Bn. later; Owners, Jn. Harrison, Wy., m.m., and Jos. Anderson, grocer; Owner, 1843, Jn. Milburn, 64; Owners, 1858, J. Milburn, 32, W. Milburn, 32. Ashore on Whitby sand, 4th Jan., 1854. Lost near Yarmouth, May, 1859.

DORIS.—Bg.; 159; Sndld., 1817; Reg. Wy., 1825; Owners, Christ. Gale, boat builder, Jn. Gale, and Jacob Johnson; Reg. Sndld., 1829.

DOWNE CASTLE.—Bg.; 156; Felling, Durham, 1818; Reg. Wy., 1848; Owners, Thos. Coggin, Geo. Granger, and Matt. Hewson. Lost near Scrbr., Feb., 1871.

DOWTHORPE.—Bk.; 320; Stockton, 1837; Reg. Wy., 1843; Owners, Marwood, Pickernell and Co.; Capt., Geo. Shaw; In Whitehall Dock, 1852. Lost, Jan., 1854, on North Uist Island, Hebrides. Crew saved. Ship's cargo transhipped the following spring.

DONNA.—Bg.; 226; Tyne, 1850; Reg. Wy., 1864; Owner, J. H. Storm.

The "Donna," Capt. Will Storm and 7 hands, left Riga 4th Dec., 1871, for Hull, deals. On the 5th, at 2 a.m., the light on Runo Island was seen about 12 miles distant, bearing N.W. by N., dipping, weather moderate and clear. At 7 a.m. the low light was seen, when a snow shower came on. At 8 a.m., being thick with snow, hove the ship to, and when just in the act of wearing she struck the ground gently and remained. Shortly after the weather cleared, and we found that she was on the reef about 1½ mile from Domesness Lighthouse. Soon after the wind increased, and blew a gale, driving the vessel further on to the reef. The vessel began to leak. Threw over some of the deck load. At 8 a.m. on the 6th found 10 feet of water in the ship. Hoisted signal of distress and got the stores on deck. About noon a large fishing boat with 18 hands got to the ship, but the wind and sea were too heavy for her to get alongside, and the crew had to slip from the end of the jibboom into the fishing boat, and were landed at Domesness village, the ship when left being a mass of ice.

DOROTHEA.—Bg.; 178; Sndld., 1830; Reg. Wy., 1835; Owners, R. Porritt, Hinderwell, and W. Walker, Runswick.

"Gravesend, 3rd Nov., 1862. The S.S. 'Harlequin,' from Gotenborg, reports speaking in Lat. 56° N., Long. 70° E., two light brigs, the 'Dorothea' and the 'Margaret,' both of Whitby, the former towing the latter."

"Before the Hartlepool Justices, 20th Jan., 1863, a claim was preferred by John Elliott Lund, master of the 'Dorothea,' against the owners of the 'Margaret' for salvage rendered that vessel from 28th Oct. to 4th Nov., 1862. It appeared from the evidence that the 'Dorothea' was blown towards the Danish coast, and fell in with the 'Margaret' with signal of distress hoisted. Her captain reported 4 feet of water in the brig, and the ballast nearly all gone, and that they wished to leave her. Capt. Lund advised their making for a Danish port, but the crew launched their boat, and came on board the 'Dorothea.' The claimant's ship then took the 'Margaret' in tow, and took her to Hartlepool. The magistrates awarded £210, including expenses—£140 for the ship, £25 for the master, £18 for men and £12 for boys.

Owners, 1871, Francis Waller, Middlesbrough, and Jn. Waller, Runswick. Lost, 10th Dec., 1872, 60 miles E.S.E. from the Spurn Light.

DOLPHIN.—Sch.; 59; Wells, 1798; Reg. Wy., 1836; Owners, Will. Taylor, Geo. Chapman, ship chandler, Will. Lister, and Sam Flintoft; Owner, 1859, Geo. Fairfoot, 64. Lost off the Humber, April, 1867.

DOLPHIN.—Sch.; 201; Sndld., 1840; Reg. Wy., 1848; Owners, Richd. Leng, and Ed. Corner, butcher, and Co. Lost on the Island of Bornholm, Dec., 1849.

DRUID.—Bg.; 249; Sndld., 1838; Reg. Wy., 1840; Owners, T. Jackson, Will. Corney, Ann Hill, and Thos. Watson. Lost, Jan., 1841.

DROGHEDA.—Bk.; 635; Reg. Shields; Owner, Jn. Taylor, Wy., 1873; Later, Frazer and Co. and W. H. Taylor.

DUKE OF YORK.—Smk.; 42; Queenborough, Kent, 1794; Reg. Wy., 1825; Owners, Will. Hunton, Lofthouse, and T. Turnbull, Wy.; A schooner later; Owner, 1851, Sam. Flintoft. Sold to Boston, 1867.

DURHAM.—Bg.; 109; Stcktn., 1814; Reg. Wy., 1832; Owner, Richd. Robinson, Kettleness. Lost, 1838-9.

DUCHESS OF KENT.—Sch.; 141; Wear, 1837; Reg. Wy., Feb., 1838; Owner, Jn. Barry; Reg. Maldon, March 28, 1838.

DUNNS.—Sch.; 50; Scrbr., 1815; Reg. Wy., 1839; Owner, Will. Foster, Wy., publican; Owner, 1842, W. Foster, 64; Reg. Scrbr., Dec., 1842.

DYSON.—Bg.; 270; Lvrpl., 1826; Reg. April, 1865; Owners, Robt. Gibson and Jn. Hall Leng. Lost off Archangel, July, 1867.

EARL MARCHMONT.—Bn.; 217; Nwcstl., 1791; Reg. Wy., May 25th, 1811; Owner, Will. Hill, jun. Lost, Nov., 1811.

EARL GREY.—Bg.; 229; Sndld., 1831; Reg. Wy., 1835; Owners, James Wilkinson and Thos. Wright; Reg. Stockton, 1836.

EARL OF MOIRA.—Bg.; 330; Wear, 1813; Reg. Wy., 1825; Owner, Benj. Hunter; Owners, 1834, Will. Clarkson, Wy., 32, James Terry, 32; Reg. Gloucester, 1836. Lost, 1837, or after.

EAGLE.—Bg.; 281; Scrbr., 1793; Reg. Wy., 1805; Owner, Chapmans, Wy.; Reg. Lndn., April, 1809.

EAGLE.—S.; 319; North Shields, 1794; Reg. Wy., 1810; Owner, Geo. Stonehouse. Lost, Oct., 1812.

ECLIPSE.—Owners, Frankland and Andrew, Staithes, 1791-5. Crew of four.

EBENEZER.—Slp.; 30; Barrow, Lincoln, 1844; Reg. Wy., 1854; Owners, James and Thos. Spink, Staithes. Lost, 1862.

EBRO.—Bg.; 202; Sndld., 1851; Reg. Wy., Feb., 1852; Owner, James Mutter. Lost at Hamburg, Aug., 1853.

EDEN.—Bk.; $\frac{235}{253}$; Bristol, 1820; Reg. Wy., 1844; Owner, Geo. Barrick; 94 by 22.4; Sq. st.; Carvel built; No head. Transferred to Hartlepool, 1866.

EDEN.—Bg.; 223; Sndld., 1854; Reg. Wy., 1863; Owners, Jn. Trattles and Susannah Liddle; Owner, 1874, Jn. Trattles, Staithes. Sold to foreigners at Ystad, Sweden, June, 1877.

EDWARD THORNE.—S.; 420; N. Scotia, 1835; Reg. Wy., Aug., 1844; Owner, T. Marwood, jun.; 111.1 by 29.1. Sold at Valparaiso, Oct., 1850.

EDWARD BOUSTEAD.—Bk.; 424; Lvrpl., 1842; Reg. Wy., March, 1865; Owner, Jos. Thompson; Owners, 1870, T. Turnbull, Robt. March Hunton, Benj. Garminsway, James David Dinsdale, Francis Anderson, Thos. Smailes, T. Turnbull, jun., John Turnbull, each 8.

Figure head was taken off the ship in Whitby and placed in the garden of the house near the railway station, built by Mr. Hutchinson, as previously stated in these records.

During a Parliamentary election the figure head was used for a practical joke. The town crier was sent round to announce that "Sir Edward Boustead" would address the electors in Station Square at a given time A great crowd assembled. People much excited when the hoax was discovered.

Captain Will. Jefferson, who was master at the time, states that the "Edward Boustead," with coals, left Grimsby for Spain, Jan., 1871. A few days later the vessel struck on the Long Sand, came off, but taking in water so fast, although the pumps were kept going, that there was soon 12 feet in the hold, and the crew had to leave her in the boats. They were soon picked up by a Belgian fishing smack, and were landed at Ostend.

ELIZABETH.—Bn.; 115; Sndld., 1799; Reg. Wy., 1835; Owner, Philip Poad, R.H.B.; Reg. Ramsgate, 1837.

ELIZABETH.—Bk.; 441; Richibucto, 1838; Reg. Wy., 1838; Owners, Richd. Wilson, Alexander Robinson, and Geo. Foggo. Lost, Dec., 1844.

ELIZABETH.—Bg.; $\frac{134}{140}$; Sndld., 1841; Reg. Wy., 1841; Owner, Will. Sanderson, m.m.

Run down off Hasebro' by brig "Lamburn," of Hastings, Sept. 26, 1849.

ELIZABETH.—Sch.; 49; Sndld., 1844; Reg. Wy., 1844; Owners, Elizabeth and Richd. Hutchinson, m.m.; Owners, 1849, Will. Fred. Mansell, 32, Elizabeth and Jane Hutchinson, Sandsend, 16 each. Lost, April, 1850.

ELIZABETH.—Bg.; 190; Sndld., 1823; Reg. Wy., 1849; Owners, Christ. and Jos. Thompson; Owner, 1873, Jos. Thompson, 64.

"Elizabeth," Capt., Will Brown, Shields for Rotterdam, lost near Fair Way Buoy, Goree, June, 1873. Crew landed at Helvoet.

ELIZABETH.—Bg.; 168; Bridport, 1840; Reg. Wy., Aug., 1855; Owner, T. Turnbull.

Total loss on Salthouse beach, near Blakeney, Nov. 19, 1875. Crew all drowned except the captain, Andrew Gatenby, he being on one of the masts which stood.

ELIZABETH.—Bg.; 182; Dundee, 1836; Reg. Wy., Dec., 1865; Owners, Ed. Storm, H. Allison, M. Bell, and Robt. Wilson.

"Elizabeth," Capt., Will. Bell, and four hands, Sunderland to New Dieppe, sprung a leak and was abandoned 22nd April, 1867. Crew taken off by the Bremen ship "Adelaide." The same day she was found derelict, and brought into Bremerhaven by two English smacks and a Hanoverian pilot boat two days later.

Sold by auction for £355, and bought by the original owner, "who has given me charge of the ship again."

Sold to be broken up, March, 1877.

ELIZABETH.—Bg.; 198; Workington, 1823; Reg. Wy., 1866; Owner, Will. Russell, R.H.B.

"'Elizabeth,' Capt., W. Porritt, and six hands, London for Hartlepool. Succession of gales, was driven over to coast of Hanover. On 3rd Nov., 1868, came to the ground on island of Norderney, with a heavy gale at W. and thick with rain, beat heavily and broke up. Crew took refuge on the bowsprit. About 11 p.m. the lifeboat came to the assistance of the crew, and on the third attempt succeeded in saving them, and landed them at Norderney."

ELIZABETH.—Bk.; 262; Scrbr., 1836; Reg. Wy., May, 1860; Owners, Middleton Cowart and Jn. Rickinson; Owner, 1868, Thos. Carlill Foxton. Sold at Hull to foreigners, June, 1869.

ELIZABETHS.—Bg.; 238; Sndld., 1854; Reg. Wy., 1865; Owners, J. K. Hill, 16, Robt. Calvert, 16, Will. Griffiths, 16, and Jn. Barry, 16.

The "Elizabeths," Capt., Robt. Claxton, and seven hands, left Shields for Swinemunde, 3rd March, 1866. Sighted the Naze on the 6th. Ship leaking badly, when a gale sprang up from the East. The ship "lay to" until the 8th, when I succeeded in getting the leak abated, and proceeded. Monday, 12th March, 11 p.m., thick with snow, Southerly wind blowing a gale, struck a sunken rock on the Swedish coast. A good look-out was kept in the hopes of seeing the Nidingen light. Ship rolled very heavily, with much water in her, and fearing she might slip off and go down in deep water, we got the boats out and left her about midnight, with the intention of remaining by her until daylight. When daylight came I could neither see ship nor land. Ran the boat before the wind and sea until the 14th, when we made the land, the Jutland coast, and got on shore. Two men from the shore came into the water and carried me and one of the crew ashore, and fetched three dead bodies of my crew to the church, they having been frozen to death in the boat. All the people were very kind indeed and most humane. Three lives lost, frozen to death, and five saved. Vessel insured for £1,500.

ELIZABETH AND MARY.—Bn.; $\frac{125}{153}$; Sndld., 1842; Reg. Wy., 1842; Owners, Robt. Goodwill and Benj. Granger; Owners, 1845, James Ellis, 32, and Jn. Tomlinson, 32; Owners, 1853, Jonathan Skerry, James Skerry and Geo. Storm; Owners, 1869, James

B. Garbutt, Hannah Jameson and Co. Foundered 6th March, 1869, about 12 miles from Havre. Capt., Will. Brown, Newcastle for Rouen.

ELIZABETH AND SARAH.—Bg.; 159; Sndld., 1840; Reg. Wy., Jan., 1857; Owner, Marshall Granger, of Rochester, Kent. Lost near Hartlepool, Feb., 1861.

ELIZABETH AND ANN.—Bg.; 215; S. Shields, 1855; Reg. Wy., July, 1861; Owner, Will. Pearson, Wy.; Off. No. 2294. Lost near Trouville, France, Jan., 1868.

ELIZABETH AND ANN.—Smk.; 20; Yarmouth, 1809; Reg. Wy., Aug., 1854; Owner, Hen. Richard Ourbridge, Wy., 64; Owners, Jan., 1855, Geo. Wardale, 32, Jn. Wallis, 32.

Run down off Redcar on night of 6th Oct., 1855. Crew drowned.

ELIZABETH MILLER.—Sch.; 66; Perth, 1863; Reg. Wy., 1905; Ketch, 1905; Owners, 1906, Burnett, 32, Clough, 32.

Wrecked in Sandgate Bay, near Caithness, N.B., Thursday, 20th July, 1906. Crew saved with difficulty, except one boy drowned.

ELLIOT.—Bg.; 208; Arbroath, 1851; Reg. Arbroath; Owner, Isaac Bedlington, W. H'pool. Wrecked at North Cheek, R.H.B., Jan., 1871.

ELIZA.—Bn.; 119; Leith, 1789; Reg. Wy., 1814; Owners, Will. Gales and John Bovill. Broken up, 1820.

ELIZA.—Bg.; 165; Pugwash, N. Scotia, 1838; Reg. Wy., 1839; Owner, James Peirson, Wy.; Owners, 1848, Jos. Bovill and James Hartley; Owners, 1854, Geo. Russell, R.H.B., 43, and Geo. J. Russell, 21; Owners, 1855, Geo. Russell, 43, James Hall, 21.

"Eliza," Capt. Jn. Mills, left Newcastle 26th Sept., 1863, for Calais, coals. Thursday, 1st Oct., at 0.30 a.m., in a S. by E. gale, struck what was thought to be a sunken wreck on the north edge of the Long Sand. After striking several times she came off and sank in deep water. Crew took to the ship's small boat, and got on board the smack "Marco Polo," and were landed at Harwich. Ship insured for £800.

It is supposed the sunken wreck was that named in notice to mariners No. 465, 26th Feb., 1863.

ELIZA.—Bg.; 179; Arbroath, 1844; Reg. Wy., 1866; Owner, Pattison Frank.

"Eliza," Sunderland for Rotterdam, running for Brouwershaven, Aug., 1873, struck Oester Bank, ebb tide, and increasing wind. Became a total wreck. Crew picked up by a Dutch pilot, and landed at Brouwershaven.

ELIZA ANN.—Bg.; 210; Sndld., 1840; Reg. Wy., 1840; Owners, Elizabeth Foster, widow, Frances Chapman Marwood, spinster, Ann Carrick, London, and James Todd, m.m., R.H.B. Lost in Riga Bay, Dec., 1851.

ELIZA ANN.—Bg.; 197; Sndld., 1831; Reg. Wy., 1864; Owner, Matt. Storm; Owners, 1882, Will Bedlington, Matt. Storm, Thos. Smith, and Will. Dixon. Foundered four miles off Cromer, 4th Sept., 1884.

ELIZA HALL.—Bg.; 192; Aberdeen, 1843; Reg. Wy., 1858; Owner, Ed. Turner. Lost at Granton, Oct., 1864.

ELIZA AND JANE.—Bg.; 192; Sndld., 1848; Reg. Wy., 1848; Owners, James Peirson and Matt. Webster; Owners, 1880, J. C. Butterwick, R.H.B.; previously J. and J. H. Barry. Lost in collision with screw steamer "Albertina," 14 miles S.S.E. of Flambro', Jan., 1892.

ELLEN.—Bg.; 194; Sndld., 1832; Reg. Wy., 1835; Owner, Thos. Trattles, Staithes; Owners, 1853, John Trattles, 11, Susannah Liddle, 11, Jn. Campion, 11, Sarah Trattles, 9, Will. Trattles, 11, Richd. Fishwick, Kirkleatham, gamekeeper, 11. Lost at Heligoland, Jan., 1854.

ELLEN.—Bg.; 156; Boston, 1827; Reg. Wy., 1840; Owners, Jn. and Geo. Rose, Wy. Lost, 1845.

ELLEN.—Bg.; 218; Leith, 1836; Reg. Wy., 1857; Owner, James Steel, R.H.B.; Owners, 1861, Robt. Parkinson, 16, J. K. Hill, 32, Matt. Boyes, W. H'pool, 16. Abandoned 150 miles S.E. of Heligoland, Oct., 1863.

ELLEN.—Bg.; 196; Sndld., 1850; Reg. Wy., April, 1858; Owners, Jos. Will Tinley, Edmund Stevenson, and Thos. Stewart, tailor; in 1862, J. W. Tinley, 48, T. Stewart, 16. Abandoned 40 miles S.W. by S. from Dantzic, Dec., 1867.

ELLEN.—Bg.; 182; Sndld., 1850; Reg. Wy., 1862; Owner, Matt. Bedlington; Owners, May, 1879, Thos. Smith, 16, Matt., Jacob, and Will Bedlington, 32 jointly, Oliver Storm, 16. Wrecked near Hornsea, 1880.

ELLEN HIGHFIELD.—Sch.; 121; Wales, 1836; Reg. Wy., 1856; Owner, Jos. Robson, jun.; Owner, 1866, Mary Jane Boyes, 64.

Oct. 21st, 1862, presented by Her Majesty's Government to Mr. Thos. Boyes, master of the "Ellen Highfield," of Whitby, a telescope for rescuing the master and crew of the "Pandora," of Middlesbrough, from their waterlogged and dismasted vessel.

"Ellen Highfield," Capt. Jn. Boyes and four hands, Newcastle for Middleburg, Saturday, 22nd August, 1868, in a gale from S.W., carried away part bulwarks, and the vessel sprung a leak. Kept pumps going till the 24th, with then three feet of water in the hold. At 10 a.m. strong gale from N.W. to N.N.W. and heavy sea. The vessel being in a sinking state and crew exhausted, ran the vessel ashore at Camperdown to save life. Part of the crew hung to the wreck. The captain and two hands reached the shore. Two drowned.

ELEANOR.—Bg.; 233; Sndld., 1839; Reg. Wy., 1858; Owner, John Mennell, Thorpe; Owners, 1871, Thos. and Eleanor Rickinson, 64 jointly. Burnt in Sweden, Nov., 1874.

ELEANOR RUSSELL.—Bk.; 306; New Shoreham, Sussex, 1836; Reg. Wy., 1848; Owner, Richd. Atkinson Robinson. Condemned and sold at Goree, W. Africa, 1850.

ELECTRA.—Bg.; 158; Perth, 1836; Reg. Wy., 1855; Owners, Miles Turnbull and Stephen Crosby. Lost near Yarmouth, Oct., 1856.

ELVIRA.—Bg.; 170; N. Brunswick, 1850; Reg. Wy., 1861; Owners, Jos. Brown and Son; Owners, 1871, Jos. Brown, 32, Jn. Robinson, m.m., 32. Sold to Blyth, 1871. Sold to foreigners, Dec., 1875.

ELOTH.—Bk.; 282; Norway, date unknown; Reg. Wy., 1862; Foreign name "Lagurtha"; Owner, James Andrew, fishmonger; later James Andrew, 8, Matt. Snowden, 7, James Pearson, 7, Jos. Thompson, 7, F. Anderson, 7, Roger Dobson, 7, Will Harland, 7, J. B. Nicholson, 7, and Will. Dotchon, 7. Stranded at Libau. Sold a wreck, Dec., 1862.

ELTHAM.—Bg.; 224; Prize, 1854; Reg. Wy., 1864; Owners, James Skerry and Jos. Steel. Lost near Newarp Sand. Run into by steamer, Jan., 1867.

EMULOUS.—Bg.; 149; Tyne, 1810; Reg. Wy., 1826; Owners, Paul Stokill and Moses Ligo. Lost on Hasebro' Sand, June, 1829.

EMULOUS.—Bg.; 179; Sndld., 1818; Owner, Andrew Clark; Reg. Wy., 1852; Reg. Stockton, 1857.

EMERALD.—Bk.; 292; N. Brunswick, 1828; Reg. Wy., 1830; Owners, Richd. Willis, Richd. Ripley, and Richd. Wilson. Sold to Quebec, Sep., 1833.

EMERALD.—Bg.; 217; Poole, 1836; Reg. Wy., 1856; Owners, Jn. and M. Y. Barnard and Thos. Feaster.

"Emerald," captain Thomas Feaster, and eight hands, left Huelva for Newcastle, manganese, 24th

Oct., 1866. Sprung a leak and foundered, 8th Nov., about 50 miles from the Portugal coast, some four miles north of river Vianna. Crew saved in the ship's boats.

EMMA.—Bg.; 261; Wear, 1836; Reg. Wy., Nov., 1836; Owner, Robt. Usherwood. Lost, 1838.

EMMA.—Bg.; 187; Chepstow, 1823; Reg. Wy., 1838; Owners, Christ. Scorra, m.m., 8, T. Turnbull, 16, Isaac Pennock, 16, Will Hunton, 16, John Witton, farmer, 8. Lost, Dec. 15, 1841.

EMMA.—Bg.; 151; Tyne, 1824; Reg. Wy., 1858; Owner, Geo. Copley Garbutt. Lost near Calais, Nov., 1861. Crew saved.

EMMA.—Sch.; 86; Ipswich, 1820; Reg. Wy., 1885; Owners, Hen. Readman and Jonathan Percival; Gill and Brown's coal hulk later. Sold to Shields, 1899. Broken up, 1904.

EMILY.—Bg.; 280; Sndld., 1846; Reg. Wy., 1858; Owners, Thos. and Jn. Coggin and Jn. and Geo. Speedy. Lost off the Texel, Nov., 1858.

EMILY.—Bg.; 231; U.S.A., 1839; Reg. Wy., 1860; Owners, Jos. Bovill and Thos. Harker; Owner, 1866, Jos. Bovill, 64. Lost in the North Sea, March, 1866.

EMSWORTH.—Bg.; 183; Sndld., 1825; Reg. Wy., 1862; Owners, Robt. Harrowing and Geo. Bilton; Owner, 1873, Jn. Harland. Sunk in the Thames, Oct., 1877.

EMMANUEL BOUTCHER.—Bg.; 193; Barnstaple, 1840; Reg. Wy., 1863; Owners, Will Walker, James Smith and H. Crosby. Wrecked at Redcar, 28th Oct., 1880.

EMPEROR.—Bg.; 243; Reg. Stcktn., 1839; Geo. Westgarth and Co.

ENDEAVOUR'S INCREASE.—Bn.; 68; Staithes, 1797; Reg. Wy., 1797; Owner, Will. Truefitt; Reg. Scrbr., March, 1809.

ENTERPRISE.—Bg.; 222; Stcktn., 1816; Reg. Wy., 1831; Owners, Will Clarkson, 32, and James Terry, 32; Reg. Lndn., Feb., 1835.

ENTERPRISE.—Sch.; 101; Sndld., 1834; Reg. Wy., 1834; Owners, Thos. Tate, grocer, Jn. Corner, grocer, and Ralph Hayes; Owners, 1840, Whitby Shipping Co.

"Enterprise," Geo. Carter, master, and three hands, left Whitby for Newcastle the 19th Oct., 1862. Lost all sails in a gale on the 20th and drifted from the land. When in latitude 55°5′ N., long. 1°49′ E., about 122 miles from land, a brig bore down to render assistance, and in doing so ran into the "Enterprise," doing much damage. The crew of the "Enterprise" boarded the brig "Ellida," of Tonsberg, which laid by all night, but the "Enterprise" being found unmanageable and having four feet of water in the hold, with both masts and bowsprit gone, was abandoned. Landed at Yarmouth from the brig.

ENTERPRISE.—Bk.; 413; N. Scotia, 1837; Reg. Wy., 1838; Owner, Hen. Boyes, Wy.; Owners, 1840, Christ. Boyes, 21, Hen. Boyes, Lvrpl., 43; Reg. at Lvrpl., 1842, June.

EQUITY.—Sch.; 82; Pwllheli, 1829; Reg. Wy., 1847; Geo. Eskdale, owner; Reg. Sndld., Oct., 1855.

ESKDALE.—Sch.; 44; Lndn., 1796; Reg. Wy., 1838; Owners, Jn. Buchannan, 42, Jonathan Eskdale, hairdresser, 22; Reg. at Boston, 1838.

ESKDALE.—Bk.; 437; Sndld., 1854; Reg. Wy., March, 1868; Owners, James Gray and Co. Sold to be broken up, Dec., 1878.

ESSEQUIBO.—Bk.; 307; N. Brunswick, 1847; Reg. Wy., Jan., 1863; Owners, James Gray, 32, Thos. Bird, Wy., 16, Thos. Storm, H'pool, 8, and Will Bird Gray, H'pool, 8. Lost on a rock off island of Bramon, Sundsvall, Oct., 1866.

ETNA.—Bg.; 268; Tyne, 1836; Reg. Wy., 1848; Owner, Will Wilson, m.m.; Owner, 1852, Jane Grant, 64; Reg. Lndn., Jan., 1855.

EUROPE.—Bg.; 178; Sndld., 1804; Reg. Wy., 1820; Owner, Richd. Wood, m.m.

Was lengthened and rebuilt at Whitby in 1835 by Messrs. Hen. and Geo. Barrick to Bk.; 231. Owner, Thos. Wood; Reg. Stcktn., 1836.

EUROPA.—Bn.; 192; Bristol, 1787; Reg. Wy., 1813; Owners, Jn. Bolton, Jn. Frank and James Wilkinson. Lost, 1818.

EUPHEMIA.—Sch.; 71; Tyne, 1829; Reg. Wy., 1845; Owners, Jn. Holliday, carpenter, and James Andrew, fishmonger; Reg. Berwick, May, 1849.

EUPHEMIA.—Bg.; 149; P. Ed. Island, 1829; Reg. Wy., June, 1848; Owner, Thos. McIntosh, m.m.; Owner, 1852, Elizabeth Cassap, widow, 32, Ann Storm, widow, 16, and Will. Taylor, joiner, 16; Owners, 1863, Elizabeth Cassap, 32, Constable Cassop, 32; Reg. West H'pool, 1863.

EUPATORIA.—Bg.; 263; Sndld., 1854; Reg. Wy., June, 1854; Owner, Marwood; Owners, 1864, T. Marwood, 51, and Jn. Wells Bowes, Mark Lane, Lndn., 13. Supposed to have foundered in the North Sea on or about 4th March, 1881.

EVERGREEN.—Bk.; 574; N. Brunswick, 1835; Reg. Wy., May, 1849; Owners, Benj. Pearson, 16, Ann Pyburn, 48; Capt., B. Pearson; Reg. Gloucester, March, 1860.

EXPERIMENT.—Ketch; 68; Knottingley, 1783; Reg. Wy., Sept., 1806; Owner, Joseph Andrew. Lost, 1807.

EXPERIMENT.—S.; 237; Canada, 1797; Reg. Wy., 1800; Owner, Hen. Walker Yeoman, Woodlands; Capt., Francis Agar; Reg. Hull, 1801, Feb.

EXPERT.—Bg.; 170; Sndld., 1839; Reg. Wy., Nov., 1860.

"Expert," owned by Jn. French, Seaham, London to Seaham, in ballast, anchored in Sandsend

Roads the 3rd Oct., 1860, with both anchors down. One cable broke, slipped the other, and ran for Whitby Harbour at 3.30 p.m. Owing to tide and strong N.W. wind drove against and round the end of the East Pier on to the Scar. Crew taken off by cliff ladders. Re-floated 16th Oct., and sold two or three times. Finally bought for £294 by Jos. Thompson, Francis Anderson, Will Dotchon, James Peirson, and J. B. Nicholson, and registered at Whitby, Nov., 1860.

"Expert," Capt., W. Usher, lying off Cookson's Quay, S. Shields, in Nov., 1868, was found to be on fire. It was put out after two hours' work. Damage about £200.

Sold foreign, Jan., 1875. Owned at Hull then.

FAME.—S.; 370; Portuguese prize; Reg. Wy., 1818, Jan.; Owners, Will Scoresby, sen. and jun.; Reg. at Hull, 1823.

FAME.—Bn.; 132; Sndld., 1796; Reg. Wy., 1818; Owners, Will and Sampson Estill; Owner, 1838, Will Estill, 64. Lost, 14th March, 1838.

FAME.—Bg.; 156; Sndld., 1814; Reg. Wy., 1826; Owner, Richd. Robinson, R.H.B.; Owners, 1840, Geo. Willis, 22, Francis Pearson, 21, and Mary Dorothy Bowes, 21; Owners, 1858, Jn. Wilkinson, sen., 22, Jos. Wilkinson, 21, and Jn. Wilkinson, jun., 21. Lost near Yarmouth, 1862.

FAME.—Bg.; 90; Wear, 1811; Reg. Wy., 1845; Owners, Geo. Harland, R.H.B., and Thos. Tomlinson, Whitby. Lost, Sept., 1851.

FALLOWDEN.—Slp.; 39; Stcktn., 1772; Reg. Wy., 1811; Owners, James Norton, Jn. Clark, and Will Hunter; Made schooner, 1811; Owners, 1819, Matt. Ord and Co.; Reg. Scrbr., Feb. 2, 1819.

FANNY.—Bg.; 115; Chester, 1782; Reg. Wy., 1801; Owners, Magnus Tait, m.m., Thos. Holt, and Thos. G. Dale, merchant; Reg. Lndn., 1805.

FANNY.—Bg.; 148; Sndld., 1818; Reg. Wy., 1828; Owner, Seaton Trattles. Lost at Cley, Norfolk, Feb., 1833.

FANNY.—Slp.; 34; Sndld., 1844; Reg. Wy., 1844; Owner, Chas. Saunders, Sneaton Castle, and R. Robinson, Sndld.; Reg. Sndld., 1850.

FANNY.—Bg.; 195; Sndld., 1848; Reg. Wy., Feb., 1859; Owners, Ed. Corner, Hen. Robinson and Matt. Gray.

"Fanny," coal laden, West Hartlepool for London, Feb., 1867, being anchored in the Lower Hope, broke her windlass and went adrift. Came into collision with the barque "Warrior," and sank. Capt. Faulkner and Jacob Clunes reported drowned.

Owners, 1870, Harrison and Co.; 1877, J. H. Storm; 1881, Robt. Harrowing. Left Sunderland for London, Jan., 1884, and not since heard of.

FAVOURITE.—Sch.; 86; Aberdeen, 1825; Reg. Wy., 1840; Owners, Thomas McIntosh, m.m., John Cassop, and Jn. Bruce. Lost near Kentish Knock, Dec., 1847.

FAVOURITE.—Bg.; 196; Bristol, 1845; Reg. Wy., 1858; Owners, Jn. Hesp, Moore Clough, Hannah Wood, and James Farrage.

"Favourite," Captain John Beadle and six hands, left W. H'pool for London, coal laden, 28th Nov., 1859. Fine weather, wind W.N.W. On Tuesday, the 29th, at 12.40 a.m., the Spurn Light bearing N.W. half W., distant eight miles, observed the green light of a vessel about 2½ points on the weather bow, and about a quarter of a mile distant. Ordered the helm to be put to starboard, and the vessel fell off from the wind about two points. The helm of the strange vessel appeared to have been put to port. Hailed her to keep her luff. No notice being taken, the two vessels came into collision, the stranger striking us on the starboard main chains, carrying away the main rigging, etc.

The two vessels immediately parted, and the stranger, whose name was not ascertained, proceeded on her course to the North. Put the helm of our vessel to port to bring her up to the wind, but on the sails filling the main mast fell over to leeward. Sounded the pumps and found 18 inches of water. Shortly after sounded again and found 2 feet 6 inches. In getting the boat out she filled and sank. Unshipped weather bulwark and launched the long boat. Again sounded the pumps, and, finding the water had increased to nearly four feet, all hands got into the boat, and about ten minutes later we lost sight of the vessel. Remained in the boat about 16½ hours, when we were taken on board the "Helen McGregor," screw steamer, Hamburg to Hull, and landed at Hull at 3 p.m. the same day. Ship insured for £1,200.

FAVOURITE.—Bg.; 185; Sndld., 1844; Reg. March, 1862; Owners, Robt. Harrowing, 48, Jn. Hardcastle, 8, Snowdon MacKuen, 8.

"Favourite," Capt., Jn. Hardcastle, Hartlepool to London, coals, 315 tons, 8th Sept., 1870. Tuesday, 13th Sept., when riding at anchor, the Swin Middle Lightship bearing N.E. by N., distant about 1½ mile, the red light of a steamer, afterwards found to be the "Viatka," of London, was seen about 2 miles S.W. Shortly afterwards the green light was seen and she came into collision, cutting the brig down to the water, and in about 5 minutes she sank. The captain and one hand got aboard the screw steamer, the others taken off by a boat from the "Atalanta," riding near. All landed at Old Haven, near Gravesend.

FAIRY.—Sch.; 87; St. Lawrence, Northumberland, 1841; Reg. Wy., 1857; Owners, Jn. Adamson, Jn. Crooks and Will Craggs.

"Fairy," owner, Jn. Adamson, Staithes, Thomas Cass, master, and three hands, left Whitby the 3rd Oct., 1860, for Port Mulgrave at 7 a.m. At 9 a.m. ebb tide weather fine, wind W.N.W. strong gale, came to anchor in Sandsend roads. Soon after let go the second anchor and all the cable. At 11 a.m. the best bower cable broke, and the vessel drove until close to Whitby rock buoy, when for the safety of the ship and crew slipped the remaining anchor. The vessel cleared the rock, but turned with head towards land, apparently having shifted her ballast. At noon she drove on the rock near Saltwick and became a total wreck. We got ashore in our own boat with the assistance of fishermen.

FALCON.—Sch.; $\frac{71}{81}$; Wear, 1813; Reg. Wy., 1840; Owners, Peter Hawksfield, Whitfield Theaker and Co.; Owners, 1861, Mary Welbank and Co. Sold to Dover, 1861.

FAMOUS.—Sch.; 47; Stcktn., 1845; Reg. Wy., Oct., 1857; Owner, Peter Moorsom, R.H.Bay.

Nov., 1861, Hartlepool for London, coal laden, sprung a leak in heavy weather and foundered 16 miles S.S.W. of Dudgeon. Crew saved by screw steamer "Onward."

FAIR MAID.—Sch.; 93; Perth, 1833; Reg. Arbroath; Owners, L. Sample, Lennard, and Lemkie. In Whitehall Dock, April, 1876.

FELICITY.—Bg.; 135; Kincardine, 1820; Reg. Wy., 1839; Owner, Thos. Andrew, plumber; Owners, 1853, Jn. Chambers, 32, Thos. Booth, East Row, 32. Foundered on passage from Chatham to Hartlepool, Jan., 1854.

FERRIS.—Bg.; 274; Bristol, 1839; Reg. Wy., 1866; Owner, James Hartley. Lost on Hasebro' Sand, Dec., 1867.

FERRET.—Sch.; 91; Sndld., 1821; Reg. Wy., 1824; Owner, Jn. Kirby, schoolmaster, and in 1836 also. Run down between Bridlington and Flambro', Oct., 1840. Crew saved.

FINDLAY.—Bg.; 180; Yarmouth, 1810; Reg. Hartlepool; Owner, 1863; James Gray, Whitby.

FLY.—Sch.; 85; Yarmouth, 1804; Reg. Wy., June, 1855; Owners, Matt. Snowdon and Matt Cummins.

1867, the "Fly," owned by Will. Smallwood and others, John Shaw, master, and three hands, Leigh, Essex, for Newcastle. Sunday, 1st Dec., blowing a N. by E. gale, whilst "lying to" about 10 p.m., heading E. by S., Scarbro' about eight miles distant, sprung a leak. The pumps choked with the sand ballast. Tried bailing with buckets until 10 a.m. on the 2nd. Hoisted signal of distress, Flambro' Head bearing N.W., distant 25 miles, when a smack hove in sight and shot up alongside. The smack in the first attempt struck the "Fly" on the starboard side. I and one of the crew jumped on board. The captain of the smack, which proved to be the "Monarch," of Hull, fearing the "Fly" was sinking, durst not venture alongside again to rescue the two men still on board, but "lay to" till 4 a.m. on the 3rd, when, not seeing the "Fly," we bore up for Hull, where we arrived at 8 a.m. on the 4th. The two men left were subsequently taken off by a smack belonging to Yarmouth on the 3rd and landed there.

The vessel afterwards picked up.

Owners, 1868, Jn. Beal, 22, Will. Booth, 22, David G. Gibson, 10, Sarah Margaret Gales, 10, Sold to Hartlepool and reg. there, 1868.

FLORENCE.—Bg.; 299; P. Ed. Island, 1862; Reg. Wy., 1873; Owner, Will. Foster, Wy., m.m. Wrecked on the island of Martinique, Sept., 1876.

FLORA.—Bn.; 194; Wemyss, Kirkcaldy, 1792; Reg. Wy., 1809; Brig, 1809; Owner, Jn. Featherstone, Wy. Lost near Kinsale, Jan., 1818.

FLORA.—Bn.; 94; Yarmouth, 1792; Reg. Wy., 1819; Owner, Jn. Richardson, Wy. Lost, Dec., 1821.

FLORA.—Slp.; 24; Maidstone, 1821; Reg. Wy., 1849; Owner, Will. Wilson, m.m. Total loss at Filey, Jan., 1851.

FLORIST.—Bg.; 217; Littlehampton, 1850; Reg. Wy., 1866; Owner, Smith Stainthorpe. Wrecked on the island of Bornholm, Sept., 1878.

FOX.—Smk.; 24; Torquay, 1813; Reg. Wy., 1857; Owners, Hen. Raw and Thos. Ward; Owner, 1860, Nesfield Hodgson; Reg. Sndld., 1861.

FOUR SISTERS.—Slp.; 60; St. Osyth, Essex, 1763; Reg. Wy., July, 1806; Owner, Anth. Twistleton; Reg. Scrbr., Sept., 1806.

FOUR SISTERS.—Sch.; 57; Rochester, 1811; Reg. Wy., May, 1854; Owner, Jn. Brown, Whitby, grocer. Lost near Dover, April, 1856.

FOUR BROTHERS.—Bg.; 133.

FOUR BROTHERS.—Lug.; 61; Scrbr., 1818; Reg. Wy., 1818; Owners, Dan Cole and Co.; Reg. Sndld., 1841.

FORTUNE.—Bn.; 66; Aberdeen, 1793; Reg. Wy., 1817; Owners, Moses Ligo, Paul Stokill, and Estill Frank. Lost, 1823.

FORTUNA.—Bg.; 93; Stcktn., 1821; Reg. Wy., 1836; Owner, Jn. Barry, Wy.

"Fortuna," owned by Jn. Wilkinson and Sons, Capt., Jn. Hunter, Dunkirk for Whitby, in ballast, in entering the harbour at Whitby, 23rd Oct., 1864, at 10 p.m., was struck by a sea and driven ashore about half a cable's length from the West Pier. Crew landed by "Fisherman's Friend," lifeboat. Vessel re-floated later.

Sold to Belfast, 28th April, 1871.

FORTUNA.—Bg.; 182; A foreign derelict owned at Wisbech, then at Scrbr., and reg. at Whitby, 1853; Owner, Samuel Flintoft. Lost near Riga, Oct., 1856.

FORTITUDE.—Bg.; 125; Sndld., 1811; Reg. Wy., 1st Aug., 1826; Owners, Jn. Mennell and Jn. Smith; Owner, 1851, Thos. Harrison, R.H.B.; Reg. Rochester, 1865.

FORTITUDE.—Bg.; 125; Sndld., 1804; Reg. Wy., 4th Aug., 1826; Owner, Thos. Hay, Wy.; Owner, 1828, Thos. Galilee Dale, 64; Owner, 1845, Will. Nicholson, 64; 1847, Ed. Granger, 64. Sold to Jersey, Jan., 1854.

FORTITUDE.—Bg.; $\frac{105}{125}$; S. Shields, 1802; Reg. Wy., 1827; Owner, Jos. Tindale, Wy.; Owner, 1853, Will. Granger, R.H.B., 64 Total wreck near Gorleston, Dec., 1855.

FORMBY.—Bn.; 175; N. Scotia, 1847; Reg. Wy., 1848; Owner, Sam. Andrew; Owners, Oct., 1864, Ann and Sam. Andrew and James Gray, 32 jointly, James Good, 16, and J. V. Andrew, 16.

The "Formby," when brought up near Aldbro', Oct., 1867, during a heavy gale from S.S.W., and being coal laden from Hartlepool, was run into by the brig "Elizabeth," of Blyth, the night very dark and a rough sea. One of the "Formby's" masts was carried away. There being a lamp and a fire burning in the cabin, it was thought that the shock of the collision had displaced the fire, for the vessel took fire, the crew became alarmed, and sprang on board the brig, two of them having a narrow escape from going overboard. The flames spread rapidly, and the "Formby" was soon destroyed and sank. The crew were landed at Hartlepool.

FOWLER.—Bg.; 137; N. Scotia, 1846; Reg. Wy., 1859; Owner, Thos. Barnard, R.H.B. Abandoned in a sinking state 80 miles from land, Feb., 1868.

FRIENDS' GOODWILL.—Smk.; 22; Brixham, 1828; Reg. Wy., March, 1851; Owner, T. Wedgewood. Lost at Sandsend, Sept., 1851.

FRIENDS' GOODWILL.—Slp.; 51; Scrbr., 1769; Reg. Wy., 1803; Owner, Benj. Miller, Wy. Lost, 1804.

FRUIT OF FRIENDS.—Slp.; 50; Buckhaven, 1777; Reg. Wy., 1799; Owner, 1808, Mary Porritt, Wy.; Reg. Sndld., Oct., 1808.

FRIENDS' REGARD.—Bg.; 171; Scrbr., 1798; Reg. Wy., 1835; Owners, Marshall and Benj. Granger. Lost after 1839.

FRIENDSHIP.—Sch.; 76; Ipswich, 1775; Reg. Wy., 1823; Owner, Geo. Thompson Lawson; Reg. Sndld., Aug., 1827.

FRIENDSHIP.—Bg.; 228; Sndld., 1837; Reg. Wy., 1856; Owner, Robt. Harrowing; 1868, Hen. Roberts and Co.

"Friendship," owned by Hen. Roberts, Capt., Francis Snaith, and seven hands, left Newcastle for Cronstadt, coals, 2nd May, 1871. At entrance to Gulf of Finland, 17th May, at 1 a.m., and about 35 miles west from Dagerort, "hove to" among drift ice, which the vessel struck shortly afterwards on the port bow, when she immediately began to leak badly. By 6 a.m., having six feet of water in the ship, were compelled to abandon her, which we did at 7 a.m., with 9 feet in her. Pulled to the "Zodiac," which was near, and got on board, when we saw the "Friendship" founder about 10 a.m. that day. Transferred from the "Zodiac" to a pilot boat off Sanhamm. Were then landed, and proceeded to Stockholm in the ship "Caroline," of Scarborough, and thence to Hull. Hen. Roberts, mate.

FRIENDS.—S.; 326; Selby, 1797; Reg. Wy., 1807; Owner, Geo. Brodrick, Wy.; three masts; 104 by 27.6. Sold to Lvrpl., 1818.

FRIENDS.—Lug.; 60; Scrbr., 1829; Reg. Wy., 1829; Owners, Jn. and Will. Harrison and Thos. Newton; Owner, 1840, Jos. Tose, Runswick, 64; Reg. Berwick, 1846.

FRIENDS.—Bg.; 151; N. Scotia, 1838; Reg. Wy., 1838; Owner, James Cowart; Owners, 1844, Jn. Bedlington Rickinson, Valentine Rickinson and Co.; Owners, 1846, Hen. and Geo. Barrick; Reg. Sndld., 20th March, 1854.

FRIENDS.—Bg.; 264; Sndld., 1841; Reg. Wy., 1841; Owners, Thos. Brown, Hinderwell, Richd. Brown, Lofthouse, and J. Smith. Left Elsinore 25th Oct., 1852. A missing ship.

FRIENDS.—Sch.; 41; Hull, 1808; Reg. Wy., 1850; Owners, Thos. Rymer, Bourne, and Co. Lost near Filey, Sept., 1851.

FRIENDS.—Bg.; 183; Sndld., 1839; Reg. Wy., Dec., 1857; Owners, Thos. Huntrods and Will. Harland. Sunk in Gravesend Reach, 10th Oct., 1858; afterwards raised and reg. anew, Nov. 29, 1859; Owners, July, 1859, T. Turnbull, 16, Benj. Garminsway, 16, Will. Knaggs, 16, and Elizabeth Hamilton, 16. Sold to foreigners, German flag, May, 1876.

FRIENDS.—Bg.; 100; Llanelly, 1798; Reg. Wy., 1860; Owners, James Terry and Hen. H. Leng; Owners, 1862, Isaac W. Sinclair, 22, Jn. Fergus, 21, and H. H. Leng, 21; Reg. Lowestoft, Aug., 1863.

FREDERICK.—Bg.; 141; Wear, 1802; Reg. Wy., 1825; Owners, James Wilkinson and Matt. Wright; Owner, 1846, Jn. Smith, 64; Owner, 1849, Jn. Iredale, carpenter, Ruswarp, 64. Lost on the coast of Norfolk, Feb., 1851.

FRANCIS.—Sch.; 53; Sndld., 1842; Reg. Wy., 1850; Owner, Geo. Copley Garbutt. Foundered in the North Sea, Oct., 1852.

FRANCES ANN.—Bg.; 259; A prize condemned at Antigua, 28th June, 1813; Reg. Wy., 1843; Owners, Isaac Mills, R.H.B., and Will. Randfield, of Harwich.

"Frances Ann," Harrison, of Whitby, W. H'pool for London, was towed into Grimsby, 29th Oct., 1861, by the smack "Petrel," of Hull, with loss of foremast, foretopmast, yards, and sails, etc.

Owners, 1875, Matt. Storm, Francis Harrison, James Skerry, Jn. Wake, Christ. Harrison, Francis Banks, John Weighill, Eliza Ebblewhite, Christ. Marwood, and Matt. Wellburn. Broken up, 1877.

FRANCES.—Slp.; 41; Staithes, 1838; Reg. Wy., 1838; Owner, Thos. Trattles, Staithes. Lost, 31st March, 1850. Reg. cancelled 26th Sept., 1850.

FUCHSIA.—Bg.; 225; Sndld., 1846; Reg. Wy., 1863; Owners, T. Longstaffe, London, R. D. Clark, W. H'pool, W. Clark, Runswick, Humphrey Orrer, Middlesbrough. Lost at Aldbro', Dec., 1868.

GALES.—Bg.; 184; Sndld., 1819; Reg. Wy., 1827; Owners, Will. and Anth. Collier; Owner, 1839, T. Kinnersley, hatter. Foundered at sea, Jan., 1845.

GALATEA.—Bk.; 305; St. John's, New Brunswick, 1828; Reg. Wy., 1837; Owners, Marwood and Willis; Reg. Gloucester, 1846.

GAZELLE.—Bg.; 193; N. Brunswick, 1826; Reg. Wy., 1842; Owners, Jos. Brown and Jn. Younghusband. Lost near the Scaw, Jutland, Oct., 1854.

GAZELLE.—Bg.; 174; Sndld., 1840; Reg. Wy., 1845; Owner, Jn. Mennell, R.H.B. Missing since Sept., 1852, Seaham for London.

GAUNTLET.—Bg.; 189; Workington, 1844; Reg. Wy., 1860; Owners, James Skerry and Jos. Steel.

"Gauntlet," Steel, of Whitby, Shields to Havre, coals, struck on the Owers Sand on Sunday, 27th Oct., 1861, came off and foundered. Crew got on board of the lightship.

GARLAND.—Bg.; 194; Arbroath, 1849; Reg. Wy., 1865; Owner, Harrison Allison, R.H.B.; Owners, 1871, H. Allison, 32, Hansell Gibson, 32. Lost in the Elbe, June, 1873.

GEORGE.—Bk.; 252; St. John's, New Brunswick, 1838; Reg. Wy., 1848; Owners, T. Turnbull and Isaac Pennock; 99.3 by 21.

Barque "George" ashore at Whitby, 1850.

The "George," coming for Whitby harbour in the evening of Nov. 20th, 1850, struck the pier end and drifted on to the beach. T. Parkinson, master, T. Caygill, mate. Re-floated.

The "George," Capt., Richd. Race, Isaac Dobson, mate, and 7 seamen, left Frederikshaven 7th Nov., 1863, with deals for Sunderland. Proceeded all well until the 3rd Dec.; at 4.30 p.m. weather very bad, blowing a hurricane from E.N.E., the ship became waterlogged, and fell over on her broadside, on which the masts all went and she righted. Next morning the decks gave way, the cargo went adrift, and the ship became a wreck. On the 6th Dec. the captain and four of the crew were taken off the wreck by a Danish schooner, the "Cito," after having been without food of any sort for 70 hours. Landed us at Christiansand, from which place we were sent to Leith by the Consul, and from thence home by the Fishermen's Society. Were it not for this timely aid the survivors of the crew would all have perished for want in a few hours afterwards, even were the vessel to hold together. Four lives lost, three from cold and want, one from drowning. Vessel insured for £800. The stern of the ship washed ashore at Heligoland ten days later.

Mr. Will Eaves, one of the crew, states that this disaster happened about 90 miles from Flambro' Head, and in about 11 fathoms of water.

GEORGE.—Bg.; 162; Peterhead, 1815; Reg. Wy., 1827; Owners, Robt. Allan, surgeon, 32, Jn. Frankland, merchant, 20, and Ann Bolton, 12; Reg. Lndn., 1828.

GEORGE.—Bg.; 144; Sndld., 1836; Reg. Wy., 1836; Owners, Geo. Thos. and Elizabeth Wood; Re-registered at Wy., 1875; Owners, Jn. Lennard, Jn. Hunter, and Geo. Milburn. A river hulk, Feb., 1897.

GEORGE.—Slp.; 60; Lancashire, 1816; Reg. Wy., 1843; Owner, Geo. Hodgson. Lost.

GEORGE.—Sch.; 155; Peterhead, 1830; Reg. Wy., 1846; Owner, Thos. Pressick. Lost on Seaton Sands, March, 1852.

GEORGE.—Bg.; 218; Sndld., 1840; Reg. Wy., 1852; Owner, Jos. Bovill. Foundered at sea, Oct., 1855.

GEORGE.—Bg.; 268; Ulverston, 1840; Reg. Wy., 1853; Owners, J. Trattles and E. Brown. Lost near Dogger Bank, March, 1870.

GEORGE.—Bg.; 217; Tyne, 1845; Reg. Wy., 1857; Owner, Will. Dotchon, Wy.

The "George," Capt., Will. Hill, from the Baltic with timber, became waterlogged in the North Sea in the gale of Dec., 1863, the same gale in which Mr. Turnbull's "George" was lost, as above recorded, and was abandoned. Crew picked up and taken to a Norwegian port. The vessel afterwards also picked up and taken to Norway. Capt. Hill was sent out to take charge of the vessel again.

Sold to foreigners, March, 1874.

GEORGE.—Bg.; $\frac{163}{175}$; Shoreham, 1839; Reg. Wy., 1861; Owner, Jn. Hoggarth. Wrecked near Hornsea, Dec., 1882.

GEORGE SMITH.—Bg.; 312; Wear, 1838; Reg. Wy., 1838; Owner, Geo. Smith, Wy.; Owners, 1846, G. Smith, 48, W. B. Smith, 16; Reg. Sndld., 1854.

GEORGE ANDREAS.—Bg.; 122; Altona, 1834; Reg. Wy., Feb., 1857; Owner, Thos. Cooper, R.H.Bay; Owner, 1858, Isaac Shadforth, R.H.B., 64. Lost, 1862.

GEM.—Bg.; 211; Stcktn., 1846; Reg. Wy., 1848; Owners, R. Verrill, Mark Hall, and Geo. Laverick. Lost on the coast of Jutland, Aug., 1862.

GEM.—Bg.; 192; Sndld., 1848; Reg. Wy., Nov., 1848; Owners, Jn. Schofield and Jos. Fletcher. Reg. Lndn., 1860.

GIPSY.—Bg.; 204; Sndld., 1837; Owner, 1853, Thos. Lancaster, Wy.

GIPSY.—Bg.; 80; Tyne, 1802; Reg. Wy., 1846; Owner, Smith Stainthorpe, R.H.Bay. Lost in St. Margaret's Bay, near Dover, Sept., 1849.

GIPSY.—Sch.; 41; Gillingham, Kent, 1801; Reg. Wy., 1848; Owner, Will. Morris, Wy.

Lost with all hands on the coast of Norfolk, 30th Sept., 1849. Whitby Beach was strewn with wrecks this day. See chronological records at end.

GILMORE.—S.; 500; Calcutta, 1824; Reg. Lndn., 1840; Owner, Robt. Barry, of Wy., residing in London. London to New South Wales, 1840.

GLEANER.—Bg.; 172; Sndld., 1815; Reg. Wy., 1832; Owner, Geo. Wood, m.m., Wy. Lost after 1833.

GLOBE.—Bg.; 227; Sndld., 1838; Reg. Wy., 1843; Owner, Addison Brown; Owner, 1869, Will. Falkingbridge.

"Globe," owned by Sarah Nesfield, Capt., Jos. Shaw, and six hands, Blyth for Sheerness, coals. Saturday, 7th Aug., 1875, was 4 to 5 miles East North East of Whitby. At 8 p.m., heading S.E. by S. and falling off with strong sea and light wind to S.S.W., and drifting bodily to the land. At 10.30 p.m., off the High Lights, calm, with heavy rain and strong sea. Found 13 fathoms, and let go the anchor to prevent the ship driving ashore. She dragged for about 20 minutes, and then held for a short time. Clewed up all sail, except lower topsails. Owing to the strong sea the anchor again dragged. Burnt a flare for assistance. About 11 p.m. the ship drifted ashore on the rocks, under Whitby High Lights. Beat heavily and carried away the rudder, and had three feet of water in the hold. Fearing the masts would go, launched the long boat, and with great difficulty, and in danger of being swamped, left the vessel and pulled out to sea, drifting North with the ebb tide, and then rowed towards Whitby. Met by a coble belonging to Thos. Cass, pilot, which took the boat in tow, and the lifeboat came alongside, but it was not required. At 5 a.m., 8th Aug., 1875, landed at Whitby. Vessel a total wreck.

GLENCOE.—Bg.; 136; N. Scotia, 1846; Reg. Wy., 1858; Owner, Will. Hall. Lost, 1858.

GLENAEN.—Bg.; 199; Tyne, 1854; Reg. Wy., 1864; Owner, Benj. Granger; Owners, 1874, Geo. Milburn and Co. Sold to be broken up, Aug., 1879.

GLADIOLUS.—Bk.; $\frac{151}{499}$; N. Brunswick, 1853; Reg. N. Shields; Owners, W. H Taylor and Co.

GLORIOSA.—Bk.; $\frac{809}{655}$; Sndld., 1849; Reg. N. Shields; Owners, W. H. Taylor and Co.

GLASGOW.—Bk.; 297; N. Scotia, 1849; Reg. Lndn. Owner, W. Elgie Corner.

In 1859 the "Glasgow" brought a cargo of guano to Whitby from the Kuria Muria Islands. The vessel was 18 months on the voyage, and lost several of her crew. One of the crew was dead on board on her arrival.

The "Glasgow" was lost soon after this.

GOOD INTENT.—Bn.; 127; N. America, 1762; Reg. Wy., 1799; Owners, Matt. Rickinson and Co., R.H.Bay. Sold about 1801.

GOOD INTENT.—Sch.; 97; Stcktn., 1782; Reg. Wy., 1802; Was owned in 1789 by William Douthwaite, m.m., Whitby. Was lengthened and re-built at Whitby in 1801, when made schooner. Owner, 1801, Thos. Wilson, tailor; Owners, 1802, Thos. Cooper, Newbegin, yeoman, and Geo. Wray, m.m. Lost, Dec., 1823.

GOOD INTENT.—Slp.; 48; Scrbr., 1785; Reg. Wy., 1805; Owners, Jn. and Anth. Twistleton, ropemakers; Owners, 1811, J. Cornforth and J. Harrison; Reg. Sndld., 1822; Reg. Wy., March, 1824; Owner, Thos. Richardson; Reg. Sndld., 24th Sept., 1824.

GOOD INTENT.—Bn.; 112; Thorne, Yorks, 1793; Reg. Wy., 1823; Owner, Moses Ligo; Reg. Sndld., Dec., 1829; Reg. Wy., July 1835, from Sndld., and made brig; Owner, T. Wilson; Owners, 1836, Ed. Corner, 16, John Corner, 16, T. Wilson, 32; Owners, 1847, Ed. Trotter, 21, Thos. Trotter, 21, Isaac Marshall, 22; Owner, 1856, Ed. Trotter, 64; Owners, April, 1859, Jos. Bovill, 32, and Will. Potter Bovill, 32. Lost on Kessingland Beach, Suffolk, May, 1860.

GOOD INTENT.—Slp.; 40; Heworth, Durham, 1827; Reg. Wy., March, 1837; Owners, Will. Nesfield and Co.; Reg. Nwcstl., May 1846.

GOOD INTENT.—Bg.; 97; Scrbr., 1802; Reg. Wy., 1841; Owner, Benj. Tindale, R.H.Bay; Sch. later; Owners, 1848, Isaac and Will. Gale. Sold as a wreck, Oct., 1860.

GOOD INTENT.—Bg.; 161; Scrbr., 1799; Reg. Wy., 1859; Owner, Matt. Seymour, Dale House; Owners, 1872, Jn., Isaac and Peter Seymour and J. Robinson. Lost on the Gunfleet sand, Dec., 1872.

GOOD SAMARITAN.—Ketch; 30; Scrbr., 1860; Owner, 1899, Hen. Hobson.

GOOD DESIGN.—Ketch; 51; Sandwich, 1877; Owner, 1897, Benj. Johnson. Sold to be broken up, June, 1900.

GORLSTONE.—Bn.; 295; Yarmouth, 1776; Reg. Wy., 1807; two masts; 67.7 by 18.5; Owner, Andrew Harrison, R.H.Bay; Reg. Campbelltown, March, 1822.

GODDENS.—Bg.; 159; S. Shields, 1841; Reg. Wy., 1841; Owners, Goddens and Steel, R.H.Bay. Lost on the Docking Sand, near Wells, Dec., 1853.

GOLDEN SHEAF.—Bg.; 225; Aberdeen, 1865; Reg. Wy., 1873; Owners, James Mills, Rillington, and Geo. Granger Turnbull, Wy. Owned at Whitstable later, then sold to Faversham, and reg. transferred there, 1881.

GRENVILLE.—Bn.; 78; Yarmouth, 1799; Reg. Wy., 1802; Owner, Matt. Stephenson, farmer, Ellerby. Lost, March, 1803.

GRATITUDE.—S.; 272; A Danish prize, 1811; Reg. Wy., 1811; three masts; 95.11 by 25.9; Owners, Seaton Trattles, Benj. Gowland, and Will. Jameson. Lost, Oct., 1814.

GRATITUDE.—Bg.; 212; Sndld., 1840; Reg. Wy., 1840; Owners, Geo. Falkingbridge and J. J. and Christ. Barnard; Owners, 1873, Will. Baxter, Matt. Storm and Co.; Capt., Stephen Hodgson. Lost with all hands on coast of Holland, 10th Aug., 1873.

GRASSHOPPER.—Bn.; 139; Selby, 1796; Reg. Wy., 1819; Owner, Francis Dobson, Mickleby. Lost with all hands, 1823, or after.

GREAT BRITAIN.—Bn.; $\frac{121}{137}$; Thorne, Lincoln, 1810; Reg. Wy., 1819; Owners, Benj. and Jos. Tindale, R.H. Bay; Owner, 1850, Jos. Tindale, 64. Foundered off Hythe, Kent, Oct., 1852.

GRACES.—Bg.; 168; Sndld., 1816; Reg. Wy., 1862; Owners, James and Samuel Andrew, Will. Harland and Matt. Snowdon; Owner, 1867, T. Anderson, 8, Will. Harland, 32, Matt. Snowdon, 16, and Will. Andrew, 8. Lost on the Kentish Knock, Jan., 1868.

GUARDIAN.—Bg.; 226; Nwcstl., 1794; Reg. Wy., 1798; Owner, Geo. Straker, jun., Gateshead; Reg. Nwcstl., 1800.

GUARDIAN.—Bg.; 208; Redbridge, S. Hants, 1823; Reg. Wy., 1851; Owner, Jn. Milburn, Wy.

"Guardian," owner, G. Milburn, Will. Breckon, master, left Newcastle for Rotterdam, coals, 24th March, 1865. Sunday, 26th March, at 1 a.m., blowing a gale at E.N.E., thick with snow, being then off Whitby, was struck by a heavy sea, carrying away port bulwarks, etc., and washing overboard an apprentice, who was not seen afterwards. At 3 a.m. was struck by another sea, and the ship began to leak. Kept the pumps going until 4.30 a.m., there then being three feet of water in the hold; cleared the boats. The sea making a clean breach over the ship, were unable to get the long boat over. Went aft to the skiff, which we lowered, and four men got into her. When the fifth man was getting in the ship went down. I jumped with the little boy to reach the skiff, calling to the men to cut the rope, and found myself drawn down by the suction of the ship as she went down. When I came to the surface I found the long boat close to me, and got into her. After driving about for about six hours I was washed ashore near Scalby Mill, where, after lying exhausted for some time, I was found and taken to the mill house by the landlord. Seven men drowned.—Master's deposition.

GUIDE.—Bg.; 222; P. Ed. Island, 1863; Reg. Wy., 1864; Owner, Matt. Snowdon; Owners, 1869, Matt. Snowdon, 48, John Swales, 8, and Will. Leng, shoemaker, 8.

"Guide" left Shields for Swinemunde, coals, March 7th, 1869. Went ashore on coast of Norway, 17th March. Re-floated.

Sold to Swansea, 1871; Reg. transferred to Swansea, June, 1874.

GWALIOR.—Bk.; 323; Wear, 1843; Reg. Wy., 1865; Owners, Jn. and Matt. Trattles and Sarah Sanderson, Staithes; Reg. Middlesbrough, 1876.

HAZARD.—Bg.; 117; N. Scotia, 1823; Reg. Wy., 1850; Owners, Will and Hen. Langstaff, Sandsend.

HAZARD.—Sch.; 53; Berwick, 1793; Reg. Wy., 1863; Owners, T. Ward and Isaac Gale; Owners. 1874, Isaac Gale, 64. Broken up, Oct., 1884.

HARMONY.—S.; 262; Scrbr., 1780; Reg. Wy., 1797; Owners, Ingram Eskdale, shipbuilder, and Gideon Smales. Captured by the French, 1797.

HARMONY.—S.; 320; Sndld., 1810; Reg. Wy., 1810; three masts; 113.8 by 28.4; Owner, Hen. Linton, East Row. Lost after 1818.

HAPPY RETURN.—Bn.; 69; Aberdeen, 1795; Reg. Wy., 1799; Owner, James Wake, lighterman. Sold to Sndld., 1799.

HAPPY RETURN.—Slp.; 66; Scrbr., 1788; Reg. Wy., May, 1815; Owner, Richd. Lines. Lost, 1822.

HANNAH.—Sch.; 70; late in H.M. service; Reg. Wy., 1820; Owner, Thos. Coates, jun., shipwright; Reg. Scrbr., 1824.

HANNAH.—Bg.; 266; Wear, 1839; Reg. Wy., 1851; Owner, Geo. Barrick; Reg. Shields, Oct., 1854. Wrecked at Tynemouth.

HANNAH AND MARGARET.—Sch.; 38; Scrbr., 1818; Reg. Wy., 1849; A lugger at first; Owner, Jn. Pearson; Owners, Sept., 1854, Jos. Tose, Runswick, and Robt. Waller, Kettleness.

Coming for the harbour, the tide getting low, and a strong "fresh" running out, struck the pier, sheared off and sank, Jan. 4th, 1855. The schooner "Shetland," coming at the same time, struck the other pier and sank.

HARPER.—Bg.; 163; S. Shields, 1813; Reg. Wy., 1826; Owner, Thos. Clark, Runswick; Owner, 1849, James Clark, 64. Lost at Yarmouth, 7th Dec., 1861.

HARRY KING.—Sch.; 116; N. Scotia, 1836; Reg. Wy., 1856; Owner, Jos. Brown, plumber; Owner, 1859, J. Brown, 32, and John Milburn, 32.

"Harry King," Capt. Harrison, Newcastle for Dunkirk, coals, went ashore near Southwold at 3 a.m., 20th Oct., 1862. Total wreck

HANTS.—Bg; 277; Hylton, Wear, 1845; Reg. Wy., 1857; Owners, T. Turnbull, and T. Turnbull, jun., 32 jointly, Jn. Webster Turnbull, 16, Robert March Hunton, 16. Lost in Ballycotton Bay, county Cork, Ireland, Feb., 1865.

HAWKHILL.—Bg.; 171; Bo'ness, 1842; Reg. Wy., 1858; Owner, Geo. Barrick, Wy. Lost at Hartlepool, Oct., 1859.

HARRISONS.—Bg.; 235; Sndld., 1839; Reg. Wy., 1864; Owners, Thos. Barnard and James Granger, R.H.B. Totally wrecked at Dantzic, Nov., 1867.

HALLYARDS.—Bg.; 313; Port Glasgow, 1818; Reg. Wy., 1865; Owners, And. Storm, sen. and jun., and Jacob Storm; Capt., J. Storm; Owners, 1875, James Trattles, Sunderland, 52, Thos. Trattles, 12. Stranded near Revel, Gulf of Finland, 3rd Oct., 1876.

HARTLEPOOL.—Bg.; 208; Sndld., 1856.

The "Hartlepool," owned by Thomas Storm, sen., R.H.B., but registered at Sunderland, Capt., T. Storm, jun., London for Shields, was driven ashore in a sudden gale a little North of Port Mulgrave, Oct., 1880. Total wreck.

HERO.—Bg.; 66; Weymouth, 1795; Reg. Wy., Aug., 1823; Owner, Will. Hebden, R.H.Bay. Lost, 19th Nov., 1824.

HERO.—Bn.; 150; Sndld., 1802; Reg. Wy., 1811; Owner, Will. Race; Owners, 1820, Robt. Appleton, Seaton Trattles and Benj. Gowland; Bg. in 1827; Capt., 1824, James Storm; 1825, M. Bedlington.

"Hero," Bedlington, of Whitby, was run down on the night of the 26th Nov., 1827, about 10 miles N. of the Float by the "Ellen," of Newcastle, which vessel went off without offering assistance to the "Hero's" crew, who took to their own long boat, and were carried into Yarmouth by the "Sprightly," of Newcastle.

HERO.—Bg.; 189; Swansea, 1814; Reg. Wy., 1828; Owner, Geo. Clark; Reg. Lndn., April, 1832.

HERO.—Sch.; 70; Lyme Regis, 1819; Reg. Wy., 1862; Owners, Ed. Turner, Ralph Horne, and J. B. B. Mead; Owner, 1864, Percy Walker Hall, 64; 1866, James Howell Seymour; Reg. at Maldon, Dec., 1866.

HEART OF OAK.—Bn.; 54; Dartmouth, 1786; Reg. Wy., 1797; Owner, Allan Burn, m.m. Sold.

HEART OF OAK.—Slp.; 45; Leeds, 1797; Reg. Wy., 1810; Owner, Gideon Smales. Lost, 1815.

HEARTS OF OAK.—Sch.; 75; Berwick, 1802; Reg. Wy., April, 1802; Owner, Robt. Stephenson, Brotton; Owner, 1825, Thos. Stonehouse, baker, 64.

Was ashore near the Salt Scar, 20th Jan., 1827, and a boy drowned. Reg. Scrbr., July, 1830.

HENRY AND MARY.—Slp.; 36; Prize called "Anna Andrina"; Reg. Wy., 1812; Owner, Hen. Barrick, jun.; Owner, 1827, Hen. Dring. Ashore at Whitby, with many others, Feb. 17, 1827; Re-floated. Lost, Oct. 14, 1838, at Runswick.

HENRY.—S.; 283; Prize, 1808; Reg. Wy., 1816; Owners, Will. Race and Francis Allison, m.m.; Reg. Nwcstl., 1820.

HENRY.—Bg.; 150; Thorne, Yorks, 1811; Reg. Wy., April, 1826; Owner, Jacob Huntrods; Owners, 1834, J. H. and Alexander Robinson. Lost, 10th Feb., 1834.

HENRY.—Bg.; $\frac{111}{137}$; Bridlington, 1811; Reg. Wy., 1835; A brigantine later; Owner, Thos. Clark, Wy.; Re-registered at Wy. for alteration of tonnage, April, 1876; Owner, 1876, Thos. Smailes. Lost on the Maplin Sand, Nov., 1876.

HERRING.—Slp.; 59; Scrbr., 1803; Reg. Wy., 1820; Owner, Will. Watson, Sandsend, alum maker; Owner, 1825, Jn. Roberts, Wy.; Reg. Yarmouth, May, 1825.

HERRING.—Sch.; 30; Scrbr., 1820; Reg. Wy., Aug., 1849; Owners, Hen. and Geo. Frank.

"Herring," Capt. Frank, coming for Whitby harbour in a sinking condition, drove on to the Scar and went to pieces in a short time, Nov. 1864.

HENRY AND HARRIOT.—S.; 257; Deptford (Durham) 1816; Reg. Wy., 1824; Owners, Will Cavillier, Matt Hill, Will. Swales; three masts; 94.3 by 25.4. Lost at the Shetlands, April, 1829.

HENRY HOOD.—Bk.; 309; N. Scotia, 1837; Reg. Wy., April, 1855; Owners, Will Readman, Will Pearson, and Will Foster. Total wreck at Karholm, near Gottenborg, Dec., 1856.

HENRY MORTON.—230; Owner, 1853, Geo. Wilson, Wy.

HEROINE.—Bg.; 239; Sndld., 1848; Reg. Wy., Aug., 1856; Owner, Robt. Harrowing.

"Heroine," Francis Snaith, master, Newcastle for Cronstadt. Proceeded till the 1st Sept., 1865. Strong gale N.N.W., struck by a sea, which swept the decks, starting a leak. Pumped about 48 hours, when she foundered at 10 a.m. 3rd Sept. Lat. 58.2 N., long. 20.58 E. Crew saved by brig "Osprey," of Inverkeithing, and landed at Cronstadt, 7th Sept.

HERALD.—Bg.; 172; Montrose, 1839; Reg. Wy., June, 1858; Owners, G. T. Knaggs, 32, Geo. Galilee, 16, T. McIntosh, 16. Lost on the Mouse Sand, Dec., 1860.

HEBE.—Bg.; 139; Leith, 1823; Reg. Wy., 1836; Owners, Stephen Pickering, John Corner, bacon factor, Thos. Jackson, weaver, and Jn. Chambers, m.m. Lost, Jan., 1841.

HEBE.—Sch.; 91; Weymouth, 1823.

"Hebe," a hulk, Will Peck, owner, with one man, left Hartlepool for Whitby, Oct., 1879, in tow of tug "Ganges." Foundered.

HEBE.—Bk.; 450; N. Brunswick, 1837; Reg. Lndn.; Owner, Edward Corner, Wy., 1853.

HEBER.—Bg.; 226; Sndld., 1830; Reg. Wy., 1837; Owners, Geo. Ward and Will Rawlinson. Lost, 1843.

HEBBLE.—Bg.; 134; Thorne, Yorks, 1796; Reg. Wy., 1838; Owner, Robt. Goodwill, Wy. Lost 1842.

HESPERUS.—Bk.; 455; N. Brunswick 1838; Reg. Wy., March, 1847; Owners, Marwoods and Pearson; Capt., B. Pearson. Lost in the Gulf of St. Lawrence, Aug., 1849.

HELEN.—Bg.; 179; Quebec, 1840; Reg. Wy., 1850; Owners, Geo. Hopper and Geo. Pyman; Owners, 1868, Jonathan Skerry and Robt. Leng. Lost, 21st Dec., 1868, Dudgeon Light bearing N.E., distant 4 miles.

HELEN.—Bg.; 329; Sutton, Yorks, 1837; Reg. Wy., Feb., 1860; Owner, Christ. Barnard; Owner, March, 1873, Thos. Smailes, 64. Supposed to have foundered in the North Sea about 20th March, 1874.

HELENE HARDY.—Bg.; Owner, T. Barnard, R.H.Bay. In Whitehall Dock, 1869.

HECTOR.—Bg.; 247; Methil, Fife, 1801; Reg. Wy., 1855; Owners, Hannah Wood, John Hesp, J. Farrage, and T. Wood.

"Hector," Gefle for West Hartlepool, became waterlogged in the North Sea, and her crew had to abandon her and take to the long boat. Picked up 10th Dec., 1870, Lat. 56° 10′ N., Long. 4.34 E., 135 miles W.S.W. from the Naze, by the "Falcon," of Tonsberg.

HEBBURN HALL.—Sch.; 85; Tyne, 1825; Reg. Wy., 1829; Owner, Zachariah Knaggs. Lost, Aug., 1845.

HERRINGTON.—Bk.; 297; Sndld., 1857; Reg. Wy., June, 1870; Owner, Jn. Bedlington, R.H.Bay; Woman figurehead. Abandoned 6th April 1885, 40 miles S. of Cape Palos.

A dispatch from Algiers, dated 13th April, 1885, reports:—The French steamer, "Forbin," which arrived at Oran 9th April, reports passing on the 7th the barque "Herrington," of Whitby, totally dismasted and abandoned, weather too bad to take her in tow.

A later dispatch from Gibraltar, dated 17th April, says:—The "River Indus" reports that on the 12th April, in Lat. 37 N., Long. 2 E., she passed the barque "Herrington" in a position dangerous to navigation.

HESSE DARMSTADT.—Bk.; 331; Sndld., 1863; Reg. Wy., Aug., 1873; Owners, J. K. Hill and Will Thompson.

"Hesse Darmstadt," from Lacepede Islands, Australia, with guano, Capt., Jn. Ebblewhite, arrived at Falmouth, reports:—"Feb. 10th, 1879, during heavy gale in the vicinity of the Western Islands, a heavy sea broke on board, carrying away 12 or 13 stanchions, bulwarks, mainrail, etc., on the port side, also the greater part of the bulwarks on the starboard side, and swept everything moveable from the deck. Vessel leaking. Jettisoned about 50 tons of cargo."

HICKMAN.—Bg.; 249; Gainsbro', Lincoln, 1813; Reg. Wy., 1835; Owners, Marwood and Willis. Lost.

HIPPOGRIFF.—Bg.; 196; Sndld., 1832; Reg. Wy., 1864; Owner, Thos. Mills, R.H. Bay. Lost off Yarmouth, March, 1870.

HINDA.—Bk.; 258; Maryport, 1834; Owner, Thos. Vasey, Wy., 1853.

HIRUNDO.—Bk.; 323; Sndld., 1845; Reg. Lndn.; Owners, 1854, H. Barrick and Co., Wy.

HILDA.—S.S.; 443; Sndld., 1866; Owners, Jn. Harrison Thomas, 48, Robt. Harrowing, 16. Stranded and total loss 5 miles South from Windau, Oct. 22, 1873. One man drowned.

HOPEWELL.—12; Skinningrove, 1783; Reg. Wy., 1797; Owners, Isaac Frankland and Jn. Teasdale. Broken up, 1816.

HOPEWELL.—Slp.; 57; Bo'ness, 1809; Reg. Wy., 1839; Owners, Geo. Harland, Jn. Kirby, and Geo. Young Kirby; Sch. afterwards; Owners, 1890, W. J. Pyman and Geo. Craggs Roberts. Broken up. Reg. closed, July, 1890.

HOPE.—Bn.; 108; Selby, 1785; Reg. Wy., 1804; Owner, Richd. Cook. Bg., 1804; Owner, 1805, Paul Cook; 1809, Mark Thompson, Staithes. Taken by the enemy, afterwards bought by a British subject. Reg. Sndld., Oct., 1814.

HOPE.—Bg.; 217; Shoreham, 1780; Reg. Wy., 1804; Owners, Jn. Wilson and Robt. Kitchinman. Lost.

HOPE.—Bg.; 243; Hull, 1789; Reg. Wy., 1805; Owners, Will Welch and Christ. Davison, m.m.; Owner, 1825, T. Benson; then Robt. Hunter, Shadwell, London; Reg. Lndn., 1825.

HOPE.—Bg.; 276; Sndld., 1797; Reg. Wy., 1810; Owners, Will Benson, Wy., and Joshua Cook, S. Shields; Reg. Nwcstl., Oct., 1814.

HOPE.—Sch.; 86; Prize, 1797; Reg. Wy., 1835; Owner, Christ. Thompson, m.m.; Reg. Sndld., Sept., 1837.

HOPE.—Bg.; 130; Sculcoates, Yorks., 1817; Reg. Wy., 1844; Owner, Will Weatherill, Wy., cabinet maker; Reg. Shields, 1852.

HOPE.—Bn.; 188; P. Ed. Island, 1837; Reg. Wy., Oct., 1847; Owners, W. H. Cramp, Appleton Stephenson, and Hen. Barrick, London; Reg. Nwcstl., 1848.

HOPE.—Sch.; 71; Perth, 1826; Reg. Wy., June, 1849; Owner, Will. Frederick Mansell. Lost near Ramsgate, Oct., 1854.

HOPE.—Bn.; 102; Dundee, 1816; Reg. Wy., June, 1849; Owner, Will Robinson, m.m. Wrecked on Whitby sand, 25th Sept., 1851.

HOPE.—Bk.; 276; N. Brunswick, 1846; Reg. Wy., 1856; Owners, Robt. Sleightholm, Wy., and Thos. Rawling, Guisbro'; Owners, 1858, Robt. Sleightholm, 16, Ann Gibson, 16, Ann E. Sleightholm, 16, John P. Sleightholm, 16. Lost in the Atlantic, Oct., 1859.

HOPE.—Bg.; 188; Sndld., 1834; Reg. Wy., 1857; Owner, Andrew Clark; Owners, 1860, Jn. Coverdale, 48, and Will. Laidler, 16; Reg. H'pool, 1860.

HORIZON.—Bg.; 227; Sndld., 1840; Reg. Wy., 1840; Owner, Jn. Clifford; Owners, 1843, Turner and Co. Lost, May, 1843.

HOLLY BOUGH.—Bk.; 324; Hylton, Durham, 1866; Reg. Wy., 1866; Owner, Thos. Thistle; Owners, 1870, Thos. Thistle, 18, T. Harwood Woodwark, 8, Matt. Thistle, 4, Thos. Huntrods, 9, David Baxter, m.m., Hull, 7. Sold to and Reg. at Swansea, 1878.

HOLYWOOD.—Bk.; 257; N. Brunswick, 1840; Reg. Wy., 1867; Owner, T. W. Parkinson. Sold to foreigners, March 27, 1875.

HUGH BOURNE.—Sch.; 70; Sndld., 1848; Reg. Wy., 1853; Owner, Thos. Seymour, Staithes. Lost on the Herd Sands, Tynemouth, March, 1855.

HUNTCLIFF.—Bg.; 182; Stockton, 1824; Reg. Wy., 1835; Owners, Geo. Willis and Thos. Marwood; Capt., J. W. Bowes. Lost, 1846.

HUMBER.—Bg.; $\frac{111}{123}$; Thorne, Yorks., 1818; Reg. Wy., 1839; Owners, Robt. Sawdon and Hen. and Jn. Ireland. Lost on the coast of Jutland, March, 1850.

HUTTON.—Bg.; 174; Sndld., 1830; Reg. Wy., 1841; Owners, Jn. Cassop and Robt. Scott; Owner, 1846, Robt. Scott, Wy., shipowner, 64; Capt., Thos. Barnard.

R. Scott dies 21st April, 1858; executors, Richd. Bradley and Francis Atkinson.

Vessel sold, 1860, to Jn. Garbutt, M'bro, 32, Charles Stewart, m.m., 16, and R. Robinson, butcher, 16.

Reg. at Stcktn.

HUMA.—Bk.; 393; Foreign; Reg. Wy., 1857; Owner, Jn. Corner, merchant; Owners, 1860, Thos. Turnbull, jun., Ed. Corner, and Ed. Kirby; Reg. at Hull, Jan., 1861.

IANTHE.—Bn.; 189; Yarmouth, 1846; Owner, Nellist, R.H. Bay. Broken up in Wy. harbour.

IDDO.—Bg.; 183; Dundee, 1848; Reg. Wy., 1862; Owner, Hansell Gibson, R.H.Bay; Owners, 1862, later in year, Harrison Allison, 48, and Hansell Gibson, 16. Lost on the Barnard Sand, near Yarmouth, Dec., 1867.

INDUSTRY.—Bn.; 86; Scarbro', 1784; Reg. Wy., 1794; Owner, Robt Richardson, R.H. Bay. Lost, 1800 or after.

INDUSTRY.—Slp.; 47; Hull, 1792; Reg. Wy., June 22, 1802; Owners, Gideon Smales and Ingram Eskdale. Lost, 1804 or after.

INDUSTRY.—Bn.; 98; Quebec, 1774; Reg. Wy., 1810; Owner, Emmanuel Parkinson; Bn., 108, 1812; Owner, 1812, Gideon Smales, shipbuilder, being one of the people called Quakers; Capt., Geo. Estill; Cost May, 1812, £1,629 3s. 3d.; Bg. then. Lost, 1816.

INDUSTRY.—Slp.; 23; Fowlis, Ross, 1832; Reg. Wy., 1845; Owner, Richd. Hutchinson, mariner; Reg. Nwcstl., 1846.

INDUSTRY.—Bg.; 196; Belfast, 1820; Reg. Wy., 1846; Owners, James Cooper, block and mast maker, and Thos. Robinson, builder. Missing since Oct. 1st, 1849.

INDUSTRY.—Slp.; 32; Sndld., 1832; Reg. Wy., 1860; Owner, Matt. Trueman.

Being towed into Whitby by the tug "Swan," drove on to the beach and became a wreck, 2nd Jan., 1868.

INDUSTRIOUS FARMER.—Shallop; 57; Sndld., 1795; Reg. Wy., 1807; Owners, Geo. Miller, mariner, and Will Heldreth; Owner, 1824, Jn. Linton, East Row. Last Capt. named is in 1831.

INTREPID.—S.; 374; Newcastle, 1809; Reg. Wy., June, 1809; Owner, Jn. Wright; 101 by 29. Sold to Lndn., 1817.

INDEFATIGABLE.—Bk.; 548; N. Brunswick, 1838; Reg. March, 1846; Owners, Marwoods and Pickernell. Lost on the island of Islay, Sept., 1867.

INDUS.—Bg.; 200; N. Scotia, 1843; Reg. Wy., 1848; Owner, Geo. Blenkhorn.

The "Beulah," of and from Hartlepool for London, coals, put into Lowestoft leaking, having been run into in the Cockle Gat by the "Indus," of Whitby.

Owner, 1864, Thos. Harland, East Row. Foundered off Scarbro' after collision, July, 1874.

IPHIGENIA.—Bg.; 273; S. Shields, 1817; Reg. Wy., 1829; Owner, Samuel Grayson, Pickering. Lost, 1833.

IROQUOIS.—Bn.; 118; Quebec, 1793; Reg. Wy., 1810; Owners, Will Hill and Jn. Boyes; Lengthened, 1814, to Brig, 151; Owner, 1840, Ann Ireland. Sold to W. H'pool, 1861. Foundered, 1865.

IRENE.—Bg.; 177; Newcastle, 1852; Reg. Wy., 1858; Owners, Geo. Calvert and Jn. Hardcastle.

"Irene," Robinson, master, London to North, was run into about 1½ miles below the Nore light about 8 p.m. on Feb. 20, 1862, by the Steamer "Pacific." The "Irene" lost bowsprit, foremast, main topmast, bulwark, anchor, and about 30 fathoms of chain and had her bows stove in. She was towed back to London.

Owner, 1869, Hen. Harrimond Leng, 64. Lost on the Cross Sand, Dec., 1871.

ISABELLA GRANGER.—Bg.; 188; Sndld., 1841; Reg. Wy., March, 1841; Owners, Marshall and Benj. Granger; Reg. Lowestoft, 1879.

ISABELLA.—Bn.; 102; Wear, 1805; Reg. Wy., 1823; Owner, Mary Tindale; Owners, 1825, Richd. Tindale, mariner, 13, Benj. Granger, fisherman, 13, and Co. Lost, Oct., 1825.

ISABELLA.—Slp.; 28; Sndld. 1820; Reg. Wy., 1827; Owner, Jn. James Jameson, R.H. Bay; Reg. Sndld., Oct., 1835.

ISABELLA.—Bg.; $\frac{218}{180}$; N. Scotia, 1837; Reg. Wy., 1838; Owners, Paul Stokill, Robt. Harrison, and Moses Ligo; Owners, 1863, Matt Snowdon, 32, Chas. Mason, London, 16, and Jn. Swales, Wy., 16.

"Isabella," Matt Snowdon and Co., Capt., Jn. Swales, H'pool for Gluckstadt, coals, struck a reef 17th Nov., 1863, on the coast of Jutland. Came off and foundered. Abandoned 21st Nov., lat. 55.40 N., long. 7.30 E., 12 miles from the shore. Crew landed in long boat.

ISABELLA.—Bg.; 166; Wear, 1827; Reg. Wy., 1839; Owners, Will Storm, 12, Coultas Storm, m.m., 10, Andrew Storm, 12, Ed. Storm, 10, Martha Storm, 10, and Thos Harrison, m.m., 10. Burnt off Hartlepool, 1840.

ISABELLA.—Bg.; 157; Sndld., 1811; Reg. Wy., 1840; Owner, Will. Hill.

"Isabella," laden, got on Whitby rock on Thursday forenoon, 13th Aug., 1857. Laid badly and filled next tide. Sea very smooth. Sold on Saturday on the Whitby pier for £7, hull and two masts. Drove on to the Scar the same night and broke up. Capt., W. Hill.

ISABELLA.—Bn.; $\frac{105}{127}$; Sndld., 1842; Reg. Wy., 1843; Owner, Jonathan Newton; Owner, 1850, Will. Newton; Owner, 1851, James Storm, R.H.Bay; Owners, 1856, Thos. Newton, butcher, 32, J. H. Storm, 32. Lost on the coast of Holland, Nov., 1868.

ISABELLA.—Bg.; 138; Hylton, Wear, 1848; Reg. Wy., 1858; Owner, Smith Stainthorpe, R.H. Bay. Sold for a hulk, 1883.

ISABELLA.—Bk.; 237; Belfast, Antrim, 1832; Reg. Wy., 1848; Owner, Sarah Nesfield; Capt., Jn. Leng. Lost in the October gale of 1861.

ISIS.—Bn.; 133; Sndld., 1843; Reg. Wy., 1852; Owners, Jn. Clarkson and Will Sample; Owner, 1860, Will Sample; Reg. at Faversham, Aug., 1872.

Lynn, Nov. 3rd, 1862. The "Wanderer," of and from this port to Hartlepool, in ballast, was abandoned to the North of the Dogger, with 7 or 8 feet of water in the hold, on the 29th ulto. The crew landed at Seaham by the schooner "Isis," of Whitby, Capt., Will. Sample.

ISIS.—Bg; 173; Sndld., 1850; Reg. Wy., Feb., 1860; Owners, Thos. Huntrods and Will Harland; Owner, 1869, Will Harland, 64; Reg. Cowes, 1882.

ISAAC AND ISABELLA.—Sch.; 33; Scarbro', 1830; Reg. Wy., April, 1830; Owners, 1854, Matt Snowdon and Co.; Owners, 1871, Jn. Wake, Geo. Ebblewhite, and Robt. Matthews; Owner, 1891, Alexander Hobson. Destroyed by fire in the river Wear, 31st July, 1891.

ISTAMBOUL.—Bg.; 269; Sndld., 1853; Reg. Wy., Feb., 1860; Owners, Marwood and Usherwood; Owners, 1865, G. T. Knaggs, 42, Geo. Galilee, 11, Thos. McIntosh, 11. Lost in the Bay of Biscay, Jan. 13th, 1865.

IVY.—Slp.; 63; Hull, 1838; Reg. Wy., 1847; Owners, Will Frankland and Hen. Simpson, of Whitby, and John Watson, of Pickering; Reg. Stcktn., 9th Aug., 1853.

Cromer, April 13th, 1862. A piece of plank, 15 feet long, 12 inches broad, and 3 inches thick, with name, "Ivy, Whitby," upon it, apparently from the stern, and part of a beam, 9 feet long and 8 inches square, painted white, apparently from the cabin, have been washed ashore at Bacton, Norfolk.

JANE.—Bn.; 248; N. Shields, 1796; Reg. Wy., 1804; two masts; 88 by 26; Owner, James Harrison, Wy. Lost.

JANE.—Slp.; 61; Sndld., 1785; Reg. Wy., 1799; Owner, Will Hildreth, mariner; Reg. Sndld., 1800; Reg. Wy., 1822, from Sndld.; Owner, Anthony Wade, R.H. Bay. Lost, Aug., 1828.

JANE.—Bg.; 130; Wear, 1802; Reg. Wy., Feb., 1825; Owner, Jacob Huntrods. Lost, Nov. 1834.

JANE.—Slp.; 18; Sndld., 1828; Reg. Wy., 1830; Owner, Will Pearson, Whitby, m.m.; Owners, 1832, Samuel Flintoft, 32, Will Lister, 32. Lost, 1837 or after.

JANE.—Bg.; 174; Sndld., 1819; Reg. Wy., 1840; Owners, Jn. Johnson and Jn. Barnard; Owners, 1849, Hannah Barnard, 42, Will Barnard, 22.

"Jane," Capt. John Barnard and 5 hands, 29th July, 1863, coal laden, Hartlepool for London, in fine weather went ashore near Staithes, and broke up next tide. The master was of opinion that the watch on deck must have been asleep.

JANE.—Bg.; 257; Stockton, 1840; Reg. Wy., 1841; Owners, Thos. and Matt Trattles, Staithes. Lost, 1845.

JANE.—Bg.; 79; Sndld., 1818; Reg. Wy., 1849; Owners, Thos. Jefferson and Will Jackson; Owner, 1859, Thos. Jefferson. Abandoned, Oct. 27, 1859.

JANE.—Sch.; 76; Blyth, 1838; Reg. Wy., 1849; Owners, Peter Hawksfield and Co.; Reg. Dover, Nov., 1851.

JANE.—Sch.; 51; Tyne, 1840; Reg. Wy., June, 1850; Owner, Jn. Corney, Wy., m.m. Lost with all the crew, Sept., 1851, when on passage from West Wemyss to Findhorn.

JANE.—Sch.; 31; Newhaven, 1797; Reg. Wy., 1853; Owner, J. J. Griffiths, East Row. Broken up at Whitby, 1868.

JANE.—Bg.; 200; Sndld., 1839; Reg. Wy., Jan., 1863; Owner, Thos. Nesfield, 64; Owners, Aug., 1868, Sarah Nesfield, 14, Stephen Nesfield, 21, Mary Nesfield, 13, Joseph Shaw, 8, Sarah Elizabeth Nesfield, 8.

"Jane," Capt. Shaw, foundered Oct., 1868, 120 miles East of Flamborough Head, through stress of weather. Crew picked up by a smack and landed at Cuxhaven.

JANE.—Bk.; 242; Littlehampton, 1858; Reg. Wy., June, 1866; Owner, Will Bedlington, R.H. Bay, 64; then W. Bedlington, 32, and Matt Storm, 32; in 1883 altered in rigging to Bqtn. and in tonnage. Sold, July, 1889, to Dixon Taylor Sharper, of W. H'pool, who dies March, 1895, and owner then, Susannah Sharper, 64. Lost April 19, 1896, by collision with screw steamer "Frederick Frank," of Havre, the Royal Sovereign light E. by N. 1 mile.

JANE.—Sch.; 136; Ipswich, 1825; Reg. Stcktn.; Owner, Hinds Thompson, Wy., 1853.

JANE VILET.—Bk.; 309; Quebec, 1826; Reg. Wy., 1827; Owners, Jn. Clark, Wy., merchant, 1, Thomas Jackson, 31, and Geo. Clark, 32; woman bust; Owner, 1830, Geo. Clark, 64; Reg. Lvrpl., 1831.

JANE WHITE.—Bg.; Sndld., 1834; Reg. Wy., 1855; Owners, Butterwick and Langborne; Owner, 1870, W. Butterwick, 64. Sold to be broken up, Nov., 1878.

JANE CLARK.—Bg.; 207; Arbroath, 1850; Reg. Wy., 1860; Owners, Bedlingtons, R.H. Bay. Lost on the coast of Holland, 1863.

JANE HEWARD.—Bg.; 171; Sndld., 1848; Reg. Wy., 1865; Owner, Jn. Barker, Sndld., then Jn. Harland and Co., R.H. Bay. Lost near the Gull Light Vessel, April, 1870.

JANE AND WILLIAM.—Bg.; 135; Howdon Pans, 1843; Reg. Wy., 1843; Owner, Jn. Richardson, Wy.; Reg. Nwcstl., 1844.

JANE AND ANN.—Bg.; 211; Sndld., 1837; Reg. Wy., 1852; Owner, Jn. Corner, Wy.; Reg. Hartlepool, 1857.

JANE AND ELLEN.—Dandy; 39; Sndld., 1839; Reg. Wy., 1867; Owner, Jn. Postgate. Total wreck, Runswick Bay, Nov. 7, 1893.

JANE AND ELEANOR.—Bg.; 196; Sndld., 1862; Reg. at Shields; Owner, J. H. Barry, Amble.

JANET.—Bg.; 280; Pictou, 1826; Reg. Wy., 1834; Owner, Geo. Smith, Wy.; Reg. Hull, Feb., 1836.

JANET AND MARY.—Bn.; 137; Leith, 1838; Reg. Wy., Aug., 1869; Owner, Robt. Granger, R.H. Bay. Foundered off Soutar Point, Dec. 16, 1880. Owned then at Middlesbrough.

JANETTA.—Sch.; 61; Bristol, 1828; Reg. Wy., 1861; Owner, Charlotte Wilson, Wy.; Owner, 1865, Will. Wilson, 64. Lost at Herne Bay, May, 1869.

JABEZ.—Bg.; 187; Sndld., 1845; Reg. Wy., 1866; Owners, Nathan Hewson, R.H. Bay, 16, T. Avery, 16, Fanny Coggin, 16, and Eliza Coggin, 16. Lost at Shields, Feb., 1871. Four drowned.

JASON.—Bg.; 119; Sndld., 1798; Reg. Wy., 1822; Owner, Will Wright, m.m.; Owners, 1840, Will Wright, 32, Matt Walker, 16, and Bennison Gales, 16. Lost off Cromer, and only one saved.

JASON.—Sch.; 99; Ramsgate, 1803; Reg. Wy., 1849, Jan. 26, from Maldon; Owner, Christ. Fewster, Wy., 64; Owner, 1852, Matt. Tinley, 64; Capt., Geo. Grantham; Owners, 1860, Matt Tinley, 48, Matt Tinley, jun., 16.

Will Barnes, captain of the brigantine "Jason," reports: "Left Shields Oct. 23rd, 1871, coal laden, for Brake. When off Heligoland caught in a severe gale and sprung a leak. The crew took to the pumps, but the leak increased until there was six feet of water in the hold and the vessel in a sinking condition. Could not leave the vessel as the boats were disabled. Happily the S.S. 'Cumberland,' of Leith, Capt. Parker, hove in sight and rescued the crew, six in number, and the captain's wife and two children. The 'Jason' afterwards foundered. She was owned by Mr. Matt Tinley, of Whitby."

JAMAICA.—S.; 391; Lvrpl., 1795; Reg. Wy., 1815; Owner, Jn. Linton, jun., East Row. Lost, 1822.

JAMES.—Bg.; 125; Redbridge, S'thampton, 1818; Reg. Wy., 1839; Owner, Tyson Coverdale, R.H.Bay. Lost, Oct., 1839.

JAMES.—Bg.; 208; Sndld., 1858; Reg. Wy., July, 1858; Owners, Jont. and James Skerry, R.H.Bay. Lost on the West coast of Jutland, March, 1863.

JAMES AND MARGARET.—Bn.; 125; Gateshead, 1789; Reg. Wy., 1798; Owner, James Dixon, Wy.; Reg. Nwcstl., 1813.

JAMES REID.—Bg.; 138; N. Scotia, 1842; Reg. Wy., Jan., 1848; Owners, Will. Dotchon, James Sayer and Francis Dobson. Abandoned in a sinking state, Dec., 1848.

JAMES CASKIE.—Bg.; 388; U.S.A., 1832; Reg. Wy., 1855; Owners, Jn. and Edward Corner and Hen. Robinson. Lost in the Atlantic, Dec., 1865; Capt. Brandth and crew.

JAMES BROOK.—Bg.; 163; Selby, 1833; Owners, Estill and Co., Wy.; later, W. Robinson. Reg. Goole, 1840.

JEANIE.—Bn.; 95; Hull, 1760; Reg. Wy., 1801; Owners, James Wake and James Hutchinson, mason. Sold to Whitehaven.

JENNY.—Bg.; 134; Kincardine, 1816; Reg. Wy., 1845; Owner, Jos. Brown, Wy.; Owners, 1860, James Cliff and Jos. Bovill, 32 jointly, Jos. Bovill, 16, and Thos. Porritt, 16. Lost on Whitburn Rocks, Dec., 1867.

JESSIE ANNANDALE.—Bn.; 123; Sndld., 1857; Owners, Messrs. Danby and Lennard, Wy.; In Boghall Dock, 1893, Dismasted, brought to Whitby, dismantled and sold a hulk.

JESSIE ANNE.—Bg.; 172; Sndld., 1842; Reg. Wy., 1848; Owner, Will. Clark, harbour master, Wy.; Owner, 1854, Jos. Bovill, 64. Wrecked on the Goodwin Sands, 1857.

JESSIE ANN.—Sch.; 53; Perth, 1826; Reg. Wy., 1860; Owner, Jn. Postgate; Enlarged at Blyth, 1839; Stranded near Boston, Lincolnshire, June, 1864, and sold a wreck.

JEAN.—Bg.; 187; Dumbarton, 1831; Reg. Wy., 1865; Owner, Robt. Brown.

"Jean," Capt., Geo. Readman, at Sunderland, Jan., 1871, being moored in Sunderland harbour, the s.s. "Belmont," which had been broken adrift by the pressure of the great quantity of ice which was going down the river, struck the "Jean," stem on, knocking away the port anchor, and cutting down the bulwark, stanchions, and top sides of the port side. Immediately afterwards the brig "Reindeer," being carried away by the ice, fell athwart the bows of the "Jean," knocking in 8 or 9 planks on the starboard bow and forced her away until about 75 fathoms of mooring chain run out, when she backed astern on to the stones below the tide gage and twisted out the sternpost, broke the lower part of the rudder, and knocked off the after part of the keel. She then swung round clear of the ground to the anchor. The "Reindeer" slipped clear, carrying away with her the bowsprit and jib-boom of the "Jean." Immediately after a French lugger drove down on the port bow, carrying away her own foremast, which, with sail attached, was left athwart the bows of the "Jean." The "Jean" during the time dragged her anchor until she fell alongside the "Cognac Packet" astern, which caused the latter to part, and drive out of the harbour. The "Jean" continued to drag her anchor until abreast of the Polka hole, when the anchor hooked something, the chain parted, and she drove out to sea leaking. A tug towed the vessel in. Next morning laid the vessel on the hard, and got her battened over and tarpaulins nailed over the bows to enable her to be removed to Whitby to dock and repair. Laid a wreck in Whitby harbour till 1875, when she was broken up.

JOHN.—Bg.; 67; Hull, 1799; Reg. Wy., Feb., 1830; Owner, Will Pearson. Sold to Richd., Will and Geo. Cass, 1830. Lost.

JOHNS.—Sch.; 79; Chester, 1805; Reg. Wy., 1837; Owner, Will. Swales, Wy.; Reg. Nwcstl., 1840.

JOHNS.—Sch.; 75; Blyth, 1841; Reg. Wy., 1846; Owner, Jn. Page, Wy. Lost in St. Margaret's Bay, Dover, July, 1849.

JOHNS.—Bg.; 299; Sndld., 1840; Reg. Wy., Jan., 1868. Lost off Yarmouth, Dec., 1872.

JOHN AND HANNAH.—Slp.; 42; Prize, 1810; Reg. Wy., 1810; Owner, Jn. Frank, Wy. Lost, 1813.

JOHN AND MARY.—Slp.; 46; Stcktn., 1785; Reg. Wy., 1807; Owners, Jn. Miller and Jn. Anderson. Lost, 1824, or after.

JOHN AND MARY.—Bn.; 125; Agnes Quay, Durham, 1801; Reg. Wy., 1817; Owners, Geo. Heselton, grocer, and Thos. Tose, mariner; Brig in 1824. Lost at Rye. Reg. cancelled 19th May, 1829.

JOHN AND MARY.—Lug.; Scarbro', 1819; Reg. Wy., 1819; Owner, 1819, Matt Dobson, Runswick. Afterwards schooner; Owner, J. Cook. Sold to Hartlepool, 1863.

JOHN AND ELIZABETH.—Bg.; 144; Sndld., 1849; Reg. Wy., 1863; Owners, Geo. Milburn, 48, Jn. Miller, 16.

"John and Elizabeth," brig, Rotterdam for Aberdeen, with sulphur and hay, took fire by spontaneous combustion off Elie, Fife, Sept., 1868, and was burned to the water's edge. Sank in Largo Bay.

JOHN AND JAMES.—Bg.; $\frac{156}{175}$; Sndld., 1827; Reg. Wy., 1827; Owners, Jn. Smith and James Storm; Owner, 1858, J. H. Storm. Lost at Cape Grisnez, Feb., 1858.

JOHN AND CATHARINE.—Sch.; 103; Hylton, 1830; Reg. Wy., 1830; Owners, Jn. Barry and Matt. Ord. Lost on Hasebro' Sand, 1836, or after.

JOHN AND AMELIA.—Bg.; 75; Lincolnshire, 1811; Reg. Wy., 1837; Owners, Robt. Hutchinson and Co. Lost, 1839, or after.

JOHN AND ELIZA.—Bn.; 127; S. Shields, 1831; Reg. Wy., 1846; Owners, Will Barker and Co.; Reg. Stockton, Jan., 1851.

JOHN AND ALICE BROWN.—Bg.; 212; Sndld., 1851; Reg. Wy., June, 1851; Owner, Alice Brown, Staithes; Owners, 1874, Will Ryder, Lavinia Brown, J. V. Laverick, and Jn. Seymour. Lost on Hasebro' Sand, April, 1876.

JOHN AND JANE.—Bg.; 187; Sndld., 1850; Reg. Wy., 1856; Owners, Bedlingtons, R.H.Bay; owned at Cardiff, 1889; sold to foreigners, Aug., 1890.

JOHN AND ANN.—Sch.; 82; Sndld., 1843; Reg. Wy., 1856; Owner, Will. Simpson, m.m. Lost on the Patch Sand near Yarmouth, Dec., 1860.

JOHN AND ANN.—Bg.; 182; Sndld., 1840; Reg. Wy., 1861; Owners, Geo. Wright and Jn. Leadley. Lost on Lowestoft beach, March, 1869.

JOHN AND WILLIAM.—Sch.; 112; unknown; Reg. Wy., 1861; Owner, Will. Jefferson.

"John and William," Jefferson, Hartlepool for Helsingborg, stranded near Hirtshals, coast of Jutland, 1862. A total wreck.

JOHN AND ISABELLA.—Bg.; 241; Sndld., 1838; Reg. Wy., 1863; Owners, Geo. Russell, of R.H.Bay, and W. Rickinson. Run down off Beachy Head, March, 1868.

JOHN FREDERICK.—Sch.; $\frac{138}{151}$; Sndld., 1831; Reg. Wy., 1837; Owners, Matt. Ord and Elizabeth Smales. Run down off Orfordness, Nov., 1845.

JOHN RICKINSON.—Bg.; 147; Wear, 1838; Reg. Wy., 1838; Owners, Elizabeth and Mary Rickinson, R.H.Bay, and Jn. Rickinson, Whitby, grocer.

Saturday, August 16th, 1851, the "John Rickinson," brig, coal laden, came ashore near Kettleness Steel. Got off next day. Lost in the North Sea about Jan. 26th, 1873.

JOHN BARRY.—Bg.; 235; Sndld., 1830; Reg. Wy., 1839; Owners, Richd. Frankland, smith, Ed. Turner, furniture broker, and W. Foster, publican; Reg. Newcastle, 1845.

JOHN BARKER.—Bg.; 162; Wear, 1839; Reg. Wy., 1839; Owner, Jos. Leng, Whitby, saddler; Owner, 1849, Samuel Andrew, 64. Lost near Aldbrough, Nov., 1855.

JOHN STAGG.—Bg.; 227; Stockton, 1837; Reg. Wy., 1844; Owner, Jn. Poad, R.H.Bay. Abandoned in the North Sea, October, 1851.

J. AND W. PORRITT.—Sch.; 99; Sndld, 1842; Reg. Wy., 1842; Owners, Jn. and Geo. Porritt, Barnby. Lost after 1845.

JOHN GIBSON.—Bg.; 259; Hull, 1842; Reg. Wy., 1850; Owner, Geo. Barrick, Whitby. Missing since Dec., 1860.

JOHN STEWART.—Bg.; 166; Kincardine, 1841; Reg. Wy., 1851; Owner, Jn. Ireland, Whitby. Lost off Harwich, March, 1855.

JOHN HAYES.—Bk.; 310; Lvpl., 1820; Reg. Wy., 1854; Owners, John Harland and Co., Thorpe. Sold as a wreck, 1862.

JOHN MURRAY.—Bg.; 200; Sndld., 1848; Reg. Wy., 1854; Owners, Ed. Corner, James Mutter, and Hen. Robinson; Owners, 1879, Ed. Corner, 32, Ann Stevenson, 32; sold to Hartlepool, March, 1879. Supposed lost in the North Sea, Jan., 1883.

JOHN CUNNINGHAM.—Bg.; 154; Belfast, 1842; Reg. Wy., 1856; Owners, Mark Frampton, Matt. Cummins, and Hugh Henwood Davey; Capt., Will Cummins; Owners, 1859, Matt. Cummins, 32, Maria Pearson, 32. Lost near Orfordness, March, 1861.

JOHN PEDDER.—Bg.; 142; Cork, 1836; Reg. Wy., 1862, from Colchester; Owner, Will. Peck. Lost on the Holm Sand, 29th Aug., 1867.

JOHN RITSON.—Bk.; $\frac{273}{305}$; Maryport, 1848; Owners, Gibson and Kerr. Lost on Mexican coast loading mahogany. Owned at Maryport in 1873.

JOLLY SAILOR.—Bn.; 70; Montrose, 1801; Reg. Wy., 1823; Owner, Henry Atty, jun.; Owners, 1829, Jn.

Thompson, Wy., 32, and Will Booth, parish of Hinderwell, 32. Total wreck at Rye. Reg. cancelled at Rye, May, 1829.

JOSEPH AND ELIZABETH.—Bg.; 209; Sndld., 1839; Reg. Wy., 1841; Owners, Geo. Young Kirby and Jn. Kirby; Owners, 1866, Robt. Kirby, 32, Will Milburn, 32. Lost on the Goodwin Sands, Nov., 1866, Shields for Dunkirk.

JOSEPH AND MARGARET.—Bg.; 200; Hylton, 1862; Reg. Wy., 1866; Owners, Jn. and Richd. Foster.

Struck on the Blanchard Rock, near Sark, Channel Islands, and foundered, 11th Feb., 1887; then owned in the Channel Islands, having been sold there by James Knott and Co., Newcastle.

JOSEPH FENTON.—Bg.; 179; Leith, 1825; Reg. Wy., 1845; Owner, Will Campion, Wy.; Owners, 1850, Joseph Bovill, 32, and James Estill, m.m., 32. Lost at Sherringham, Jan., 1852.

JOHN WICKLIFFE.—S.; $\frac{542}{881}$; Dumbarton, 1841; Reg. Lndn.; Owner, Ed. Corner, Wy., 1853. A missing ship in the Atlantic about 1854.

JOHANNES.—Sch.; 49; Schulan, near Hamburg, 1849; Reg. Wy., 1875; Owner, Jn. Lennard.

Left Brussels for Berwick, 90 tons of bones, 9th Oct., 1874.

"Emu," tug boat, Capt., Francis Davison Forrest, owned by the Whitby Steamboat Co. Monday, 19th Oct., 1874, at 9 a.m., weather fine, wind W., strong breeze, proceeded out of Whitby harbour to cruise for vessels, and about noon, when under Whitby High Lights, observed a schooner bearing East about 6 miles distant, having lost foretopmast, and a smack apparently towing the vessel. At once proceeded to the smack which was towing the ship, afterwards found to be the "Johannes," of Hamburg, Brussels for Berwick, with bones, and asked the smack whether they required assistance.

The master of the smack was then on board the schooner, the remainder of his crew being with him, or in a boat alongside, except one man, who was in charge of the smack, and referred deponent to the master. Deponent then went alongside the schooner and asked whether they wanted assistance, and was informed by the master that the ship was sinking, and that it was no use trying to save her. Deponent observed the mate take up an axe and begin to chop into the deck, and at once jumped on board the vessel and prevented the mate from doing further damage. He found the water within six inches of the forecastle deck, the foretopmast was gone, the head stays and gear cut away, marks of an axe on the foremast, and everything moveable taken to the smack, and the pump gear thrown overboard.

Deponent then tried to make the holes on deck secure, and having seen the mate come out of the forepeak and the water appearing to enter the hatch, he closed it. He then passed a towline from the tug, and towed the ship, being greatly impeded by the mate and fishermen in so doing. Fearing that a fisherman who was steering would run into some other vessel, he set the engineer of the "Emu" to steer, and succeeded in running the vessel on to the sand near Whitby West Pier to prevent her from sinking.

When off Saltwick the mate slipped the tow line, and got into the ship's boat, and, together with the master, rowed to Whitby. Deponent engaged a coble and five men to assist in pumping and getting the ship into harbour, and they continued to work the pump, which they obtained from the "Emu," and to bail until 8.30 p.m., when they towed the ship into the harbour after grounding nearly the entire length of the channel.

The vessel was safely moored, and they were employed in pumping and attending to the ship all night until the 20th, when deponent reported the vessel to the Receiver of Wreck as derelict, and claims £400 for the services of the "Emu" and her crew and a coble and crew.

On examining the vessel he finds two holes in the forepeak, which he believes have been knocked in with the windlass handle, and three holes on deck, one completely through, chopped with an axe, and one of the main hatches drove in and the battens taken off and the foremast chopped with an axe.

Wrecked at Orfordness, Feb., 1880.

JUNO.—Bn; 69; Stockton, 1805; Reg. Wy., 1809; Owner, Hen. Hutton, Whitby; Capt., Walker Tindale; Owner, 1818, Jn. Gill, R.H.Bay; in 1809, 117 tons. Lost 1819.

JUNO.—Bg.; 212; U.S.A., date unknown; Reg. Wy., 1862. Owners, Jos. Steel and James Skerry.

"Juno," Capt., Matt. Steel, and seven hands, left Hamburg, Oct. 28th, 1863, for Newcastle. Proceeded as far as Little Vogel Sands, where we came to anchor, moderate breeze. Tuesday, Oct. 30th, the weather became thick, with strong wind from W.S.W., the ship riding with one anchor. Gave her 70 fathoms of cable and got the starboard anchor ready. At 8.30 let go the starboard anchor and paid out all the port cable with 70 fathoms of starboard cable. The wind was now a complete hurricane.

Found the ship was driving towards the Vogel Sands. Sounded ¼ less 3 on the edge of the Sand. The vessel still driving, we cut away both masts, when the anchors held until 10 p.m., when the port cable parted and soon after the starboard one. The ship then struck the Sand and drove about all night on the Sands until about 6 a.m., when she filled and sank. The sternpost started and rudder unshipped. At 1 p.m. left the ship in the long boat, rowed for three miles, and landed safe at 2 p.m. at Frederick VII. Koog, Holstein. Vessel insured for £950.

JUPITER.—Bg; 147; Sndld., 1817; Reg. Wy., 1832; Owner, Geo. Barrick, Wy.; Owners, 1860, Elizabeth Anderson, Jn. Corney, Jn. Gale, and Thos. Tindale; transferred to H'pool, 1860.

JUNIA.—Sch.; 73; Findhorn, Moray, 1824; Reg. Wy., 1838; Owner, Benj. Tindale, R.H.Bay. Lost, 1841.

JULIA.—Bg; 146; P. Ed. Island, 1848; Reg. Wy., 1855; Owners, Jn. Holliday and Will. Bain, sailmaker.

Lost on the Long Sand, 31st Dec., 1856; Reg. closed, 11th Feb., 1862, Wy. Custom House.

The master, Isaac Wilson, his wife, daughter of Will. Robinson, and a child and Will. Bain, mate, his wife, Sarah Gatenby, and two children, and some of the crew, were drowned. Two only saved. Tombstone Whitby Churchyard says lost 31st May.

JUDITH MILBANK.—Bg.; 199; Sndld., 1837; Reg. Wy., 1855; Owner, Jos. Tindale; Owners, 1872, Jn. and Will. Bedlington. Sunk after collision, off the South West Reach, Oct. 21st, 1874.

JUDITH.—Bk.; 251; Lvpl., 1829; Reg. Wy., June, 1857; Owner, Rich. Wetherill, m.m., 39, Mary Carling, 25. In Messrs. H. and Geo. Barrick's dock at Whitby in 1858, and made brig. Mizen lower mast sold for mainmast of schooner "Oak." Lost on Falsterbo Reef, Baltic, Jan., 1860.

JULIA.—S.; 973; Quebec, 1851; Reg. at Lvrpl.; 160.1 by 31; Owner, Chas. Wright, Wy.; Capt., T. Smailes.

KATE EVELYN.—Bk.; 364; Sndld., 1851; Reg. Wy., 1862; Owners, Richard Verrill, Staithes, 22, Jn. Laverick, 21, Mark Hall, 21.

"Kate Evelyn," Pomaron for London, mineral, sprung a leak, Cape St. Vincent N.N.W., distant

18 miles, 8th December, 1866. Long boat got out and passed astern with crew and master's wife in her; master, mate and boatswain remaining to try and get the ship to land. One a.m. 9th Dec. found the ship settling and abandoned her, when she sank shortly after, about 14 miles from land. Crew saved by the boat.

KATE.—Bn.; 197; P. Ed. Island, 1864; Reg. St. Ives; Owner, Geo. Hopper; Capt., A. Gatenby; Bqtn. later; Foundered off Flambro' Head. Washed ashore further South and became a wreck, Oct., 1889.

KEZIA.—Bg.; 205; Sndld., 1847; Reg. Wy., 1855; Owners, Will Steel and Matt. Storm. Lost at Burntisland, Jan., 1866.

KELLO.—Bg.; 219; Sndld., 1838; Reg. Wy., Jan., 1858; Owners, Mary Parkinson and Jn. and Richd. Foster. Lost in the North Sea, Dec., 1863. Owners, 4th March, 1863, Matt. Scrafton, M'bro, 32, Richd. Foster, 16, Jn. Foster, 16.

KING WILLIAM.—Smk.; 22; Cowes, 1798; Reg. Wy., July, 1849; Owner, Geo. Copley Garbutt; Reg. Exeter, Oct., 1849.

KILBLAIN.—Bk.; 435; Greenock, 1839; Reg. Wy., 1857; Owners, James Sayer, Ed. and J. B. Dale and Levi, P. Mead; Abandoned, Nov., 1860; Owners, July, 1860, Ed. Corner, 32, Hen. Robinson, 16, W. E. Corner, Albert Square, Stepney, 16.

KING GEORGE.—Slp.; 23; Scrbr., 1791; Reg. Wy., 1819; Owner, Jn. King, Wy., m.m.; Owners, 1822, Garbutt Coates Robinson, Robert Coates and Clark Coates, mariners. Lost with all crew, 1822, or after.

KINGFISHER.—Sch.; 61; Sutton, Yorks., 1836; Reg. Wy., 1853; Owners, Stevenson and Eaton, Skinningrove and Lofthouse.

"Kingfisher," Shakeshaft, of Whitby, Newcastle for Lowestoft, coals, lost 29th Oct., 1860, on the Barber Sand. Crew landed in their own boat at Sratby, near Winterton.

KITTY.—Bg.; $\frac{90}{108}$; Stockwith, Notts, 1812; Reg. Wy., 1841; Owners, Robt. Jackson, Will Dotchon and Jonathan Eskdale; Owners, 1848, Francis Dobson, tailor, 22, Will Pearson, m.m., 21, and Joseph Pearson, Middlesbrough, 21. Lost on the coast of Lincolnshire, Oct., 1849.

KITTY.—Bn.; 116; Pwllheli, 1785; Reg. Wy., 1805; Owner, James Cullen, Redcar; Owners, 1825, Thos. Marwood, Rich. Ripley, surgeon, and Richd. Willis. Brig, 169 tons, in 1839. Lost, Oct., 1839.

KITTY.—Slp.; Owner, Fairfoot, Wy.

During a strong breeze on the 3rd Oct., 1860, the sloop "Kitty," coal laden, came to the sand between 12 and 1 o'clock in the day near Lector Nab, and soon became a wreck. The lifeboat got the crew and a woman.

KOH-I-NOOR.—Bk.; 303; Wales, 1852; Reg. Wy., March, 1855; Owners, Hen. Robinson and Edward Corner; Capt. Summerson. Sold to Melbourne, 1863. Liverpool to China, 1860.

LAUREL.—Bn.; 106; Yarmouth, 1790; Reg. Wy., 1797; Owner, Jn. Hudson, Wy.; Reg. Sndld., Dec., 1800.

LAURA.—Bg.; 122; Gattcombeth, 1785; Reg. Wy., 1807; Owner, Will. Dalton, m.m. Lost, 1807, or after.

LAURA.—Bg.; 274; Sndld., 1861; Reg. Wy., April, 1871; Owners, R. K. Smith and Jacob and And. Storm, R.H.Bay. Sold to Norway, 1880

LAVINIA.—Bk.; 249; Stcktn., 1832; Reg. Wy., 1832; Owner, Addison Brown, Staithes; Owners, 1838, Addison Brown, Staithes, 53, and Richd. Brown, Lofthouse, m.m., 11; Reg. Stcktn., March, 1846.

LATONA.—Bg.; 173; Hylton, 1812; Reg. Wy., 1835; Owners, Will. Swales and Jn. Schofield. Reg. Newcastle, May, 1839.

LATONA.—Sch.; 81; Tyne, 1836; Reg. Wy., Oct., 1844; Owner, Jos. Fletcher; Brigantine later; Reg. Faversham, Oct., 1846; Reg. Wy., from Rochester, 18th April, 1853; Owners, 1853, Will. Hill and Matt. Cummins, innkeeper; Owners, 1855, J. K. Hill and Francis Davison Forrest, m.m.; Reg. Yarmouth, 1856.

LANCET.—Bg.; 199; Hylton, 1855; Reg. Wy., Feb., 1873; Owner, Geo. Sinclair Willis. Sold to be broken up, Dec., 1899.

LADY MILNER.—Bn.; $\frac{44}{94}$; Hull, 1790; Reg. Wy., 1804; Owner, Michael Cockerill, Whitby; Owner, 1824, Christ. Granger. Lost, Sept., 1833.

LADY NORMANBY.—Bg.; 236; Deptford, Durham, 1827; Reg. Wy., June, 1827; Owners, Thos. Newton, Barnby, Will Brown, Wy., and Co.; Reg. Lndn., Oct., 1833; Reg. Wy. from Lndn., 26th Feb., 1838; Owners, 1838, Will Brown, 25, Robt. Porritt, Hinderwell, 5, and Thomas Newton, Barnby, 32, Fraction, 2, Wy. Custom House. Lost, 5 miles E.S.E. of Soderham Lighthouse, May 28, 1867.

LADY RIDLEY.—Sch.; 46; Sndld., 1823; Reg. Wy., 1838; Owners, Thos. Watson, Kettleness, and Will Watson, Lythe; Owner, 1861, J. Scarth, Sandsend. Lost in Runswick Bay, Dec., 1863.

LADY NAPIER.—Bg.; 230; N. Scotia, 1843; Reg. Wy., Feb., 1848; Owners, Jn. Corner, 2, W. Rose, 16, and W. E. Corner, 46; Reg. Lndn., Sept., 1848.

LADY BULLER.—Sch.; 50; Salcombe, 1842; Reg. Wy., Feb., 1858; Owner, Will. Sanderson, Whitby. Sold to Goole, 1868.

LADY SALE.—Bk.; 388; Tyne, 1843; Reg. Wy., Nov., 1850; Owner, Thos. Jackson, Wy. Wrecked in Torres Straits, March, 1853. Certificate delivered at Batavia as per letter dated 14th March, 1853.

LADY SANDYS.—Bk.; 300; St. Mary's, Scilly, 1844; Reg. Wy., 1861; Owners, Jn. and Charles Wright; made brig, 28th Feb., 1862; London to Ceylon, 1851; To West Indies, 1860; Abandoned at sea, Dec., 1863. Afterwards sold a wreck at Ameland, Netherlands.

LADY JOCELYN.—Bg.; 259; Lynn, 1847; Reg. Wy., 1857; Owners, James Pearson and Will Pennock; Owners, 1861, Mary Pennock, James Peirson, Jn. Larkin and Geo. Grantham; Owners, 1871, Mary Pennock, 16, James Peirson, 24, Jn. Larkin, 16, and Matt. Thistle, 8; Reg. Sndld., 1872.

LADY STANLEY.—Bg.; 333; S. Shields, 1851; Reg. Wy., April, 1864; Previously Bk.; Female bust removed, 1867; Owner, James Skerry, R.H.Bay. Sold to Hartlepool, 1879.

LADY ANNE.—Bg.; 97; Wells, 1827; Reg. Sndld.; Owner, Will. Peck, Wy.

"Lady Anne," not in Lloyd's list, always in tow when on a voyage; Owner and Capt., Will Peck, and one hand, East Hartlepool for Whitby, with 150 tons of coal, in tow of tug "Cupid," Feb., 1881. When off Runswick, the sea increased in strength, preventing the tug towing so fast. At 8 a.m., 19th Feb., arrived off Whitby, and not seeing any warning signal, was induced to enter. In entering the harbour, and while in tow, took the ground on the West Bar, and owing to a heavy fresh running out, the vessel at once turned athwart. The tug tried to get us out again, but could not.

She struck the pier, tearing her stern and quarter away, the water rushing in, the cargo began to wash out. Assistance was given to haul the mate and myself ashore. I then gave permission for anyone to take the coals as payment for their services. About 7 p.m. the mast fell, and the ship soon broke. Part of the bow and of the bottom now lying in the channel.

LANCASHIRE LASS.—Sch.; 88; Ilfracombe, 1836; Owners, Danby and Lennard, Wy.; In Boghall Dock, Sept., 1891; A missing ship; Capt. Porritt.

LEITH PACKET.—Slp.; 35; Leith, 1771; Reg. Wy., 1800; Owner, Jn. Walker, Wy. Lost, 1805, or after.

LEVERET.—Bg.; 150; Sndld., 1819; Reg. Wy., 1824; Owner, Thos. Hay. Lost.

LEVERET.—Sch.; 191; Sndld., 1839; Reg. Wy., April, 1848; Owners, Ann and Christ. Harrison; Afterwards a brig; Owners, 1855, Isaac Gale, m.m., 22, Christ. Harrison, 21, and Jn. Weighill, 21; Capt., E. Clark. Lost on Sherringham Shoal, March, 1867.

LEEDS.—Bn.; 111; Stockwith, Notts, 1815; Reg. Wy., 1828; Owners, W. Clark, Humphrey Orran, and Ann Dawson, all Runswick; Owner, 1849, Joseph Bovill, 64. Lost off Sndld., Dec., 1849.

LEVANT.—Bg.; 165; Maryport, 1809; Reg. Wy., 1831; Owner, Geo. Barrick. Lost. Reg. cancelled Sept., 1844.

LEVANT.—Bg.; 210; Dundee, 1853; Reg. Wy., May, 1865; Owner, Smith Stainthorpe, R.H.Bay. Previously owned at London, 1862. Sold to the Tyne, 1880. Totally lost off Egmond, Holland, 5th Sept., 1884. Reg. lost with the vessel.

LEANDER.—Bg.; 190; Sndld., 1817; Reg. Wy., 1833; Owner, Thos. Wright; Owners, 1837, T. Wright, 32, James Willkinson, 32. Lost at Cromer. Reg. cancelled 28th Jan., 1841.

LEO.—Bg.; 205; Maryport, 1839; Reg. Wy., 1855; Owners, James Sayer, Levi P. Mead, Joseph B. and Ed. Dale. Lost on the coast of Jutland, March, 1856.

LEVEN.—Sch.; 33; Stockton, 1828; Reg. Wy., 1861; Owner, George Fairfoot. Sold to W. H'pool, 1876. Dismantled and sold for a lighter, March, 1877.

LEDA.—Bg.; 202; Dundee, 1828; Reg. Wy., 1865; Owner, Ed. Storm, R.H. Bay.

"Leda," Champley, master, coal laden for Stockholm, lost on the Kopparstend. The crew were saved by the Norwegian brig "St. Olaf," except the mate, who died. The master had his leg broken. Sept., 1871.

LEONARD DOBBIN.—Bk.; 611; Quebec, 1837; Owner, Wilkinson.

Capt. Wm. Foxton died in this vessel when off the Shear Light on passage to Gottenborg, Nov., 1856.

LIBERALITY.—Bn.; 216; Sndld., 1812; Reg. Wy., 1816; Owner, Will Usherwood.

Bound to Quebec, sprung a leak and was accidentally burnt in the Atlantic, April 15, 1825. Crew carried to Quebec.

LIZZIE.—Smk.; 37; Goole, 1855; Reg. Wy., 1859; Owner, Will. Wright, Abbey Farm; Owner, 1869, Jn. Rowland, 64. Lost on Woolcot Beach, Oct., 1882. Crew drowned.

LIGO.—Bg.; 118; Wear, 1829; Reg. Wy., 1834; Owners, Paul Stokill and Moses Ligo; Owners, 1856, Joseph Shaw, m.m., 32, Jn. Groves, 32; Owners, 1864, J. Shaw, 32, and And. Chapman, 32; Reg. Lowestoft, 1865.

LITTLE HENRY.—Slp.; 62; Stockton, 1835; Reg. Wy., 1835; Off. No. 8981; Owners, Addison Brown and Ralph Sanderson, both of Staithes. Sold to H'pool, 1864, by Ant. Jackson. Lost near Sunderland, Nov. 20, 1879.

LIBERTY.—Bg.; 152; Poole, 1819; Reg. Wy., 1838; Owner, Will Todd, R.H. Bay.

"Liberty," Todd, lost at Warberg, Sweden, 9th Sept., 1870.

LIBRA.—Bg.; 291; Dundee, 1845; Reg. Wy., 1854; Owners, Thos. Brown and Co., Staithes; Reg. Sndld., 1861.

LIVELY.—Bg.; 182; Blythnook, 1817; Reg. Wy., 1826; Owner, Will Cavillier, cabinet maker. Lost, 1831 or after.

LINDA.—Bk.; 242; Foreign, date unknown; Reg. Wy., 1855; Owner, Will. Raw.

Foreign name "Maruela" and Bill of Sale dated Aug. 20, 1855, now produced in favour of Wm. Raw, jun., from Fred Huth and Co., of Lvrpl., in pursuance of power of attorney from Saucher Hermaus, dated at Valparaiso 12th Oct., 1854, and produced this day.

Lost near Yarmouth, Oct., 1860.

LINDISFARNE.—Sch.; 75; Fisherrow, Edinburgh, 1831; Reg. Wy., 1856; Owners, T. Turnbull, jun., Matt. Gray, Brown Marshall, and Sam. Andrew; Capt., Jn. Gatenby; Owners, April, 1866, J. B. Nicholson, 22, Sarah Ann Westgarth, 42. Lost near the Kentish Knock, June, 1867.

"Lindisfarne," owned by Richard Verrill, of Staithes, and others, Faversham to Port Mulgrave, Feb. 18, 1861, there being too much sea to enter Port Mulgrave, was being towed to Whitby when the tow rope broke and the vessel drove on to the beach at Whitby. Re-floated.

LIGHT AND SIGN.—Bg.; 161; Sndld., 1845; Reg. Wy., 1863; Owner, Isaac Seymour, Kettleness. Wrecked on Palling Beach, Oct., 1882. Crew drowned.

LIZZIE BARRY.—Bk.; 498; Hylton, 1875; Reg. Wy., Sept., 1875; Owners, J. H. Barry, 24, James Gardner, James Maul, and Jn. and Robt. Robinson, Mickleby. Sold foreign, May, 1887.

LLEWELLYN.—Bg.; 262; Teignmouth, 1841; Reg. Wy., 1866; Owners, Jn. Brown Cole, Staithes, 32; Will. Thompson, 32. Lost near Archangel, July, 1867.

LOUISA.—Bg.; $\frac{104}{122}$; Sndld., 1809; Reg. Wy., 1830; Owner, Jn. Tose, m.m., Whitby; Owner, 1847, W. Moorsom, R.H. Bay. Lost at Caistor, near Yarmouth, Nov., 1852.

LOUISA.—Bg.; 149; Sndld., 1817; Reg. Wy., 1830; Owner, Geo. Barrick, Wy. Lost at Holderness, Nov., 1852.

LOUISA.—Bg.; 235; Sndld., 1852; Reg. Wy., 1853; Owners, Sam Flintoft and Will. Gale; Owners, 1871, Isaac Gale, 18, Jn. Crowe Gale, 7, Dorothy Ann Gale 7, Will Ward 16, and Hen. Burton, m.m., 16. Lost with all hands in the great gale of March 19-20, 1874, in the North Sea.

LONDON.—Bg.; 138; Sndld., 1817; Reg. Wy., Aug., 1835; Owner, Jn. Mennell, R.H. Bay. Lost near Aldbro', 1852.

LONDON.—Bg.; 185; Mevagissy, Cornwall, 1826; Reg. Wy., 1850; Owners, Peter Hawksfield and Co. Lost, July, 1851.

LORD EXMOUTH.—Sch.; 25; Lowestoft, 1816; Reg. Wy., 1857; Owner, Joseph Bovill; Owner, 1863, Philip Elliott, R.H. Bay, 64. Lost, 1863.

LORD GOUGH.—Bg.; 211; N. Brunswick, 1849; Reg. Wy., Aug., 1857; Owners, Ed. Corner, Joseph Jackson, Jn. Yeoman, and Elizabeth Wood, 16 each; Owners, 1862, Ed. Corner, 24, Jn. Yeoman, 24, and Elizabeth Wood, of Hunstanton, 16. Sold to foreigners, Feb., 1874.

LOWESTOFT MERCHANT.—Sch.; 61; Southtown, Suffolk, 1834.

In collision and put ashore on the South Cheek, R.H. Bay, April, 1874. Got off and brought into Whitby.

Lost off Lossiemouth and all hands. Owner, Leonard Leng, Whitby.

LUCERNE.—Bg.; 263; Sndld., 1840; Reg. Wy., 1842; Owners, Will Thompson, Sarah Nesfield, and Dorothy Wilson.

"Lucerne," Capt. Sinclair, was abandoned in the North Sea about 20 miles off the Texel, Jan., 1863. Crew taken to Yarmouth.

LUCY AND MARY.—Bg.; 74; Sndld., 1807; Reg. Wy., 1843; Owners, Will and Matt Wright; Owners, 1846, Peter Hawksfield, 43, and Thos. Bingham, Kent, coal merchant, 21. Lost near the Kentish Knock, Aug., 1849.

LUNA.—Bg.; 248; N. Scotia, 1827; Reg. Wy., 1858; Owners, Trattles and Co. Lost off Leba, Baltic, Nov., 1864.

LUCY.—Bg.; 190; Sndld., 1851; Reg. Wy., 1866; Owner, Jn. Harrison, R.H. Bay; Owner, March, 1881, Jos. Peacock, W. H'pool, 64. Lost on the Gunfleet Sand, Feb., 1882.

LUTTERWORTH.—S.; 883; H'pool, 1868; Reg. Lndn.; Owners, James Gray and Co.

LYRA.—Bg.; 194; Greenock, 1839; Reg. Wy., 1856; Owners, Geo. Young Kirby and Jn. Younghusband; Owners, Feb., 1865, Jos. Bovill, 48, Will Nelson, 16; Owners, 1866, Joseph Bovill, 48, and James Strong, S. Shields, 16. Lost off Egmoudzee, Aug., 1868.

MARY.—S.; 240; Scarbro', 1788; Reg. Wy., 1797; Owners, Mich. and Robt. Cockerill; afterwards a brig; Capt., Will Stonehouse; Reg. Hull, 1799.

MARY.—Bn.; 149; Conway, 1789; Reg. Wy., 1805; Owners, Gideon Smales and Ingram Eskdale, shipbuilders. Sold to foreigners.

MARY.—Slp.; 32; Howdon Dyke, 1800; Reg. Wy., 1810; Owner, Jonathan Oyston, Wy.; Owner, 1825, Christ. Thompson; Capt., Thos. Coulson; Reg. Nwcstl., 1831.

MARY.—Bn.; 147; Swansea, 1784; Reg. Wy., 1811; Owner, James Hutchinson, Wy. Lost, 1822 or after.

MARY.—Slp.; 50; Prize, 1813; Reg. Wy., 1813; Owner, Oct., 1813, Ed. Wilson, Wy., carpenter; Foreign name "Trende Soskende." Condemned at Hull, Aug. 23, 1813; Owner, 1847, Anth. Jackson.

Ashore and broken up at Staithes, Oct., 1857.

MARY.—Galliot; 44; A prize, March, 1813; Called "Ebenezer"; Owner, 1813, Geo. Miller; Capt., Robt. Jackson; Lengthened 1815 to Schooner, 67 tons; Owner, 1834, Jn. Wilson, Wy., 64; Owner, Feb., 1844, Richd. Purvis, 64. Lost at Bacton, Norfolk, June, 1869.

MARY.—Slp.; 41; Sndld., 1787; Reg. Wy., May, 1791; Owner, Jn. Welburn, R.H. Bay; Reg. Greenock, June, 1798.

MARY.—Slp.; 71; Stockwith, 1808; Reg. Wy., March, 1822; Owner, Jn. Sayers, East Row; Owner, 1825, Zachariah Knaggs. Lost, 1827.

MARY.—Bn.; 137; Gainsborough, 1798; Reg. Wy., 1822; Owner, Thos. Clark, Runswick; Owners, 1826, Geo. Heselton, grocer, 22, Jn. Tose, m.m., 21, James Wood, m.m., 21. Lost; Reg. cancelled, March, 1835.

MARY.—Bg.; 87; Sndld., 1817; Reg. Wy., 1826; Owners, Will Sanderson and Dan. Robinson; Reg. at Cley, Jan., 1838.

MARY.—Bg.; 125; Hylton, Durham, 1798; Reg. Wy., 1826; Owners, W. and C. Storm, R.H. Bay; Owners, 1838, J. Todd, Staithes, 48, J. Harland, R.H. Bay, 16; Reg. Stockton, 1840.

MARY.—Bg., then Bn.; 62; Yarmouth, 1817; Reg. Wy., 1838; Owner, Jn. Hardy, Wy., cordwainer; Owner, 1851, Thos. Jackson. Lost on Middleton Sand, H'pool, Sept., 1860.

MARY.—Slp.; 38; Stockton, 1825; Reg. Wy., 1840; Owner, Hen. Attley, coal merchant; Owner, 1841, Jn. Agar, 64. Lost.

MARY.—Slp.; 22; N. Shields, 1833; Reg. Wy., 1840; Owners, Thos. and Richd. Wright; Reg. Stockton, 1843.

MARY.—Bg.; 233; Sndld., 1826; Reg. Wy., 1842; Owner, Thos. Clark, Runswick; Owners, 1849, Andrew Clark, 32, James Clark, 16, and Will. Hardy, Runswick, 16.

Sept. 25, 1851, about 5 p.m., the wind flew round and blew a gale, quickly raising a heavy sea. The brig "Mary," of Whitby, coal laden, was riding at anchor, but soon came to the sand near the Battery Steps and became a wreck.

MARY.—Slp.; 51; Newbegin, Yorks., 1841; Reg. Wy., 1847; Owners, Will Frankland, Hen. Simpson, Wy., and Jn. Watson, Pickering; afterwards Whitby Stone Co. Lost at Palling, Sept., 1852.

MARY.—Bg.; 161; Sndld., 1847; Reg. Wy., June, 1847; Owners, Richd. Wilson and Thos. Rickinson, Whitby; Owners, 1852, T. Rickinson, 43, Chas. Wilson, draper, 21.

"Mary," owner, Thos. Rickinson, Capt. Will Rickinson, Seaham for Dunkirk, Oct., 1869, sprung a leak, and the crew, being unable to keep her off a lee shore, ran her aground 1½ miles West of Gravelines harbour.

MARY.—Bg.; 171; Yarmouth, 1826; Reg. Wy., 1855; Owners, Ed. Storm, Will Baxter, and Thos. Jameson; Owners, 1869, Mary A. Hartley, Geo. Hartley and Co. Lost on the island of Bornholm, 10th Nov., 1869.

MARY.—Bg.; 181; Alloa, 1845; Reg. Wy., 1877; Owner, James Page; Owner, 1879, Will Frankland. Run down off Dover, April, 1881.

MARYS.—Bg.; 109; Southwick, Durham, 1839; Reg. Wy., 1839; Owner, Jn. Barry, Whitby, shipwright, and Jn. Prowse, Kent. Lost, 1841.

MARYS.—Bg.; 209; Dundee, 1838; Reg. Wy., July, 1851, Owners, Jos. Tindale and Jn. Hall Leng.

Jan. 4, 1854, a strong breeze from the East. In the evening the brig "Marys," of Whitby, coal laden, came to the sand beyond Lector Nab. Refloated later.

Owner, 1872, Nathan Hewson, 48, Thos. Avery, 16. Lost off Aldbro', Oct., 1881.

MARYS.—Sch.; 126; Selby, 1839; Reg. Wy., Sept., 1861; Owner, Thos. Mills, R.H. Bay. Abandoned in a sinking state 50 miles from the Spurn, Nov., 1863.

MARYS.—Bg.; 150; Dundee, 1849; Reg. Wy., 1864; Owner, Matt. Peacock, who sold her to Newcastle in 1875. Stranded and total loss at Falmouth, 22nd Oct., 1880.

MARYS AND ANN.—Sch.; 84; Fifeshire, 1831; Reg. Wy., 1856; Owners, T. Turnbull, Matt. Gray, Brown Marshall and Samuel Andrew. Lost with all hands, Jan., 1857.

MARIA.—S.; 310; Scarbro', 1793; Reg. Wy., 1802; Owners, Hen. Noddings, m.m., and Jos. and Jn. Addison; Reg. Nwcstl., Jan., 1808.

MARIA.—Sch.; 82; Place and date unknown; Reg. Wy., April, 1866; Owners, Geo. Laverick, sen. and jun. Broken up, July, 1880.

MARY STOWE.—Bg.; 200; Gloucester, 1861; Reg. Wy., 1881; Owners, Thos. Pritchard and Geo. and Will Hopper; Owners, 1893, Geo. Hopper, 24, Will Hopper, 20. Stranded and became a total wreck on Corton Beach, Norfolk, March, 1897.

MARY ANN.—Bn.; 105; Workington, 1780; Reg. Wy., 1816; Owner, Walker Tindall, R.H. Bay. Lost, 1818.

MARY ANN.—Bg.; 142; Wear, 1813; Reg. Wy., March, 1819; Enlarged, 1822, to 177 tons; Owner, Nathaniel Langborne. Lost, 1830.

MARY ANN.—Bg.; 191; Hylton, 1830; Reg. Wy., May, 1830; Owner, Jn. Storer, Wy., grocer; Reg. Nwcstl., 1833.

MARY ANN.—Sch.; 34; Southtown, 1811; Reg. Wy., 1837; Owner, Will. Smith, Wy.; Owner, 1840, Jn. Agar, Wy., 64. Lost, 1840.

MARY ANN.—Bg.; 216; Coxgreen, Durham, 1841; Reg. Wy., 1848; Owners, Sampson Storm and Jn. Corner and Co.; Owners, 1863, S. Storm, 22, J. Corner and Ed. Corner, and Christ. Harrison, 21 jointly, and Mercy Harrison, 21; Owner, 1864, J. K. Hill, 64. Lost off Cromer, Dec., 1869.

MARY AND ANN.—Slp.; 33; Scarbro', 1816; Owners, 1836, Jn. Wright, 32, Richd. Wright, 32; Reg. cancelled, vessel lost off Staithes, Custom House, Wy., 16th Sept., 1866; Off. No. 8925.

MARY AND ANN.—Lug.; 55; Scarbro', 1799; Reg. Wy., 1824; Owner, Robt. Ward, Staithes, 64. Lost, 1835.

MARY AND ANN.—Slp.; Scarbro', date unknown; 22 tons; Owner, Will Hutchinson; Capt., Isaac Marshall; Off. No. 8902.

"Mary and Ann," owned by W. Hutchinson, Isaac Marshall, master, and one hand, left Middlesbrough 1st June, 1860, at noon. Light breeze at W. Saturday, 2nd, weather stormy, thick with rain, wind E.N.E. fresh. When off Whitby sprung a leak. Set the pumps on and kept continually pumping. About 9 p.m., the vessel having reached towards the land, saw one of the Whitby High Lights. Told the man at the helm to put it down. Attempted to ware the vessel, but being too near the land she came to the ground near the West Bar. The coastguard boat then came off, and the crew were landed on the beach. Expected to become a total wreck. Not insured.

MARY ELIZA.—Bn.; 127; P. Ed. Island, 1845; Reg. Wy., 1848; Owners, Jos. Harrison, m.m., Elizabeth and Jn. Andrew; Owner, 1869, Matt. Tinley, 64.

"Mary Eliza," owner Matt. Tinley, Hartlepool for London, coals, struck on Kettleness Steel, Aug., 1869, during a thick fog about 7.30 a.m. on the 27th.

Lost in the North Sea, 1872.

MARY DICK.—Bg.; 162; Fraserburgh, 1840; Reg. Wy., March, 1848; Owners, Benj. Garminsway, Richd. Moon, m.m., and Francis Knaggs. Run down off the Dudgeon light, Dec., 1849.

MARY MITCHESON.—Bg.; 277; Sndld., 1836; Reg. Wy., 1849; Owners, Thos. and Geo. Harrison, R.H. Bay. Sold to Lndn., 1866. To St. Heliers, Jersey, in 1871. To Falmouth in 1873. Sold to foreigners at W. H'pool, Nov., 1873, and the register closed at Whitby.

MARY CLARK.—Bg.; 177; Sndld., 1845; Reg. Wy., 1860; Owners, Ed. Wood, Whitby, and Thos. Day, Hartlepool; Reg. W. H'pool, 1864.

MARY ANT.—Sch.; 50; Hull, 1832; Reg. Wy., 1862; Owners, Sam. Andrew, T. Anderson, T. Smales, and James Andrew; Owners, 1864, T. Anderson, 32, T. Smales, 24, R. J. Milestone, 8; Reg. Grimsby, 1869.

MARY BRACK.—Bg.; 294; Sndld., 1838; Reg. Wy., Feb., 1866; Owners, Jn. Wilson, 32, Jn. Yeoman, 16, Ann Pressick, 16. Sold to foreigners, Feb., 1872.

MARY YOUNG.—Bg.; 258; Shields, 1832; Owner, Matt. Todd, R.H. Bay, 1867.

MARY LOUISA.—Bk.; 321; Hylton, 1850; Reg. Wy., Feb., 1871; Owners, Robt. Gibson and Jn. Kerr; Reg. Lvrpl., Oct., 1877.

MARY AND AGNES.—Bg.; 174; Sndld., 1842; Reg. Wy., 1853; Owner, Will. Baxter, R.H. Bay; made brigantine; Reg. Scarbro', 1879.

"Mary and Agnes," registered at Scarborough, owned by Will Baxter, of Alpha Villa, Falsgrave, Scarborough, master, Thos. Pearson, London for Newcastle, scrap iron, got embayed, and could not work off the land on either tack, and with sails blown away came ashore at Whitby, Oct. 24, 1885.

MARY AND EMILY.—Bg.; 203; Middlesbrough, 1853; Reg. Wy., March, 1866; Owner, Christ. Moorsom, R.H. Bay. Sold to D. T. Sharper, West H'pool, Nov., 1888.

MARY AND ELIZABETH.—Bk.; 326; Sndld., 1858; Reg. Wy., 1863; Owner, Francis Robinson.

"Mary and Elizabeth," Capt. Robt. Greenbury and ten hands, Thos. Oxley Boyes, mate. Left Cardiff 9th Nov., 1868, for Syra, 545 tons of coals. At 10 a.m. passed Lundy. On the 20th Nov., at 4 p.m., passed Cape St. Vincent. On the 22nd Nov., blowing a gale from S.W. and thick with rain, saw a light supposed to be Cape Trafalgar. At 8 p.m. tacked to W.N.W., and at 11 p.m. tacked to S.E. At 2.30 a.m. on the 23rd saw the same light at intervals, being thick with rain. At 4 a.m. the light bore E. by N. distant about 8 miles. The vessel heading S.E. by S. At 5.15 a.m. the vessel struck the ground. Put the helm hard down, but the vessel would not answer her helm. At daylight found we were 6 miles South of Cape Spartel, Africa. About 7 a.m. launched a boat. Master and five of crew got in, and when about 50 yards from the vessel the boat capsized, all being drowned. About 11 a.m. the mate and four hands left the vessel in the long boat, and succeeded in reaching the shore. On the 25th Nov. mate and four hands left for Tangier, the vessel then a wreck, and sold for 400 Spanish dollars. Six drowned, 5 saved. Thought the wreck was occasioned by Cape Spartel light being mistaken for Cape Trafalgar, the weather being so thick with rain.

MARGARET.—Bg.; 145; Sndld., 1825; Reg. Wy., 1837; Owners, Thos. and Mary Foxton and Will. Barker. Lost, Feb., 1843.

MARGARET.—Sch.; 64; Leith, 1809; Reg. Wy., 1841; Owner, James Sneaton, m.m. Missing since Nov., 1849.

MARGARET.—Sch.; 101; Arbroath, 1830; Reg. Wy., 1844; Owner, Benj. Gales; Owner in 1846, Richd. Gibson Gales, 64.

MARGARET.—Bg.; $\frac{137}{182}$; Pembroke, 1818; Reg. Wy., 1846; Owners, Will Dotchon, James Sayer and Geo. Hopper; Owner in 1855, J. Milburn.

Abandoned in the North Sea, Jan., 1863, 120 miles from Flambro'. Crew landed at Grimsby.

MARGARET.—Bg.; 175; Sndld., 1825; Reg. Wy., 1846; Owner, Jos. Brown and Co. Sold to Rye, August, 1871.

MARGARETS.—Smk.; 16; Ferryport, 1828; Reg. Wy., 1837; Owner, Will Booth, Borrowby; Owner in 1839, Robt. Linsey, 64; Reg. at Wisbech, 1839.

MARGARETS.—Bg.; 236; Hylton, 1837; Reg. Wy., 1864; Owners, Geo. Stevenson and Co. Wrecked at Bidding, S. Coast of Sweden, Dec., 1875.

MARGARETS.—Sch.; $\frac{112}{92}$; Wthrn., 1839; Owner, R. Lawrie, Wy., 1854; Capt. Cumming.

MARGARET AND JANE.—Galliot, prize; 67 tons; Reg. Wy., 1812; Owner, T. T. Granger, R.H.Bay. Lost.

MARGARET AND ELIZABETH.—Slp.; 28; Sndld., 1834; Reg. Sndld.; Owner, C. J. Horner, Tunstall, Stafford; Capt., George Corner. Total wreck near Port Mulgrave, Aug., 1874.

MARGARET SOPHIA.—Bg.; 178; Sndld., 1842; Reg. May, 1846; Owner, Jn. Trattles, Staithes. Lost off Heligoland, Aug., 1859.

MARGARET RAIT.—Bk.; 308; N. Brunswick, 1831; Reg. Wy., 1844; T. and Jn. Marwood. Lost at the Lewis Islands, Dec., 1851.

MARGARET PRYDE.—Bg.; 288; N. Scotia, 1849; Reg. Wy., April, 1857. Lost off Heligoland, April, 1861.

MARGARET NIXON.—Bg.; 188; Tyne, 1861; Reg. Wy., March, 1876; Owners, Matt. Peacock and Jn. Wallis.

This vessel, now owned by Messrs. Isaac and Jn. Mills and Co., of R.H.Bay, is the last brig registered at Whitby.

Mr. W. M. Dawson, writing to the "Whitby Gazette," says:—"Having joined the 'Margaret Nixon' as a boy apprentice in 1861, passed 5½ years, less 21 days holiday, in her. She was a smart vessel in those days, had a gilt streak all round her, a full figure head, and carried royal yards.

Mr. Will Fletcher, of Whitby, commanded this brig for nearly 30 years.

MARGARET CUNNINGHAM.—Sch.; 40; Inverkeithing, 1824; Reg. Wy., 1859; Owners, Jn. Smith, mariner, and Jn. Cross, blacksmith; Owners in 1863, T. Anderson, 32, and James Andrew, 32. Wrecked at Cat Beck, Kettleness, near Whitby, July, 1868.

MARGARET ELIZABETH.—Bg.; 295; S. Stockton, 1852; Reg. Wy., 1866; Owners, Will. Dale, Jn. Weighill and Richd. Brown. Sold, Dec. 20, 1871, to Mr. Page for £1,450. Owners in 1877, James Page, 24, Will. Frankland, 40.

Condemned as unseaworthy, and sold to be broken up in Aug., 1879.

MARTHA KAY.—Bk.; 337; Sndld., 1853; Reg. Wy., 1864; Owners, Sam. Andrew, 32, J. V. Andrew, 8, Ann, Sam. and Isabella Vickers Andrew, and James Gray, 16 jointly, and James Good, 8. Lost, Lat. 29.22 N., Long. 40.30 W., July, 1868.

MARTIN.—Bg.; 115; Selby, 1790; Reg. Wy., March, 1824; Owners, Hen., Frank and Thos. Ayre. Lost, Dec., 1833.

MARTIN.—Slp.; 68; Selby, 1785; Reg. Wy., Oct., 1797; Owner, Christ. Richardson; Reg. Leith, 1800, or after.

MARTHA.—Bn.; 123; Appledore, 1819; Reg. Wy., July, 1865; Owners, James Terry, 22, Thos. White, Seaham, 42. Sold to foreigners, Dec., 1874.

MATCHLESS.—Bg.; 133; Bridport, 1810; Reg. Wy., 1837; Owner, Geo. Barrick; Owned at Seaham in 1866. Wrecked near Hornsea, March, 1883.

MANTURA.—Bg.; 216; Wear, 1826; Reg. Wy., 1826; Owner, Francis Dobson, Mickleby; Owners in 1831, Thos. Anderson, miller, 32, and Cornelius Clark, of Lythe, farmer, 32. Lost.

MARWOOD.—Bg.; 224; Wear, 1835; Reg. Wy., 1835; Owners, Jn. Marwood, Geo. Marwood, ship chandler, Thos. Marwood, m.m., and Fran. Pickernell, engineer; Reg. Sndld., 1853.

MALTA.—Bg.; 144; Sndld., 1822; Reg. Wy., 1836; Owners, Storm and Co., R.H.Bay; Owners in 1854, David Gullon Pinkney, 32, Thos. Pinkney, 32; Reg. Colchester, 1854.

MAGDALANE.—Slp.; 33; Dundee, 1777; Reg. Wy., 1837; Owner, Jos. Bovill, Wy. Lost, 1838.

MATILDA.—Bg.; 211; Sndld., 1828; Reg. Wy., 1837; Owner, Geo. Clark. Lost, 1844.

MATILDA.—Bg.; 141; Hull, 1818; Reg. Wy., 1858; Owners, James and Geo. Estill. Lost off the Dudgeon, Sept., 1863.

MARSINGALE.—Bg.; 247; Sndld., 1839; Reg. Wy., 1839; Owners, Will. Frankland, banker, Thos. Wright, James Wilkinson, and Will. Marsingale Wilkinson, Manchester. Lost near Cromer, Jan., 1855.

MALTON.—Bg.; 231; Middlesbrough, 1839; Reg. Wy., 1843; Owner, Will. Cavillier. Lost, 1844.

MALVINA.—Bg.; 186; Hythe, S'thampton, 1825; Reg. Wy., 1848; Owners, Isaac Calvert, Runswick, and Jn. Clark, H'pool. Broken up, 1879. Owned at Hartlepool then.

MALVINA.—Bk.; 249; P. Ed. Island, 1846; Reg. Wy., 1850; Owners, Brown and Co.; Owners, 1852, April 21st, Will Gales, 32, James Brown, 32. Lost, Long Island Reach, New York, April 21, 1852.

MAGNIFIC.—Bg.; 242; Stcktn. 1850; Reg. Wy., July, 1850; Owners, James Hindson, Ugthorpe, and Jn. Newton, Hinderwell, and Will Brown, of Staithes; Reg. M'bro., 1861.

MANCHESTER.—Bg.; 111; Thorne, Yorks., 1819; Reg. Wy., 1851; Owners, Jos. Harland, of Gillamoor, and Jonathan Andrew, Wy., m.m. Sold to Woodbridge, 1865.

MARION.—Sch.; 88; Montrose, 1843; Reg. Wy., 1852; Owner, Jn. Goodill; Reg. Hartlepool, 1855.

MARIOUPOL.—Bg.; 267; Sndld., 1853; Reg. Wy., April, 1853; Owner, Marwood. Lost in the Dardanelles.

MAYFLOWER.—Bg.; 112; Scrbr., 1818; Reg. Wy., Sept., 1862; Owners, Will. Potter Bovill, 16, Will Hall, 16, Ed. Corner, 16, and J. Bovill, 16. Sunk off Scrbr., Aug. 11, 1866, Shields for Zuider Zee.

MAYFLOWER.—326; Owner, Hen. Barrick, Wy., 1853.

MARIQUITA.—Bk.; 329; Foreign, date unknown; Reg. Wy., 1864; Owners, Geo. Wright, York, 48, Jn. Leadley, Wy., 16; Owner, 1869, Geo. Wright, 64. Sold foreign, 1871.

MALCOLM.—Bk.; 277; P. Ed. Island, 1856; Reg. Wy., April, 1868; Owners, Jos. Bovill, James Thompson and Geo. Graham; Owner, 1869, Jos. Bovill, 64. Sold foreign, July, 1872.

MANDARIN.—Bk.; 785; Quebec, 1864; Reg. Wy., Sept., 1864; Owner, Thos. Marwood. Sold to Gloucester, Aug., 1880. Round stern; Head a scroll.

MAGGIE.—Bk.; 292; Ilfracombe, 1852; Reg. Wy., March, 1870; Owner, Geo. Russell, R.H.Bay. Sold to Holland, March, 1882.

MATTHEWS.—Bn.; 83; Tyne, 1803; Reg. Wy., 1822; Owners, Jn. Fenwicks and Co.; 59.3 by 18.5; Reg. cancelled Nov., 1825. Vessel broken up on Whitby beach.

MATER DEI.—Ketch; 49; Dunkirk, date unknown; Reg. Llanelly; Owners, R. H. Burnett and Co., Wy., 1905.

MAESE.—Bg.; 206; Yarmouth, 1841; Reg. Hartlepool; Owners, Emerson and Barnard, R.H.Bay; In Whitehall Dock in 1875.

MERCURY.—Bn.; 101; Sndld., 1785; Reg. Wy., 1800; Owners, Benj. Tindale and Jn. Walker, farmer; Owner in 1832, Richd. Robinson, R.H.Bay. Lost in 1833.

MEANWELL.—Bg.; 116; Blythnook, 1821; Reg. Wy., 1832; Owner, Thos. Barker; Owner in 1835, Geo. Barrick, 64. Lost, 1836.

MEANS.—Bg.; 99; Thorne, Yorks., 1803; Reg. Wy., 1836; Owner, Robt. Goodill, Wy., m.m. Lost, Dec., 1837.

MEDUSA.—Bg.; $\frac{158}{168}$; Sndld., 1816; Reg. Wy., 1837; Owners, Jn. Schofield, 48, and Jn. Walker, 16. Lost, 1839.

MEAD.—Bg.; 198; Wear, 1847; Reg. Wy., June, 1847; Owners, J. B. B. Mead, W. E. Corner and Mark Weighill; Reg. Lndn., 1855.

MEMPHIS.—Bk.; 327; N. Brunswick, 1856; Reg. Wy., April, 1871; Owners, Thos. and Hannah Wood. Total wreck on island of Bornholm, April, 1884.

MEDORA.—Bg.; 201; Sndld., 1845; Reg. Wy., Jan., 1856; Owners, Robt. Simpson Adamson, 32, Ann Adamson, 16, and F. K. Robinson, 16; Owner in 1868, Constable Cassap, 64.

During a heavy gale from the East, Jan. 4th, 1857, came ashore, light, at Lector Nab. Re-floated later.

"Medora," owner and captain, C. Cassap, Hartlepool for Cronstadt, 18th July, 1870. Aug. 1st brought up in Copenhagen roads, 4th proceeded with variable winds and rough weather till 30th, when about 30 miles N. of Dagerort, Gulf of Finland, at 10 p.m. was struck by a heavy sea, doing much damage and causing the vessel to leak some two or three feet per hour. Men constantly pumping. At 8 a.m., 31st Aug., made Fillsand S., distant 4 miles. Drifting towards the reef near Fillsand left the pumps to make sail, and cleared the reef, but the vessel having 2½ feet water in her and the crew exhausted, ran her ashore about 5 p.m. on N. end of island of Oesel. Total wreck. Landed in ship's boat. Insured for £800.

MEDORA.—Bk.; 211; N. Scotia, 1840; Reg. Wy., July, 1857; Owners, Harrison Allison, and Hansell Gibson, R.H.Bay. Lost with all hands at N. Sunderland, Nov., 1865.

MECCA.—Bg.; 240; N. Brunswick, 1841; Reg. Wy., 1857; Owner, Ed. Wood, Wy., m.m. Lost at West H'pool, Oct., 1859.

MERMAID.—Bg.; 198; Montrose, 1844; Reg. Wy., 1865; Owner, Smith Stainthorpe, R.H.Bay. Sold by S. S., 1881, to F. Towers, of Bolsam, Sussex, and Jn. Wilson, Hartlepool. Wrecked at Donna Nook, May, 1886, master, mate and two lifeboatmen drowned. Owned at Whitstable when lost.

MEG LEE.—Bg.; 174; Sndld., 1840; Reg. Wy., March, 1869; Owner, Will. Russell, R.H.Bay. Foundered off Southwold after collision, Dec., 1871.

MINERVA.—Bn.; 95; Dundee, 1785; Reg. Wy., 1794; Owner, Newark Andrews; Reg. Nwcstl., May, 1798.

MINERVA.—Bg.; 148; Yarmouth, 1805; Reg. Wy., 1828; Owner, Jn. Craven, grocer; Reg. Scrbr., 1839; Reg. Wy. from Scrbr., Feb., 1848; Owners, Matt. Stevenson, 48, Jn. Wake, 16. Lost in the North Sea, 1849.

MINERVA.—Bg.; 119; Jersey, 1826; Reg. Wy., 1846; Owner, Benj. Gales, m.m.; Reg. at Faversham, 1852.

MINERVA.—Bg.; 143; Lynn, 1802; Reg. Wy., 1855, Owners, W. and T. Harker. Foundered on passage London to Shields, Nov., 1864.

MIRANDA.—Bg.; 309; Sndld., 1851; Reg. Wy., July, 1851; Owners, Matt. Gray, Matt. Rickinson and Co. Lost on the coast of S. America, near Rio Janeiro, May, 1862.

MILLMAN.—Bg.; 273; N. Brunswick, 1832; Reg. Wy., April, 1864; Owners, Jos. Thompson and Co.; Owners in 1866, Jos. Thompson, 8, Thos. Clegg, 8, W. Dotchon, 8, J. B. Nicholson, 8, T. Ward, 8, J. Peirson, 8, Is. Cooper, 8, Matt. Snowdon 8. Sold a wreck at Gottenborg, Dec., 1866.

MIKADO.—Bk.; 804; Baltimore, 1860; Reg. Wy., March, 1865; Owners, T. and W. H. Marwood, Will, and Eliza Jane Usherwood, and Geo. Bardo, Troon. Sold foreigner at Antwerp, Jan., 1874.

MONTE VIDEO.—Bg.; 191; Prize, 1806; Reg. Wy., 1808; Owner, Thos. Seaton, Wy. Taken by enemy, 1809.

MOSCOW.—Sch.; 52; Scrbr., 1813; Reg. Wy., 1837; Owner, Thos. Douglas, Wy., pilot. Lost, Nov., 1842.

MONICA.—Bg.; 231; Wear, 1835; Reg. Wy., 1840; Owner, Will. Thompson, Wy. Lost.

MONICA.—Bg.; 135; Wear, 1814; Reg. Wy., May 14th, 1840; Owners, Ed. Turner, cabinet maker, 32, Will. Butterwick, 24, and Simon Butterwick, 8. Lost on Warkworth Bar, 28th March, 1847.

MOUNTAINEER.—Bk.; 370; P. Ed. Island, 1846; Reg. Wy., Jan., 1847; Owner, T. Turnbull; Capt., Thos. Smailes, 1847. Arrived at Whitby from St. Lawrence, timber, 1850; Man bust; 102 by 22; Altered at Whitby in 1850 to brig and figure taken off; Capt., 1854, Will. Pearson. Sold to foreigners at Ystad, Sweden, June, 1877.

MORA.—Bg.; $\frac{186}{200}$; Sndld., 1848; Reg. Wy., 1851; Owner, T. Wilson; Reg. Sndld., 1855.

MUTUAL.—Bg.; 197; Sndld., 1846; Reg. Wy., Dec., 1858; Owners, Robt. Harrowing and Snowdon Mackuen; Reg. Middlesbro', 1889.

NANCY.—Bn.; 107; Prize, 1811; Reg. Wy., May, 1820; Owner, Jn. Gill, R.H.Bay. Lost, 1823, or after.

NANCY.—Slp.; 27; Scrbr., 1814; Reg. Wy., 1848; Owner, Geo. Peterkin, Lythe, and Jn. P. Linton, Sandsend. A lugger when first built, owned by Porritt, Staithes. Lost on the island of May, Feb., 1849.

NANCY.—Sch.; 23; Yarmouth, 1819; Reg. Wy., 1855; Owner, Hen. Durbridge, Wy. Supposed lost about 1860.

NAVARIN.—Bg.; 183; Sndld., 1828; Reg. Wy., Jan., 1837; Owner, Geo. Barrick. Total loss on the Brake Sand, Oldenburg, Dec. 30, 1849.

NAMELESS.—Bg.; 249; Coxgreen, Durham, 1841; Reg. Wy., 1843; Owner, Will Watson, Lythe; Reg. Lndn., 1844.

NAIAD.—Bg.; 177; Wear, 1844; Reg. Wy., Feb., 1857; Owner, Will Storm, R.H.Bay. Supposed to have foundered off Flamborough Head about Jan. 23rd, 1844.

NAUTILUS.—Bg.; 134; Sndld., 1834; Reg. Wy., 1857; Owner, Jn. Chambers. Lost, 1862.

NAYLOR.—Bg.; 135; Paull, Yorks., 1815; Reg. Wy., 1857; Owner, Jn. Adamson, Southwick, Durham. Lost, Dec., 1857.

NELLY.—S.; 295; Hull, 1784; Reg. Wy., 1797; Owners, Jn and Thos. Holt, Wy. Lost, 1803.

NELLY.—S.; 338; G. Yarmouth, 1800; Reg. Wy., 1820; Owner, Richd. Atkinson Robinson; three masts; 104.1 by 27.3. Lost, and all hands, in 1822.

NEPTUNE.—Bn.; 117; G. Yarmouth, 1793; Reg. Wy., 1810; Owner and Capt., Will. Gibson; Owners, 1824, Matt. and Isaac Marwood; Owners, 1835, Jn. Langborne, 32, Will. Jameson, 32; Owner, 1843, Will Jameson, 64; Owner, 1847, Moore Clough, 64; Owner, 1856, Moore Clough. Lost on Southwold Beach, Oct., 1859.

NEPTUNE.—Bn.; 135; Stockwith, Notts, 1786; Reg. Wy., 1814; Owner, Thos. Newton, R.H.Bay; Owners, 1847, Robt. Parkinson, R.H.Bay, and Sampson Storm. Lost at Pakefield Gat, Sept., 1850. Nicknamed "The Bay Pulpit."

NEPTUNE.—Sch.; 62; Bideford, 1812; Reg. Wy., 1820; Owner, Thos. Goodwill, Lofthouse; Reg. Sndld., April, 1824.

NEPTUNE.—Bk.; 484; N. Scotia, 1839; Reg. Wy., Feb., 1848; Owners, T. Turnbull and Co. Lost in the St. Lawrence, 1850.

NEUTRAL FISHER.—Sch.; 54; Yarmouth, 1801; Reg. Wy., 1823; Owner, Thos. Rawling.

NELSON.—Bk.; 244; Stcktn., 1799; Reg. Wy., Feb., 1826; Owner, Will Gibson; Reg. Nwcstl., 1833.

NEW SPEEDWELL.—Sch.; 59; Scrbr., 1819; Reg. Wy., 1819; Owners, J. Smith and J. Avery, and T. Harrison, R.H.Bay. Sold away. Re-registered at Whitby in 1845; Owner, Will. Simpson. Broken up at R.H.Bay, Nov., 1848.

NEWCASTLE.—Bg.; 124; Ipswich, 1802; Reg. Wy., 1846; Owner, Will Robinson, m.m., Whitby.

On the night of Feb. 20th—21st, 1849, the brig "Newcastle" was making for Whitby harbour, when the tide swept the vessel against the East Pier. Being light, she was driven close up under the cliffs to the South of the pier. Lieut.

Bainbridge, of the Whitby Coastguard, immediately threw two rocket lines on board, but the crew landed on a shelving piece of rock by means of a line. The wind was N.W., blowing fresh. The brig a total wreck.

NEW COMMERCIAL.—Bg.; 204; Sndld., 1847; Reg. Wy., 1847; Owner, Thos. Wilson, Wy. Lost off Penzance, Jan., 1851.

NEWTON.—Bg.; 205; Sndld., 1840; Reg. Wy., 1859; Owners, Jn. Chambers and Jn. Beal, butcher.

The "Newton," brig, Scotland for London, came into collision with a barque at 1 o'clock 28th June, 1862, near the South West Buoy, off Bardsey, much damage. Proceeded, and was the following day in the Swin.

"Newton," brig, owner, Jn. Beal, master, Jn. Chambers, and 8 hands, struck Sherringham Shoal, May, 1867, filled, sank clear of the shoal in 10 fathoms. On passage Sunderland for London.

NEWTON.—Bg.; 184; Southtown, 1828; Reg. Wy., 1863; Owner, Alfred Walker; Capt. Power. Foundered in the North Sea, Feb., 1866, 140 miles off Hartlepool.

NEW BRUNSWICK.—Bk.; $\frac{574}{557}$; Bathurst, 1860; Reg. Lndn.; Owners, 1871, Andrew and B. R. Frazer.

NINA.—Bg.; 260; Sndld., 1850; Reg. Wy., 1859; Owner, Addison Brown, Redcar. Lost at Gluckstadt, March 24, 1871. Owned at Shields, 1869.

NIGER.—Bg.; 298; Sndld., 1835; Reg. Wy., 1863; Owner, Benj. Granger, R.H. Bay. Stranded on Island of Oland, Nov., 1875.

NILE.—Bg.; 227; Whitehaven, 1838; Reg. Wy., 1865, from Glasgow; Owners, April, 1865, B. T. Robinson, 22, B. Granger, 21, and Richd. Robinson, 21; Same in 1870. Broken up, June, 1880.

NICARAGUA.—Bk.; 421; N. Brunswick, 1844; Reg. Wy. 1870; Owner, James Gray, Whitby; Transferred to Jn. Blumer Bushell, of S. Shields, Sept., 1879. Sold to Norway the same month.

NICHOLAS SMIRK.—Bg.; 193; Sndld., 1849; Owner, 1860, J. W. Lennard; Reg. Sndld., 1873.

NORVAL.—Bg.; 186; West Wemyss, 1805; Reg. Wy., 1822; Owner, Peter Cato, shipbuilder; Owner, 1824, Robt. Harrison, m.m. Lost, 1829.

NORTH BRITAIN.—Bg.; 240; Sndld., 1838; Reg. Wy., 1838; Owner, Hen. Barrick, jun.; Reg. Nwcstl., 28th Nov., 1844.

NORTHUMBERLAND.—Bg.; 212; Sndld., 1844; Reg. Wy., 1849; Owners, Storms and Co., R.H. Bay; Owners, 1871, Matt. Coultas Storm, Thos. Newton, and James Steel.

"Northumberland," owner, Ed. Storm, Capt., Archibald Martin, and six hands, left Sndld. 28th April, 1871, for Cronstadt, coals. 16th May, at 6 p.m., clear and fine, moderate S.W. breeze, being about 25 miles W. from Dagerort, met with a quantity of drift ice. "Laid to" until midnight, being unable to see the ice in the dark. At 2 a.m. she was kept away, and at 4 a.m. passed a little loose ice. About noon an extensive mass of ice was met with. At 5 p.m. Hango Udd lighthouse was sighted E.N.E. 10 to 12 miles distant. Soon after we were surrounded by the ice, which was setting towards the land. Tried to get the ship through to Hango Udd harbour, having wood fenders over the bow. About 8 p.m. all hands on deck, when endeavouring to clear a large piece of ice, she would not pay off, with the little way she had on, she lightly struck the ice with stem and port bow. Sounded the pumps, but found no water, but shortly after found the ship settling by the head. Ordered the boats to be got out, but kept the pumps going; by the time the boat was in the water and through the ice some 100 feet, the vessel went down head first, then about 8 miles from Hango Udd. Managed to get the boat through the ice to Hango harbour, where we got on board the "Isabella," of Montrose, at 11.30 p.m. Casualty caused by the ship getting among a mass of ice, which she accidentally struck, and had her lower bow port knocked in, which was no doubt a weak part of the ship.

NORTH OF SCOTLAND.—Bk.; 252; Sndld., 1845; Reg. Wy., 1861; Owners, Ed. Harrison and Co., R.H. Bay. Lost near Libau, Gefle for London, Dec., 1867.

NORTH WIND.—S.; 783; Quebec, 1865; Reg. Wy., 1866; Owner, Benj. Pearson; Made Bk., 1871. Sold to Norway, Dec., 1879.

NORMANBY.—Bg.; 222; Sndld., 1836; Reg. Stockton; Owners, Craggs and Co., Stockton; Geo. Westgarth part owner, 1839.

Late on the 11th or early on the 12th Oct., 1844, a vessel ran down the brig "Normanby," of Stockton. Crew saved and landed at Whitby.

NYMPH.—Bg.; 88; Aberdeen, 1799; Reg. Wy., 1826; Owner, Jn. Cole, Staithes; Owners, 1829, Ed. Wood, Runswick, 32, Will Jackson, of Goldsbro', 32. Lost, 1830.

NYMPH.—Sch.; 61; Gainsborough, 1828; Reg. Wy., 1840; Owner, Jos. Barker, Wy.; Reg. Yarmouth, 1842.

NYMPH.—Bg.; $\frac{188}{206}$; Sndld., 1847; Reg. Wy., 1850; Owners, Ed. Storm and Thos. Phillips, minister; Owner, 1871, Coultas Storm. Lost 26th Aug., 1871, near Lysekchl.

OAK.—Slp.; 50; Sndld., 1807; Reg. Wy., 1818; Owner, Hen. Dring; Owner, 1827, Jn. Dring. Total wreck at Whitby, Feb., 1827.

OAK.—Bg.; 226; Montrose, 1851; Reg. Wy., 1861; Owner, Thos. Huntrods, Thorpe; Owners, 1873, James Trattles, 48, Thos. Trattles, 16. Sold to Sndld., 1873. Wrecked 1 mile S. of Souter Point, Durham, May, 1877.

OAKHAMPTON.—Bg.; 112; Prize, 1809; Reg. Wy., March, 1819; Owner, Thos. Nicholson, Wy.; Reg. Dover, April, 1823. Lost, 1824.

OCEAN.—Bg.; 193; Sndld., 1837; Reg. Wy., 1840; Owners, Simon Tose and Co.; Owners, 1879, Will. and Margaret Clark, T. Clark Tose, and Jane Tose. Sold to Seaham, 1879. Totally lost near Marshchapel, Lincoln, Oct. 29, 1880.

OCEAN.—Bg.; 165; Montrose, 1840; Reg. Wy., 1849; Owner, Jn. Pearson; Owners, 1854, Thos. Harrison, 16, Geo. Harrison, 16, both of R.H.B., Will. Harrison, Ewe Cote, 16, Francis Harrison, 16. Lost off Huntcliffe Foot, Feb., 1860.

OCEAN.—Bg.; 211; Sndld., 1825; Reg. Wy., March, 1863; Owner, Coultas Storm. Lost on the Bar of Faro, Jan., 1868.

OCEAN.—Bg.; 126; Montrose, 1818; Reg. Wy., 1833; Owners, Jos. Tindale and Richd. Robinson, R.H. Bay; Owners, 1852, Jos. Tindale, 40, Robt. Bentley Tindale, 16, and Jn. Hall Leng, 8. Total wreck at Southwold, Nov., 1855.

OCEAN.—Bn.; 80; Staithes, 1835; Reg. Wy., 1835; Owner, Thos. Trattles; Builder at Staithes, Jn. Spencelayh; Owner, 1852, T. Walker, Wy.; a sch., 1852; Reg. Stockton, 1852.

OCTAVIA.—Sch.; 66; Southtown, 1817; Reg. Wy., 1862; Owner, Matt Trattles, Staithes. Sold to the Tyne, 1865.

ODESSA.—Bg.; 256; Sndld., 1849; Reg. Wy., March, 1861; Owner, Matt. Snowdon; Owners, 1866, Will. Watson, Stainsacre, and Will. Hill, Ruswarp. Lost on the island of Bornholm, Nov., 1866.

OKEANOS.—Bg.; 181; Wear, 1854; Reg. Wy., 1865; Owners, P. G. Rayne and Co.; Owners, 1868, P. G. Rayue, 16, David G. Pinkney, 16, W. Smallwood, 8, Will. Booth, 8, and Christ. Thorpe, of West H'pool, 16. Lost near Aldbro', Jan., 1869.

OPHELIA.—Bg.; 196; Sndld., 1845; Reg. Wy., April, 1848; Owners, Benj., Thos., and Harriot Jones. Lost, 1862.

OPAL.—Bg.; 166; Greenock, 1845; Reg. Wy., Dec., 1865; Owners, Jonathan Skerry and Jn. Hesp; Owners, 1893, Geo. and Will Hopper. Ashore at Dieppe, Dec., 1867; Capt., James Power. Sold, 1899, to the Cleveland Flour Mills Co. for a lighter.

ORLANDO.—Lug.; 15; Newlyn, 1868; Reg. Wy., Oct., 1881; Owner, Thos. Dryden. Wrecked on Whitby Sand, Dec., 1882.

ORLANDO.—S.; 351; Blyth, 1802; Reg. Wy., 1810; Owners, Robt. Campion and Jn. Pyman; three masts; 100.9 by 28.8. Lost, Nov., 1813.

ORIENTAL.– Bk.; 241;Hartlepool, 1851; Reg. Wy., Oct., 1872; Owner, Will. Foster, m.m., Wy. Lost near Sndld., Nov., 1872.

ORANGE BOVAN.—Slp.; 55; Prize, 1813; Reg. Wy., 1818; Owner, Jn. Anderson, jun., Whitby; afterwards Gordon McLachlin. Ashore in Runswick Bay, July 20. Wrecked there, Sept., 1852.

ORIENT.—Bn.; 121; Sndld., 1805; Reg. Wy., 1821; Owner, Jn. Bogue, m.m. Lost, reg. cancelled Jan. 17th, 1822.

ORIENT.—Bk.; 265; Sndld., 1855; Reg. Wy., 1855; Owners, Jn. Schofield, Mary Dobson, and Chas. Cockburn. Sold foreign, April, 1865.

ORION.—Bg.; 201; Sndld., 1838; Reg. Wy., 1840; Owners, Matt. Peacock and Hilda Agar, R.H. Bay, and T. Fletcher, Durham. Abandoned in the N. Sea, Texel S.S.W. 38 miles, April, 1874.

ORONOCO.—Bg.; 193; N. Scotia, 1847; Reg. Wy., Oct., 1847; Owner, Geo. Barrick; Capt., 1848, Will. James; Reg. Scarbro', 1866.

ORCHID.—Bk.; 215; Bristol, 1864; Owners, R. H. Burnett and Co., 1901.

OSCAR.—Bg.; Owner, Jn. Ripley.

OTHELLO.—Bk.; 361; St. Peter's, Northumberland, 1844; Reg. Wy., Dec., 1854; Owners, T. Turnbull and Co. Sold to be broken up, Feb., 1880.

OTTERBURN.—Bg.; 198; Sndld., 1849; Reg. Wy., Feb., 1859; Owner, Francis Banks; Owners, 1869, Geo. Milburn, Jos. Brown, J. Lennard, Will Milburn. Lost on the Long Sand, Nov., 1881.

"Otterburn," owner, Jn. Lennard, Capt., Will Brown, and six men, Newcastle for Boulogne, 6th Nov., 1881. On the 16th blowing a gale, ship reaching to W.N.W. till midnight, when, in the act of wearing, she took the ground on the S.W. edge of the Long Sand. Came off immediately. Found one foot of water in the hold. Got out the long boat, putting two apprentices in her. At 0.30 a.m., 17th Nov., finding the water increasing in the hold, decided to run her ashore to save life. At 2 a.m. ran her ashore on the S.W. edge of the Long Sand. Remained by the ship till daylight, when we were obliged to slip and run before the wind and sea as the vessel was breaking up. Got on board the Kentish Knock Light Vessel at 11.30 a.m., 17th Nov. Finally landed at Gravesend by Trinity yacht "Argus."

PALAMBAM.—S.; 394; S. Shields, 1819; Reg. Wy., April, 1825; Owner, Hen. Simpson, banker; Capt., Lotherington, at one period. Lost with all hands, 1838.

PALLAS.—Bg.; 194; Sndld., 1831; Reg. Wy., 1831; Owner, Richd. Atkinson Robinson; Owners, 1837, R. A. Robinson, 48, Will Terry, 16. Lost, 1837.

PALESTINE.—Bg.; 176; Sndld., 1841; Reg. Wy., 1848; Owners, Richd. Charles and Jn. Wright; Owner, 1869, Will Steel, R.H.Bay. Lost at Scrbr., Nov., 1872.

PALEMON.—Bg.; 243; P. Ed. Island, 1828; Reg. Wy., April, 1828; Owners, Ed. Turner, cabinet maker, Ralph Horne, printer, Will Dotchon, tailor, and Jn. Richardson, printer; Reg. Hull, 1847.

PARAGON.—Bn.; 163; P. Ed. Island, 1847; Reg. Wy., April, 1855; Owners, Robt. Harrowing and Geo. Bilton; Later, Paul Stamp and T. Shimmins. Abandoned at sea in a sinking state 20 miles S.S.E. of Lowestoft, March 12th, 1876.

PARAGON.—Bg.; 199; Sndld., 1834; Reg. Wy., Feb., 1877; Owners, Will Bedlington, Matt. Storm and Co.; Owner, 1885, Christ. Marwood; Owner, 1889, J. H. Harrowing, March; May, 1889, H. McDomels, Stockton. A sailing lighter, abandoned off Flambro' Head, 17th Oct., 1895.

PAX.—Bg.; 180; Sndld., 1856; Reg. Wy., June, 1856; Owner, Gideon Smales. Lost off Flambro' Head, Jan., 1860.

PATCHETT.—Bn.; 108; Goole, 1838; Reg. Wy., Feb., 1863; Owner, W. B. Smith, Whitby Shipping Co. Sold a wreck, Nov., 1881.

"Patchett," Thomas Newton, master, riding with both anchors down in the lower Thames, Nov., 1881, dragged them. The masts were then cut away. A smack came to assist and sent a tug. When the cables were hove in the anchors had gone. Sold as above.

PANOPE.—Bg.; 154; N. Brunswick, 1842; Reg. Wy., May, 1865; Owners, T. Wardell and Eleanor and Jn. Frank, Ruswarp; Owners, 1871, Gideon Smales, jun., 22, Geo. W. Smales, 21, Chas. Smales, 21. Lost on the Gunfleet Sand, March 16th, 1871.

PALLADIUM.—Bg.; 191; Sndld., 1814; Reg. Wy., April, 1868; Owners, Jas. Page, m.m., Will Frankland, Paul Stamp and Geo. Mather, Nwcstl. Lost in the North Sea, Dec., 1872.

PALESTINE.—Bk.; 322; Sndld., 1857; Reg. W. H'pool; Owners, Jos. Bedlington, West H'pool, and Jn. Bedlington.

PEGGY.—Slp.; 40; Arbroath, 1789; Reg. Wy., 1824; Owner, Ambrose Bell; Reg. Lynn, March, 1826.

PEGGY.—Bn.; 103; Yarmouth, 1798; Reg. Wy., 1798; Owners, Jn. and Matt. Porritt, Runswick. Lost, 1798, or after.

PEGGY.—Sch.; 62; Montrose, 1802; Reg. Wy., 1811; Owner, Jn. Estill, R.H.Bay; Reg. Scrbr.

PEGGY.—Bg.; 98; Inverkething, 1784; Reg. Wy., 1842; Owner, Jn. Mennell, R.H.Bay; Owner, 1853, Betsy Hill, 64.

"Peggy," brig, of Whitby, went ashore on Corton Sand on Monday morning, Jan. 5th, 1857. All drowned, except the master, who washed ashore lashed to the tiller.

PEGGY.—Slp.; 14; Cromarty, 1822; Reg. Wy., Aug., 1846; Owners, Robt. Tiplady, publican, and Thos. Williamson, sweep. Lost in Runswick Bay, Dec., 1846.

PEGGY.—Slp.; 31; Dundee, 1767; Reg. Wy., 1864; Owner, Philip Elliott, R.H.Bay. Sold a wreck at Scrbr., 1865.

PEIRSONS.—S.; 319; S. Shields, 1799; Reg. Wy., 1799; Builders, Lockwood and Brodrick; Owners, Thos. and Geo. Peirson; Bk. in 1825; Owners, 1825, Thos. and Harrison Chilton. Lost, 1827, or after.

PEACE.—Bg.; 178; Sndld., 1826; Reg. Wy., 1834; Owners, Seaton Trattles and Matt. Bedlington. Sold to Seaham, 1879. Lost near Grimsby, Oct., 1880.

PEACE.—Bg.; $\frac{149}{188}$; Sndld., 1827; Reg. Wy., 1837; Owners, Adamson and Corner; Owners, 1858, Jos. Bovill, 16, and Jos. Bovill and James Cliff, 48 jointly. Lost off the Dudgeon, Dec., 1859.

PETER AND JANE.—Sch.; 85; N. Shields, 1825; Reg. Wy., 1839; Owner, Jn. Wear, m.m.; Reg. Sndld., 1849.

PETER AND MARY.—Sch.; 72; Youghal, Cork, 1827; Reg. Wy., 1856; Owners, T. Turnbull, jun., Matt. Gray, Brown Marshall, and Sam Andrew. Foundered somewhere off Runswick, Crew drowned, 4th Jan., 1857.

PELION.—Bg.; 233; Sndld., 1832; Reg. Wy., 1840; Owner, Geo. Craven. Sold March, 1863, by Will Jameson,. of Wy., to W. M. Fawcett, of London,

PET.—Bg.; 175; Sndld., 1843; Reg. Wy., 1843; Owner, Sampson Storm. Run down off Flambro' Head, Nov., 1855.

PET.—Bg.; 176; Sndld., 1837; Reg. Wy., July, 1865; Owners, Isaac Pennock, Benj. Garminsway and And. Gatenby. Lost off Southwold, Dec., 1869.

PERO.—Bg.; 195; Sndld., 1850; Reg. Wy., Jan., 1864; Owners, Jn. Bedlington and Co. Lost on Yarmouth Sand, Feb., 1866.

PEARL.—Bk.; 192; Whitehaven, 1852; Reg. Wy., 1858; Owner, Andrew Banks; Reg. W. H'pool, 1863.

PEARL.—Bg.; 199; Wear, 1846; Reg. Wy., 1858; Owner, Jn. Ireland.

"Pearl," Capt., Richd. Leng, Hartlepool for Bremerhaven. March 5th, 1868, moderate gale, hoisted jack for a pilot, but were compelled to run for the Weser, being unable to keep the ship to the windward. About 5 p.m., not being able to find the buoys, were driven ashore at the mouth of the river Weser, Wanderoug light distant about 13 miles N.W. by N. At 6 p.m. the crew left the ship, and at 9 boarded the "Bremen" lightship.

PETREL.—Sch.; 60; Wear, 1859; Reg. Wy., June, 1859; Owner, Geo. Westgarth; Lengthened in 1862; Owner in 1866, Sarah Ann Westgarth. Sold to Wick, 1867.

PELHAM.—Bk.; 317; Sndld., 1849; Reg. Wy., March, 1866; Owners, Robt. Robinson and Benj. Parkinson; later, R. Robinson, 43, Francis Parkinson, 21.

A Board of Trade inquiry was held at Shields concerning the loss of this barque, owned by Mr. R. Robinson, of Whitby, and Mrs. Francis Parkinson, of Thorpe. She left Bordeaux, Mr. Will Breckon master, on the 23rd Feb., 1867. On the 25th she suddenly struck on the Laverres Reef off the coast of Brittany. Rolling badly, she sprung a leak. The crew then got the boats out, and all but the master and one seaman left the barque before midnight. At noon on the 28th the master and seaman had to jump and swim for their lives, as the vessel rolled right over. The master at the time was going down into the cabin for papers, and had to get through the skylight. The decision of the Court was suspension of the master's certificate for six months.

PERCY.—Sch.; 126; Sndld., 1855; Reg. Sndld.; Owners, Barry and Co.

PHŒNIX.—Shallop; 55; G. Yarmouth, 1767; Reg. Wy., 1807; Owner, Thos. Atkinson, Wy., m.m.; Owner, 1815, Thos. Mills, Wy. Lost, 1815.

PHŒNICIAN.—Bg.; 198; Sndld., 1852; Reg. Wy., 1858; Owners, Richd. Leng, Christ. Harrison and Jn. Weighill.

The "Phœnician" sailed from Hartlepool for Dantzic early in March, 1863. A dreadful storm swept over the Baltic about the time the vessel was due there. She was found stranded near Leba, not far from the Gulf of Dantzic. Capt. Leng and crew, many of them Whitby men, were drowned.

PHŒBUS.—Bg.; $\frac{187}{192}$; Sndld., 1815; Reg. Wy., 1841; Owner, Francis Thompson. Lost near Aldbro', Jan., 1848.

PHŒBE.—Bg.; $\frac{148}{138}$; Thorne, 1807; Capt., J. Pearson. Lost with all hands, about 1842.

PHILO.—Bk.; 344; Sndld., 1853; Owners, Jn. Mills, Sndld., and Bedlington.

PILGRIM.—Bg.; 228; Sndld., 1853; Reg. Wy., 1866; Owner, James Skerry; Owner, 1876, Sarah Skerry. Burnt in the Humber, Dec., 1876.

PILGRIM.—Bg.; 166; Sndld., 1866; Reg. Wy., 1884; Owner, Christ. Marwood. A hulk, Oct., 1885, being sunk at Woolwich after collision. Owner, Sept., 1885, T. F. Wood, Gravesend, manager.

PLOUGH.—Bn.; 93; Scarbro', 1769; Reg. Wy., 1816; Owners, Will Moorsom, m.m., Will Robinson, and Thos. Cropton, R.H.B.; Reg. at Sndld., 1823.

PLOUGH.—Sch.; 69; Aberdeen, 1811; Reg. Wy., 1838; Owner, Christ. Thompson, Wy.; Owners, 1840, Thos. Newton, R.H. Bay, 32, and F. Newton, Peak, farmer, 32; Owners, 1858, James Steel, 42, Jn. Peacock, 22. Wrecked at Shoreham, June 2nd, 1860.

PLANET.—Bg.; 184; Pugwash, N. Scotia, 1847; Reg. Wy., Jan., 1848; Owner, Robt. Sleightholm. Lost near Fecamp, Dec., 1849.

POLLY.—Bn.; 77; Gt. Yarmouth, 1772; Reg. Wy., 1808; Owner, Will Storm; Reg. Sndld., 1818.

PORTIA.—Bk.; 294; Stockton, 1839; Reg. Wy., 1839; Owner, Geo. Clark, Whitby. Lost, June, 1844.

PORCIA.—Bg.; 136; Newcastle, 1829; Reg. Wy., 1838, from Lvrpl.; Owner, Mennell, R.H. Bay.

"Porcia," from Trouville, put into Clayhole with the Captain (— Emmerson) dead on board. After giving the vessel's course and directions for going into Boston Deeps the captain went below and died very suddenly. He was interred at Boston, Oct., 1871.

Sold to Hartlepool, 1876.

PORT GLASGOW.—Bn.; 95; Port Glasgow, 1832; Reg. Wy., Jan. 22, 1846; Owner, Jn. Elder, Whitby, shoemaker; Owner, 1846, Jan. 24, Jos. Bovill, publican, and James Hartley, m.m., and Geo. Pyman, sailmaker; Owners, 1859, Thos. Seymour and Jos. Bovill.

During the gale of Jan. 4th, 1857, when many vessels came ashore at Whitby, the "Port Glasgow," dismasted and apparently abandoned, drove past Whitby and went ashore at Deepgrove, beyond Sandsend. Crew found to be shut up in the cabin, having despaired of life.

"Port Glasgow," Capt. Storr, Warkworth for Boulogne, drove ashore at Sizewell, near Aldbro'. Being opposite the coastguard station, a line was thrown over the vessel by the mortar and the crew landed, Oct., 1862.

PROVIDENCE.--Bn.; 71; Shoreham, 1772; Reg. Wy., 1797; Owner, Geo. Lawson, Hawsker; Owner, 1799, Will Boult and Will Jackson; Reg. Nwcstl., 1799.

PROVIDENCE.—Bn.; 69; Wells, 1775; Reg. Wy., 1796; Owner, Willson Bedlington; Capt., Isaac Bedlington. Lost after 1799.

PROVIDENCE.—Bn.; 102; Sndld., 1814; Reg. Wy., 1817; Owner, Jn. Seaton; Capt., Thos. Seaton; Reg. Sndld., Sept., 1825.

PROVIDENCE.—Hoy, 36; Prize; Reg. Wy., 1811; Owners, Thos. Worthy and Co. Lost.

PROVIDENCE.—Bg.; 157; Hull, 1819; Reg. Wy., 1840; Owners, Will Butterwick, Will Langborne, and Simon Butterwick; Owners, 1870, Will. and Richd. Butterwick. Sold to Yarmouth, Jan., 1870.

PROVIDENCE.—Slp.; 55; Scarbro', 1773; Reg. Wy., 1802; Owner, 1821, Jn. Main; Owner, 1829, Benj. Miller; Owners, 1840, Will. and Benj. Garminsway; Reg. Hartlepool, 1857.

PROVIDENCE PROTECTOR.—Yl.; Scarbro', 1834; Reg. Wy., 1845; Owners, Will Storm and Geo. Harrison, R.H. Bay; Reg. Boston, 1880.

PROVIDENT.—Sch.; 113; Newcastle, 1839; Reg. Wy., 1847; Owners, Jos. Fletcher, Whitby, and James Croft, Margate; Reg. Hastings, Jan., 1849.

PROSPEROUS.—Slp.; 68; Southampton, 1776; Reg. Wy., 1802; Owner, Jn. Taylor, Whitby; 1806 a Brigantine, and Owners, Francis Emblington, joiner, and Jn. Burden, mariner; a Brig, 1808; Owner, Isaac Salton, Thorpe, who sold 16/64 to Edmund Stevenson, Hawsker. Lost near Scarbro', 1808.

PRINCE.—S.; 386; Tyne, 1793; Reg. Wy., 1804; Owner, Will Chapman, sailmaker; 108.8 by 29.8; Reg. Lndn., March, 1839.

PRINCE OF WALES.—Slp.; 46; Stockton, 1794; Reg. Wy., 1816; Owners, Will Harland and Geo. Wilson, mariners; a Schooner, 65 tons, in 1821; Owner, 1837, Will Tyerman, m.m., Whitby, 64. Lost, 1840.

PRINCE KUTOUSOFF.—Bg.; 290; Wear, 1813; Reg. Wy., 1825; Owner, Robt. Usherwood.

Quebec for Lvrpl., Dec., 1829, went ashore on Long Strand, near Castle Freyke, Ireland. Wreck.

PRINCE LABOO.—Bg.; 266; N. Scotia, 1829; Reg. Wy. from Lvrpl., March 9, 1836; Owners, Will Swales, Jn. Raw, and Jn. Schofield; Reg. at Hull, March 14, 1839; Reg. at Wy., March 20, 1839, and Owners, Will Swales, 32, and Jn. Raw, S. Shlds., 32. Lost. Reg. cancelled 7th May, 1840.

PRINCE LEOPOLD.—Bg.; 106; Stockton, 1816; Reg. Wy., 1842; Owner, Jonathan Eskdale; Owners, 1848, Jos. Wray, m.m., 21, Jn. Milburn, 22, Miles Hall, 21; a Brig, 97 tons. Lost and all hands on coast of France, Feb., 1853.

PRINCE ALBERT.—Bg.; 185; Perth, 1842; Reg. Wy., 1857; Owners, Sam. Smith, London, and Benj. Hall and Jn. Leng, Wy.; Owners, 1869, Leonard Leng, 32, James Ainslie, 16, Jn. Leng, 16. Lost at Lowestoft, Feb., 1870.

PRINCE OF SAXE-COBURG.—Bg.; 163; Ramsgate, 1819; Reg. Wy., 1858; Owner, David Baxter; Owners, 1867, W. Bedlington and Matt. Storm. Lost off Cleethorpes, 1867.

PRINCE WALDEMAR.—Bk.; 463; Quebec, 1863; Reg. Wy., April, 1864; Owner, T. Marwood; Figure head, a dog. Sold to Dartmouth, March, 1883.

A coal hulk there, June, 1883.

PROMISE.—Bg.; 153; Tyne, 1847; Reg. Wy., 1848; Owner, Ed Turner; Reg. Exeter, 1854.

PROMISE.—Bg.; 395; N. Brunswick, 1824; Reg. Wy., Oct., 1865; Owner, James Terry.

"Promise," Capt., James Terry, jun., and 11 hands, left Cardiff 13th March, 1866, for Alicante, coals. At 6 a.m. 17th March, a squall blew away the sails and the ship began to leak. Set the crew to the pumps. Bore up. When off St. Ubes hoisted signal for pilot, but none came. At 10 p.m. anchored, being then only 1½ miles from the breakers. Hoisted ensign Union down for assistance. At 3 p.m., 19th March, having 7 feet of water in the hold, and being unable to obtain assistance, abandoned the ship in my largest boat. At noon on the 20th the vessel was seen to go down.

PRINCESS.—Bg.; 186; Sndld., 1841; Reg. Wy., 1848; Owners, Matt. Storm and Co., R.H.Bay; Owner, 1880, J. H. Storm. Sold to Seaham, Oct., 1880.

Wrecked at Hasebro' Sand, Jan., 1882.

PROBLEM.—Sch.; 65; Russian Prize, 1855; Reg. Wy., 1855; Owner, Jn. Cockerill, Wy. Sold to Scrbr., 1855.

PRIMA DONNA.—Bg.; 195; Sndld., 1848; Reg. Wy., Oct., 1869; Owner, James Hall, R.H.Bay. Lost on west coast of Jutland, May, 1872.

PROTHEROE.—Sch.; {109 / 138}; Cardiff, 1834; Reg. Lndn.; Owner, R. Gale.

PRIMUS.—S.S.; 520; Sndld., 1865; Owners, J. H. Thomas, 48, and Robt. Harrowing, 16.

The first screw steamer registered at Whitby.

PUNJAUB.—Bk.; 563; N. Brunswick, 1863; Reg. Wy., 1879; Owner, Geo. Willison, Wy. Lost at Tangier Bay, Dec., 1883.

Just sold, or about to be sold, to Bahia, S. Am., for £700.

PYTHO.—Bg.; 173; Sndld., 1840; Reg. Wy., 1852; Owners, Benj. Tindale Robinson and Benj. Granger; Reg. Sndld., 1863.

PYTHAGORAS.—Bg.; 236; N. Scotia, 1843; Reg. Wy., 1848; Owners, Mark Weighill, 12, Jn. Weighill, 12, Jn. Miller, 8, Anth. King, 8, Hannah Webster, Runswick, widow, 24. A missing ship after 1855.

QUAYSIDE.—Bg.; 223; Wear, 1832; Reg. Wy., 1866; Owner, Thos. Nesfield, Wy.; Owners, 1886, Will Craven, 32, Thos. Hardcastle, 32.

Sunk 6 miles S.E. by E. of Spurn Light, Jan., 1886.

QUEEN.—Bg.; 249; Hartlepool, 1854; Reg. Wy., 1854; Owners, Sam. Flintoft, 22, Isaac Greenbury, 11, Geo. Falkingbridge, 10, Will. Stonehouse, painter, 10, and Will Gale, 11. Lost on Island of Hoyland, Oct., 1857.

QUEST.—Bg.; 102; Scrbr., 1810; Reg. Wy., March, 1825; Owners, Jn. Rose, whitesmith, 13, Will Lord, cabinet maker, 13, Will Turnbull, watchmaker, 13, Gideon Buck, tinner, 13, and Jos. Brown, 12; Capt., James Rayment.

"Quest," Captain Rayment, towed into Shoreham, Jan., 1829, with loss of foremast, etc., through collision with "Gen. Palmer," E. Indiaman.

Wrecked at Shoreham, 1829.

QUEBEC PACKET.—Bg.; 196; Aberdeen, 1822; Reg. Wy., March, 1851; Owner, Robt. Parkinson, R.H.Bay; Owners, 1863, Sampson Storm, 32, Benj. Parkinson, m.m., 32.

"Quebec Packet," Capt., B. Parkinson, and six hands, Riga for London, timber. On Thursday, 5th Nov., 1863, during a S.S.W. gale, was struck by a sea carrying away part of deck cargo and doing much other damage. On 6th Nov. abandoned the ship in a sinking state, with 7 feet of water in the hold. Lat. 58.8 N., Long. 20.20 E. Crew taken on board the barque "Lubinka," of Riga, and landed at Elsinore.

RAMBLER.—S.; 245; Scrbr., 1793; Reg. Wy., Aug., 1793; Owners, James Harrison and Jn. Anderson, grocer; Builder, Sam. Wharton. Reg. Lndn., 1813.

RAMBLER.—Bg.; 239; Nwcstl., 1789; Reg. Wy., 1824; Owners, T. Turnbull, Jos. Turnbull and Will Hunton.

Brig "Rambler."

"Rambler," Capt. March, of Whitby, Quebec for Dublin, timber, was fallen in with by the brig "Grace," Capt. Maine, on the 1st Oct., 1827, Lat. 51 N., Long. 29 W., waterlogged and abandoned. She was boarded by the crew of the "Grace," who took out sundry articles. The crew have not been heard of, and it is supposed they have been taken off by an outward bound vessel.

"The crew of the 'Rambler,' March, of Whitby, which was abandoned on 27th Aug. in the Western Ocean, waterlogged, were taken off by a vessel and landed at Philadelphia. Lost at sea. Register cancelled."—"Whitby Magazine."

RANGER.—Bn.; 144; Wear, 1805; Reg. Wy., 1810; Owners, James Wood and Co. Lost on Pakefield Beach, Nov., 1829.

RACHEL.—Sch.; 154; Sndld., 1841; Reg. Wy., 1841; Owner, Robt. Hill, m.m. Lost on the coast of Denmark, Oct., 1849.

RACHEL LOTINGA.—Bg.; 242; Sndld., 1855; Reg. Wy., Oct., 1874; Owner, Jn. Brown.

A hulk, foundered 1½ miles S.E. of Eyemouth, Aug., 1889.

RAPID.—Bg.; 165; Aberdeen, 1834; Reg. Wy., 1843; Owners, Isaac Bedlington and Co. Lost on the Holderness Coast, Feb., 1871.

RATCLIFF.—Bk.; 288; Prize, 1807; Reg. Wy., 1844; Owner, Geo. Barrick; Capt., Will Barrick. Wrecked at Filey, Jan., 1857.

RAINBOW.—Bg.; 157; S. Shields, 1832; Reg. Wy., 1849; Owner, James Storm, R.H.Bay. Lost on Stranton Sands, Jan. 4, 1854.

RAVENSWORTH.—Bg.; 204; Sndld., 1845; Reg. Wy., May, 1851; Owner, Samson Estill Clark; Reg. Hartlepool, 1861.

RAISBECK.—Bg.; 209; Stcktn., 1836; Reg. Wy., Feb., 1864; Owner, Hannah Barnard.

"Raisbeck," Capt., Jn. Barnard, London for Shields, ballast, was in collision with a barque, unknown, on the 25th Oct., 1869, Whitby lights S.E. by S., distant 10 miles.

Lost in the North Sea, Sept., 1872.

RESPECT.—Slp.; 20; Sndld., 1821; Reg. Wy., Feb., 1827; Owner, Thos. Grayston, Park Gate, stonemason; Reg. Nwcstl, Dec., 1827.

RENOWN.—Slp.; 17; Sndld., 1818; Reg. Wy., 1827; Owner, Thos. Robinson, East Row. Lost on the Salt Scar, Oct. 28th, 1827.

REWARD.—S.; 347; Deptford, Kent, 1789; Reg. Wy., March, 1832; Owners, Geo. Barrick and Richd. Kneeshaw; Reg. Hull, 1837.

REBECCA.—Slp.; 17; Stcktn., 1839; Reg. Wy., 1847; Owner, Aaron Johnson; Lengthened, 1842; Owners, 1850, Geo. Cook, mariner, 32, Geo. Corner, publican, 32; Owners, 1851, Will. Kennett, 32, Aaron Johnson, 32; Owner, 1855, Aaron Johnson, 64; Owner, 1861, Geo. Corner, 64.

Lost at Runswick, April, 1861, owned by Spence and Burton.

REBECCA.—Bg.; 193; Sndld., 1852; Reg. Wy., March, 1852; Owner, James Storm, R.H.Bay; Owners, 1866, Matt. Storm, 48, Will Bedlington, 16. Lost on the coast of Hanover, Feb., 1868.

RECOVERY.—S.; 494; Batavia, 1799; Reg. Lndn.; Owners, Chapmans, 1816; 120 by 30.

REGARD.—Bg.; 223; Sndld., 1851; Reg. Wy., June, 1851; Owners, Benj. Granger and Co., R.H.Bay. Lost in the Gulf of Venice, Jan., 1854.

REGALIA.—Bg.; 186; Montrose, 1835; Reg. Wy., 1854; Owners, Will Taylor, Ann Storm, Robt. Mills; Owners, 1862, Will Trattles, 39, Susannah Liddle, 25. Lost in the North Sea, Oct., 1869.

RESOLUTE.—Bg.; 167; Barmouth, 1819; Reg. Wy., June, 1856; Owners, Isaac Wood Sinclair and Francis Banks, 32 each. Wrecked island of Oeland, Nov., 1856.

RELIANCE.—Bk.; 226; Peterhead, 1840; Reg. Wy., June, 1858; Owners, Will. Dale, Hannah Charter and Jn. Weighill. Lost at Yarmouth, Feb., 1866.

RELIANCE.—Bk.; 783; N. Brunswick, 1845; Reg. Wy., March, 1870; Owner, Chas. Henry Wright, Wy.; Reg. Barrow, 1872.

REGINA.—Bg.; 273; Sndld., 1851; Reg. Wy., Nov., 1859; Owners, F. Robinson, Christ. Harrison and J. Weighill. Lost end of 1861, or early in 1862.

RELIEF.—S.; 660; N. Brunswick, 1857; Reg. Wy., March, 1864; Owners, J. P. Hay, Jn. Weighill and Christ. Harrison. Lost at Newfoundland, 1865.

RETRIEVER.—Bg.; 318; Quebec, 1847; Reg. Wy., 1866; Owner, Jn. Leng, Wy.; Owners, 1870, J. Leng, 56, Matt. Young Barnard, 8.

"Retriever," Capt., M. Y. Barnard, Tunadal, near Sundsvall, deals, etc., for West Hartlepool, Nov., 1872. Encountered heavy weather. Got on a lee shore, drove ashore, and became a wreck in Faxoe Bay, between Stevns Head and Moen Island, Zealand, Denmark, 14th Nov., 1872.

REMEMBRANCE.—Bg.; 251; S. Shields, 1847; Reg. Wy., March, 1868; Owner, B. H. Tindale, R.H.Bay. Sold to Middlesbrough, 1874.

REMEMBRANCE.—Bg.; 208; Middlesbrough, 1862; Reg. Wy., 1875; Owner, Jn. Foster, Wy.

Hartlepool for Greenwich, coals, April, 1904, struck Bawdsey sand and foundered. Crew got to Harwich.

RHODA.—Bg.; 145; Sndld., 1819; Reg. Wy., 1832; Owners, Will Clark, Isaac Calvert and Jn. Clark, Runswick; Owners, 1859, Alfred Walker, m.m., and Jn. Wake. Lost at Dungeness, Dec., 1862.

RHONDDA.—Bk.; 179; Cardiff, 1848; Reg. Wy., March, 1869; Owners, Jn. Cummins, Will. Hutton, James White, Will. Cuthbert, and Geo. Ebblewhite; Made Barquentine, Sept., 1869; Owners, March, 1874, Elizabeth Ebblewhite and Christ. Marwood, executors of Geo. Ebblewhite, who died April, 1872; Owner, April, 1874, James Ward, 64. Lost 6 miles N.N.W. of Goree Church, Holland, Sept., 1875.

RICHARD.—Bg.; 196; Prize taken at Malta, 1808; Reg. Wy., 1811; Owner, Thos. Brown, Kirbymoorside. Captured by the enemy in 1812.

RICHARD.—Sch.; 95; Deptford, Kent, 1775; Reg. Wy., 1816; Owner, Robt. Leng, m.m. Lost, 1816.

RICHARD.—Smk.; 30; Govt. Hulk, built at Plymouth, date unknown; Reg. Wy., 1860; Owner, Alfred Ardown. Lost, 1862.

RICHARDS.—Ywl.; 41; Scrbr., 1878; Reg. Wy., July, 1878; Owners, Jn. Miller and Co. Lost in the North Sea on or about Oct. 28, 1880.

RIENZI.—Bg.; 188; Sndld., 1846; Reg. Wy., May, 1858. Lost on the Island of Bornholm, Dec., 1867.

ROBERT.—Bn.; 142; Canada; 1810; Reg. Wy., 1811; Owner, James Atty; Reg. Whitehaven, 1812.

ROBERT AND HANNAH.—Slp.; 37; Tyne, 1833; Reg. Wy., 1841; Owner, Geo. Blinkhorn. Lost. Sept., 1846.

ROBERT AND MARY.—Bg.; 217; Sndld., 1849; Reg. Wy., March, 1874; Owners, Jn. Knaggs, Elizabeth Elder and Jn. Jackson. Wrecked on Middleton Sand, W. H'pool, Dec., 1874.

ROSE.—Slp.; 33; Stcktn., 1770; Reg. Wy., Oct., 1822; Owner, Oliver Suggitt, 64. Broken up, Sept., 1823.

ROSE.—Sch.; 74; French prize, 1808; Reg. Wy., 1808; Owner, T. King, farmer, Redcar; Capt., T. T. Granger. Lost.

ROSE.—Bn.; 93; N. Biddick, 1811; Reg. Wy., 1821; Owner, R. Robinson, R.H.Bay; Owner, 1836, James Watt, grocer, 64. Lost, Oct., 1845.

ROSE.—Sch.; 56; Stcktn., 1821; Reg. Wy., Sept., 1858; Owners, Will. Walker and Isaac Seymour.

The "Rose," Stevens, of Whitby, left Yarmouth, 19th Oct., 1860. When off the Newcome Sand was caught by a gale at W.N.W. On Saturday morning, the 20th, tacked and stood to the Southward, very leaky and pumps choked. At 7 p.m. on Sunday the crew were taken off by the "Racehorse," smack, of Yarmouth, and soon after transferred to the "Swift," of Yarmouth, which landed them at Sunderland on the Tuesday following.

ROSE.—Bg.; 185; Sndld., 1848; Reg. Wy., March, 1869; Owner, Jn. Mills, R.H.Bay. Ashore at Hartlepool, Dec., 1874. Broken up at Sunderland, 1906.

ROSS-SHIRE.—Bg.; 306; N. Scotia, 1843; Reg. Wy., 1844; Owners, T. Jackson, Barnby, Will. Watson, Lythe, and T. Watson, Goldsbro'; Afterwards, W. Wilkinson and Co.

A missing ship in the Atlantic, 1859, Capt., T. Robinson, mate, J. Garbutt.

ROSEBERRY.—Slp.; Stcktn., 1807; Reg. Wy., Feb., 1819; Owner, Will. Hunton, Lofthouse, alum maker. Lost, 1824.

ROSEBERRY.—Bg.; 208; Stcktn., 1838; Reg. Wy., 1844; Owner, Geo. Wood; Owners, 1851, Hannah Wood, widow, 40, Jn. Hesp, 8, Will Rawlinson, Lndn., 16. Lost on the coast of Sweden, Dec., 1852.

ROVER.—Bg.; 139; Aberdeen, 1840; Reg. Wy., 1850; Owner, Ed. Clark; Owners, 1861, Mary Watson and Elizabeth Clark; Owners, 1868, M. Watson and E. Clark, 32 jointly, and Ed. Prodham, West H'pool, 32. Lost, 20th March, 1872, the North Foreland bearing W.S.W., distant 30 miles.

ROMP.—Bg.; 169; Hull, 1841; Reg. Wy., 1852; Owners, Jn., Robt. and Isaac Bedlington. Lost on Hasebro' Sand, Jan. 10, 1872.

ROYAL SAXON.—Bk.; 277; Sndld., 1856; Reg. Wy., April, 1856; Owners, Jn. Rickinson and Middleton Cowart. Lost at Newfoundland, Oct., 1862.

ROE.—Sch.; 84; Dundee, date unknown; Reg. Wy., 1861; Owner, Will. Smallwood, blacksmith; Later, Jn. Harding, boat builder, 22, Hen. Burton, 32, and Jackson Harding, boat builder. 10. Ashore at Whitby, 1861. Wrecked on the Kentish Knock, Jan., 1866.

ROBINSONS.—Bg.; 213; Sndld., 1865; Reg. Wy., March, 1865; Owner, Francis Robinson, 64; Owners, 1872, F. Robinson, 32, Will Brown, Staithes, 32; Owners, 1877, F. Robinson, 43, Geo. Galilee, 11, W. H. Taylor, 10. F. Robinson died 7th Nov., 1876; G. Galilee and W. H. Taylor, executors, sold the ship 15th Feb., 1877, to Richd. Allix, of St. Heliers, Jersey, licensed pilot. Reg. transferred to Guernsey, 3rd May, 1877.

ROSANNA.—Bk.; 135; Charlestown, Fife, 1838; Reg. Wy., Dec., 1865; Owner, W. B. Smith; Made brigantine; Sold, Aug., 1870, to W. C. Murrell, jun., London, by W. Jameson, Hen. Simpson, G. T. Knaggs, joint owners. Lost in the North Sea, 1872 or 1873.

ROSEBUD.—Bg.; 218; Wear, 1836; Reg. Wy., Sept., 1867; Owners, Jn. Elliott and Ed. Lowery, Monkseaton; Later, Matt. Storm and Co. Lost on Sizewell Bank, near Aldbro', Nov., 1881.

ROSAMOND.—Bk.; 327; Lvrpl., 1852; Reg. Wy., March, 1875; Owners, Christ. Harrison, J. Weighill and Jn. Brand, who sold to Will Thompson, Thos. Bryan and Geo. Hopper. Totally wrecked on the East coast of Barbadoes, Feb., 1876.

ROSELLA.—Bk.; 283; Sndld., 1859; Reg. Shields; Owner, J. H. Barry, Amble.

RUBY.—Slp.; 48; Blythnook, 1797; Reg. Wy., 1817; Owner, Ed. Dale. A schooner, 70 tons, in 1818. Lost, 1822.

RUNSWICK.—Bg.; 188; Sndld., 1819; Reg. Wy., June, 1819; Owners, Jn. Bovill and Will. Brown, Runswick; Reg. Nwestl., March, 1833.

RUNCINA.—Bn.; 74; Garmouth, Moray, 1840; Reg. Wy., 1852; Owner, Geo. Copley Garbutt. Woman bust. Lost in North Sea, June, 1858.

RUNO.—Bg.; 177; Dundee, 1849; Reg. Wy., 1863; Owner, Will Steel, R.H.Bay; Owners, Feb., 1879, Matt. Storm, 32, Will Bedlington, 32.

Sunk in Yarmouth Roads after collision with the "Warrior Queen," Oct., 1882.

SAINT JOHNS.—Bn.; 119; Bristol, 1786; Reg. Wy., 1793; Owner, James Atty. Sold to Nwestl., 1794.

SAINT ANDREW.—Slp.; 34; Pallion, Durham, 1804; Reg. Wy., 1852; Owners, Hen. Bennison and Co.; Reg. Aberdeen, 1857.

SAINT CATHERINE.—Bg.; 196; N. Brunswick, 1827; Reg. Wy., 1853; Owners, Ed. Corner, butcher, and Robt. Kilvington, m.m. Lost, Nov., 1857.

SAINT CLAIR.—Bk.; 264; Dysart, 1855; Reg. Wy., May, 1867; Owners, Will. Hill, Ruswarp, and Will Watson, Stainsacre; Owners, 1880, Will Hill, 32, and W. Hill, jun., 32.

Left Shields for Middleburg, Holland, 19th March, 1881. On the 22nd passed West Happel Pilot Station at 10.30 a.m., and while taking in sail she came to the ground about 11 a.m., on what proved to be Zouthlander Bouken, about 3 miles from Flushing. At 2.30 p.m. five tugs came, but were of no avail. At 3 p.m. the ship, having five feet of water in her, was abandoned. Crew taken off by a tug and landed at Flushing Total wreck.

SAINT BEDE.—Bk.; 321; Blyth, 1859; Reg. Wy., June, 1870; Owner, Thos. Huntrods, Thorpe. Sold to Blyth about 1872, but still registered at Whitby. Lost on St. Anna Bar, Bay of Camphecy, Jan., 1879.

SALLY.—Bg.; 140; Sndld., 1816; Reg. Wy., 1816; Owner, Richd. Unthank, Staithes; Reg. Nwcstl., May, 1821.

SAPHIRAS.—Bg.; 275; Wear, 1838; Reg. Wy., 1838; Owners, Addison Brown and Co.; Reg. Stcktn., 1849.

SARAH.—Bg.; 152; Nwcstl., 1815; Reg. Wy., 1838; Owner, Will. Poad, R.H.Bay. Lost.

SARAH.—Bg.; 172; Sndld., 1818; Reg. Wy., 1840; Owners, Messrs. Tose, Calvert and Clark, Runswick.

Wrecked near Yarmouth, Dec., 1874.

SARAH.—Sch.; 98; Wells, 1828; Reg. Wy., 1858; Owner, Geo. Weetman. Lost, Sept., 1862.

SARAH MARGARET.—Bg.; 199; Sndld., 1851; Reg. Wy., April, 1857; Owners, Storm and Skerry, R.H.Bay; Owners, 1876, Isaac Storm Harrison, 16, Oliver Storm, 16, Jn. Storm, 16, Sarah Skerry, 16.

"Sarah Margaret," owned by Geo. Hopper, Capt., Thos. Pritchard, Dover for Shields, chalk, drove ashore on Whitby Scar, 10th Dec., 1880. Crew and pilot, 9 in all, brought ashore by pier rocket apparatus, and ladders.

SARAH AND MARGARET.—Bg.; 191; Hylton, 1849; Reg. Wy., 1858; Owner, Christ. Moorsom, R.H.Bay.

Rochester for Whitby, in entering the harbour in Nov., 1872, the tow rope broke, and she drove on to the sand. Re-floated later.

Owner, 1885, Granger Moorsom. Broken up, Oct., 1888.

SARAH ANN.—Bg.; 144; Hull, 1844; Reg. Wy., July, 1865; Owners, Peter Geo. Raine, Will. Booth, and David Gray Gibson, roper.

"Sarah Ann," Lund, of Whitby, Shields for Rotterdam, sunk off Flambro' Head, after collision with the "Helen," 23rd August, 1865.

SARAH JANE.—Bg.; 206; N. Brunswick, 1838; Owner, 1853, Jos. Pearson, Whitby; Capt., R. Foster.

Sunk off Whitby after collision with s.s. "Rennie," Aug., 1890, and two lives lost.

SAREPTA.—Bg.; 259; Sndld., 1839; Reg. Wy., 1841; Owners, Will. and Francis Thompson, Sarah Nesfield and Dorothy Wilson. Lost, 1844.

SAMUEL AND SARAH.—Bg.; 158; S. Shields, 1821; Reg. Wy., June, 1846; Owner, Moore Clough; Owners, 1847, Geo. Carter, 32, Richd. Bradley, 32. Lost at Wick, May, 1851.

SANDWICH.—Bk.; 253; Cowes, 1823; Reg. Wy., Nov., 1849; Owners, Lawsons and Rothwell; Reg. Lvrpl., 1853.

SAMSON.—Sch.; 118; Lvrpl., 1841; Reg. Wy., Dec., 1860; Owners, Jn. Beal and Geo. Manson; Owners, 1867, Leonard Leng, 32, Geo. Manson, 32.

Struck a sunken wreck and foundered 1 mile S.S.E. of Havre Piers, Sept., 1868.

Sold as a wreck.

SANTIAGO.—Bk.; 247; Guernsey, 1845; Reg. Wy., April, 1861; Owner, Jn. Trattles, Coatham; Reg. Middlesbrough later in same year.

SALUS.—Bg.; 148; Sndld., 1817; Reg. Wy., Aug., 1858; Owners, Jn. Wake, Robt. Oliphant, Hannah Stephenson, and Will. Oliphant.

Sunk, and total loss, in River Seine, Dec., 1879.

SANCHO.—Bg.; 167; Blyth, 1839; Reg. Wy., 1866; Owner, Jos. Bovill; Owners, 1880, Christ. Harrison, T. P. Yeoman, Jn. Rowland and Co. Lost, with all hands, at Yarmouth, Jan. 17th, 1881.

SCHIEDAM.—Bg.; 216; Sndld., 1840; Reg. Wy., March, 1840; Owner, Francis Watkins; Reg. Stcktn., 1848.

SCEPTRE.—Bg.; 218; Stcktn., 1850; Reg. Wy., June, 1850; Owner, Thos. Trattles, Staithes; Reg. Stcktn., 1857.

SEA NYMPH.—Bg.; 224; Sndld., 1849; Reg. W. Hartlepool; Owner, Isaac Bedlington, West H'pool.

SEA NYMPH.—Bg.; 125; Southtown, 1827; Reg. Middlesbro'; Owner, Stephen Crosby, R.H.Bay. On the patent slip at Whitby, 1873.

SEA.—Bg.; $\frac{107}{143}$; Wthrn, 1840; Owner, 1854, R. Lawrie, Whitby.

SEVEN.—Bg.; 227; Hylton, 1838; Reg. Wy., June, 1875; Owner, Will. Baxter. Total wreck at the Scaw, March, 1878.

SEAHAM.—Bn.; 144; Rye, 1860; Owner, Miles Hall; Reg. Faversham, 1873.

SHEPHERD.—Bg.; 105; Southtown, 1811; Reg. Wy., 1826; Owners, Thos. Harland, m.m., Eleanor Pearson, and Thos. Garbutt; Brigantine, 1843; Owners, 1836, Jn. Cassap, 32, Geo. Lennard, 32; Owner, 1843, Geo. Lennard, 64; Reg. Stcktn., April, 1847.

"A Whitby trader to London."—Dr. Young.

SHEPERDESS.—Bg.; 194; Sndld., 1841; Reg. Wy., 1850; Owners, Verrill and Laverick; Owner, 1856, Will. Wear, 64; Reg. Scrbr., 1856.

SHERATON.—Sch.; 140; Sndld., 1836; Reg. Wy., 1846; Owner, Thos. Jackson, Wy.; Owners, 1848, T. Jackson, 43, Hen. Dale, m.m., 21. Foundered in the North Sea, Sept., 1856.

SHETLAND.—Sch.; 51; Yarmouth, 1810; Reg. Wy., July, 1852; Owners, Richd. Pinkney and Thos. Marshall, each 32.

Coming for the harbour, the tide getting low, the wind light, and a "fresh" running out, struck the pier, sheared off and sank, Jan. 4, 1855, Custom House date.

SIR DAVID MILNE.—Sch.; 89; Pictou, N. Scotia, 1818; Reg. Wy., 1841; Owners, Christ. and Chas. Thompson; 1848, C. Thompson, 64. Lost at Dungeness, June, 1848.

SIR COLIN CAMPBELL.—Bg.; 160; N. Scotia, 1838; Reg. Wy., Sept., 1848; Owners, Will. Cooper, spirit merchant, and Will. Dale, m.m.; Owners, 1861, J. Wilkinson, sen., 22, J. Wilkinson, jun., 21, and J. Wilkinson, 21. Lost at the North Foreland, Dec., 1866.

SIR HENRY WEBB.—Bg.; 202; Sndld., 1845; Reg. Wy., April, 1857; Owners, W. Jameson, 48, Richd. Mate, m.m., 16. Lost on the Dudgeon, Jan., 1860.

SIR JOHN ANDERSON.—Bk.; 245; Foreign, date and place unknown; Reg. Wy., Oct., 1857; Owners, Elizabeth Cassap, and Geo. Read Ellison, m.m. Lost on the coast of Jutland, March, 1859.

SIR ROBERT PEEL.—Bg.; 174; Sndld., 1839; Reg. Wy., 1859; Owner, Miles Turnbull, R.H.Bay; Owners, 1863, Robt. Harrowing, 48, John Mackuen, 16. Lost on the Bawdsey Sand, Jan., 1866. Crew saved.

SISTERS.—Bg.; 187; Sndld., 1832; Reg. Wy., May, 1848; Owner, Benj. Granger, R.H.Bay. Lost at Bridlington Quay, Oct., 1849.

SILISTRIA.—Bg.; 203; Sndld., 1853; Reg. Wy., Aug., 1853; Owners, T., Will. and Jn. Marwood; Reg. Sndld., 1863; Owners, 1865, Zach. and Robt. Granger, R.H.Bay; Owners, 1874, Zach. Granger, jun., 42, and Zach. Granger, gentleman, 22.

Run into by a steamer at Boulogne, and sold as a wreck, Dec., 1876.

SILISTRIA.—Bk.; 394; Sndld., 1854; Reg. Wy., 1857; Owners, Hen. Robinson, W. E. Corner, James Mutter, and Jn. Yeoman.

Burnt at sea, as per letter from St. Helena, dated Aug., 1862. Crew landed at St. Helena.

SKIDDAW.—Bk.; 356; Workington, 1852; Reg. Wy., Aug., 1871; Owner, J. H. Storm.

Sold to Germany, Dec., 1880.

SKY LARK.—Bg.; 121; S. Shields, 1817; Reg. Wy., 1828; Owners, Zachariah Knaggs, 40, M. Granger, 24; Owner, 1829, Z. Knaggs, 64. Lost, 1829, or after.

SNOWDON.—Bg.; 152; Carnarvon, 1818; Reg. Wy., 1835; Owner, Will. Jones, Whitby, m.m. Supposed to have foundered in the North Sea.

SNAKE.—Slp.; $\frac{65}{22}$; Nwcstl., 1773; Reg. Wy., 1836; Owner, Will. Todd, m.m.; Reg. Sndld., 13th March, 1840.

SOLEBAY.—Bn.; 91; Southwold, 1798; Reg. Wy., 1811; Owner, Benj. Tindale. Lost, 1837.

SOLON.—Bg.; 177; Sndld., 1849; Reg. Wy., April, 1850; Owner, Benj. Granger. Sold to Hartlepool, 1861.

SOLWAY.—Bg.; 300; Hylton, 1842; Reg. Wy., May, 1842; Owners, Geo. Falkingbridge, J. Barnard and Co. Lost in the Atlantic Ocean, Sept., 1853.

SOVEREIGN.—Bg.; 239; Dumbarton, 1854; Reg. Wy., 1858; Owner, Robt. Bedlington. Lost off the Scaw, Nov., 1872.

SPEEDWELL.—Slp.; 52; S'hampton, 1771; Reg. Wy., July 6, 1799; Owner, Will. Webster, Wy.; Reg. Sndld., July 11, 1799.

SPRING.—Bn.; 137; Portrack, near Stockton, 1801; Reg. Wy., 1801; Owner, J. Atty; Builder, Dan. Cole; Reg. Guernsey, 1803.

SPRING.—Bg.; 166; Sndld., 1833; Reg. Wy., 1833; Owner, Gideon Smales; Owners, 1855, Will. Hill, and trustee for family of Hen. and Betsy Hill; Owner, 1862, Miles Hall, 64; Owners, 1864, J. Hall, Sndld., greengrocer, and James Hall, R.H.B., shoemaker, executors of M. Hall, who died Feb. 15, 1863.

"Spring," owner, Mrs. Dorothy Hall, Capt. Peacock, and five hands, Amble for Dunkirk. Sat., 2nd Nov., 1867, weather stormy, wind N.W. by N. a fresh gale, was in sight of S. Foreland, and the N. Sand lightship, when he was relieved by the mate at 4 a.m. At about 7.55 a.m. he was called by the mate, as the vessel was in broken water, was on deck at once, and put the ship before the wind, but the ship immediately came to the ground, and became a total wreck on the Dye Bank, about 7 miles N.N.E. from Dunkirk. The Dunkirk lifeboat came and took off the crew from the maintop.

SPECULATOR.—Slp.; 38; Plymouth, 1818; Reg. Wy., 1820; Owner, Jn. Turnbull, block and mast maker. Lost, 1824, or after.

SPECULATION.—Slp.; 93; Redbridge, S'thampton, 1807; Reg. Wy., 1843; Owner, Geo. Hall, Wy.; Reg. Shields, April, 1850.

SPRIGHTLY.—Bg.; 106; Kincardine, 1812; Reg. Wy., 1849; Sch. later; Owner, Will Tyerman, stonemason. Lost at Wainfleet, Dec., 1856.

SPECTATOR.—Bk.; 295; Southwick, 1844; Reg. Wy., 1866; Owner, Thos. Harrison, R.H.Bay; Owner, March, 1873, Mercy Harrison. Sold to a foreigner at Elsinore. Lost at Elsinore, 1873.

SQUIRREL.—Bg.; 122; Hull, 1794; Reg. Wy., 1811; Owner, John Middleton; Owners, 1824, J. Coward, 32, Matt Corner, 32; Owner, 1827, Samson Storm. Lost, 1827 or after.

SQUIRREL.—Bg.; $\frac{116}{132}$; Pictou, 1836; Reg. Wy., 1837; Owners, Paul Stokill, Robt. Harrison, and Moses Ligo; Owner, 1868, Will Simpson, 64.

Jan. 11, 1856, a brig was seen to the north of Whitby, with only one mast. The tug "Goliah" went to her assistance. It proved to be the "Squirrel," of Whitby, abandoned by her crew. She was towed to Scarbro', accompanied by the tug "Hilda." Two boys had got on board a vessel; the others of the crew were landed at Bridlington. The vessel had been in collision.

Wrecked at Bridlington, and four of the crew drowned, Feb., 1871.

Great loss of vessels and seamen at this time.

STORK.—Bn.; 158; Prize in 1798; Reg. Wy., 1820; Owner, Robt. Kirby, Whitby. Broken up, 1820.

STOREY.—Sch.; 29; Sndld., 1821; Reg. Wy., 1824; Owner, Will. Carling; Owner, 1826, Jn. Estill, carpenter, 64. Lost, 1826.

STANSFIELD.—Slp.; 90; Sndld., 1827; Reg. Wy., 1841; Owner, Thos. Johnson, wine merchant. Lost. Reg. cancelled, June, 1842.

STRANTON.—Bg.; 182; Hartlepool, 1850; Reg. Wy., 1856; Owners, Matt. Storm, Will. Steel, Will. Bedlington, and Thos. Storm. Lost off Cromer, Nov., 1860.

STEERWELL.—Sch.; 64; Stockton, 1842; Reg. Wy., 1856; Owners, T. Turnbull, jun., Matt. Gray, Brown Marshall, and Sam. Andrew. Sold as a wreck, Dec., 1860.

STOCKTON PACKET.—Sch.; 37; Stockton, 1826; Reg. Wy., Aug., 1859; Owners, Jn. Ebblewhite and Co. Sold to Scrbro', Nov., 1866.

STANLEY.—Bg.; 188; Pitea, 1832; Reg. Wy., 1865; Original Swedish name "Christine"; Owners, Robt. Harrowing, 40, J. Hardcastle, 8, Sn. Macquen, 8, and Jn. Harland, Sandsend, 8. Lost at Equion, Sept., 1867.

STAR IN THE EAST.—Bk.; 277; Sndld., 1850; Reg. Wy., 1869; Owners, Will. Steel, James Storm, and Jn. Nellist. Man figure head. Lost at Sturge, Denmark, Oct., 1875.

SUCCESS.—Bn.; 129; Deptford, Durham, 1810; Reg. Wy., 1811; Owner, Addison Brown, Staithes; Owners, 1827, Hezekiah Godden, James Skerry, T. Coggin; Brig, 162 tons, 1825. Lost at Bridlington, Oct., 1852.

SUCCESS.—Bg.; 257; Workington, 1786; Reg. Wy., 1811; Owner, Jn. Marshall; Reg. Plymouth, 1815.

SUSANNAH.—Bg.; 114; Newcastle, 1792; Reg. Wy., 1832; Owners, Thos. and Christ. Walker; Reg. Stockton, Oct., 1854.

SUSANNAH DIXON.—Bg.; $\frac{222}{211}$; Sndld., 1852; Owner, Francis Robinson, Wy., m.m. Totally wrecked at Lowestoft, Oct. 28, 1882. Owned at Shields when lost.

SUFFOLK.—Bk.; 339; N. Shields, 1795; Reg. Wy., 1836; Owners, Richd. Wilson and Geo. Foggo. Broken up, Dec., 1844.

SWIFT.—Sch.; 81; S. Shore, Durham, 1829; Reg. Wy., 1848; Owners, Miles Turnbull, Moses Bell, cordwainer, both of R.H. Bay. Foundered on Dogger Bank, Sept., 1853.

SYLPH.—Bg.; 148; Sndld., 1818; Reg. Wy., 1839; Owners, Zach. Granger and Christ. Moorsom; Owners, March, 1865, Will. Ramsdale, 22, W. H. Boase, 21, and Sam Lonsdale, 21, the two last both of London. Seized by the Prussians at Rouen to sink her in the Seine, Dec., 1870.

SYBIL.—Bn.; 195; P. Ed. Island, 1855; Reg. Wy., 1865; Owners, Benj. Tindale Robinson, 16, B. Granger, 16, Geo. Leng, m.m., 16, Richd. Robinson, 16. Sailed from Middlesbrough for Riga, May, 1865. A missing ship.

TAR.—Sch.; 93; Sndld., 1837; Reg. Wy., 1841; Owner, Jn. Turner, butcher; Owners, 1843, Geo. Hopper, mariner, 42, Will Dotchon, tailor, 22. Lost near Harwich, Sept., 1852.

TANNER.—Bg.; 195; Wear, 1840; Reg. Wy., 1852; Owner, Geo. Mennell, R.H. Bay; Owner, 1873, Robt. Rowton, 75, Clapham Road, London. Lost on the Mouse Sand, July, 1873.

TAY.—Bk.; 515; N. Brunswick, 1840; Reg. Wy., March, 1856; Owners, Ed. Corner, Hen. Robinson, and W. Elgie Corner. Wrecked on the island of Anticosti, St. Lawrence, Sept., 1857.

TASMANIA.—Bk.; 251; Stockton, 1825; Reg. Wy., 1825; Owners, James Dixon, jun., Brotton, and Jn. Williamson Mennell, Wy., m.m. Lost. Reg. delivered at Lndn., Aug., 1835.

TEES.—Sch.; 58; Stockton, 1813; Reg. Wy., 1843; Owners, J. Tate, Stockton, and Will. Gale, Wy.; Owners, 1854, Geo. Ebblewhite, 22, Will. Ebblewhite, 21, and Will. Cuthbert, 21; Owner, 1870, Geo. Ebblewhite 64. Broken up, Aug., 1870.

TENNANT.—Bg.; 234; Stockton, 1834; Reg. Wy., 1846; Owners, Robt. Swales and Co.; Reg. Stockton, 1848. Ashore at Wy. early in 1849.

TENTERDEN.—Bg.; 118; Nwcstl., 1815; Reg. Wy., April, 1846; Owner, Will Watson, Lythe; Reg. London, May, 1846.

TELEGRAPH.—Bg.; 191; Middlesbrough, 1847; Reg. Wy., 1865; Owner, Jn. Spence, m.m. Lost, Lat. 56.20 N., Long. 4.45 E., Jan. 19, 1872.

TEAZER.—Bk.; 283; Dartmouth, date unknown; Reg. Wy., Dec., 1873; Owner, J. H. Storm.

Oct. 18, 1875, when towing into Whitby, drifted too far behind the West Pier when the tug was inside. Slipped the tow rope, and tried to sail off, but the vessel came on the sand. Capt., Will Storm. Vessel refloated afterwards.

Condemned as unseaworthy at Fayal, April, 1880.

THOMAS AND ANN.—Sch.; 37; Scarboro', 1793; Reg. Wy., 1849; Owner, Jn. Atkinson, m.m.; Reg. Sndld., 1850.

THOMAS AND JANE.—Slp.; 46; Blythnook, 1774; Reg. Wy., 1795; Owner, Geo. Potts. Lost, 1802, or after.

THOMAS AND JAMES.—Bn.; 64; Staithes, 1777; Reg. Wy., 1800; Owners, Jn. Dalton and Geo. Pharaoh, of Wy., shipwrights. Captured by the enemy.

THOMAS AND MARY.—Slp.; 47; Stcktn., 1785; Reg. Wy., 1807; Owner, Geo. Sanderson, Whitby; Owners, 1855, Will Laverick, 32, Thos. Taylor, 32, both of Staithes.

Total wreck on the Herd Sand, Tynemouth, and all the crew drowned, March, 1855.

Certificate of Reg. lost as per letter from J. Corner, jun., the owner, dated 27th April, 1855, Whitby Custom House.

THOMAS AND MARY.—Sch.; 34; Wakefield, Yorks, 1824; Reg. Wy., Feb., 1862; Owner, James Andrew; Reg. Nwcstl., 1864.

THOMAS AND BETSY.—Bg.; 171; Sndld., 1829; Reg. Wy., 1856; Owner, Jn. Ireland. Lost, Oct., 1857.

THOMAS AND MARGARET.—Bg.; 176; Sndld., 1830; Reg. Wy., 1857; Owners, Jn. Harland and Co. Lost off the Nore, Jan., 1865.

THOMAS AND ADAH.—Bg.; 170; Sndld., 1813; Owners, 1853, J. Fidler and Co., Whitby.

THOMAS WILLIS.—Bk.; 365; Stcktn., 1825; Reg. Wy., 1826; Owner, Will Benson, Whitby. Fitted out by Gideon Smales, Wy.

"Thomas Willis," of Whitby, Capt. Hughes, was totally lost, with all hands, about 7th Jan., 1828, on the Sunk Sand, when on passage from Hamburg to London.—Wy. Panorama.

THOMAS RICHARDSON.—Bg.; 180; Stcktn., 1832; Reg. Wy., May, 1842; Owner, Will. Watson, Lythe. Lost, Dec., 1842.

THOMAS.—Sch.; 77; Wear, 1803; Reg. Wy., 1818; Owner, Ambrose Bell; Owner, 1824, Thos. Dotchon; Owner, 1835, Mary Dotchon, widow; Owner, 1838, Geo. Hopper, 64; Owners, 1848, T. Watson and Geo. Peterkin, Lythe and Goldsbro. Later, Jn. Chambers, 32, Jn. Costy Wishart, 32; Owner, 1873, Mich. Thurlbeck, sen., Sndld. Foundered off Dunbar, May 6, 1873. Reg. closed.

THOMAS.—Bg.; 266; Lvrpl., 1790; Reg. Wy., 1837; Owners, Marwood and Pickernell.

March 28, 1842. Began to break up this old brig in Campion's dock. She belonged to Marwood and Co., who would not repair her.

THOMAS.—Bg.; 220; Sndld., 1849; Reg. Wy., May, 1849; Owners, Thos. Brown and Co., Staithes.

Driven ashore near Libau, Oct., 1854, and taken as a prize by the Russians.

THOMPSON.—Bg.; 190; Sndld., 1823; Reg. Wy., 1852; Owner, James Estill; Owners, 1865, Richd. Jackson, Lythe, 16, Will. Baxter, 16, James Gray, solicitor, 16, Christ. Richardson, m.m., 16. Lost on the Dutch coast, Oct., 1865.

THREE BROTHERS.—Lug.; 55; Scarbro', 1805; Reg. Wy., 1805; Owners, Isaac and Will. Storm; Reg. Newcastle, Aug., 1829.

THREE SISTERS.—Bg.; 119; N. Brunswick, 1846; Reg. Wy., 1849; Owners, Matt. and Richd. Dobson, Mickleby; Reg. Lvrpl., Feb., 1850.

THORNE.—Bn.; 105; Thorne, Yorks, 1802; Reg. Wy., 1815; Owner, Stephen Crosby, Whitby. Lost, 1833.

THORNTONS.—S.; 273; Stockwith, Notts, 1807; Reg. Wy., 1824; Owner, Jn. Holt; Owner, 1825, Richd. Brown, 64; Reg. Newcastle, 1830.

THANKFUL.—Bg.; 80; Sndld., 1827; Reg. Wy., 1829; Owners, Jane, Richd. and Anth. Wade. Lost on Corton Sand, Dec., 1836.

THETIS.—Bg.; 163; Dundee, 1834; Reg. West H'pool; Owner, Isaac Bedlington.

THISTLE.—Sch.; 77; Grangemouth, 1804; Reg. Wy., 1831; Owner, Christ. Thompson, Whitby, m.m.; Owner, 1848, Hen. Streeting. Lost on the coast of France, April, 1849.

THETFORD.—Bg.; 78; Lynn Regis, 1814; Reg. Wy., 1838; Owner, Will. Taylor, Whitby; Owners, 1843, Geo. Eskdale, m.m., 42, and Jn. Gibson, shipwright, 22. Lost at Scarbro', Jan., 1847.

THESSALIA.—Bg.; 271; Sndld., 1854; Reg. Wy., Oct., 1854; Owners, Marwood and Pickernell; Owners, 1865, Eliza Mary Marwood, 16, Thos. Marwood, 32, and Emily W. Marwood, 16.

Wrecked at Craster, Northumberland, Oct., 1875.

THALIA.—Bg.; 300; Sndld., 1864; Reg. Sndld.; Owner, Isaac Bedlington, West H'pool. Abandoned at sea, 1883.

TORRIDGE.—Bn.; 112; Prize, 1810; Reg. Wy., 1810; Owner, Richd. Hutchinson.

TOWN OF DUNDEE.—Sch.; 98; Dundee, 1840; Reg. Wy., April, 1849; Owner, Jn. Goodwill, Whitby, m.m. Lost on the coast of Courland, Baltic, May, 1851.

TOWN OF LIVERPOOL.—Bk.; 313; S. Shields, 1851; Reg. Wy., 1865; Owners, J. Walker, James Gray, and Christ. Barnard, 1874; Later, W. Hill. Wrecked at Palling, Nov., 1884.

TRAVELLER.—Bn.; 111; built in N. Britain; Reg. Wy., 1801; Owner, Francis Rudd, Whitby; Lengthened at Scarbro', 1775; Re-built at Whitby, 1783; Owner, 1823, Jn. Kearsley, m.m. Lost, 1823.

TRITON.—Bn.; 89; Yarmouth, 1800; Reg. Wy., 1816; Owner, Richd. Robinson, R.H.Bay. A brig in 1824. Owners, 1824, R. Robinson, 32, Geo. Stainthorpe, Park Gate, 32; Reg. at Bridlington, July, 1837.

TRANBY.—Bg.; 253; Sndld., 1809; Reg. Wy., 1824; Owners, Jn. Pennock and Geo. Smith; Owner, 1845, Geo. Smith, 64; Reg. Newcastle, 1845.

TRYPHENA.—Bg.; 150; Sndld., 1817; Reg. Wy., 1825; Owners, Geo. Clark, 53, and Will. Martin, Whitby, mariner, 11. Lost at Cadiz end of 1826.

TRIMMER.—Slp.; 28; Stcktn., 1808; Reg. Wy., 1827; Owner, Jn. Estill, Whitby, shipwright; Reg. Stockton, April 25, 1838; Reg. Wy. from Stockton,

June, 1838; Owners, Jn. Moorsom, R.H.Bay, tailor, 32, Sampson Thompson, of R.H.Bay, butcher, 32. Foundered at R.H.Bay, crew saved, Oct., 1838.

TREBIZOND.—Bg.; 284; Sndld., 1854; Reg. Wy., Oct., 1854; Owners, Marwood and Pickernell.

A missing ship—supposed to have struck on Laesoe Island, in the Cattegat, on or about Nov. 7, 1876.

TRUE LOVE.—Dy.; 28; St. Ives, 1879; Reg. Wy., 1879; Owner, J. Thompson, Staithes.

TRAVELLER.—Slp.; 14; Blythnook, 1820; Reg. Wy., Aug., 1828; Owner, Geo. Harrison, Whitby; Owners, 1831, Richd. Frankland, and Will. Lister, blacksmith, 16 each, Jn. Rickinson, grocer, 16, James Cowart, 16; Owners, 1832, Flintoft and Lister. Lost, 1832, or after.

TUTELINA.—Slp.; 18; Stcktn., 1836; Reg. Wy., 1852; Owners, Thos., Frank and Will. Adamson, shoemaker.

Friday night, or early on Saturday morning, Oct. 21 or 22, 1854, the "Tutelina," sloop, was found wrecked in Collier Hope, part of her having come through the Spa Ladder. The crew, two in number, drowned. The craft was in the roads on Friday evening, too late for the tide.

TWO SISTERS.—Bn.; $\frac{102}{87}$; Berwick, 1790; Reg. Wy., 1800; Owner, James Atty; Capt., Geo. Addison; Owner, 1805, Thos. Backas, mariner; Owner, 1852, Matt. Walker, 64; Capt., Isaac Bedlington; Owners, 1861, Jn. Beal, butcher, 32, Will Hovington, mariner, 32; A schooner in 1861. Lost, 1861.

TWO SISTERS.—Bg.; 132; Sndld., 1807; Reg. Wy., 1817; Owner, Thos. Nicholson, brazier, Whitby. Lost, 1818, in Boston Deeps.

TWO FRIENDS.—Slp.; 40; Plymouth, 1789; Reg. Wy., July, 1821; Owners, Robt. Brough and Robt. Leng. Lost with all hands.

TWO FRIENDS.—Slp.; 29; Scarbro', 1812; Reg. Wy., 1849; Owners, Geo. Peterkin and Co., Lythe; Owner, 1868, Will. Simpson, 64. Broken up at Whitby, 1877.

TWO BROTHERS.—Slp.; 60; Scarbro', 1772; First Reg. at Whitby, 1794 · Re-built and enlarged and Re-reg. at Whitby, 1800; Owners, James Naylor, brewer, Jn. Fewster, jun., yeoman, and Jn. Boanson, whitesmith; Owner, 1809, Jn. Summerson, cordwainer. Lost, 1809.

TWO BROTHERS.—Slp.; 59; Prize, 1811; Reg. Wy., 1811; Owner, Jonathan Oyston; Owners, 1835, T. Turnbull, 32, Will. Hunton, 32. Lost, 1839.

TWO BROTHERS.—Slp.; 35; Knottingley, Norfolk, 1827; Reg. Wy., 1857; Owner, George Pyman. Missing since 1863. Widow of owner denied all knowledge. Supposed sold.

TWEED.—Bg.; 167; Sydney, Cape Breton, 1836; Reg. Wy., 1838; Owner, Hen. Barrick, Wy.; Owner to Sept. 3, 1838, Jn. Sanderson, 64; after Sept. 3, J. Lawson, 64; Owner, 1843, Jn. Sanderson, 64; Owners, 1856, Jn. Ripley, 48, and Matt. Boyes, 16; Owners, 1881, Christ. Harrison, T. P. Yeoman, W. Edwards, G. Remmer, J. Rowland, Christ. Marwood, Will. Wood and T. Langdale.

Supposed to have been lost in the North Sea about 28th Oct., 1882.

TYCOON.—Bk.; 352; Sndld., 1863; Reg. Wy., March, 1863; Owners, T. Marwood, 40, James Mutter, 16, T. N. Marwood, 8. Sold to London, Nov., 1882.

UHLA.—Bg.; 341; Hull, 1841; Reg. Wy., 1863; Owners, Sarah Nesfield, 38, Andrew Gatenby, 16, and Will. Falkingbridge, 10. Sold to Quebec, 1871, by Ed. Theaker Weatherill.

UNDINE.—Bk.; 315; Lynn, 1849; Reg. Wy., 1857; Owner, Robt. Parkinson, R.H.Bay.

Master and crew of the barque "Undine," of Whitby, wrecked on the Sunk Sand, in the gale of Sunday, 28th Dec., 1862, were landed at Deal from the brig "Nautilus," of S. Shields. The crew were in a very exhausted state, and did not abandon the vessel until she was full of water.

UNDINE.—Bk.; 309; Sndld., 1860; Reg. Wy., 1879; Owners, Matt. Peacock and Will. Sample. Sold to Norway, April, 1881.

UNA.—Bg.; 170; Sndld., 1856; Reg. Wy., May, 1856; Owner, Gideon Smales; Owner, 1879, Will. Bedlington. Abandoned at sea, Nov. 7, 1881, picked up and sold as a wreck at Ostend.

UNITED.—Bg.; 300; Hartlepool, 1846; Reg. Wy., Feb., 1864. Owners, Stephen Crosby, M. Burrows, Moses Bell, and Ch. Wright. Sold to Norway, 1881.

UNITY.—Bg.; 193; Sndld., 1840; Reg. Wy., Feb. 29, 1840; Owners, Matt. Bedlington and Isaac Storm. Lost on the Lincolnshire Coast, Nov., 1861.

UNITY.—Bg.; 80; Bridlington, 1817; Reg. Wy., 1844; Owners, Geo. Russell and Jn. Hoggarth; Owners, 1862, Matt. Hoggarth, 16, Jos. Hoggarth, 16, Thos. W. Denne, 16, and Robt. N. Reynolds, 16. Lost in Boston Deeps, October, 1869.

UNION.—Bn.; 134; Topsham, Devon, 1782.; Reg. Wy., 1798; Owner, Hen. Bennison, Whitby; Reg. Newcastle, 1818.

UNION.—Bn.; 95; Southtown, 1806; Reg. Wy., 1814; Owner, Francis Dobson, Mickleby; Owners, 1824, F. D. and M. Trowsdale, Northallerton. Lost, 1829.

UNION.—Bn.; 122; Newcastle, 1800; Reg. Wy., 1825; Owner, Jos. Wood, Wy., m.m.; Owner, 1831, James Wood, 64. Lost on the Shipwash Sand, June, 1856.

UNION.—Slp.; 77; Pallion, 1801; Reg. Wy., 1827; Brigantine, 1837; Owners, Will. Hill and Jn. Boyes; Owner, 1832, Peter Appleton, Whitby, 64; Owners, 1834, Geo. Lennard, Lythe, 16, T. Douglas, Wy., 16, and Robt. Miller, Scarbro', 32; Reg. Scarbro', Oct. 16, 1835; Reg. Wy. from Scarbro', Oct., 1837; Owners, Whitwell Theaker, 32, and Hen. Reynolds, Deal, 32. Stranded at Deal. Reg. cancelled, Dec., 1841.

UNION.—Bg.; 149; Sndld., 1812; Reg. Wy., 1837; Owner, Will. Granger, R.H.Bay; Owner, 1851, James Granger. Lost off the Dudgeon lightship, Nov., 1860.

UTILITY.—Bg.; 150; Sndld., 1842; Reg. Wy., from London, June, 1861; Owner, Jos. Bovill. Lost at the entrance to the Humber, Jan. 22, 1871. Came ashore at Whitby Feb. 9, 1861, the day the lifeboat upset.

VANGUARD.—Bk.; 459; P. Ed. Island, 1836; Reg. Wy., 1845; Owners, T. and Jn. Marwood. Lost, Sept., 1845.

VANGUARD.—Bg.; 255; Sndld., 1840; Reg. Wy., 1848; Owners, Isaac Bedlington and Co., R.H.Bay. Lost on the beach near Aldbro, 3rd May, 1860; Reg. cancelled and closed, 29th May.

VALLISNERIA.—Bk.; 236; Aberdeen, 1849; Reg. Wy., 1861; Owners, Jn. Walker, Wy., and Christ. Walker, Sndld. Lost at Lowestoft, Nov., 1867.

VENUS.—Slp.; 70; Hull, 1787; Reg. Wy., October, 1804; Owner, Robt. Adston, Whitby. Lost, 1807, or after.

VENUS.—Fishing boat; 41; Reg. Wy., 1801; Owners, J. T. and R. Brown, Staithes. With "Cockpit," formerly the "Hirondelle," a ship of war condemned Oct., 1800; Reg. Scarbro'.

VECTIS.—Bg.; 206; Isle of Wight, 1833; Reg. Wy., 1848; Owners, Will. Tose and Son, Wy.; Reg. Southampton, Feb., 1854.

VERNON.—Bg.; 181; Stockton, 1846; Reg. Wy., 1852; Owners, Matt. Trattles and Thos. Rodham, Staithes; Owners, 1880, Robt. Rowton, Clapham Road, London, and Will. Chas. Murrell, of Bermondsey, London. Totally wrecked at Cleethorpes, 28th Oct., 1880.

VESTA.—Bg.; 177; Sndld., 1827; Reg. Wy., 1856; Owners, T. and Robt. Mills; Owner, 1866, Robt. Mills, 64. Lost in Swansea Bay, March, 1866.

VERONICA.—Bg.; 232; Sndld., 1840; Reg. Wy., 1860; Owner, Moore Clough, Whitby. Ashore at R.H.Bay, North Cheek, Jan., 1860; Owners, 1867, Harrison Allison, 32, and Hansell Gibson, 32.

"Veronica," coal laden, 7 hands, left Hartlepool Sept. 25th, 1871. On the 26th a strong easterly gale and heavy sea, ship leaking badly and the crew constantly at the pumps. At 2 p.m. sighted a French fishing vessel, and hoisted ensign for assistance, as the vessel was now in a sinking condition. With difficulty the crew were got on board the "Frenchman," about 70 miles from Whitby, and were landed at Bridlington Sept. 28th.

VIGILANT.—Bg.; 216; Sutton, 1806; Reg. Wy., May, 1824; Owners, Geo. Watson, 22, Robt. Davison, 21, Will. Weatherill, butcher, 21. Lost. Last capt., named in 1831, James Dunbar.

VIGILANT.—Bn.; 74; Fishlake, 1785; Reg. Wy., 1797; Owner, Jn. Pearson, R.H.Bay. Lost.

VIGILANT.—Sch.; 62; Yarmouth, 1801; Reg. Wy., 1857; Owners, James Page and Will. Wright, Abbey Farm. Lost in the Humber, Sept., 1860.

VINE.—Bn.; 233; Sndld., 1793; Reg. Wy., 1817; Owner, Robt. Corner, Lofthouse. Lost, Dec., 1822.

VIOLET.—Slp.; $\frac{39}{58}$; Stockton, 1831; Reg. Wy., 1831; afterwards a schooner; Owner, Geo. Westgarth, Boulby; Owner, 1850, James Roberts; Owner, 1854, Hen. Roberts.

"Violet," of Whitby, with a general cargo, ashore at Hummersea, near Staithes, Oct., 1861. Total wreck.

VIOLET.—Bg.; 189; Sndld., 1850; Reg. Wy., 1867; Owners, Will. Baxter, James Gray, Christ. Richardson, and Richd. Jackson; Owners, 1871, Nathan Hewson, Thos. Avery and Fanny and Eliza Coggin. Wrecked at Wells, Norfolk, Oct. 29th, 1880.

VICTORIA.—Cutter; 19; Scarbro', 1840; Reg. Wy., May, 1864; Owner, Jn. Fergus; Reg. West Hartlepool, 1866.

VIBILIA.—Bk.; 360; Quebec, 1826; Reg. Wy., 1838; Owners, Jn. Lawson, jun., and Mary Garbutt. Capt. Terry. Lost in the Mozambique Channel.

VISITOR.—Bg.; 209; Sndld., 1823; Reg. Wy., 1840; Owners, Anth. Adamson, Jn. Corner, Jn. Stevenson, and Robt. Simpson Adamson; Owners, Oct., 1855, Mary Ann Adamson, Francis Kildill Robinson, Geo. T. Knaggs, Chas. Wrightson, 16 jointly, Ann Adamson, 16, Jn. Stevenson, 16, and T. Robinson, 16.

"Visitor," owner, Trueman Robinson, R.H. Bay, Capt., Will Todd Anderson, and five hands, left Shields for London, Jan. 16th, 1881, with coals. 18th, close to Flambro' Head, when at 4 p.m. the wind changed and began to blow a gale from S.E. to E. with snow. During the night, blowing a gale, all the sails were blown away except main trysail and main staysail, and the ship drove North.

About 2 a.m. on the 19th sounded and found 20 fathoms. To prevent the ship driving ashore, brought up with both anchors down about 4 miles off R.H. Bay town, and on sounding the pumps found two feet of water in the vessel. The sea broke quite over the ship, the wind a hurricane from the East. About 8 a.m. found five feet of water in the hold, and to save life got out the long-boat, and all hands got into her, and hung by a kedge and two warps near the vessel.

Soon afterwards the vessel foundered. The crew continued in the boat until about 3 p.m., when the lifeboat which had been brought from Whitby by land to R.H. Bay and there launched, came out and succeeded in rescuing the crew, who were so exhausted by exposure to the cold, and wet with the sea, that they had to be carried from the lifeboat to the shore at R.H. Bay. Ship a total loss.

(This is the incident Miss Linskill utilises in her tale "Between the Heather and the Northern Sea.")

VICTORIA.—Bg.; 154; Sndld., 1844; Reg. Wy., 1844; Owner, Alice Brown, Staithes. Foundered in the North Sea, Jan., 1851.

VIATKA.—Bg.; 210; Hull, 1841; Reg. Wy., Jan., 1855; Owners, Hannah Stephenson and Co. Lost on island of Gottska Sando, Baltic, Nov., 1867.

VICTOR.—Sch.; 85; Russian Prize; Reg. Wy., Jan., 1857; Owner, Mark Frampton, Whitby. Lost, Nov., 1857.

VICTOR.—Bg.; 208; Sndld., 1848; Reg. Wy. Feb., 1858; Owners, Matt. Storm, Will. Bedlington, and Will. Steel; Owners, 1866, Matt. Storm, 32, Will. Bedlington, 32. Lost in Boston Deeps, Oct., 1869.

VIXEN.—Bg.; 184; Quebec, 1840; Reg. Wy., Feb., 1859; Owner, Mark Frampton. Lost off Yarmouth, Aug., 1870.

VIRTUE.—Sch.; 46; Wear, 1845; Reg. Wy., Feb., 1862; Owner, Hen. Roberts; Owners, 1894, Will. Roberts, m.m., 32, and Francis John Roberts, grocer's assistant, 32. Converted into a lighter, 1899.

VIVID.—Bg.; 212; Sndld., 1846; Reg. Wy., 1876; Owner, Jn. Harrison, R.H.Bay; Owners, 1890, W. Milburn and Co., North Shields. Wrecked at Waterford, Dec., 1893.

VICTORIA.—Bk.; 237; Prize; Reg. Newcastle, 1840; Owners, 1840, Will Todd and Co.; Capt., James Wood; Capt., 1863, Zebulon Hodgson.

VOYAGER.—Bg.; 223; Sndld., 1832; Reg. Wy., 1857; Owners, Ed. Storm and Matt. Peacock; Owners, 1877, Matt. and Isaac Peacock, and James Simpson. Lost on Juist Island, Germany, July 18th, 1877.

VOLTA.—Bk.; 318; U.S.A., date unknown; Reg. Wy., May, 1864; Owner, Sampson Storm; Owners, 1865, Jn. and J. H. Storm, 64 jointly. Condemned at Gibraltar, June, 1866, as unseaworthy, and sold.

WALMER CASTLE.—Slp.; 57; Hull, 1801; Reg. Wy., 1808; Owner, T. Verrill, Staithes; Capt., Isaac Bedlington. Taken by the enemy. Re-taken and sold to Yarmouth, 1814.

WATERLOO.—Bg.; 153; Lvrpl., 1815; Reg. Wy., 1836; Owner, Martin Granger, R.H.Bay; Owner, 1842, E. Mackenzie, R.H.Bay, school-master, in right of his wife, Alice Granger, widow of Martin Granger. Reg. Stockton, 16th March, 1847.

WATERLOO.—Sch.; 45; Southtown, 1815; Reg. Wy., 1861; Owners, Geo. Ayre and Will. Smallwood; Owners, 1865, Francis Cornforth, 10, Jn. Legg, 32, and Jn. Hovington, 22; Reg. at Scarbro', 1868.

WANDERER.—Bg.; 221; Sndld., 1840; Reg. Wy., 1840; Owners, J. and M. Rickinson and Co. Lost on the coast of Sweden, May, 1847.

WANDERER.—Bg.; 247; Sndld., 1841; Reg. Wy., 1841; Owners, Will. Corney, Thos. Jackson, Ann Hill, and T. Watson; Owner, 1872, Will. Steel, 64.

"Wanderer," Capt., Ed. Lothian, and eight hands, Leith for Dantzic, went ashore in thick rain on the Island of Bornholm, 18th Sept., 1873.

WANDERER.—Bg.; 173; P. Ed. Island, 1847; Reg. Wy., Feb., 1848; Owners, Jn. Schofield and Jos. Fletcher, m.m.; Reg. London, Nov., 1848.

WANDERER.—Bg.; 234; Wear, 1848; Reg. Wy., 1857; Owner, Jos. Bovill. Lost on Island of Krangelsholm, Baltic, Oct., 1858.

WATERWITCH.—Bg.; 204; Sndld., 1840; Reg. Wy., 1848; Owners, Will. Brown, Staithes, and Jn. Liddle, Sndld; Owners, 1863, Geo. Wright, 48, Jn. Leadley, 16.

"Waterwitch," Capt., Fred. Leng, Shields for Rotterdam, coals, foundered through stress of weather. Crew saved by an Ostend fishing smack, which left fishing to save life, Feb., 1869. Landed at Ostend, March 3rd.

WALLACHIA.—Bg.; 276; Sndld., 1854; Reg. Wy., Jan., 1854; Owners, T. and J. Marwood. Lost in the Black Sea, 1864.

WANNAN.—Bg.; 184; Lvrpl., 1840; Reg. Wy., 1855; Owner, Robt. Dawson Clark, Runswick. Lost in S.W. Reach, Oct. 22nd, 1865.

WATERS.—Bg.; 174; Sndld., 1833; Reg. Wy., 1865; Owner, James Hartley, Whitby; Owners, 1870, P. G. Rayne, Will. Booth and Will. Smallwood. Lost near Browershaven, Aug. 26, 1871.

WARDS.—Bg.; 161; Wear, 1846; Reg. Wy., 1876; Owners, Jn. Bedlington, sen. and jun., and Jane Skinner Jackson. Missing, supposed foundered in N. Sea, about 28th Oct., 1882.

WARRIOR QUEEN.—Bg.; 220; Sndld., 1852; Reg. Wy., 1879; Owner, James Rayment. Sold to Newcastle Sept., 1881. Foundered in Yarmouth Roads, Oct., 1882, after collision with brig "Runo," of Whitby.

WATER NYMPH.—Bg.; 205; Walker, Tyne, 1840; Reg. Sndld.; Owner, Will. Peck, Whitby, 1873.

WATER HEN.—Bk.; 353; Hull, 1825; Reg. London; Owners, 1853, Brown and Robertson, Whitby.

WEAR.—Bn.; 94; Sndld., 1785; Reg. Wy., 1794; Owners, James Wake, lighterman, and Hen. and Thos. Barrick; Reg. at Sndld., Nov., 1795.

WEAR.—Slp.; 35; N. Shields, 1855; Off. No. 10184.

"Wear," owned by Jn. Lennard, Robt. Brockett, master, and one hand, drove ashore half a mile N.W. of the piers at Whitby, May, 1885, at 5.30 p.m., and became a total wreck. The two men took to the rigging till 5.45, when they were taken off by the lifeboat. The sloop was bound from West Hartlepool for Maudesley, Norfolk, with coals.

WESTMORELAND.—S.; 376; Yarmouth, 1783; Reg. Wy., 1797; Owners, Robt. Gill, m.m., Hen. Barrick, sen., gentleman, and Jn. Watson; Reg. Lvpl., Feb., 1800.

WEDDELL.—Sch.; 101; Thorne, 1785; Reg. Wy., 1806; Owner, Francis Spence, Wy., 1809; previously, Jn. Ayre, m.m.; enlarged from Sloop; Owner, 1824, Jn. Holt, 64; Reg. Sndld., 1825.

WELLINGTON.—Bn.; 123; Prize, 1810; Reg. Wy., 1823; Owner, Ed. Bell, Wy., m.m.; a brig in 1824; Owner, 1824, Robt. Cockerill, 64; Reg. London, 1827.

WELLINGTON.—Bg.; 208; Aberdeen, 1815; Reg. Wy., 1835; Owners, T. Harland and Jn. and Ed. Corner. Lost.

WELLINGTON.—Slp.; 21; Boston, 1814; Reg. Wy., April, 1869; Owner, Jn. Winspeare, Glaisdale.

"Wellington," sloop, Geo. Corner, master, riding in Sandsend Roads, 15th June, 1869, was driven ashore by a sudden gale from the N.E. Total wreck.

WELLINGTON.—Bg.; 227; P. Ed. Island, 1856; Reg. Wy., 1883; Owner, Christ. Marwood; Owner, 1891, J. W. Laws, S. Shields. Lost off South Pier, Shields, Jan., 1892.

WEST HENDON.—Bg.; 151; Stockton, 1839; Reg. Wy., 1846; Owners, Christ. Thompson and Co. Lost on Goree Beach, Dec., 1854.

WELTHIN.—Bg.; 171; Sndld., 1840; Reg. Wy., 1856; Owner, Will. Granger, R.H.Bay. Lost near Gunfleet Light, Aug., 1869.

WELCOME.—Bg.; 228; Hylton, 1838; Reg. Wy., 1852; Owner, Thos. Moorsom, R.H.Bay; Owners, 1857, Robt. Stainthorpe, Christ. Moorsom, and T. Barnard, 64 jointly. Lost off the Gunfleet, Feb., 1866.

WHITBURN.—Slp.; 38; Sndld., 1789; Reg. Wy., April, 1795; Owners, Geo. Potts and Co., Whitby; Reg. Sndld., July, 1795.

WILLIAM.—Bn.; 72; G. Yarmouth, 1794; Reg. Wy., 1810; Owner, Jn. Gill, R.H.Bay.; Reg. Sndld., 1815; Reg. Wy. from Sndld., May, 1817; Owner, Will. Porritt, Lofthouse. Lost.

WILLIAM.—Bn.; 103; Sndld., 1815; Reg. Wy., 1815; Owner, Zachariah Knaggs, cordwainer. Lost, 1821, or after.

WILLIAM.—Bn.; 134; Sndld., 1800; Reg. Wy., 1817; Owner, Thos. Clark, Runswick. Lost in 1822.

WILLIAM.—Slp.; 50; Wear, 1802; Reg. Wy., 1818; Owner, Sam. Holsey, R.H.Bay, 27th May, 1818; Owner, 22nd Sept., 1823, Rich. Robinson, R.H.Bay; Owners, 23rd Jan., 1830, Jn. Milburn, 32, W. Robinson, 32; Owners, 4th March, 1846, Jn. Ireland, 16, and James Robinson, Scarbro', 48; Schooner, 50 tons, 1846; running bowsprit; Owners, 5th March, 1847, Will. Pearson, R.H.Bay, 16, James Robinson, 48; Capt., Will Pearson; Owners, 26th Aug., 1854, Thos. Frank, 32, Will. Harrison, 32; Capt., Jos. Harvey; Owners, March, 1856, T. Frank, 16, W. Adamson, 16, Robt. Sawdon, 32; Owner, Feb., 1860, Robt. Sawdon, 64; Sold 5th March, 1873, to Hen. K. Upclere, of Sherringham Hall, Norfolk; Reg. Cancelled, Dec., 1878. Vessel used for inland navigation.

WILLIAM.—Sch.; 19; Yarmouth, 1826; Reg. Wy., Aug. 21, 1855; Off. No., 9012; 46.4 by 14.5; Owners, Will. Adamson, shoemaker, 42, T. Frank, tailor, 22; Later, Mary Ann Frank, widow; Sold, March, 1861, to Jackson Adamson, shoemaker, and Will. Latimer, grocer, both of Lofthouse; Sold by them 20th Aug., 1861, to West Hartlepool.

WILLIAM.—Bg.; 244; Sndld., 1825; Reg. Wy., 1825; Owner, Edgar Richardson, m.m. Lost.

WILLIAM.—Bg.; 121; Fowey, 1824; Reg. Wy., 1838; Owners, Robt. Robinson, R.H.Bay, and Hen. Sutton, Middlesboro'; Reg. Stockton, Oct., 1846.

WILLIAM.—Slp.; 27; Berwick, 1821; Reg. Wy., 1840; Owners, Thos. and Will. Belcher, coal merchants; Reg. H'pool, Feb., 1847.

WILLIAM.—Sch.; 75; Aberdeen, 1831; Reg. Wy., 1856; Owners, Matt. Trattles, Thos. Rodham and Will. and Geo. Laverick; Reg. H'pool, 1868.

WILLIAM.—Bk.; 284; Sndld., 1845; Reg. Wy., 1862; Owners, Sanderson, Brown and Co. Lost off Scarbro', Nov., 1864.

WILLIAM.—Bg.; 234; Dundee, 1841; Reg. Wy., 1864; Owners, Will. Bedlington, 24, and Matt. Storm, 40, in 1866. Lost off East Coast of Jutland, March, 1866.

WILLIAM AND MARY.—S.; 209; Sweden; Reg. Wy., 1800; 3 masts; 88.6 by 23.9.

Made free, pursuant to Attorney General's opinion, April, 1778, then called the "Providence."

Owners, Isaac Chapman and Thos. Marwood, a cooper, of Whitby. Sold to Newcastle, 1809.

WILLIAM AND MARY.—Bg.; 178; Sndld., 1841; Reg. Wy., 1841; Owners, Will Granger and Co., R.H. Bay; Owners, 1853, Will Granger, 32, Mary Hunter, 16, and Jn. Mowbray Gales, Sndld., 16. Lost near Harwich, Nov., 1855.

WILLIAM AND HANNAH.—Galliot; 77; Danish Prize, 1810; Reg. Wy., 1810; Made a schooner; Owner, Will. Hodgson, Whitby; Danish name "Fraw Magdalena." Lost, 1812.

WILLIAM AND HANNAH.—Bg.; 224; Sndld., 1838; Reg. Wy., 1841; Owners, Jonathan and James Skerry, R.H.Bay; Reg. Shields, 1859.

WILLIAM AND NANCY.—Bg.; 90; G. Yarmouth, 1791; Reg. Wy., 1818; Owner, Will. Robinson, R.H.Bay; Owner, 1836, Jn. Christopher Farndale; Owner, 1855, Ann Farndale. Foundered off Dimlington, June, 1866, after collision. Capt. Polly and crew drowned.

WILLIAM AND ANN.—Sch.; 166; Sndld., 1840; Reg. Wy., 1840; Made a brig; Owner, Matt. Storm, R.H.Bay. Lost near Winterton, Nov., 1849.

WILLIAM AND HENRY.—Bg.; 268; Sndld., 1841; Reg. Wy., 1841; Owner, Addison Brown.

Left Malta, Feb. 24th, 1849. A missing ship.

WILLIAM AND ISABELLA.—Bg.; 189; Sndld., 1840; Reg. Wy., 1849; Owners, W. and D. Baxter and Co.; Owners, 1853, David Baxter, 22, Robt. Sawdon, 21, Matt. Storm, 21. Lost on Seaton Beach, April, 1856.

WILLIAM AND JANE.—Bg.; 185; Sndld., 1829; Reg. Wy., 1852; Owner, Thos. Pressick. Lost on the Gunfleet Sand, Jan., 1865.

WILLIAM AND JANE.—Sch.; 78; Sndld., 1849; Reg. Wy., 1862; Owner, W. P. Bovill. Sold by Jn. Harding, 16, Jn. Glaves Hodgson, 16, Jackson Harding, 16, and Thos. Marshall, 16, to James Gilroy, Berwick-on-Tweed, July 7th, 1868. Lost in Yarmouth Roads, June, 1869.

WILLIAM AND RICHARD.—Bg.; 175; Stcktn., 1839; Reg. Wy., 1854; Owner, Philip Poad, R.H.Bay; Owner, 1857, J. H. Storm, 64. Lost off Yarmouth, Feb., 1864.

Found derelict, with no trace of crew, and afterwards sank with a salvage crew on board from the s.s. "Ryhope" in Lowestoft Roads. Mate and four men drowned.

WILLIAM ASH.—Bg.; 250; Sndld., 1853; Reg. Wy., Dec., 1864; Owners, Robt. Harrowing, 56, and J. Mackuen, 8. Lost at St. Nicholas Gat, Jan., 1871.

WILLIAM BOTSFORD.—Bk.; 553; N. Brunswick, 1842; Reg. Wy., Feb., 1848; Owner, Will. Usherwood; Lad. June 28, 1842.

Sailed for Quebec, Aug., 1859; A missing ship.

WILLIAM MAITLAND.—Bg.; 159; Aberdeen, 1839; Reg. Wy., 1852; Owner, Samson Storm; Owners, 1856, James Skerry, 21, Jn. and Jn. H. Storm, 22 jointly, and J. H. Storm, 21; Owners, 1865, J. Skerry, 21, Jn. Corner, Christ. Harrison and Ed. Corner, 21 jointly, and J. and J. H. Storm, 22 jointly.

"William Maitland," Anth. Newton and five hands, left Hartlepool 9th Feb., 1871, for Chatham, coals. Proceeded with favourable weather till 2 a.m. on the 10th, when the wind veered to the South, and at 6 a.m. increased to a gale from S.S.E. to E.S.E., the ship being then about 20 miles South of Flambro' Head. Put the ship under snug canvas with her head to the sea until noon, when they were about 9 miles South of Bridlington. At noon E.S.E. gale thick with snow, a heavy sea struck the ship, doing great damage and making a clean sweep of the deck and causing the vessel to leak. Wore towards land, keeping the pumps going. At 2 p.m. hoisted signal of distress to a Screw Steamer, but the latter could not assist on account of the heavy sea. The water rapidly increased in the ship, and finding we could not keep her afloat ran her ashore for the safety of their lives about 4 p.m. about 7 miles South of Bridlington. The vessel struck heavily, the sea making a clean breach over her. Tried to persuade the crew to leave the ship, and to try to reach the shore on spars. About 4.15 p.m. jumped overboard with a lifebuoy and succeeded in reaching the shore. The coastguard came to the wreck, but were unable tc reach the ship with a rocket line. The crew took to the rigging until 6.30, when they were carried overboard with the masts and drowned. The vessel broke up, and the stores washed ashore were sold by auction. Five men drowned.

WILLIAM BARKER.—Sch.; 53; Nwcstl., 1836; Reg. Wy., 1860; Owner, Jos. Cook, Sandsend.

Feb. 1st, 1858, about 5 p.m., blowing hard, very dark, and sea heavy, the schooner "William Barker," of Newcastle, came to the sand between the Battery and the first nab. Crew saved. Re-floated.

Owners, 1867, Jos. Cook, 16, Sarah S. Armstrong, Sandsend, 32, and Chas. Bell, Sandsend, m.m., 16.

The "William Barker," schooner, coming for the harbour, Feb. 20th, 1868, struck the East Pier and went on to the Scar. The crew were rescued with great difficulty by ropes from the cliff, the master's leg being broken, and the other men exhausted. Total wreck.

WILLIAM PITT.—Bg.; 183; Canada, 1840; Reg. Wy., 1866; Owners, Will Dotchon and Messrs. Wilson, Nicholson, Varley, Jefferson, Cooper, and Anderson.

"William Pitt," Will Wilson, master, and six hands, left Hartlepool 9th Feb., 1871, for London, coals. On the 10th brought up in the Humber, wind E.S.E. blowing a hurricane. On the 12th proceeded. On the 18th, off Gravesend at 10 p.m., weather fine, wind W.S.W., proceeding up the river under all plain sail, on reaching Northfleet Hope saw a light about 350 yards ahead belonging to the vessel "Tamesa," of London, brought up in mid stream. Considered there was not room to pass with safety and let go the anchor, and backed the yards, but the anchor dragged on hard soil, and the vessel drifted on the tide and came into collision athwart hawse with the "Tamesa." The vessel immediately filled, and was only held up by the cable of the "Tamesa" for about 10 minutes, when the cable slipped and the "William Pitt" sank. The crew got on board the "Tamesa" and landed at Gravesend. Considered the "Tamesa" to blame in bringing up in mid channel.

WILLEY.—Bg.; 178; Sndld., 1831; Reg. Wy., 1852; Owners, Sarah, Rachel, and Thos. Nesfield.

Capt. Outzen, of the Danish vessel "Ernest," which has arrived in the Thames, reports that on the 26th Oct., 1862, he picked up the master and crew of six hands of the brig "Willey," of Whitby. They were picked up off the Texel, and were on board the "Ernest" 8 days.

WILLIE AND ETTIE.—Bg.; 253; P. Ed. Island, 1865; Reg. Wy., Oct., 1865; Owners, J. H. Storm, 48, Thos. Newton, 16. Sold foreign, May, 1880.

WITHAM.—Bn.; 125; S. Shields, 1793; Reg. Wy., 1816, Owner, Will Grant, R.H.Bay; Owners, 1859, Isaac Pennock, 48, Benj. Garminsway, 16; Capt., Andrew Gatenby. Lost on the Gunfleet Sand, Sept., 1864.

WILLING MIND.—Ketch; 23; Scarbro, 1840; Reg. Wy., Jan., 1876; Owner, Will Featherstone; Ashore near Runswick, July, 1876; Owners, 1883, Hen. Readman and Chas. Wittup; Capt., Francis Dobson, and one hand. Wrecked R.H.Bay, March, 1883.

WILLIAM BROWN.— Bk.; $\frac{403}{439}$; Sndld., 1852; Owner, W. Brown, Whitby.

WINGS OF THE MORNING.—Bk.; 344; Sndld., 1857; Owner, Isaac Bedlington. In Whitby Harbour, Oct., 1878.

WOODHALL.—Bg.; 209; Hull, 1817; Reg. Wy., 1828; Owners, James Wilkinson, Matt. and Thos. Wright; Reg. Nwcstl., April, 1832.

WORKSOP.—Sch.; 74; Stockwith, Notts, 1805; Reg. Wy., 1830; Owner, Jn. Terry. Broken up; Reg. cancelled Jan., 1833.

YARM.—Slp.; 78; Stcktn., 1802; Reg. Wy., 1817; Owners, Jn. Turnbull, block and mast maker, Thos. Turnbull, watchmaker, and Will Hunton, Lofthouse, alum maker. Wrecked at Shields, Nov., 1828.

YAR.—Bg.; 155; Sndld., 1842; Reg. Wy., 1850; Owners, Thos. and Robt. Mills. Total loss on Kessingland Beach, Lowestoft, Dec., 1855.

YORK UNION.—Bg.; 91; Thorne, Yorks, 1787; Reg. Wy., 1803; Owner, Paul Cook, jun. Lost, 1809, or after.

YORK PACKET.—Sch.; 102; Bo'ness, 1806; Reg. Wy., 1824; Owner Ed. Bell, Whitby, m.m.; Reg. Hull, Aug., 1828.

YTHAN.—Bg.; 166; Newburgh, Aberdeen, 1825; Reg. Wy., Jan., 1857; Owner, Miles Turnbull, R.H.Bay. Lost near the Spurn, Nov., 1858.

YTHAN.—Sch.; 84; Aberdeen, 1839; Reg. Deal; Owner, Will Farndale, Whitby, 1869.

"Ythan," Owner, William Farndale, Jacob Porritt, master, and three hands, left Hartlepool 27th April, 1885, for Hythe, coals. On Thursday, 30th April, foggy, run into and sunk by the s.s. "Francis," of Stavanger, Rochester for Tyne. Cut down to water's edge right aft, mainmast falling soon afterwards. Launched the boat, all hands getting in, and in five minutes the "Ythan" foundered 10 miles off Spurn point. The Steamer brought the crew to Whitby, where we landed at 9.30 p.m. on the 30th.

ZEALOUS.—Sch.; 65; Ferryport, 1819; Reg. Wy., 1838; Owners, Joseph Lines Wodham, marine store dealer, 32, Geo. Lockey, whitesmith, 32. Reg. cancelled 23rd Sept., 1842.

ZEPHYR.—Bg.; 184; Stcktn., 1845; Reg. Wy., June, 1845; Owner, Thos. Trattles, Staithes. Lost off Yarmouth, Feb., 1860.

ZEPHYR.—Slp.; 27; Scarbro, 1801; Reg. Wy., 1850; Owner, Thos. Bean, Whitby, mariner. Wrecked at Skinningrove, Oct., 1858.

ZILLA.—Bg.; 191; Sndld., 1833; Reg. Wy., 1857; Owners, James Watson, m.m., and Co. Lost, 1862.

ZODIAC.—Bk.; 317; Salcombe, 1852; Reg. Wy., 1865; Owners, Geo. Galilee and Co.; Owners, 1870, Geo. Galilee, 22, Geo. T. Knaggs, 31, and Thos. McIntosh, 11; Reg. Sunderland, 1881.

ZOUCH.—Slp.; 67; Thorne, 1785; Reg. Wy., 1798; Owner, Jn. Holt, jun., sailmaker; Owners, 1799, Ed. and Aaron Chapman and Robt. Campion; Re-built 1801; Reg. Sndld., 1803.

WHALE FISHING.

Whitby Whalers among the Icebergs in Davis Straits.

As before stated, many of the larger Whitby sailing vessels found employment in the Arctic whale fishery, which was first begun from Whitby in 1753 by two vessels. According to Dr. Young, in his history of Whitby, the fishing was continued by a few ships until 1758, but from 1759 to 1766, both included, it was given up except for one only in 1760, the vessels being withdrawn for the transport service, a less precarious source of gain. After the return of peace in 1769 the industry was renewed, and was continued year by year by varying numbers of vessels, 20 in one year being the greatest number, until 1837. For three or four years before this the fishing had been unprofitable, the price of whale oil having fallen to a low figure. It had varied from some £23 to over £50 per ton, and whalebone from about £30 to £150 per ton. Of the two vessels proceeding to the fishery that year, 1837, one unfortunately drove ashore on leaving Whitby, and the voyage of the other proving a failure, the whale fishing from Whitby finally ceased.

After a few years the only evidences of the industry remaining about the neighbourhood were some of the oil houses, often constructed of the whale jawbones and boarded over; and the jawbones used all about the country for gateposts and for rubbing posts for the cattle in the fields. Several of these are yet in existence.

Moorsom's Storehouse. From a Sketch by George Weatherill.
This Storehouse was built of Whale jawbones, as can be seen.

WHALE SHIPS.

A list of vessels, and the years in which they were sent to the Whale Fishery :—

Henry and Mary 1753-7
Lost, Oct., 1757.
Sea Nymph ... 1753-8
Lost about 1758.
Dolphin ... 1754-6
Ann 1754-6
Sold, 1762.
John and Ann ... 1757-8
1773-5
Leviathan ... 1757-8
Lost, 1758.
Henry and John 1758-60
James and Mary 1767-75
Jennie 1767-1784
Porpoise ... 1769-1772
Lost, 1772.
Peggy ... 1769-1771
Lost, 1771.
Volunteer ... 1772-1825
Hope 1772-1775
1784-1790
Lost, 1790.
Loyal Club ... 1774-9
Delight ... 1774-1780
Providence ... 1774-7
Hercules ... 1775-9
Addison ... 1775-8
1780-3
Free Love ... 1775-89
1792
Speedwell ... 1775
1777-1780
Esk 1775

Two Sisters ... 1775-6
1785-90
British King ... 1775-6
Rachel ... 1776
Henrietta ... 1776-1819
Perseverance ... 1776-9
Providence and Nancy ... 1776-9
Friendship ... 1776-9
1784-90
Marlborough ... 1777-1792
Lost, 1792.
Adamant ... 1778-81
1784-9
1791-4
Chance ... 1780-1788
Lost, 1788.
Earl Fauconberg 1784-99
1805
Unity 1784-8
Jenny's Adventure 1784-6
Lively 1785-1826
Lost, 1826.
Loyalty ... 1785
Nautilus ... 1785-1794
Burnt in Whitby Harbour, Feb., 1795.
Resolution ... 1785-9
Prospect ... 1786-1790
Ann & Elizabeth 1786-9
Whitby ... 1786-1790
Harpooner ... 1786-1792

Martha ... 1787-9
Unity 1787-9
Experiment ... 1800-10
Reg. Hull, 1801.
Aimwell ... 1802-1824
Oak 1803-1806
Resolution ... 1803-25
1827-8
William & Ann... 1805-8
1810-30
Lost, 1830.
James ... 1811-1825

Esk 1813-1826
Lost, 1826.
Valiant ... 1815-25
Phœnix ... 1816-37
Mars 1816-21
Fame 1818-19
Harmony ... 1819-29
Camden ... 1833-37
Lynx ... ...
Sailed from Whitby, 1797, but delivered at Hull.

Several other Whitby-built ships were whalers, but sailed from other ports. Further particulars of all the above ships are in the catalogue.

Late in the year 1835 painful anxiety arose as to the fate of several ships engaged in the whale fishing in Davis Straits, whose protracted absence caused fearful apprehensions for their safety. The vessels belonged to the ports of Hull, Newcastle, Berwick, Kirkcaldy, and Aberdeen. The two Whitby whalers of that season, the "Phœnix" and the "Camden," had returned all well. The Hull merchants offered to equip a vessel to be sent to the relief and succour of the missing whalers if the Admiralty would supply provisions, stores, and a competent naval commander. Capt. James Clark Ross, R.N., having volunteered, was appointed to the command with Lieuts. Ommany and Crozier (the latter afterwards second in command of the sad Franklin expedition of 1845). The ship "Cove," belonging to Messrs. Spivey and Cooper, of Hull, built at Whitby in 1798, and of 374 tons, was selected. During the time occupied in fitting out the "Cove," two of the absent ships arrived in England, and reported four vessels frozen in the land ice of the west coast, and four beset in the pack, and drifting to the southward. It was at first proposed by the Admiralty to send out two bomb vessels, the "Erebus" and the "Terror" (of future fame), to assist Capt. Ross, but this was afterwards considered unnecessary. The "Cove" sailed from Hull on the 5th Jan., 1836, and in the Pentland Firth the Captain was informed by some fishermen of the arrival at Stromness on the 2nd of another of the missing whalers. After calling in at Longhope harbour and sailing again on the 11th the ship was fairly in the Atlantic. On the 14th, in Lat. 61 N., Long. 6 W., two very large icebergs were

sighted, never before known so near the British Isles. Encountering violent gales and the bowsprit being carried away, the "Cove" was compelled to put back to Stromness for repairs on the 5th February. A few days later two more of the missing vessels arrived. The scene of misery that presented itself on board the "Viewforth," of Kirkcaldy, was very terrible. She had rescued 27 men from the "Middleton," of Aberdeen, making with her own crew 84 men. Of these 14 had died of scurvy and from cold. Many were in their beds in the last stage of disease, and only seven were able to do duty. A few more days at sea and probably all would have perished. Still another ship arrived before the "Cove" sailed, leaving two only missing. The "Lady Jane," of Newcastle, arrived after the "Cove" had sailed, thus leaving only the "William Torr," of Hull, unaccounted for. The "Cove" spent the season in unavailing efforts to find the latter vessel, which was never heard of. During the summer the crew of the "Cove" received letters from various whale ships, and, among others, from the "Resolution," previously a well-known Whitby whaler, but then owned at Aberdeen. The "Cove" returned to Hull 31st Aug., 1836.

The Ship "Cove."

About the middle of August the "Antilles," of Greenock, on her way home from the Mediterranean, and in Lat. 45.11 N. and Long. 13.79 W., picked up a large oil cask branded "William Torr," and which afterwards proved to be a new cask which had been put on board just before that vessel sailed. It was much rubbed and covered with seaweed and barnacles. Several other of her casks have been picked up at sea, confirming the lamentable fate of her crew.

"Tales of Shipwrecks and Adventures at Sea."

The ship "Judith," built at Whitby in 1825, was owned in 1840 by Mr. T. W. Torr, of Hull. A Mr. H. J. Torr was living at Horton Hall, Swinderby, Lincolnshire, in 1906.

CAPT. COOK.

Capt. Cook, although not a native, was so closely connected with the sailing vessels of Whitby that he must necessarily be included in these records. Moreover, some errors and inaccuracies both as to Cook himself and the ships he sailed in having from time to time appeared and been repeated in public accounts, a correction of these is desirable, especially as I have had the advantage of a source of information apparently never previously examined.

James Cook was born at Marton-in-Cleveland, Oct. 27, 1728. When about 17 he was placed with Mr. William Sanderson, shopkeeper, in Staithes. He was not apprenticed, as is often erroneously stated, but was on the footing of a verbal agreement with no indenture. The absurd statement that Cook stole a shilling from Mr. Sanderson's till has been repeated *ad nauseam*. He is said to have exchanged, for a shilling of his own, a newly coined one from the till; but of course this was wrong, unless he asked permission to do so. This had little, if anything, to do with his leaving Mr. Sanderson; this arose from association with the seafaring youths and from residing in a seaside town, where all were occupied or interested in a sea life, and also, no doubt, from his own adventurous disposition. After about 18 months Cook, having determined to adopt a seafaring life, Mr. Sanderson assisted him, and he was bound servant, then so-called, or apprentice, to Mr. John Walker, of Whitby. His first vessel was the "Free-Love" (more of this vessel in the next section) in the coal trade. Then he sailed in the "Three Brothers," a new ship.

In May, 1753, then a little over 24 years of age, he was mate of the "Friendship," owned by Mr. John Walker, having spent nearly three years after the expiration of his apprenticeship, in July, 1749, in various vessels as a seaman. In 1755 he volunteered into the Navy, "having a mind," as he said, "to try his fortune that way." In 1758 he was master's mate in the "Pembroke," which vessel was at the taking of Louisburgh. In 1759 he was master of the "Mercury," and was at the siege of Quebec. Here he took soundings of the St. Lawrence, a perilous service, executed much to the satisfaction of his officers. He afterwards constructed a chart of the whole river below Quebec. In 1768 he was appointed to command an expedition to the Pacific to observe a transit of Venus, and made Lieutenant. He sailed in July, 1768, in the ship "Endeavour." During this voyage he sailed all round New Zealand, verifying its geographical position, as also the East coast of Australia from Cape Howe to Torres Straits, over 2,000 miles, discovering the Great Barrier Reef by getting ashore on it, and narrowly escaping total shipwreck. He returned home in 1771.

Being selected to command an expedition to determine the disputed question of the existence of a great continent about the South Pole he was now made post-Captain. He had two ships for his second voyage, the "Resolution" and "Adventure," his narrow escape of shipwreck above stated proving the advisability of a consort. He sailed from Sheerness June 22nd, 1772. In this voyage he sailed all round the South Pole as near as he could, establishing the fact of land there, and of its being completely icebound. He returned to Spithead July 30th, 1775.

A voyage for the discovery of a northern passage between the Pacific and Atlantic Oceans being proposed, Cook volunteered his services, and was appointed to command it. He sailed from Sheerness on his third voyage June 25th, 1776, in the "Resolution." At the Cape of Good Hope he was joined by Capt. Clark in the "Discovery." He found a Northern passage impracticable, and on returning for repairs to the Sandwich Islands, which he discovered the previous year, he, having some quarrel with the natives, was massacred by them Feb. 14, 1779, at Owhyhee.

Capt. Cook is often described as a great discoverer. This he certainly was not. He was great as a navigator of his day, and for the careful accuracy of his observations. He did, indeed, discover many groups of small islands in the Pacific, especially that of the Sandwich Islands, as above, which was his most important discovery as such. Had the Spaniards known of these islands lying about midway between the Philippines and California they would have been valuable for refreshment to their treasure ships.

SHIPS IN WHICH CAPT. COOK SAILED.

It is repeatedly stated that Cook first went to sea in a vessel or Brig called the "Brotherly Love." This is incorrect. "Free-Love" was the name, a full rigged ship of 341 tons, built at Great Yarmouth in 1746, as fully stated in the Whitby Custom House Registry, owned by Mr. Jn. Walker, of Whitby, and commanded by Mr. Jn. Jefferson. See catalogue in this Book. In a list of the crew of the ship "Free-Love" for Feb., 1747, still preserved in the Muster Roll Book at the Whitby Seamen's Hospital, there is, among nine others, the name of "Jas. Cook," servant or apprentice, as now called, of Marton, Great Ayton. His name is also in the list of the crew for June, 1748. In Nov., 1748, he is among the crew of the ship "Three Brothers," a new vessel also owned by Mr. Jn. Walker, and commanded by John Jefferson. In Sept., 1749, he is entered as a seaman, as his apprenticeship expired in July, 1749. According to Dr. Young he now went before the mast for two years or so, but not under Mr. Walker. In 1750 the list of the crew of the "Mary," owned by Mr. John Wilkinson, Will. Gaskin, master, contains the name of James Cook, seaman. I believe Dr. Young in his life of James Cook gives the vessel's name as "Maria." In May, 1753, Mr. John Walker gave Cook the place of mate in the "Friendship," duly stated in the list of the crew. Last entry as such, July, 1755.

"Endeavour" was built at Whitby in 1764 by Mr. Thomas Fishburn for Mr. Thomas Milner, and then named "Earl of Pembroke." When Cook was appointed to command the expedition to the Pacific, the choice of a suitable vessel was entrusted to Sir Hugh Palliser and Lieut. Cook, who selected a Whitby built ship, not from any sentimental predilection on Cook's part for such, but because their build allowed them to be beached for repairs without injury, a necessary quality in places far removed from civilisation, and also for their capacity for large crews and stores, and their strength. The "Earl of Pembroke" was bought of Mr. Milner and re-named "Endeavour," manned with 84 seamen, furnished with provisions and stores, and armed with ten carriage guns and twelve swivels. Her register was 370 tons.

When the "Endeavour" was stranded on the Great Barrier Reef as before mentioned, she was so much injured that it was with the utmost difficulty and danger that she was got into a place suitable for beaching and repairing, but fully carried out Cook's opinion of her qualities. He named the river where she was beached after the vessel, and the cape opposite the place of stranding he named Cape Tribulation.

THE AFTER HISTORY OF THIS SHIP.

Cook himself says in his own journal, that when the second voyage was determined on the "Endeavour" was not available, having been sent to the Falkland Islands as a storeship.

She is said to have been re-named "Amphitrite."

To be laid a hulk at Oban.

To be in New York Harbour and named "Rubens."

To have sailed for many years as a collier in the North Sea.

At one time a notion got abroad that she was lying in the Thames in front of Somerset House doing duty as a police hulk. Inquiry was made of the Admiralty, who replied: "The vessel referred to is the 'Royalist,' built at Bombay in 1839, and has never been known by any other name." The only "Endeavour" on the list of the Navy in 1770 was a sloop (so called) of that name which was purchased by Government in 1768, and sold in 1775, and the Admiralty records throw no light on that vessel subsequent to the sale.

Another Account:

"The 'Endeavour,' remaining in the Navy for nearly four years after, was twice sent out with stores to the Falkland Islands. Her next voyage was as a store ship for Boston to take the place of the 'Britannia,' which had been burnt. When she returned from Boston she was paid off at Woolwich in September, 1774. Early in the following year she was sold by the Admiralty, and with this sale all information from the Admiralty records ceases."—"Melbourne Argus."

Letter from the Admiralty dated 2nd Feb., 1888, addressed to Mr. G. W. Waddington:—"With reference to your letter asking for information respecting the 'Endeavour,' she was purchased for £2,800. After her return in 1771 she was fitted as a storeship, but for what station is not known. She was sold at Woolwich in March, 1775, for £645."

"During a recent visit to Newport, R.I., U.S.A., my attention was attracted by a paragraph in the newspaper referring to the unveiling of the statue of Capt. James Cook in England, and stating that his old ship 'Endeavour' was finally broken up in the harbour of Newport. As a native of Whitby I was sufficiently interested to follow the matter up, and I trust the result of my investigations may interest your readers. Through the courtesy of Mr. William Gilpin I was placed in possession of the main facts relating to the vessel's previous career and final disposition after passing out of English hands, as follows:—In 1790 the French Government, desirous of competing with Great Britain in the whale fisheries, offered bounties to such vessels as should engage in that business under the French flag. Capt. William Hayden, of New Bedford, Mass., then in Europe, through the firm of De Bacque Freres, of Dunkirk, bought the 'Endeavour,' and, having registered her under French colours as 'La Liberté,' sailed for Newport with a cargo of oil. The vessel was consigned to Messrs. Gibbs and Canning, prominent merchants in that day, and after discharging her cargo safely, took in a return load, but meeting with an accident in going out of the harbour was run ashore where Sherman's Wharf is now located, and upon inspection being found unseaworthy, was condemned. Gradually she fell to pieces, and the recollections of her famous career passed from the memories of all save a few of the old inhabitants. One day Mr. Gibbs, of the firm of Gibbs and Canning before mentioned, and then an old man, walking in the vicinity of Sherman's Wharf with Mr. Gilpin, British Consul at Newport at that time, and father of my informant, called the latter's attention to the remnant of an old hulk embedded in the mud, and told him that what he saw was all that remained of the good ship 'Endeavour,' in which Capt. Cook first circumnavigated the globe."—Letter to the "Whitby Gazette," Dec. 27, 1878, from Geo. Merryweather, 111, Broadway, New York.

"Resolution" and "Adventure," apparently so named when bought for Capt. Cook's second voyage, were both built by Mr. Thos. Fishburn at Whitby in 1770, and when bought were owned by Mr. Will. Hammond, of Hull. The "Resolution" (one of many of that name) was 462 tons, and manned with 112 men. The "Adventure" was 336 tons, and carried 81 men, under the command of Lieut. Furneaux, subject to Capt. Cook's orders. Little is known of the after history of the "Resolution." The following seems probable:

"When young John Barrow, who was afterwards for 50 years a Secretary of the Admiralty, was on his way out as Controller of the Household to Lord Macartney's sumptuous embassy to China (1792), he saw the 'Resolution' a Portuguese coal hulk, at Rio de Janeiro, and wrote some indignant sentences thereon."—"Melbourne Argus," Feb. 25, 1879.

The "Adventure," though not admitted to accompany the "Resolution" in her last voyage, outlived the other vessels then employed (*i.e.*, the "Resolution" and the "Discovery"). She belonged for several years to a Mr. Brown, of Hull, and more recently to Messrs. Appleton and Trattles, of Whitby. She underwent a thorough repair in the dock of

Messrs. Langborne in 1810, but was wrecked in the Gulf of St. Lawrence in 1811.—Dr. Young.

"The 'Adventure,' Snowdon, of Whitby, from Leith for Quebec, lost May 24, 1811, in the Gulf of St. Lawrence."—English Chronicle, June 25, 1811.

"Discovery," consort to the "Resolution" in Cook's third voyage, was built at Whitby by Messrs. G. and N. Langborne for Mr. William Herbert, of Scarborough, in 1774, and first named "Diligence." She measured 295 tons and carried 80 men. Later history unknown.

None of the four vessels employed by Cook for his three voyages were specially built for that purpose.

"Discovery" sketched by E. W. Cook, R.A., as a convict hulk.—("The ship, her story," Clark Russell, "Pall Mall Magazine," Volume 17, 1899).

Letters and date on Mr. Jn. Walker's house, Grape Lane, Whitby, where Cook spent his winter evenings.

WILLIAM SCORESBY.

Born 3rd May, 1760, at a farm called Nutholm, in the township of Cropton, near Pickering, began life in Whitby sailing ships, being apprenticed when about 19 years old to the ship "Jane" (owned by John Chapman, a Quaker) in the Baltic trade. He joined the Navy in 1781, was taken prisoner, but escaped. He remained at home about two years, and then went to sea in the whale ship "Henrietta," in which he remained till 1797, since 1791 as captain. Being a man of great resource and observation, he considered that many more whales might be secured in a season than was then usual, six or seven being thought good. His first year of command was an entire failure, his crew mutinying and the season being unpropitious. On his second voyage as commander, having selected his crew himself, he proved the correctness of his opinions by bringing home eighteen whales, much the largest cargo up to that date. Being so successful he received tempting offers to command ships from other ports. From 1798 to 1802 he commanded the "Dundee," of London, in which vessel, being a large one, he caught 36 whales the first voyage.

1803 to 1810, he commanded the "Resolution," built and owned by Messrs. Fishburn and Brodrick, of Whitby. It was in this vessel in 1806 when in the Greenland Seas West of Spitzbergen in search of whales he reached Lat. 81° 30′ N., the furthest Northerly point ever attained up to that date by sailing, being about 510 miles from the Pole. The sea was open, and he might have got further North, but he considered it his duty to attend to the object of his voyage.

He made four voyages in the "John," of Greenock, 1811-1814, the proceeds of one of them being £11,000. He afterwards bought a vessel, the "Fame," registered at Whitby, Jan., 1818, in his own and his son's name. He died 28th April, 1829.

WILLIAM SCORESBY, JUN.

Born Oct. 5, 1789, went to sea with his Father when 10 years old, to the Arctic Seas. In 1822, when commander of the ship "Baffin" (not a Whitby vessel), he surveyed part of the East coast of Greenland. Later in life he took Holy Orders, and was Vicar of Bradford. He was a scientist. He made the voyage to Australia in 1856 for magnetical investigations as to the effect of the metal on the compasses of iron ships. He sailed in the "Royal Charter," of Liverpool, then a new vessel. This was the vessel that, in Oct., 1859, was wrecked near Moelfra, Anglesea, homeward bound from Australia with passengers and gold valued at £350,000. Some 500 passengers drowned, most of the gold recovered.

Dr. Scoresby died at Torquay, March 21, 1857.

GEORGE CHAMBERS.

George Chambers, as an Artist, has done much to preserve the memory of sailing vessels by his paintings.

Born at Whitby in 1803, he (according to a memoir published by Will. Forth in 1837), at 8 years of age, was employed in concert with another boy to hold the mouths of the bags open until they were filled with coal by the shovelman on board a little coal vessel, earning 2s. 6d. for his services for perhaps a week's work. At 10 years of age he went to sea in a small coaster, and in 1816 was bound apprentice for seven years to Capt. Storr, of the brig "Equity," and now his genius for painting began to develop. When at St. Petersburg he ornamented some buckets for Capt. Braithwaite, of the ship "Sovereign," of Whitby, who was so pleased with them that he persuaded Capt. Storr to release him from his indenture that he might gratify his wish to be a painter. When the "Equity" arrived in London that was done, and Chambers worked his way home by sea. At Whitby he was bound for three years to learn house painting with Mrs. Irvine, a widow. During this period he devoted all his spare time to the study of his favourite propensity, and executed a painting of his native port from the sea. After this he determined to take his chance in London, and having worked his passage in a new ship called the "Valleyfield," Capt. Gray, in 1825, and owned by Messrs. Chapman, to whom he had a letter of recommendation, they kindly bought his picture, which was afterwards engraved by Messrs. Fisher.

The Whitby captains when in London, meeting together at the house of Mr. Crawford, formerly a doctor in one of the whale ships out of Whitby, but then a spirit merchant in Wapping, were wishful to possess a view of their native town, and made application to Mr. Huggins, the marine artist, but his terms were beyond their means. Capt. Gray mentioned Chambers, and Mr. Crawford bespoke a picture for himself. He was employed by the captains to paint the portraits of their ships, etc., and he also painted a panoramic view of the coast

North and South of Whitby on the walls of the smoke room at Mr. Crawford's, that the captains might enjoy the representation of their native seaport.

Study by Geo. Chambers.

Chambers afterwards got engaged to paint at the Coliseum, and as a scene painter at the Royal Pavilion Theatre, which soon brought him before the public. Lord Mark Kerr procured him the royal patronage of King William and Queen Adelaide. He painted a view of Greenwich Hospital for the Queen and the opening of New London Bridge for the King. He was elected Associate, and, later, Member of the Water Colour Society. There is a fine picture in the Painted Hall, Greenwich, by him, of the Battle of La Hogue, 1692. His early life gave him structural truth in his ships, and correctness in their manœuvres. He died in 1840.

THE SEAMEN'S HOSPITAL

originated as under

An agreemt . . . of a New yeares gift to the distressed Seamen, and to the relief of theire widdows and the education of theire children in the Towne of Whitby in the county of Yorke this first day of January Anno Domini 1675.

In the name of God Amen We whose names are hereunto subscribed Burgesses of the towne of Whitby aforesaid and the Masters and Owners of the Shipps in and belonging to the said towne of Whitby haueing taken into serious consideration the sad and deplorable condition of our poore distressed disabled and decayed seamen whose livelyhood haus depended upon the Seas theire wives and children and not knowing to what straits wee ourselves may in the future be reduced to, it is our desires and intentions to raise and provide for a future provision to assist and be helpful to such whose necessities doe or may require.

And therefore wee doe lay impose and enjoine every Master of any vessel above the Burdon of twentie Tunns belonging to the towne of Whitby to pay unto such as are and shall be yearly appointed Collectors such summs of Moneys as is imposed and laid . . shipp for her Profitt. The Master for his wages and portadge and the sailors for theire wages upon every voyage as is hereinafter agreed and sett down to pay viz. :—

ffor every voyage past Whitby

The shipp to pay out of its profit	00	01	00
The Master for his wages and portidge	00	00	06
And every sailor who receives twentie shillings or above as wages to pay every man	00	00	02

ffor every voyage to any alloms worke or to the towne of Whitby

The shipp to pay out of its profitt	00	00	06
The Master for his wages	00	00	03
And every sailor who receives ten shillings or above for his wages	00	00	01

And wee doe hereby . . ourselves and authorise every respective Master with full power and libertie to receive and

.... as doe willingly

and with it to pay his own and the shipps ....

unto such as be then ....Collectors Provided

Allways that in case any owner doe refuse to allow his proportion then the Maister only to pay such owner's part as theire Charities are willing to contribute

And we doe . . hereby . . ourselves and those our successors whose inclinations may tend for a charitable .... every .... new yeare's day to choose by the major part ffower able and responsable Maisters or owners to be collectors for .... after theire election are hereby authorised to gather and receive from every responsable Maister theire charitable collections every voyage or as opportunity shall present it selfe And of what money they soe receive to give a true and just account every yeare and for the disposeing of such moneys soe by them collected it is hereby injoined .... the same new yeares day the collectors are chosen and appointed that ffower more able Owners or Masters be yearly elected .... to which ffower overseers and ffower collectors we do yearly give full power and authority to distribute and pay such summs of moneys as by them or the major part of them shall be thought fit towards the relief of poor travailing Seamen with the poor Seamen and Seafaring men theire wives widdows education of theire children belonging to the towne of Whitby as they shall find yearly theire necessities require and the stock will allow of **In** confirmation of this wee have hereunto sett our hand .... January 1675

Cri Ffairfax	John Jefferson
Linskill	Bartholomew Pinder
Dring	Geo. Lotherington
Bagwith	W. Kitchingman 1709
Jacob Hudson	Geo Meggison

John Conyers
Will Linskill, jun
Richard Marsingale
Thos Harrison
Daniel Yeoman
Thos Rogers
Thos Huntrods
Geo Weatherill
Thos Lindslay
Will Gaskin
Ingram Chapman
Henry Simpson
John Watson
Richd. Lotherington
Robert Harrison
Francis Barker
John Walker
John Gill
Jonathan Hammond
Richd. ffrost
James Yeoman
John Yeoman
— Noddings
Jos Scarth
Will Rudd
John Smales
Will Oxley
John Stokesley
John Allaton
Hen Linskill
Cornelius Nickols
John Chapman
Marmaduke Marwood
Mark Noble
John Jackson
Christopher Thompson
Jonathan Waynman

and others undecipherable.

Signatures of a later date.

1726
Christ. Yeoman
Hen. Brown
— Coates
Geo Widgett
— Harrison
— Smallwood
— Brown
— Marlan
Will. Brown
Solomon Chapman
Will Hill
Will Webster
Antho ....
John Walker

1727
John Lotherington
James Wear
Thos Jackson
Benj Chapman
Jacob Linskill

1728
Leonard Wild
Francis Coates
Robt. Middleton
Geo. Gill

1729
Benj Bridnall
Jn Moxam
Nickall Jackson
Ingram Chapman

1730
Robt Boulby
Thos Alily
Richd Richardson
Jos Scott

1732
Jonthan Lacy
Jn Wilkinson
T. Sleightholm
Thos Taylor

1735
Will Addison
Israel Blackburn
Matt. Brown
Geo. Hill

1736
John Mellar
Christ. Blackbourn
Witham Boynton
Benj. Chapman

1739
John Kildill
Corns. Clark
Benj. Hunter
Thos. Benson

1743
Adam Boulby
Hen. Cockerill
Jonthan Porritt
Will. Reynolds
John Yeoman
John Lacy

Dr. Young says:—"In a few years the funds thus provided were found sufficient for the erection of Hospital Houses, as well as for pecuniary relief to the distressed. The amount in the year 1676 was £36, but it was much greater in some succeeding years. Some Hospital Houses were built prior to 1684, their number gradually increasing by building or purchasing."

In 1747 an Act of Parliament was passed—20 Geo. 2—"For the relief and support of maimed and disabled seamen, and the widows and children of such as shall be killed, slain, or drowned in the merchant service."

This Act providing funds from sailors' wages for the same purposes as the Whitby agreement, and the subscriptions having somewhat fallen off, the agreement of 1675 was rescinded in Feb., 1748. The document is signed by—

B. Adam Boulby, Thos. Boulby, Miles Breckon, James Blackburn, Matt Brown.

C. Will. Chapman, Abel Chapman, Hen. Clark, Aaron Chapman, Ingram Chapman, Cornelius Clark, Benj. Chapman, Solomon Chapman, Hen. Cockerill.

D. Jn. Dale, E.T.G., T. Emlington, A. Fotherly, F.G., Jacob Hudson.

K., L. Robert King. L. Robt. Linskill, Jacob Linskill, Will Lyth.

M. Robt. Middleton, jun., Jn. Moorsome, Jn. Mellar, Will. Presswick, Benj. Presswick, Will. Reynolds, Hen. Thompson, Geo. Skinner.

W. Hen. Walker, Will. Webster, Jn. Waller, Thos. Williamson, Jn. Wilkinson, Jn. Walker, Henry Wilkinson.

Y. James Yeoman, jun., Jn. Yeoman.

Some, however, continued their voluntary subscriptions until January, 1756, when the charity, as such, finally closed, having distributed about £4,459 and provided 42 Hospital Houses.

After the close of the original agreement the Hospital was vested in Trustees—ship owners and ship masters of Whitby; who at one time disbursed some £700 per annum of the Seamen's Fund or Muster Roll, as it was called, not only to the residents in the Hospital, but also to the widows and children who needed it, of those who had lost their lives in the merchant service.

There was also another fund provided by Act of Parliament for the relief of indigent sailors, known as Greenwich money.

In the reign of William III., whose wife, it is said, suggested the plan of founding an asylum for disabled seamen belonging to the Royal Navy, it was determined, upon the recommendation of Sir Christ. Wren, that the unfinished Palace of Greenwich should be enlarged and adapted to the purpose. It was forthwith vested in the hands of Trustees. £2,000 per annum was granted by the King, the trustees contributed nearly £8,000, and Sir Christ. Wren undertook the work gratuitously. It was opened for pensioners in 1705. In the year of the foundation (1696) an Act was passed—7 & 8 William III. cap. 21—by which 6d. per month of the wages of all seamen in the Navy was appropriated to the

Institution. By the 10 Anne cap. 27 it is enacted that the seamen of the merchant service shall contribute equally with those of the Navy, and that such of the former (merchant seamen) as may be wounded in the defence of property belonging to Her Majesty's subjects, or otherwise disabled while capturing vessels from an enemy, shall also be admitted to the benefits of the Institution. The money received from visitors to be appropriated to the support of a school for boys.

Now in Aug., 1851, the "Seamen's Fund Winding Up Act" was passed, after which no sailor could benefit from any seamen's fund, unless he had been at sea a given number of years. Neither could he receive from the funds of both the above. The Trustees of the Whitby Seamen's Hospital, since the last named Act was passed in 1851, have had no funds to disburse, except the interest of certain bequests, but they have now 52 tenements available as free houses for indigent seamen or their widows.

The front of the Hospital was re-built in 1842 from a design made by Messrs. Scott and Moffat—afterwards Sir Gilbert Scott. It is in the Elizabethan style. At the top of the building over the central arch is a fine model of the hull of a ship.

COPY OF LETTER.

2, Dean's Yard, Westminster.

DEAR SIR,

When your letter about the Seamen's Hospital reached me, I feared it would be impossible for me to get the information you ask for, but a list has been found of Scott and Moffat's works, and among them is the Seamen's Hospital at Whitby.

Yours very truly,

(Signed) J. O. SCOTT.

Feb. 22, '07.

By a document preserved in the Seamen's House *i.e.*, the Committee Room, it appears that in 1688, the masters and mariners of Whitby being often in Shields Harbour, built a gallery for themselves in South Shields Church, which was long after called "The Whitby Gallery." This gallery was appropriated to another use several years ago.—Dr. Young.

South Shields Parish Church, dedicated to St. Hilda. The present church is modern.

THE SEAMEN'S HOSPITAL.
Drawn by Mary Weatherill.

WHITBY TRADERS.

1823. The Steam Packet "Tourist," from London to Edinburgh every Thursday. To London every Sunday. J. Lempriere, agent, St. Ann's Staith, Whitby.

Bains' "Directory and Gazette," Volume 2.

1827. The Sloop "Lark," bought by the Whitby New Shipping Co.

1840. The Whitby traders to London—"Enterprise," "Astrea," "Dispatch," and "Shepherd." The Steamer "Streonshalh" once a week to Newcastle and to Hull. Registered Shields, 1858.

1850. Traders from Toppin's Wharf, London—The "London," Capt., Thomas Postgate; "Pickering," Capt., James Girdwood; "Whitby," Capt., Robt. Kilvington. Mr. Matthew Wright, agent.

From Chamberlain's Wharf—"Astrea," Capt., Will Sanderson; "Dispatch," Capt., Jn. Newton; "Enterprise," Capt., Robt. Sanderson. Mr. Edward Dale, agent.

1871-3. S.S. "Captain Cook," 154 tons, built at Willington Quay. Sold to Dublin, 1873.

1876. S.S. "Lady Hilda," 450 tons, built at Whitby, 1876. S.S. "Tilsco."

WHITBY TUG STEAMERS.

MARY.—Owned by Mr. James Swallow.

MARY AND JANE. About 1847.

SAMSON.—Built at North Shields, 1839. Reg. Whitby, 1851; Owner, Charles Swallow; Later, James Swallow; Reg. at Inverness, 1855.

HILDA.—Built S. Shields, 1853; Reg. Whitby, May, 1853; Owners, W. and R.H.B. S. P. Co.; Capt., James Peirson; Capt., June, 1853, Geo. Robinson Hodgson; Capt., April, 1854, Will. Jameson; Reg. Grimsby, 1867.

GOLIAH.—Built N. Shields, 1854; Reg. Whitby, April, 1854; Owners, Whitby and R.H.B. S. P. Co.; Capt., Gordon Walker; Capt., Dec., 1854, Jn. Douglas; Reg. at Shields, Dec., 1858.

On Wednesday night, August 29, 1866, the "Goliah" broke adrift and was carried down the river by a strong "fresh," swept through the bridge with the loss of funnel and mast, and coming in contact with the tug "Hilda" below bridge broke her adrift also, but the crew of the latter being on board she was brought up in Collier Hope. The "Goliah" drifted out to sea and became a wreck on the Scar. A boy who was on board was with difficulty rescued as the boat was passing out near the East pier end.

MARSHALL.—Built at North Shields, 1852; Reg. Wy., 1857; Owner, Charles Mark Palmer; Reg. Newcastle, 1862.

ESK.—Built S. Shields, 1857; Reg. Wy., Dec., 1857; Owners, Whitby and Robin Hoods Bay S. P. Co. Sold to Middlesbrough, 1872.

EMU.—Built at Low Walker, Tyne, 1871; Reg. Wy., Aug., 1873. Sold to North Shields, 1895.

WHITBY LIFEBOATS.

Dr. Young says:—"Whitby is supplied with a lifeboat procured by subscription about 18 years ago (*i.e.*, 1798-9). It has saved several lives and would have saved many more had it been smaller, for being large and clumsy it requires too much time to launch and man.

In 1840 there was one on each side of the harbour.

In 1850 the same. One built at Sunderland on the West side, and one built by Mr. Gale on the East.

In 1860 the Sunderland built boat on the West side of the harbour being thought hardly worth repairing was sold to Messrs. Andrew and Co. for £3 13s. 6d., and a new one built by Mr. Falkingbridge was launched in October, 1860. This boat capsized on the 9th February, 1861, and twelve of the crew were drowned. The boat was subsequently broken up.

The Sunderland-built boat above mentioned was bought and repaired for use by the fishermen and called "Fishermen's Friend." The one on the East side, built by Mr. Gale, which had capsized in 1841, four of the crew being drowned, as fully recorded further on, was repaired and named "Petrel," and was used to save the crew of the barque "Royal Rose" in December, 1862. It was afterwards sold away. After the terrible accident of the 9th February, 1861 (see further on in these records), Whitby was supplied by the Royal National Lifeboat Society with a self-righting boat, and later with two for Whitby, both kept on the West side, and one at Upgang, one mile North.

Capt. Manby's life-saving apparatus was obtained at Whitby in 1816.

NOTATU DIGNA.

1614.—5th Oct. By an inquisition then taken before Sir Geo. Selby, Sheriff of Durham, it is found that a vessel called a "Hoy," bound from Whitby for Sunderland, was by tempest overset, and that the master and one of the sailors were drowned, and that two others of the seamen escaped to land in the boat, and the vessel thus became derelict, and was cast upon Ryhope Sands, and that John Rand, water bailiff, had seized the said vessel and materials to the use of the Bishop, and that the owners had supplicated the Bishop to restore the same.

1721.—William Pearson, of Whitby, blacksmith, by will Sept. 7 directed his body to be buried in linnen—his 64th part of the ship "True Love" to his sister Dorothy.

1722.—John Jackson, of Whitby, Innkeeper and Master mariner, by will June 16, gave to his son "one full and fourth part of all my ship called the 'Happy Returne,' with one-fourth part of the stock and profits,

Rights, Titles, members and appurtenances, to the said pinque belonging."

1776.—Charlton, the Whitby historian, says :—"The harbour is capable of containing all the shipping owned at the port, *i.e.*, some 250 vessels."

1796.—Jan. 23rd. A sand boat with decks was driven to sea with an old man and his wife only on board. The next day the vessel was found near Whitby, the poor old couple having perished through cold and fatigue. They were found lashed to each other and to the mast.

1807.—Thomas Baxter was killed on board His Majesty's ship "Scout" by a shot from a Spanish gunboat off Cape Trafalgar in November.

1823.—Preventive men first came to Whitby in February.

1826.—During the gale of Sept. 6-7 (in which the "Esk," whaler, of Whitby, was wrecked near Redcar), the brig "Air Balloon," Capt., James Brown, of Sunderland, came on shore near the Battery a little after 4 o'clock in the morning of the 7th. Crew saved. She was afterwards got off. Between 7 and 8 o'clock the brig "Quintilian," Kemp, of S. Shields, in ballast, was coming for the harbour. Her topsails split, which rendered the vessel unmanageable. She missed the entrance and drove behind the East Pier, where she became a total wreck. The master perished with his wife in attempting to save her. Their infant, about 10 months old, was saved with the rest of the crew.

At 1 o'clock in the morning the brig "Rochdale," Watson, of Sunderland, drove ashore at Hawsker Bottoms, about 2 miles south of Whitby. The crew not knowing where they were, and it being nearly low water, thought they might save themselves in the boat. They cut the lashings and lowered her over the side, when all hands got into her, and almost directly after they had got in, the brig began to part. The mainmast came over her side and sunk the boat. Seven of the men got hold of the rigging, the eighth of the topgallant halyards. The rope being loose he was drowned, leaving a wife and five children. The survivors got on to the mainmast, and having crept along it, to their very great surprise found that it washed upon a large rock which the sea had left. They proceeded towards the shore until they found a footpath, where they sat down, nearly exhausted. Soon after they attempted to secure some shelter from the storm. After walking about for some time they again sat down, exposed to the heavy wind and rain, some of them without jackets. After being in the cliff about eight hours they got down upon the Scar, and soon after found a road up the cliff, which place they recognised as being where they first were on coming ashore. They succeeded in reaching the cliff top and got to Mrs. Petty's, where they were kindly treated.

"John Wilson, who died at Whitby, Oct., 1826, was upwards of 40 years a Master in the Royal Navy, and during the years 1793-4-5-6 served in H.M.S. 'Agamemnon,' of 64 guns, commanded by Lord Nelson, whose heroic deeds in that ship must be too well-known to need comment."

1827.—July 13, at Abergavenny, Mon., aged 87 years, Jonathan Lacy, formerly of Larpool Hall, and shipbuilder, of Whitby.

1828.—On Friday, the 9th of May, a small smuggler called the "Goode Hoope," of Ostend, laden with contraband goods, was brought into Whitby, having been captured by Lieut. King, of the Preventive Service, with three men and two pilots. The cargo, which was immediately landed at the Custom House, consisted of about 300 kegs of spirits and 100 packages of tobacco, snuff, tea, etc. There were five men on board, and three others, supposed to belong to the vessel, were taken by two of the Preventive boatmen on the preceding night as they were landing from a boat on the sand near Upgang.

Friday evening, August 1st, a suspicious vessel was seen by the coastguard at Whitby standing in for Runswick Bay. Lieut. King at once went for the vessel, with a boat's crew, on which she stood out to sea. After a tedious chase the boat reached the vessel, which proved to be the "Francois," of Ostend, of about 28 tons, with contraband goods. She was brought into Whitby the following morning, and discharged 21 tubs of Geneva, 7 tubs of brandy, 3 casks of tobacco, two chests of tea, and twenty-eight casks of salt. The men, four in number, were fined £100 each, but, in default, were committed to York Castle. When examining the cargo one of the Preventive men was accidentally wounded, a ball from his own pistol in his pocket lodging in his thigh. It was extracted by Mr. Mewburn, surgeon.

Two or three nights after this last capture a large lugger was seen. The coastguard immediately went in pursuit, but were unable to overtake her.

1828.—Between 5 and 6 o'clock in the morning of Sept. 13, during a strong gale from the North East, two vessels ran into Whitby for shelter, and a small craft to the Southward bore up to do the same, but probably from not knowing the port stood across the rock. About halfway to the harbour she was thrown on her beam ends. The crew, some three men, and a woman got into the boat, which soon upset, and before assistance could be rendered the people were drowned. The vessel drove ashore and went to pieces on the Scar. She proved to be the "Elizabeth," of Hull, Thompson, master, with 50 tons of coals from Sunderland for Hull.

1829.—Oct. 14th, Thomas Johnson, master of the schooner "Prince of Wales," and Matthew Skelton, one of the crew, were endeavouring to make the vessel more secure, it being a strong gale from the N.E., when the boat upset, and Johnson was drowned. Skelton was saved by some men in a coble.

1830.—Jan. 17. Mr. Johnson, aged 47, many years a successful master in the Davis Straits and Greenland fisheries, and lately harbour master at Whitby. He sailed in the "Aimwell."

Dec. 12. John Brown blown off the hearse and over the bridge—the horse also; the latter saved, but Brown perished, and his body was never found.

1835.—March 25. The new bridge opened.

June 24. The brig, "Sierra Leone," came into the roads dismasted. She had a cargo of African oak and palm oil. Came to the sand next morning and became a total wreck.

1836.—Feb. 16. Shrove Tuesday. Extraordinary high tide. Much damage done to piers, etc.

1836.—April 16th. The brig "Spring" stranded on the rock in thick fog but smooth sea. The crew left the vessel and were all drowned.

1837.—Dec. 21. A gale. The vessel "Middlesbrough" came ashore on the sand at Whitby, and the brig "Friendship," near Sandsend. Three vessels at Robin Hood's Bay, a schooner, a vessel called the "Fame," and another called "Matilda."

1838.—Feb. 24th. Saturday, about 4 o'clock in the afternoon, the two brigs "Betsy" and "Derwent," both coal laden, came ashore on the sand, in stormy weather. Crews saved by the lifeboat. The "Derwent" was sold to Mr. Thomas Wright, and refloated March 2nd. The "Betsy" re-floated March 10th.

Sept. 26. Whilst a shooting party were at sea off Whitby one of them, Mr. Will Mann, was so seriously injured by his gun being accidentally discharged, that he shortly after died.

Oct. 11. A Dutch vessel lost off Whitby. A great quantity of wreckage came ashore and a small cask of wine. The wreckage was seen in the forenoon floating about. The vessel's hull washed ashore on the Scar next day, and the body of a man was found in the hold.

Oct. 12. Strong Westerly and N.W. wind. Many light vessels on the coast. The sloop "David," of Whitby, and a sloop owned at Sunderland, came ashore at Newholm Beck, the latter a total wreck, the "David" re-floated. The red buoy at the pier end broke adrift and washed into the harbour.

Oct. 17. 39 light vessels took refuge in Whitby harbour. A strong gale came on in the evening, and the brig "Ivanhoe," coal laden, came ashore at Upgang. Crew saved. Total wreck next day. She was owned at Sunderland.

1838.—Oct. 28. During the night a gale came on, and next forenoon the brig "Jupiter," of Whitby, came ashore on the sand, laden. Crew taken off by the lifeboat. Vessel re-floated Nov. 2nd. The brig "Kitty," of Whitby, narrowly escaped getting on the rock, but she got out to sea. Several cobles damaged in the harbour by the heavy "fresh" which came down.

About the end of October, or early in November, the two sloops, "Boulby" and "Magdalane," were lost.

1839.—Jan. 6th, Sunday. Late at night a heavy gale of wind came on, the worst off-shore gale ever known at Whitby up to that time. Much damage done. The Parish Church flagstaff blown down.

Jan. 16th. The brig "Daphne," of Whitby, came in during a strong sea. She had been missing some ten days, being blown off the land by the gale of the 6th.

Jan. 27th. The schooner "Jane Lyme," coal laden, grounded on Whitby rock. Crew saved. Vessel washed up under the cliff and broke up.

Feb. 2nd. The Sunderland brig "Automatia" on the rock. Crew taken off by the "George," of Whitby.

Nov. 29. A strong gale. The laden brig "Thames," of Scarborough, came to sand leaking. Two Humber keels riding at anchor in the afternoon began to drive. The lifeboat went out and brought away the crews. One went ashore at Sandsend and the other drifted away. The brig and keel sold as wrecks next day.

1841.—Feb. 11. The brig "Shakespeare," of Shields, grounded on "Filly Tail," laid all night, but was re-floated next morning by throwing overboard some of the cargo of coals.

Feb. 19. Brig "Sceptre," of Blyth, on the rock. Got off without damage.

May 1st. Three vessels on the rock. All got off the next day.

July 3rd. The schooner "Barbara and Ann," of Dover, laden, got on the rock about 8 a.m. Got off in the afternoon.

August 11. About 6.30 p.m. a French sloop came for the harbour, too soon for the tide, and drove on to the Scar. Became a wreck. Sold the next day. The pilot, Bilton, having his coble astern of the sloop when coming in, it was much damaged.

Oct. 6th. The Whitby lifeboat being rowed out to assist two yawls upset on the harbour bar, with thirteen men in her, and before the other boat could be got out, four were drowned. The sea was not very high, but there was a "fresh" running out. Wind S. or S.E. 7 men on the boat, one upon an oar, and one underneath the boat were saved. The four drowned were Walker, Storr, Wilson and Pattison.

Nov. 11. Sunday morning the brig "Miriam," of Sunderland, came to the sand about 10 o'clock. Crew taken off by the lifeboat. Vessel re-floated Dec. 1st.

Nov. 30. The brig "Shakespeare," of Sunderland, coal laden, got on Upgang Rock. Came off.

1842.—March 31st. During a fresh breeze from N.N.W. a sloop was seen off Whitby to "lie down" and turn over about 12 o'clock. Four men supposed to be on board. A fleet of between 40 and 50 vessels ran into Whitby harbour for shelter.

April 25. Monday, thick weather, the brig "Glasgow," of London, got on Upgang rock. Came off without damage, and came into the harbour.

Oct. 17. A Sunderland brig on the rock. Came into Whitby. Coal laden.

The crew of the "Economy," of Blyth, landed at Whitby, the vessel having sunk after collision.

Dec. 6. Three vessels on the rock. All got off. The "Edward" took assistance, and went to Shields.

Dec. 15th. A schooner on the rock in the middle of the day. No damage.

1843.—Jan. 9th. A brig on the rock. Got to Scarborough.

Feb. 4, Saturday. The R.H.Bay lifeboat returning with the rescued crew of the brig "Ann," of London, upset, and twelve were drowned—six of the brig's crew, five men belonging to Bay town, and Lieut. Lingard. (Will. Bedlington, of R.H.B.)

A light brig, the "Elizabeth," of Sunderland, came to the sand. Was re-floated.

Mr. Will Pearson, captain of the brig "Lune," of Shields, a Whitby man, was unfortunately drowned by the upsetting of a boat off the island of Orleans in the St. Lawrence.

Oct. 18th. About 8 a.m. a boat was seen close in. There being a high sea the lifeboat was got out, but before she could be got afloat the boat came near the beach and filled. Three men drowned. Two saved. Their vessel was the "Success," of Ipswich. They had been in the boat all night and were quite benumbed with the cold.

Dec. 16th. A boat was seen at sea coming for the harbour. There being a high sea the lifeboat went to their assistance. They were the crew of the "Neptune," of Berwick, which had struck on the Salt Scar. They had got on board of a brig, which brought them to Whitby.

1844.—Jan. Two brigs were riding at anchor in Sandsend roads sheltering from a North West wind. One of them, which belonged to Scarbro', slipped her cable and came to the sand about 1.30, the sea being high. The other one, which belonged to Shields, parted from her cables and came ashore, both near Newholm Beck. Both re-floated.

Feb. 13th. A brig on the rock. Got off. The "Sneaton," schooner, owned at Ruswarp, also on the rock. Got off at 4 p.m. Brig "Neptune," of Sunderland, coal laden, on the rock about 6 p.m. She drove up near the Spa Ladder, and broke up on the 17th. Materials saved.

Nov. 11th. A heavy sea. A sloop making for the harbour got on to the Scar. Crew were saved by men going down the cliff with lines. Three saved. Proved to be the "Brothers." A total wreck.

1845.—Feb. 1st. Very cold. About 10 a.m. a boat, containing 5 men and a boy, came into the harbour, having lost their vessel, the "Ann," of Ipswich, about 2 a.m. A rough night. The men were nearly naked.

July. 70 vessels and twenty large fishing boats came into Whitby harbour for refuge.—Evidence of Lieut. Brittain, R.N., given Oct. 28, 1845.

Evidence of James Wood, pilot master—"When

master of a vessel took refuge in Whitby, with 76 others." Evidence Oct. 28, 1845.

A buoy laid at the rock by the Trinity House.

Dec. 11. A gale. The brig "Mercury," of Colchester, laden, from Shields, came ashore at Newholm Beck. Two men washed overboard previously. One found dead, five saved by a line.

Dec. 29. John Barritt and Thomas Oxley, pilots, went off looking for vessels. Never heard of. Their coble was cast up near the Skaw.

1846.—July 8. A man named Plews fell from the mast of Mr. Smales' new brig "Nio," and died a few days after.

1847.—The bottom of the brig "Lord Nelson," which had been on the beach covered with sand for very many years, was laid bare and taken up.

Nov. 29. The schooner "Pilot," of Sunderland, coal laden, got on the rock in thick weather and soon broke up. Two of the crew were saved.

Dec. 7. A brig belonging to Rochester went ashore about Hawsker bottoms. The crew were in the cliff all night, not knowing where they were, it being so dark.

1849.—Sept. 30. Strong wind and heavy sea. In the afternoon the light brig "Wrangel," of Stettin, the brig "Black Diamond," of Stockton, and the schooner "Rocket," both these laden, came to the sand. A little foreigner lost his bowsprit on the bar, either by the sea, or it caught the ground as she nearly turned completely end over. The "Black Diamond" broke up, the others re-floated.

Two brigs, the "Victoria," of Shields, and "Sisters," of Rochester, on Upgang Rock. One broke up immediately, the other stood a tide.

Prussian Brig "Wrangel."

Dec. 3rd. The laden brig "White," of Sunderland, wrecked on Upgang rock.

Dec. 23rd. The brig "Doubtful" lost at Runswick, and two laden schooners on Whitby rock, one owned at Yarmouth, the other at Sunderland. Both total wrecks.

1850.—Nov. 26th. A small laden brig, the "Norwich Merchant," of Yarmouth, came on to the rock. Only a dog on board. Crew taken on board another vessel. Wrecked next tide, and sold.

1851.—March 3rd. The fine large brig "Saxon Maid," of Sunderland, coal laden, ran on Whitby rock. She was coppered, and going a long voyage. She washed up on the Scar and her sails were got away, but a gale coming on she broke up.

March 4. The brig "Samuel and Sarah" wore round and came into Whitby much damaged, having been in collision with a laden brig, whose mast and bowsprit were carried away. She put back to the north.

March 19th. A new flagstaff put up on the West Cliff.

March 22nd. The laden brig "Matchless," of London, got on the rock. Came to the pier end and sank. Coals discharged, and the vessel got into the harbour.

Sept. 3rd. Very thick weather. A brig, owned at Scarbro', ashore near "Filly-Tail" and sank. A schooner on the Salt Scar, but got into Whitby. A brig and a French vessel ashore at Whitby. Both got off.

Sept. 26. About 1 p.m. a Scotch sloop got behind the East Pier, not having sufficient sail set to bring her into the harbour. The crew left her. Men then got on board, and with a rope she came under the Spa Ladder into Collier Hope, but broke up about 5 p.m.

Wedgewood's sloop, "Friend's Goodwill," was riding in Sandsend Roads, the master ashore, one man only on board. A gale coming on, the sloop capsized, but the man was rescued.

1852.—Jan. 9. A very great tide, strong wind and high sea. Stonework on pier, etc., carried away. Dock End and Angel Inn much damaged.

Feb. 22nd. A wreck discovered on the rock. Proved to be the "Mary," of Shields, abandoned. The crew got to Bridlington.

May 26. Schooner "Isabella," of Shields, on the rock. Total wreck.

Oct. 26-7. Heavy gale. Great loss on the coast. A schooner was seen to founder off Sandsend. She proved to be the "Acorn," of Newcastle. Several Whitby vessels ashore and wrecked.

Dec. 17. A large brig ran against the bridge and did damage.

Dec. 25. The "Duke of York" assisted into

Whitby by Staithes fishermen. One mast had given way and the other followed. Agreement £20.

1853.—Dec. 10. The laden schooner "Flora," of Sunderland, was on fire off Whitby. Crew left her. Got into Whitby by fishermen, who succeeded in extinguishing the flames and discharged the cargo.

1854.—Jan. 4th. Strong breeze from the East. Several vessels could not fetch the harbour. The "Beta," Tyerman, "Bedlington," Seymour, brig "Mary Jane," and schooners "Donnington" and "X.L." In the evening the brig "Marys," of Whitby, coal laden, came to the sand just beyond the Lector Nab. All re-floated later on.

Jan. 14th. A large ship laden with guano was off Whitby with loss of rudder. The Whitby tug, after a hard tow, succeeded in getting her to the Humber.

April. A schooner belonging to T. Harland got on to the rock, came off and sank in deep water.

June 30th. The little schooner "Ant," of Sunderland, drove from her anchor and went on the Scar. Neglect.

October. During a strong gale from the N.E. a barque passed Whitby and went ashore at R.H. Bay. Eight of the crew rescued, four drowned. The vessel was the "Emporium," timber laden, which had been blown from Sunderland, to which port she was bound. She was got off the beach without the bottom part, floated by the timber, no masts standing, and towed into Whitby. The wreck sold to Mr. Thos. Wright, Dec. 8th, for £330. The timber was sold later.

Dec. 30. The brig "Champion," of Lynn, foremast and bowsprit gone, was being towed North from Bridlington. Put into Whitby through stress of weather.

1855.—The ship "Beemah," $\frac{887}{1021}$, built at Dundee for Messrs. Willis, Marwood and Co., Liverpool and Whitby; Capt., Jonathan Pickernell.

May 6th. The ship "Edward," Thornhill, the last full-rigged ship built at Whitby and fitted with Manilla running rigging, towed from Messrs. Barrick's to Shields. She was for London owners.

"Betsy," brigantine, laid on at Newholm Beck jetty to load ironstone, August 24th.

Oct. 30. About 3 p.m. a billybuoy sloop, the "Hannah," of Goole, was coming for the harbour, when she was capsized by a heavy sea. There was a family on board as well as the crew. All perished. The vessel washed up at Newholm Beck, bottom up. A man's and a child's body found.

The same night the brigs "Friendship," "Findlay," and "Content," came on the sand, and the next day a foreign sloop came ashore near East Row having lost two of crew of five. She was from Newcastle. The "Hannah" was sold Nov. 3rd for £74, and re-floated Nov. 9th. The foreign sloop broke up. The brigs were re-floated.

Dec. 15. The laden brig "Hibernia," of London, coals, was seen inside the rock, abandoned. Broke up. Crew got to Scarborough.

1856.—Jan. 28th. Schooner "Mary and Ann," of Lynn, ashore at Peak. No one on board. A wreck.

1857.—Jan. 2nd. The brig "Fanny Huntley" was running for Whitby harbour in a fresh gale at N.E. when she struck the East pier and carried away her figure head and stem, then got above the bridge and sank.

Jan. 4. Gale from E.N.E. The following vessels ashore: On Whitby Sand, "William Pitt," of Stockton, the "Medora," at Lector, the "Lively," of Guernsey, at Newholm Beck, the "Abeona," of London, at Sandsend, and the "Port Glasgow," at

Red Shale, Deepgrove. The brig "Amelia" lost near Runswick. Crew drowned. The "Peter and Mary" went down, crew drowned, somewhere off Runswick. The schooner "Mary and Jane," of Teignmouth, at Saltwick. The "George," of Colchester, at R.H.Bay, and many wrecks all along the coast.

January. The brig "Ariel," of Whitby, Thomas Reed, master, towed into Shields harbour bottom up. Crew missing.

Jan. 24th. The schooner "Triumph," of Ipswich, supposed to have struck Kettleness Steel and foundered, with crew.

March 14th. Brig "Ryhope," of Sunderland, towed into Whitby with loss of mainmast.

The "Goliah," tug, towing three iron boilers from Whitby for Port Mulgrave, near Staithes, two of them filled with water and sank off Kettleness point. Valued at £300 each.

The fine ship "Dunbar," of London, lost at the Gap, Sydney heads, in August. Terrible loss of life, only one man saved. Mr. William Snowdon, of Whitby, was carpenter on board this vessel.

1858.—Aug. 21. The brig "Amulet," of Blyth, coal laden, got inside the rock about 9 p.m. Alarmed the inhabitants. Crew taken off by lifeboat. Total loss. Sold for £56.

1859.—"Ætna," schooner, 82 tons, built at Gainsborough, date unknown, owned at Knottingley, registered at London, "Left Leith, 13th Dec., for Sandwich, with barley. Weather foggy, wind light from N.N.W. At 9 p.m., when off the Farne Islands, sprung a leak. About 5 a.m. on the 14th the pumps choked, and in order to save vessel and life determined to put into the first port. At 7 a.m. saw Tynemouth light, bearing N.N.W., distant about 16 miles. Altered the course for the Tees, but made

Huntcliff foot, then ran for Whitby. At 3.30 p.m., tide flood, wind N.N.E., a strong gale with snow showers, when close to the harbour was struck by a sea and driven on to the beach. Crew saved, vessel broke up."

Dec. 17th. Five light vessels went ashore at Robin Hood's Bay, all re-floated. Two brought into Whitby, the "Belford," three-masted schooner, and "John Henry Yates," schooner.

December. The men working at High Bell Shoal found a skeleton.

1860.—Jan. 26th. During heavy snow showers 10 light vessels ran ashore inside the North Cheek, Robin Hood's Bay. Two of them broke up, the other eight were variously disposed of. A company of 23 carpenters, who appointed John Marshall their captain, contracted to re-float two; the "Earl Bathurst," for which they had £150, was got safely into Whitby Harbour, and the "Will Watson" for £250, a few days later. The "Emily" was sold to Messrs. Harrowing and Co., and re-floated, as was also the "Veronica," for which they paid £205. The carpenters then got off the "Swan," and received £300 for the work and brought her to Whitby. The "Miriam" was sold for £300, but became a wreck, as well as the "Marion" and the "Clemence."

March. The "Conquest," tug, in search of vessels, anchored in the "Roads," parted from her cable, the crew apparently asleep and no look-out man, and drifted on to the Scar, breaking up a day or two later.

May 28th. Blowing a gale from the North, a brig was seen early in the morning dismasted and riding to her anchor. Brought into Whitby by two tugs, and proved to be the "Phesdo," of 245 tons, built at Aberdeen, and owned at Shields.

Oct. 25th. Brig "Thetis," Norris, master (registered at West Hartlepool, owner, Isaac Bedlington), got on Kettleness Steel. Got off and brought into Whitby.

1861.—Jan. 1st. The masts and wreck of a vessel seen off Newholm Beck. Belonged to Yarmouth. Crew drowned.

Saturday, 9th February, 1861.

"On Friday evening, the 8th of Feb., 1861, the wind began to blow strong from the North East, and continued to increase during the night, until it was blowing with intense fury on the morning of the 9th. The large fleet of sailing vessels known to be on the coast caused grave fears that serious calamities might occur, and these fears were alas! too fully verified, but in a manner in one respect not at all contemplated."—"Whitby Gazette."

About 8 a.m. the brig "John and Ann," of Sunderland, came ashore at Sandsend. Crew of five saved by a coble manned by John Storr, Robt. Leadley, Geo. Martin, Will Tyerman, John Dixon, Henry Freeman, and Will Dryden;

all these, except Dryden, were in the lifeboat when she upset, as hereafter stated, and the first five perished.

The schooner "Gamma," Middleton, of Newcastle, coals, for London, came to the sand about 10. Crew of four taken out by the lifeboat. Soon after the Prussian barque "Clara," Sunderland built, owned at Memel, Newcastle for Madeira, came ashore, crew of twelve landed by lifeboat. This vessel went to pieces very suddenly and disappeared.

The brig "Utility" next came ashore, and was closely followed by the schooner "Roe," Ritchie, of and from Dundee for Newcastle. The lifeboat brought ashore the crews of these two vessels at one trip.

About 2 p.m. the brigantine "Flora" succeeded in entering the harbour, but ran aground in "Collier Hope." The "Merchant," schooner, seemed likely to come safely in, but her sails giving way, she came to the beach close to the "Roe." The lifeboat, when attempting to save the crew of the "Merchant," was struck by a heavy sea and capsized. John Storr succeeded in getting on to the bottom of the boat, and others were washing about struggling for their lives with thousands looking at their unavailing efforts. Although only some 50 yards from the pier, and lifebuoys being thrown and rockets fired over them by Captain Butler, not the least aid was obtained by the drowning men, some of whose wives and children were among the helpless multitude. One after another the men perished. But soon Henry Freeman, who had on a cork jacket (the only one among the crew), was seen slowly working towards the shore, and men rushing in, holding each other, he was got ashore, the only one saved. Those drowned were John Dixon, Robert Leadley, Robert Harland, Will. Walker, Isaac Dobson, John Philpot, Will Storr, Will Tyerman, Matt Leadley, Geo Martin, John Storr, and Christ. Collins, twelve in all.

In the meantime the crew of the "Merchant" were calling for help, and the mortar had to be used to throw a line over the vessel, when the crew of five were hauled ashore, just as the vessel was falling to pieces.

About 4 p.m. the brig "Urania" came ashore. A rocket line was thrown over her, but as the tide was falling the crew remained on the vessel till it left her dry.

At 8 o'clock the brig "Tribune" came ashore not far from the West Pier. Rockets were tried, but could not reach her. The old East Side lifeboat was therefore lowered into the harbour, rowed across and lifted on to the pier by the Scotch Head crane, and a volunteer crew being called for, the following men took charge of her:—Thos. Boyes, Alfred Walker, Joseph Wood, George Milburn, Will. Hutton, and Thomas Harker, all master mariners, Will. Walker, mate, Daniel Clark, Will. Burton, and Robt. Wardle, seamen, Jn. Hodgson, fisherman, and Edwin Turnbull and John Carr, jet ornament manufacturers. They rescued the crew except one.

Next morning, Sunday, 10th February, the brig "Memnon" was seen riding in Sandsend roads, and about 7 p.m. she slipped her cable and came ashore, having ten feet of

Sunday, 10th February, 1861.

water in the hold. The old lifeboat was again used and brought the crew ashore, one of the above volunteers being in her this time also.

The Rev. W. Keane, then incumbent of Whitby, wrote the following appeal to the "Times" newspaper on behalf of the bereaved families of the lifeboat crew :--

"Will you allow your newspaper to add another tale of anguish to the many which have recently called forth the sympathy of the public? We have had a fearful storm to-day at Whitby. Half a mile of our strand is already strewed with seven wrecks. Our new lifeboat was but launched a few months ago, and was manned with the old crew of the finest picked seamen in Whitby. Five times during the day had they braved the furious sea, and five times returned with crews from vessels in distress. A sixth ship was driven in behind the pier. The men, all exhausted though they were, again pulled out, but before they had gone fifty yards a wave capsized the boat. Then was beheld by several thousand persons—within almost a stone's throw, but unable to assist—the fearful agonies of those powerful men buffeting with the fury of the breakers till one by one, twelve out of thirteen sank, and only one is saved. I have to add that eleven out of these twelve were married and have left families, and I am sorry to say that I myself know that owing to the severe winter to fishermen nearly all are left destitute. Whitby will do its duty to its bravest hands, but I feel assured that an old lifeboat's crew who have saved hundreds of our fellow creatures from such a fate as this, and at last perished in the noble discharge of duty to the public, will have the wants of their bereaved families cared for by the readers of the 'Times.'"—Saturday night, Feb. 9, 1861.

"Merchant," schooner, 103 tons, owned at Maldon, George Young, master, coals, Sunderland for Maldon. "Left Sunderland, 8th Feb., 1861. At midnight blowing a gale at E.N.E. At 8.30 a.m. wore to the North, jib and fore trysail adrift, bulwarks carried away, and boats smashed. At 3 p.m. the gale having increased to a hurricane, the sea tremendous, and finding the ship could not be kept off the land, the crew exhausted, determined to run the ship, then off Whitby, for the harbour, on nearing which the ship was struck by three heavy seas and driven past to the North side. On striking, the crew took to the rigging, the sea making clean breaches over them. In about 20 minutes the lifeboat was launched, and had come so close that one of the crew of the boat with a boathook struck the stern of deponent's vessel. The mate of deponent's ship, who was at the stern, had a rope in his hand ready to throw to the lifeboat, when a man in the latter requested it to be passed before the main rigging. Deponent and mate then went forward, and on looking for the boat, found her upset and the crew in the water. They were all drowned but one. The rocket apparatus was then used, but without effect. The mortar was then carried to the pier, and a line having been thrown over our vessel, the crew were successively drawn to the shore."

"Tribune," schooner, 132, registered Dartmouth, owned by Mr. Nicholas Browse, of Brixham, Newcastle to Brixham with coals. "Left Tyne 8th Feb., 1861, at 2 p.m. A light wind from E.N.E. Midnight off Huntcliff. About this time the wind increased. At 8 next morning, the wind still increasing, stowed the topsail. 11 a.m. the main sheet block carried away, and broke two guard irons in the main rigging. At 3 p.m. the mainsail began to give way at the leach. 5 p.m. saw Whitby light, very hazy, sea running fearfully high, wind E.N.E. blowing a hurricane. Finding the ship would not weather Whitby rock ran for the harbour, but recollecting that there was not sufficient water put the vessel on the north side of the pier. She struck about 7 p.m. The crew took to the rigging. Several rockets were fired from the shore, but did not reach the vessel. The crew still clung to the rigging. The ship was about 200 yards from the shore, and their cries for help distinctly heard. At 10 p.m. the old lifeboat was launched, and the crew taken off the ship with the exception of one. This man, James Allan, of Cowes, is supposed to have been drowned in the act of jumping into the lifeboat, or washed off the deck by a sea. Deponent being the last to quit the ship, states that no one of the crew was on board when he left. It is the opinion of the master that had there been a harbour of refuge at Hartlepool or Whitby his ship would have been saved, as well as the above seaman.

"Gamma," schooner, 79, bt. Newcastle, 1847.

"Clara," barque, 354 tons, built Sndld., 1850.

"Utility," brig, 156, built Sndld., 1843, owned at London.

"Urania," brig, 209, built Sndld., 1837.

Great loss of life and property by this storm all along the coast. About 70 vessels near Hartlepool, ten of them with loss of all hands. A large ship at Redcar, a brig at Staithes. Two or three vessels at R.H.Bay, with loss of life. (See Miss Linskill's tale, "The Haven under the Hill.").

1862.—Jan. 11th. The schooner "Little Ben," 46 tons, registered at London, owned at Brotton, went behind the East Pier and broke up.

Feb. 23. The Dutch brig "N. R. Gas Taberek," De Goede, master, left Shields on Saturday, 22nd Feb., coal laden, for Rotterdam, where she was owned. During a dense fog she went on the rocks South of Whitby High Lights, about 4 o'clock on Sunday morning, the 23rd Feb. The crew took to the boat, four of them just out of bed, and rowed to Whitby. Efforts were made to save some stores, but unavailing, as the brig had settled in deep water. During the afternoon the mainmast fell, the foremast with all the sails standing remained over Monday, but the vessel entirely disappeared that night. Crew forwarded by Mr. J. N. Lawson to the Dutch Consul at Hull.

March 13. S.S. "Deptford" on the rock. Refloated, but while towing to the North sank off Boulby.

March 20. The bridge fenders now being made by Messrs. Smales Bros. will soon be finished, and placed in position, and the old "dolphins" removed.

Sept. 25. The laden schooner "Polka" on the rock near Saltwick. Owned at Maldon. Sold to Messrs. Andrew and Co., and brought into Whitby. Sold again to Maldon.

"Chandernagore," barque, 564 tons, built at Sunderland, 1851, owned by Messrs. Harris and Co., Middlesbrough, Capt., J. Lynas, arrived at Whitby July 5th, and was docked at Whitehall, July 11th.

She was also at Whitby to dock in January, 1865.

Lloyd's agent at Portland, Dorset, telegraphs on June 18, 1886:—Barque "Chandernagore," of Hongkong, London for Pescadores, China, with cement, put into Portland leaky.

A telegram from Pernambuco, Sept. 30, 1887, states that the British barque "Chandernagore," Macau, S. America (Lat. 5 S.), for Rio de Janeiro, has been totally lost off Roccas. Crew picked up by the Brazilian steamer "Gequia" and landed at Pernambuco.

The Roccas reef is in Long. 33.46 W., Lat. 3.51 S., distance from Cape San Roque 129 miles N.E. ½ N., from Pernambuco 250 miles, and 84 miles West of Fernando Noronha.

1862.—December. "Duke of Buccleuch," brig, 163 tons, built at Leith, 1829, owned at Aberdeen. Left Aberdeen for London, 19th Dec., 1862, with granite and about 100 tons of oats. At 11 a.m. moderate breeze from N.W. Saturday, 20th, 1.30 p.m., wind N.W., and blowing at times a hurricane, and being then off Hartlepool, the ship was struck by a heavy sea, which swept the decks, carrying away the longboat, bulwarks, etc., and washing overboard Alexander Duncan, A.B., and David Williamson, apprentice. Soon after this sighted Whitby lights and kept away for R.H. Bay, as she was fast settling down in consequence of the hatches having been stove. About 10 p.m. ran the ship ashore on the North side of R.H. Bay, it being then low water. Drifted round the Bay about 5 miles, though the vessel was sometimes half mast down in the water. The remainder of the crew clinging to the rigging. Having again drifted to the North of the Bay, the lifeboat there came off and took us all safely on shore, about 10 a.m. on Sunday morning, the 21st Dec., 1862.

1863.—Feb. The brig "Ann," of Shields, coal laden, wrecked on "Filly Tail."

June 10th. The Dutch barque "Zeemenw," Shields for Sourabaya, came on the rocks South of the Spa Ladder. Thick fog, but smooth sea. Threw some cargo over and came off.

Dec. Great storm in the North Sea. Mr. Dotchon's, and Mr. Turnbull's "George," the latter foundered.

1864.—Jan. "Lady Mary," barque, 178 tons, built in N. America, owned by Jn. Mowbray, of Hartlepool, West Hartlepool for London, coals, was brought up in Whitby Roads. About 10.30 p.m. the master felt the vessel touching the ground, and shortly after she struck heavily and filled. She was afterwards got off, and getting near the Pier, washed up and was sold a wreck.

Jan. 29th. Early in the morning a boat with five or six men came into Whitby. They were not seen until in the harbour. Their vessel had foundered.

Feb. 12th. "Queen Victoria," barque, owned in Norway, Kars, master, Hull for Shields, wrecked on the rock.

Feb. 13th. A thaw and a great "fresh" down the river. A laden lighter went to sea. A small vessel behind the pier.

March 15. In the afternoon four cobles and crews went out to get some anchors, but a strong sea coming on, the fishermen's lifeboat had to go to their assistance. When being lowered down by the crane, the strop broke, and the boat was damaged. A man, Thomas Gaines, was also much hurt.

May 10. The brig "Sherwood Ranger," 160 tons, built at Sunderland in 1852, owned by Mr. Baines, of Shields, Shields for Lisbon, coals, could not clear the land, and drifted ashore at Kettleness. A total wreck.

Nov. 25. The schooner "Oak," 132 tons, owned at London, Sunderland for Portsmouth, coals, when off R.H. Bay was struck by a heavy sea, whilst beating South against a strong S.S.E. wind, which stove the boat, carried away part of bulwarks, gangway, etc., and split main and mizzen sail. Putting back to the North, when off Huntcliff, the wind changed to W.N.W. Stood for Whitby, where she arrived about 1 p.m., the 26th.

1865.—A little schooner bound to Scarborough with coals ran into Whitby for shelter. She touched the sand inside the pier and fell to leeward. Beating against the Scotch Head she became a wreck. The coals were sold.

May 10th. "Maria Soames," barque, 600 tons, built at Southtown, G. Yarmouth, 1841, owned by Seymour Peacock and Co., London, Geo. Lambton, master, and 17 hands. "Left Sunderland for Alexandria, coal laden, 9th May, 1865, at 2.30 p.m. Proceeded with a North Sea branch pilot in charge, steering S.E. by E. At 6 p.m. the course altered to S.E. a fresh breeze with rain. 11 p.m. very thick. At midnight S.E. by S. Wednesday, 10th May, at 12.15 a.m., tide half flood, weather very thick, wind N.N.E. a fresh breeze, the ship struck the ground. In a few minutes after saw Whitby West Pier Lighthouse about 400 yards to the N.W. Showed signal for assistance, a pilot light, which was answered. The sea increasing, and the ship striking very heavily, after taking every means to get the ship off without effect, she filled with water, and at 3.30 a.m. was forced to abandon her, the sea increasing, and the vessel falling over to the sea. Some cobles came off and ran a warp to the pier head to endeavour to get if possible into the harbour, but without effect. At 1 a.m. 17 of crew taken off by the National lifeboat "Lucy." The cobles forced by the heavy sea to leave the ship. Lifeboat left the ship at 3.30 a.m. The lead was never used. Cannot tell the cause of casualty, unless it was local attraction on this coast, in consequence of the ironstone which affected the compass.

Oct. 19th. About 1 p.m., during a gale and high sea, a schooner to the North of Whitby was seen to founder. A boat with men in it was then seen. The lifeboat was immediately got out, but before it could reach the boat the latter was overwhelmed and the men drowned. It was afterwards ascertained that the vessel was the "Elizabeth," of Goole. The body of the mate was found at Boghall, Nov. 6, 1865.

Oct. 25th. The tug "Pearl," towing an ironstone hulk (the schooner "Sovereign") to the North, when a gale came on, was obliged to run for Whitby, but missed the harbour and went on to the Scar. Crew saved.

Dec. The sloop "Nancy," of West Hartlepool, anchored in Runswick Bay, waiting for suitable weather for "lying on" at Staithes. Three men and a woman got into the boat to go ashore, when it upset, and one man only got ashore by swimming.

1866.—Jan. 12. "Cora," schooner, of Aberdeen, Aberdeen to Whitby, with oats. "Friday, the 12th, wind W.N.W. blowing strong, being then off Whitby, was, in consequence of the falling snow, unable to see that a heavy sea was breaking on the Bar. The weather clearing a little as I approached, and then seeing the state of the Bar, I was unable to stand off, having lost some canvas. The vessel struck heavily outside the piers. The port bow then struck the East pier, and afterwards the port quarter, and the vessel gradually drove into the harbour, striking and dragging as she drifted. Sailed up the harbour and took the ground above bridge in mid-channel, and lay with a strong list to port. Sounded and found 2 feet of water in hold."

June. S.S. "Lady Borriedale" ashore at Whitby.

1867.—March 30. "Isabella and Jane," schooner, of Dundee, left Whitby in tow of tug "Powerful" for Seaham. A gale coming on, the tug had to let go the rope. The schooner brought up in Whitby roads. At tide time, the tug "Esk" towing her in, she struck East pier and went on the Scar.

Dec. "Sir Richard Jackson," barque, 384 tons, of North Shields, built in Canada in 1843. Carthagena (Agulais) for Tyne, lead ore, etc. "Sunday, Dec. 1, 1867, took the steam tug 'Rescue' off Whitby, and when five miles from the Tyne, a gale came on from the N.N.E., causing the tug to cast us off. Wore the ship with her head to S.E., and set close reefed main topsail, being all we could show to the gale. At 7 p.m., off Seaham, the foremast went over the side, carrying the bowsprit end along with it, and the main top gallant mast. At 7.30 p.m. the main topsail burst and blew away. Soon after the ship became unmanageable. At 10.30 p.m. saw the cliffs under our lee, which proved to be Huntcliff. At 11.45 p.m. she struck very heavily, when the mainmast went over the side, taking mizen topmast. In about 10 minutes she washed over the reef into comparatively smooth water and drifted on to the scar at Boulby, where she now lies, bilged, with the whole of her cargo aboard. Crew saved by rocket apparatus worked by the coastguard and inhabitants of Staithes, unto whom I shall ever feel a debt of gratitude."

1868.—March 1. Soon after 12 o'clock, during a strong gale, the schooner "Eleanor," of Colchester, from Hartlepool for London, coals, struck on Kelder Steel, where she remained for some time. Signals were made for assistance, and a Sandsend coble and two from Whitby put off, one of the latter returning. The vessel was got off, but so leaky that she was beached at Sandsend, and will doubtless break up.

June 26. During a strong breeze the brig "Sceptre," of Seaham, went ashore at Kettleness, but with the assistance of Runswick fishermen, was got off on Thursday, the 27th, with little damage, and towed into Whitby by the tug "Esk." The salvors received £18 and the tug £70 by agreement.

Nov. The "Blanche," of Scarborough, left Hartlepool on the 18th, and it is supposed foundered or was run down, crew of three. Portions of wreck washed up at Whitby and R.H.Bay.

Nov. "Favourite," brig, of Sunderland, Sunderland for London, coals, stranded at Kettleness. Total loss. Crew supposed themselves seven miles from the land.

1869.—March. "Palladium," Capt. Stamp, arrived at Dundee from London, reports:—"March 20th, at 1.45 a.m., "Dudgeon" bearing S.E. by E., 5 miles distant, vessel on the starboard tack, under close reefed topsails and reefed foresail, double reefed main trysail, and foretopmast staysail, side lights burning brightly, observed a vessel on the port bow showing no lights. On drawing near she proved to be a schooner on the port tack, and continued her course, evidently trying to cross our bow. Our jibboom came between her masts, carrying it and all gear attached away, as also the schooner's mainmast, and doing other damage unknown. She falling alongside of us we hailed her several times, but received no answer, neither did we see any person on board of her. After clearing away our own gear, wore ship to try and find her, but saw nothing of her.

June. "Severn," smack, of Scarborough, was caught by a heavy gale from the N.E. about midnight on the 15th, and was driven ashore at the back of Whitby East pier at 2 a.m. on the 16th. Became a wreck.

1871.—"Hopewell," schooner, owned by Mary Harland, Richd. Barker, master, and two hands, left Whitby for Middlesbrough in tow of tug "Reaper." When off Huntcliff the stem head broke off, and both masts came down, owing to being towed against a head sea. Arrived at Middlesbrough at 5 p.m., 14th March, 1871.

1872.—October. "Lucy," brigantine, of Yarmouth, Bremerhaven for Newcastle, trying to enter Whitby harbour, being leaky and having lost sails, struck East pier and went on to the Scar. A wreck. Crew saved.

1874.—November. "Ann Rankin," barque, 448, built at Quebec, 1840, owned at Christiania by Hans Andersen, Shields to Christiania, came ashore a mile North of Staithes. Total wreck.

November. "Star," schooner, of Faversham, sprung a leak in heavy weather and came ashore on Whitby sands.

Dec. 9th. A gale visited the North East Coast unequalled for severity and disasters to shipping since that of Feb. 9th, 1861. "Danube," brig, of Whitby, Price, master, arrived and anchored in the roads on the evening of the 8th. About midnight it began to blow, and so rapidly increased that soon after 2 a.m. the vessel drove ashore near Upgang. The crew remained on board till daylight, as the vessel was light and drove close up to the cliff.

About 3 a.m. the brig "Lord Saumarez," John Harrison, master, owned by Mr. H. M. Cockerill, of Scarborough, bound from London for Shields, in ballast, came to the sand. The crew, six in number, were landed by rocket lines.

This vessel was soon followed by the "Pride," ketch, of Southampton, Charles Parsons, master, Northfleet for Dundee, with 50 bags and 480 barrels of cement. The master had been washed overboard. One man and a boy saved by lifeboat.

At daybreak the schooner "Excelsior," of and from Whitstable for Sunderland, in ballast, came for the harbour. On reaching the entrance she was carried by the "fresh" against the East Pier, carrying away bowsprit and jibboom, and then lurched over to the West Pier, just inside, and came to the ground on the sand, striking heavily. Deponent and crew got on the pier with the assistance of ropes.

"Isabella," brigantine, of Amble. "At 1.45 a.m., Whitby pier light bore West, distant a mile, steered through the Sledway and succeeded in entering the harbour, and came to the ground in Collier Hope."

"Britannia," brig, of Shoreham, Stephen Kennard, master, came on the Scar about 3.30 a.m. Half of the hull was seen at daylight underneath the Spa Ladder, and it was feared that the crew had perished. But soon after this they were discovered by George Cowens, miner, in a cleft on the rock.

"Drove past the harbour, and under the cliff, deponent and crew jumped from the rail to a ledge of the cliff and remained there until daylight, when they were discovered by some men from the top of the cliff, and one man descended with a pick and cut a road for deponent and crew, by which they ascended safely, and walked to Whitby about 8 a.m."

"Blakeney and Hull Packet," a billyboy, is supposed to have struck on the Scar, lost her crew, and broke up. Part of her, keel uppermost, with a portion of the cargo (flour), underneath, was found inside the Spa Ladder.

"Indian Queen," schooner, of Portsmouth, Charles Gardiner, master, from Beaulieu, near Southampton, with pit props for Sunderland, came ashore at Newholm beck. A boy washed overboard as the vessel was running for the sand.

"Debut," a French vessel, Capt. Mason, of and from Gravelines, with a cargo of 54 tons of apples for Hartlepool, stranded at Deepgrove. One man washed overboard before she came to the beach.

The barque "Rosamond," lying at Mr. Barrick's dock gates ready for entering, was driven on to a mudbank and left very badly laid. Only just bought to the town.

1877.—"Penguin," barque, 347 tons, built at Sunderland in 1855, owned by Robt. H. Potts, of Sunderland, Alexander Trotter, master, and ten hands. Left Sunderland, 5th Feb., for Trinidad, West Indies, 200 tons of coals and 20 tons of pig iron. Proceeded S.E. by S. under all plain sail until about 11.30 a.m., then off Huntcliff foot on the Yorkshire coast, from five to six miles distant, the course then altered to S.S.E. About 12.45 p.m., last quarter ebb, weather fine and clear, wind W., moderate breeze with a smooth sea, the ship was to the Westward and abreast of Whitby rock buoy, and about 3 cables lengths from it when first seen, the helm was then put hard a-weather, shivered main yard, and took in the after sails, but the ship would not answer her helm, and shortly afterwards she went aground. Agreements were subsequently made with 20 men in two boats for the sum of £50, and for the assistance of the steam tug "Emu," of Whitby, also for £50, to get the vessel off and take her into a place of safety, with which assistance the vessel was got off when the tide flowed, and taken into Whitby harbour at 9 p.m. the same day, taking in little or no water. The land was distinctly seen, and the course by compass should have taken the vessel outside of Whitby rock buoy. Thought the compass must have been affected by the iron in the hold. There was no special look-out appointed, the deponent being on deck from the time the vessel left Sunderland until she came to the ground off Whitby, the crew being employed clearing and securing things about the decks."

"Christopher Housteen," brig, built at Bergen in 1855, bound from Drobak (near Christiania) with pit props for Leith, made the land off Huntcliff in heavy weather, and the vessel leaking badly, the crew abandoned her on the 28th February with six feet of water in the hold, about 15 miles N.E. from Whitby, and at 6.30 a.m. on the 1st March were taken from the boat outside Whitby rock by the "Robert Whitworth," lifeboat, the sea being too heavy for the ship's boat to land.

1878.—January. S.S. "Oscar," of Leith, Newcastle for Cadiz, coals, ashore on Whitby rock.

1879.—S.S. "J. H. Lorentzen" on Whitby rock.

1880.—A gale of great force blew on this coast on the 28th October, doing much damage on shore and causing the wreck of many vessels.

"Sarah," schooner, of and from Portsmouth for Hartlepool, in ballast, ashore near Upgang, crew of four saved.

The "Reaper," schooner, 82 tons, built at Peel, 1864, owned at Douglas, James David Clark, master, Ostend for Sunderland:—

"Thursday, 28th October, wind E.N.E., stormy, with hail and heavy sea. Under double reefed topsail, reefed foresail, and double reefed mainsail, which were set under very great difficulty with the object of keeping her off the shore, was driven by the sheer violence of the gale on to Whitby beach, where she now lies. Upon the vessel taking the ground a lifeboat (R. N. Society) put off and succeeded in rescuing three of the crew of five, the master and mate remaining on board. The rocket apparatus having been previously made fast to the foremast, the mate got into the breeches buoy, but before he had got well clear of the ship the buoy capsized, and a running sea passing at the time, carried him away from the buoy. He then clung to the back rope chain, which was broken, but was unable to hold on more than a minute or two, when he was swept away and drowned."

"Elizabeth Austen," schooner, of Rye, Gifford, master, crew of five saved by lifeboat.

"Comet," schooner, Petersen, master, of Mental, in Sweden, cement in bags, struck near the end of Saltwick Nab, and the men who saved the crew by rocket lines, under the superintendence of Chief Boatman Taylor, were in great risk of their lives, as the vessel's crew did not understand the working of the rocket.

"Good Intent," yawl, of Staithes, near coastguard station, crew of nine rescued by lifeboat.

"John Snell," schooner, Craven, master and owner, of and from Yarmouth for Newcastle, grain, ashore towards Upgang. Crew, four in all, saved by lifeboat.

"Ianthe," schooner, of Faversham, 174 tons, Gravesend for Shields, ballast, 2 miles North of Staithes. One man drowned, another had his leg broken. Vessel total wreck.

It fell to the lot of the light-keepers at High Whitby to witness a painful sight. A schooner, which afterwards proved to be the "Sarah and Mary," was overwhelmed a few hundred yards from the shore, and her crew drowned.

A few days later a vessel came ashore bottom up a little distance from the Spa Ladder. Her name was found to be the "Corsolus," of Mollosund, Sweden.—Partly from the "Whitby Gazette."

1881.—Jan. 15. "Lumley," brig, wrecked on Upgang rock in the evening. Strong gale and thick snow. Not seen at first. Both Whitby and Upgang lifeboats proceeded off, but returned, and the ship's crew were drowned.

1885.—Oct. 24. The Russian schooner, "Dmitry," of Narva, with silver sand, came in splendidly, in heavy weather, but going ashore in "Collier Hope," became a total wreck.—"Whitby Gazette."

1896.—S.S. "Clydesdale" ashore, through fog, under the High Lights. Re-floated.

ADDENDUM.

Screw Steamers built at the Whitehall Yard, Messrs. Turnbull and Sons.

25 sailing vessels having been previously built by this firm, the second is the yard number of the steamers.

Name, when Launched, Length & Breadth, Tonnage & Owners.

1871.

1. 26 WHITEHALL; June 20th; 200 by 28½; 1,100; Turnbull and Co.
2. 27 ISAAC PENNOCK; Dec. 7th; 209 by 28½; 1,200; Turnbull and Co.

1872.

3. 28 ALICE; March 9th; 225 by 30; 1,400; J. Gray and Co.
4. 29 R. M. HUNTON; June 8th; 225 by 30; 1,400; Turnbull and Co.
5. 30 ROBIN HOOD; August 16th; 209 by 30½; 1,300; Turnbull and Co.
6. 31 SCORESBY; Nov. 14th; 225 by 30; 1,400; Turnbull and Co.

1873.

7. 32 DOUGLAS; March 15th; 232 by 30; 1,450; Pyman and Co., West H'pool.
8. 33 DAISY; May 24; 180 by 28; 850; Turnbull and Co.
9. 34 PANSY; Sept. 6th; 183 by 28; 900; Turnbull and Co.

1874.

10. 35 FOAM; Feb. 28th; 181 by 28; 875; Watson and Co., Newport.

11. 36 KATE; June 1st; 247 by 33; 1,800; J. Gray and Co.

12. 37 CONSTANCE; July 13th; 225 by 30; 1,400; Pyman and Co., W. H'pool.

13. 38 UNITY; Aug. 29th; 225 by 30; 1,400; R. Harrowing, Whitby.

14. 39 SIR GALAHAD; Oct. 14th; 225 by 30; 1,400, Richards, Power and Co., Swansea.

15. 40 KING ARTHUR; Dec. 23rd; 225 by 30; 1,400; Turnbull and Co.

1875.

16. 41 DARENT; Feb. 20th; 225 by 30; 1,400; Turnbull and Co.

17. 42 COSMOPOLITAN; May 6th; 267 by 33½; 2,300; Turnbull and Co.

18. 43 SYRA; June 19th; 225 by 30; 1,400; Turnbull and Co.

19. 44 EMMA LAWSON; Aug. 18th; 225 by 30; 1,400; Turnbull and Co.

1876.

20. 45 LADY HILDA; Jan. 25th; 147 by 22; 450; W. and L.S.S. Co.

21. 46 NELLIE; March 11th; 247 by 33; 1,800; J. Gray and Co.

22. 47 STAINSACRE; June 24th; 225 by 30; 1,400; Turnbull and Co.

23. 48 SHILDON; Sept. 20th; 250 by 33½; 1,900; G. Pyman, West H'pool.

24. 49 LIZZIE; Dec. 2nd; 250 by 33½; 1900; J. Gray and Co.

1877.

25. 50 GOLDEN GROVE; Feb. 28th; 250 by 33½; 1,900; Turnbull and Co.

26. 51 MELROSE ABBEY; Sept. 14th; 235 by 32; 1,600; Pyman, Watson and Co., Newport.

27. 52 RAVEN HILL; June 13th; 250 by 33½; 1,900; Turnbull and Co.

28. 53 JAMES GRAY; Aug. 25th; 252 by 33½; 2,250; J. Gray and Co.

29. 54 CÆDMON; Oct. 23rd; 235 by 32; 1,600; Turnbull and Co.

30. 55 STREONSHALH; Dec. 22nd; 250 by 34; 2,200; Turnbull and Co.

1878.

31. 56 PEACE; Feb. 19th; 252 by 33½; 2,250; Turnbull and Co.

32. 57 NORTHCOTE; April 17th; 1,500; Holman and Son, Exeter.

33. 58 ZOE; June 15th; 250 by 33; 2,200; Turner, Brightman and Co., London.

34. 59 No. 59; Aug. 29th; 270 by —; 2,700; Benyon and Co., Newport.

35. 60 WILFRID; Oct. 26th; 235 by 32; 1,650; Turnbull and Co.

36. 61 EUSTACE; Dec. 23rd; 260 by 34; 2,200; Pyman and Co., West H'pool.

1879.

37. 62 ANNIE; March 10th; 270 by 34½; 2,800; J. Gray and Co.

38. 63 EDGAR; May 6th; 240 by 33; 2,100; Turnbull and Co.

39. 64 MILDRED; June 5th; 240 by 33; 1,900; Turnbull and Co.

40. 65 KATE; Aug. 20th; 270 by 34½; 2,800; J. Gray and Co.

41. 66 BEATRICE; Sept. 2nd; 240 by 34; 1,850; Turnbull and Co.

42. 67 JANE; Dec. 13th; 240 by 34; 1,850; Turnbull and Co.

1880.

43. 68 T. TURNBULL; Feb. 28th; 276 by 36½; 3,000; Turnbull and Co.

44\. 69 LIZZIE ENGLISH; June 22nd; 259 by 34; 2,200; Pyman and Co., West H'pool.

45\. 70 CHOLMLEY; July 23rd; 240 by 34; 1,900; Turnbull and Co.

46\. 71 SOLON; Sept. 18th; 240 by 34; 1,900; Robinson, Rowland and Co.

47\. 72 NEMESIS; Dec. 30th; T. Parker, Melbourne.

1881.

48\. 73 BARON ARDROSSAN; April 14th; 243 by 34; 1,950; H. Hogarth, Ardrossan.

49\. 74 FLORENCE; May 29th; 280 by 38; 3,100; Pyman and Co., West H'pool.

50\. 75 SHARON; July 27th; 240 by 34; 1,900; Robinson, Rowland and Co.

51\. 76 ZENOBIA; Sept. 24th; 286 by 36; 2,800; Turner, Brightman and Co., London.

52\. 77 SAXON; Nov. 23rd; 260 by 34½; 2,200; Robinson, Rowland and Co.

1882.

53\. 78 MATTHEW BEDLINGTON; Jan. 21st; 280 by 38; 3,100; Turnbull and Co.

54\. 79 HIGHGATE; March 4th; 240 by 34; 1,950; Turnbull, Scott and Co., London.

55\. 80 EVERILDA; April 17th; 240 by 34; 1,950; Turnbull Bros., Cardiff.

56\. 81 B. GRANGER; June 3rd; 240 by 34; 1,950; Robinson, Rowland and Co.

57\. 82 MOSS BROW; July 29th; 260 by 35; Pyman and Co., London.

58\. 83 WYKEHAM; Aug. 29th; 240 by 34; 1,950; Robinson, Rowland and Co.

59\. 84 HENRIETTA; Oct. 26th; 240 by 34; 1,950; Best, Wyley and Co., London.

60\. 85 CAIRO; Dec. 11th; 260 by 37; 2,400; Turnbull and Co.

1883.

61. 86 GWENDOLINE; Jan. 23rd; 260 by 37; 2,400; Turnbull Bros., Cardiff.

62. 87 INVERALT; March 8th; 240 by 32; Stoddart and Co., Liverpool.

63. 88 SOUTHGATE; April 23rd; 260 by 37; 2,400; Turnbull, Scott and Co.

64. 89 BARON CLYDE; June 5th; 260 by 37; 2,400; H. Hogarth, Ardrossan.

65. 90 ZEPHYRUS; July 21st; 286 by 36; 2,700; Turner, Brightman and Co., London.

66. 91 ALBANY; Sept. 17th; 240 by 34; 1,900; T. W. Woodhead and Co., Hull.

67. 92 MARCH; Nov. 14th; 286 by 36; Turnbull and Co.

68. 93 ZURICH; Dec. 15th; 245 by 34; Turner, Brightman and Co.

1884.

69. 94 BERNARD; Jan. 26th; 260 by 37; 2,350; Turnbull Bros., Cardiff.

70. 95 JOHN STEVENSON; March 11th; 240 by 34; 1,900; T. Smailes and Co.

71. 96 INVERMAY; May 24th; 240 by 34; 1,950; Stoddart and Co., Liverpool.

72. 97 FLOWERGATE; Dec. 3rd; 286 by 36; 2,800; Turnbull, Scott and Co.

1885.

No launches this year.

1886.

73. 98 MANDALAY; Feb. 18th; 258 by 37; 2,350; Turnbull and Co.

99 Hopper.

1887.

74. 100 ZARATE; April 7th; 300 by 38; 3,300; Turner, Brightman and Co., London.

75. 101 DORA; Nov. 15th; 300 by 38; 3,600; Turnbull and Co.

First steel steamer (Mr. Alder).

1888.

76. 102 FALSHAW; March 27th; 288 by 38; 3,350; H. Baxter and Co.

77. 103 NORTHGATE; May 26th; 288 by 38; 3,350; Turnbull, Scott and Co.

78. 104 EXCELSIOR; July 23rd; 258 by 37; 2,550; H. Baxter and Co.

79. 105 CYRIL; Sept. 20th; 288 by 38; 3,350; Turnbull Bros., Cardiff.

80. 106 THORDISA; Nov. 17th; 288 by 38; 3,400; Turnbull and Co.

1889.

81. 107 GEORGE CLARKSON; Jan.; 258 by 37; 2,570; H. Baxter and Co.

82. 108 CONCORD; March 2nd; 258 by 37; 2,570; T. Smailes and Co.

83. 109 EASTGATE; April 17th; 258 by 37; 2,550; Turnbull, Scott and Co., London.

84. 110 ILLTYD; June 13th; 258 by 37; 2,550; Turnbull Bros., Cardiff.

85. 111 PARKGATE; Aug. 27th; 288 by 38; 3,440; Turnbull, Scott and Co., London.

86. 112 ZOE; Nov. 7th; 288 by 38; 3,440; Turner, Brightman and Co., London.

87. 113 OSWIN; Dec. 23rd; 258 by 37; 2,550; Turnbull Bros., Cardiff.

1890.

88. 114 FAIRMEAD; March 6th; 288 by 38; 3,350; Turnbull and Co., Wy.

89. 115 NETHERGATE; May 6th; 288 by 38; 3,350; Turnbull, Scott and Co., London.

90. 116 OSWALD; July 3rd; 258 by 37; 2,600; Turnbull and Co.

91. 117 VERA; Dec. 12th; 288 by 38; 3,420; W. H. and T. Marwood.

1891.

92. 118 RAVENSWOOD; March 10th; 288 by 38; 3,450; T. Smailes and Co.

93. 119 KENDAL; May 23rd; 288 by 38; 3,420; H. Baxter and Co.

1892.

94. 120 WHITEHALL; Jan. 14th; 321.9 by 40.6; 4,150; Turnbull and Co.

95. 121 ERIC; March 29th; 321.9 by 40.6; 4,150; Turnbull Bros., Cardiff.

96. 122 MUTUAL; Aug. 10th; 280 by 40.6; 3,000; Smailes and Jackson.

97. 123 PETERSTON; Oct. 19th; 321.9 by 40.6; 4,200; Radcliffe and Co., Cardiff.

1893.

98. 124 WESTGATE; March 2nd; 321.9 by 40.6; 4,200; Turnbull, Scott and Co., London.

99. 125 GENA; June 15th; 321.9 by 40.6; 4,200; Turnbull and Co.

1894.

100. 126 PHŒBE; Nov. 14; 321 by 40.6; 4,200; Turnbull Bros., Cardiff.

1895.

101. 127 PENELOPE; March 12th; 321 by 40; 4,200; H. Baxter and Co.

102. 128 EDDIE; July 23rd; 3,900; Turnbull and Co.

1896.

103. 129 GLASGOW; Feb. 27th; 318 by 43; 3,980; McLay, McIntire and Co., Glasgow.

104. 130 ALTON; Aug. 25th; 344.4 by 42.6; 5,150; Turnbull and Co.

1897.

105. 131 TRONGATE; May 3rd; 4,000; Turnbull, Scott and Co.

1898.

106. 132 EMMA; March 9th; 319 by 44; 4,160; Turnbull Bros., Cardiff.

107. 133 HUTTON; Oct. 29th; 361 by 43; 5,660; Pyman and Co., London.

1899.

108. 134 BRINKBURN; May 11th; 361 by 43; 5,675; Harris and Dixon, London.

BARGES.

135 ADVANCE; Sailing; launched May 18th, 1898.

136 DIAMOND; Sailing; launched Aug. 9th, 1898.

109. 137 JOHN; Screw; launched Dec. 12th, 1898.

110. 138 ONWARD; Screw; launched March 3rd, 1899.

139 PEARL; Sailing; launched July 7th; 1899.

111. 140 SOUTHGATE; Nov. 4th; 361.3 by 43; 5,675; Turnbull, Scott and Co., London.

1900.

112. 141 BERNARD; April 14th; 361 by 43; 5,675; Turnbull Bros., Cardiff.

113. 142 OLIVE; Sept. 10th; 361 by 43; 5,675; Turnbull Bros., Cardiff.

1901.

114. 143 WARRIOR; Feb. 10th; 361 by 44; 5,700; Turnbull and Co.

115. 144 THEODOR WILLE; Aug. 3rd; 5,700; Heinrich Diederichen, Kiel.

1902.

116. 145 BROOMFIELD; April 10th; 310 by 44; 3,860; Turnbull and Co.

SS. "Theodor Wille," 5,700 tons, passing through Whitby Bridge, stern first.

Valeat quantum valere potest.

LIST OF SUBSCRIBERS.

A

Andrew, Mrs. J. V., 7, St. Hilda's Terrace, Whitby.
Anderson, E. E., The Firs, Wellclose Square, Whitby.
Arnett, Miss Mary P., Widdrington, Acklington.
Attlay, Col. W. H., V.D., Stainsacre Hall, Nr. Whitby.
Austen, George, Rev. Canon, M.A., R.D., The Rectory, Whitby.
Austen, H. C. M., C.E., The Rectory, Whitby.

B

Bagshawe, J. R., The Old Rectory, Whitby.
Bagshawe, E. T. G., The Old Rectory, Whitby.
Barber, Mrs., Ryston Vicarage, Downham Market, Norfolk.
Barker, Miss, 20, St. Hilda's Terrace, Whitby.
Barker, Miss Ella, 24, St. Hilda's Terrace, Whitby.
Barker, E. A., Sandbeck, Duchy Road, Harrogate.
Bartholomew, C. W., Blakesley Hall, Nr. Towcester.
Barton, George, Calcutta, India.
Barton, William, Master Mariner, 15, Esk Terrace, Whitby.
Baxter, John, 159, Folkestone Road, Dover, Kent.
Baxter, Harrison, Master Mariner, Melrose, Bagdale, Whitby.
Batchelor, W. H., 176, Church Street, Whitby.
Beadnell, Miss, 24, Skinner Street, Whitby.
Beckett, The Hon. Gervase, M.P., 1, Hyde Park Place, London, W.
Benson, Mrs., 8, Woodville Gardens, Ealing.
Benson, Wm. Thos., 56, Kingscourt Road, Streatham, London, S.W.
Blenkey, Mrs., Beach Hotel, Sandsend.

Bolton, J. S., County Asylum, Rainhill, Lancs.
Bourdas, J., Duncan House, Clapham Common, London, S.W.
Boulby, Rev. Adam, Aislaby, Nr. Whitby.
Braithwaite, David, 71, Church Street, Whitby.
Braithwaite, Wm., 26, Endymion Road, Brixton Hill, London, S.W.
Brand, Thomas, Stoneleigh, Whitby.
Breckon, George, Master Mariner, Southend Gardens, Whitby.
Bridges, G. H., 4, The Esplanade, Whitby.
Briggs, Wm., 4, South Parade, Wakefield.
Brodrick, Thos., 47, Brunswick Square, Hove (Sussex).
Brodrick, Miss, 18, Talbot Square, Hyde Park, London.
Brodrick, J., J.P., Tainui, Cockatoo Creek, Victoria, Australia.
Brodrick-English, Mrs., Sleights.
Brodrick, Cecil, Ormond House, 63, Queen Victoria Street, London, E.C.
Brockett, J. W., Master Mariner, Esk Terrace, Whitby.
Brough, J. R., 27, George Street, Whitby.
Brown, The Misses, 6, St. Hilda's Terrace, Whitby.
Brown, William, The Hut, Stakesby Vale, Whitby.
Brooksbank, Wilman, 87, Church Street, Whitby.
Bruce, John, Hillcrest, Whitby.
Buchannan, Miss Sarah M., 12, Bagdale, Whitby.
Buchannan, George, Flowergate Cross, Whitby.
Buchannan, Chas., 6, East Crescent, Whitby.
Buchannan, Mrs. Chas., 6, East Crescent, Whitby.
Buchannan, Alexander, 6, East Crescent, Whitby.
Buchannan, Rev. Malcolm, 6, East Crescent, Whitby.
Buchannan, Charles, Junr., 6, East Crescent, Whitby.
Buck, Joseph, M.D., Mulgrave House, Rothwell, Nr. Leeds.
Buckler, F. J., Fairhaven, Carr Hill Lane, Whitby.
Burgon, Mrs., Stainforth Vicarage.
Burnett, R. H., Orchid House, Green Lane, Whitby.
Burton, Mrs., 1, Crescent Place, Whitby.
Burnett, Joseph, Birtley S.O., County Durham.

C

Cave-Day, Mrs. W., Kewsid Ho, Harrogate.
Calvert, Robert, 6, Hanover Terrace, Whitby.
Campion, George, 96, Church Street, Whitby.
Chapman, E. G. C., Combe, Dulverton, Somerset.
Chapman J. J., J.P., 17, St. Hilda's Terrace, Whitby.
Chapman, E. H., 3, Hare Court, Temple, London, E.C.
Chapman, H. C.

Chapman, W. H.

Chapman, Arthur, Iver, Bucks.

Chapman, J. E. P., Kenmure, Allenby Road, Forest Hill, London, S.E.

Chapman, Abel, Houxty, Wark-on-Tyne.

Chapman, Major, M.V.O., Arthur's Club, St. James' Street, London, W.

Chapman, E. H., Cobrey Park, Ross, Herefordshire.

Chapman, Major F. R. H., Balgonie, Camberley, Surrey.

Clark, Mrs. G. W., 89, Kensington Gardens Square, London, W.

Clarkson, Thomas, Thordisa House, Nr. Whitby.

Clarkson, J. N., Riddlesden Hall, Keighley.

Clarkson, Misses, Alverthorpe Hall, Wakefield.

Clough, Fred, 9, Sandgate, Whitby.

Coble, Miss, Bagdale House, Whitby.

Collier, Wm., 2, Baxtergate, Whitby.

Collier, W. G., 12, Esk Terrace, Whitby.

Collier, Raymond, 3, Newton Street, Whitby.

Connell, Rev. A. J. C., M.A., 14, Royal Crescent, Whitby.

Conroy, R., Master Mariner, 1, Wellclose Terrace, Whitby.

Cooper, Mrs. A. E. D., Grosmont.

Cooper, Rev. R. Jermyn, M.A., Fylingdales Vicarage, Robin Hood's Bay.

Co-operative Holidays Association, The Abbey House, Whitby.

Corner, Walter William, 10, Marisfield Gardens, South Hampstead, London, N.W.

Corner, Fred, Master Mariner, Crownthorpe, Whitby.

Corner, Ed., 19, Wellclose Square, Whitby.

Corner, Cursham, M.D., 113, Mile End Road, London, E.

Corney, H. D., Master Mariner, Brambletye, Stakesby Road, Whitby.

D

Dale, Miss, 1, Crescent Avenue, Whitby.

Debenham, Mrs., The Old Rectory, Great Warley, Brentwood.

Debenham, A. M. G., Clough Bank, Bollington, Nr. Macclesfield.

del'Strother, Mrs., 26, Bagdale, Whitby.

Dickson, Mrs., Porch House, Sleights.

Dingle, Rev. A. T., M.A., Egglescliffe Rectory, Co. Durham.

Dobson, Robert, Ugthorpe House, Ugthorpe.

Don, Mrs., Sleights Hall.

Duck, Henry, 9, Flowergate, Whitby.

Duck, John, 1, Sandgate, Whitby.

Duell, W., Lawns Farm, Ugthorpe.

Dyson-Moore, Miss, Heath Crest, Westcott, Nr. Dorking, Surrey.

E

Edwards, Beilby, Glenwood, Whitby.
Edwards, William, 10, St. Hilda's Terrace, Whitby.
Elliott, Miss, Oak House, West Haddon, Rugby.
Ellis, Miss, Hovingham, Wimbledon Common, London, S.W.
Ellis, Mrs. R. H., St. John's, Wakefield.
Ellis, Rev. J. H., 29, Collingham Gardens, South Kensington, London, S.W.
Else, Miss, 2, Belmont Villas, Leicester.
Emerson, Jno. J., LL.D., J.P., Easby Hall, Yorks.
Emmerson, William, Eden House, Robin Hood's Bay.
England, Mrs., Welton Manor, Brough.

F

Fairfoot, C. Wrightson, 28, Rodney Street, West Hartlepool.
Falkingbridge, William, 1, Lombard Street, London, E.C.
Falkingbridge, Harold, Wellclose Square, Whitby.
Farndale, J. T., Barclay's Bank, Thirsk.
Farside, William, 17, Burton Court, Chelsea, London, S.W.
Fennell, Miss B., 2, Broomfield Terrace, Whitby.
Flamstead, Dr. W. Dodsley, 4, Belle Vue Terrace, Whitby.
Fletcher, Wm., White Horse Yard, Whitby.
Fletcher, William, "Glenesk," Water Street, Deal (Kent).
Ford, William, Lythe, Nr. Whitby.
Forrest, Mary E., Mrs., The Moorings, Wellclose Square, Whitby.
Foster, John, Coombe Park, Whitchurch, Reading
Frank, John, 3, The Esplanade, Whitby.
Frankland, Henry, Linthorpe, Middlesboro'.
Fulford, Frank H., 15, Greek Street, Leeds.

G

Galleway, W. M., 3, Havelock Place, Whitby.
Gallilee, George, Chubb Hill Road, Whitby.
Gill, J. Armstrong, Gray Street, Whitby.
Gladstone, Mrs., Sterling House, Whitby.
Gray, Jas., J.P., The Shrubberies, Whitby.
Gray, G. B., 2, Lansdowne Street, Withington, Manchester
Gray, Alfred, Ingleneuk, Prospect Hill, Whitby.

Gray, Arthur T., 5, High Street, Barnes, London, S.W.
Gray, Miss Amy T., Lyndhurst, Argyle Road, Whitby.
Gray, R. E., 10, Wellclose Square, Whitby.
Gray, George A., Balgoney, Woodside Park, London, N.
Gray, W. Seaton, 16, St. Hilda's Terrace, Whitby.
Gray, E. N., Master Mariner, 7, Broomfield Terrace, Whitby.
Grimshaw, Walter E., 1, Esplanade, Whitby.

H

Harburn, J. E., L.R.C.P. Edin., J.P., Broad Walk, Buxton.
Harland, John, 12, Clapton Common, London. N.E.
Harland, John Crowe, Eltingville Boulevard, Staten Island, U.S.A.
Harland, Rev. W. G. and Mrs., The Vicarage, Lythe Hall, Whitby.
Harmston, J. Egan, Westgrove, Prospect Hill, Whitby.
Harmston, F. E., 5, Bridge Street, Whitby.
Harrison, Mrs. Chris., 14, St. Hilda's Terrace, Whitby.
Harrison, George, The Firs, Ashton-under-Lyne.
Harrowing, Miss, 2, Union Place, Whitby.
Harrowing, J. H., Low Stakesby, Whitby.
Hawes, J., 8, Frederick Street, Edinburgh.
Hermon, James Milne, M.D., Southgate, Wakefield.
Hick, Thos., Esk House, Whitby
Hill, Fredk., Park House, Southwell, Notts.
Hill, Miss S. J., Fernhill, North Park Avenue, Roundhay, Leeds.
Hinchcliffe, Geo. Wm., 23, Avenue Crescent, Leeds.
Hodgson, G. Wright, Cedric House, Whitby.
Hodgson, Mrs. J., 4, Sandgate, Whitby.
Horne, F. W., "Whitby Gazette" Office, Whitby
Horne, H. S., "Whitby Gazette" Office, Whitby.
Horne, Wm. Mackenzie, Wellclose Terrace, Whitby.
Horne, Miss Evra, 8, Hanover Terrace, Whitby.
Hubbard, E. Isle, Brook Park, Sleights.
Hutton, Mary P., Thorpe Hall, Robin Hood's Bay.

I

Ingham, Chas. H., Dalton Holme, Beverley.
Ingham, Miss E., Esk House, Whitby.

J

Jackson, R. K., Abyssinia, Prospect Hill, Whitby.
Jackson, J. B., Fishburn Park, Whitby.
Jameson, Wm. Storm, Master Mariner, Saxonville, West Cliff, Whitby.
Jefferson, W., Master Mariner, Malabar House, Bagdale, Whitby.
Jefferson, J. Foss, Bank House, Whitby.
Johnson, J. R., 89, Church Street, Whitby.

K

Kaye, Mrs. M. L., 12, Abbey Hill, Bury St. Edmunds.
Keighley, Miss Marion, Spring Hill House, Whitby.
King. L. H., A.M.I.C.E., Prospect Villa, Whitby.
Kirby, E. H., Parkgate, Roker, Sunderland.
Kirby, Thos., Master Mariner, Sunny Lea, Chubb Hill Road, Whitby.

L

Langborne, Miss, 4, Newbold Terrace, Leamington Spa.
Lawson, Sir John, Bart., Whitby.
Lawson, W. H., 33, Skinner Street, Whitby.
Lawson, Philip H., St. Eilian, Newton, Chester.
Leck, Wm. W., 19, Park Crescent, North Shields.
Leng, Richard, Master Mariner, "Mulgrave," Connaught Road, Cardiff.
Linton, H. P., 3, Llandaff Place, Cardiff.
Loraine, R., 10, Park Terrace, Stockton-on-Tees.

M

Marlow, Benjamin, 38, Dane Castle, Tow Law, Co Durham.
Marr, R. Johnson, Thornfield, Kingsbridge, Devon.
Martineau, Miss Mary, Brathay, Thornton Road, Clapham Park, London, S.W.
Marwood, Chris., J.P., The Stone House, Whitby.
Marwood, George, 6, Broomfield Terrace, Whitby.
McNeil, James, White Horse Yard, Church Street, Whitby.
Mennell, George, 17, Baxtergate, Whitby.
McGregor, Chas., Master Mariner, Chubb Hill Road, Whitby.
Mellor, Miss P., Weevors, Sleights.

Merryweather, George, c/o Railway Exchange Bank, Chicago, U.S.A.
Milestone, Mrs. F. E., 12, Downside Crescent, Hampstead, London, N.W.
Millburn, John, Master Mariner, 28, Esk Terrace, Whitby.
Mitchell, G. B., M.B., 1, Skinner Street, Whitby.
Moss, Mrs. Gilbert H., The Beach, Aigburth, Liverpool.
Moss, Mrs., The Mill House, Goathland.

N

Nesfield, George, Sandybed, Scarborough.
Newbitt, Thomas, 20, Crescent Avenue, Whitby.
Newton, George, Brentwood, Ash Street, Southport.
Nicholson, H. W., 18, George Street, Whitby.
Nielsen, Mrs., Eskside, 26, Adelaide Road, Leamington Spa.
Normanby, Rev. Marquess of, Mulgrave Castle, Nr. Whitby.
Norton, George, Master Mariner, 3, Park Terrace, Whitby.

O

Oliphant, Mrs. W. S., 3, Talbot Square, Hyde Park, London, W.
Ormston, Thos., Master Mariner, Mindello, Ocean Road, Whitby.

P

Pannett, Alderman R. E., J.P., Whitby.
Pawle, F. C., Northcote, Reigate, Surrey.
Parkinson, Mrs., 11, Gloucester Road, South Kensington, London, S.W.
Peace, Mrs. J. A., "Ravenscar," 606, Barnsley Road, Sheffield.
Peacock, Arthur, Castleton, Grosmont.
Pearce, George Harper, Darton Hall, Nr. Barnsley.
Peart, Thos., Master Mariner, Whitby House, 74, Hunter Street, Cardiff.
Percival, Miss, 9, Skinner Street, Whitby.
Pickering, George Henry, Hilda Cottage, Sleights.
Pinkney, Thos., Sleights and Sunderland.
Piper, Thomas, 319, Bath Road, Hounslow, Middlesex.
Popple, Lawrence, Whitby.
Power, Henry, M.B., F.R.C.S., Bagdale Hall, Whitby.
Preston, T. N., Flowergate, Whitby.
Prudom, Miss M., St. Ann's Staith, Whitby.
Puckrin, T. E., Leicester House, Whitby.
Pyman, Mrs. W. H. S., Raithwaite Hall, Whitby.

R

Raw, H. H., M.R.C.S., L.R.C.P., Bridge Street, Whitby.

Raw, Mrs. John, South View, Moorsholm, Boosbeck, S.O.

Rayment, W., 3, South Terrace, Whitby.

Reid, John, 9, Cleveland Terrace, Whitby.

Richardson, W., Solicitor, Guisborough.

Richardson, Mrs. E. G., Lealholm, Clifton Avenue, West Hartlepool.

Richardson, Mrs. Henry, 14, John Street, West Cliff, Whitby.

Rippon, C., Master Mariner, 3, Esk Place, Whitby.

Robinson, A. H., Whitteron House, Low Moor, Bradford.

Robinson, Rev. F. W., Paston Rectory, Peterboro'.

Robinson, F. Kildale, Frickley Colliery, South Elmsall, Doncaster.

Robinson, Frank Kildale, Frickley Colliery, South Elmsall, Doncaster.

Robinson, R. A., J.P., L.C.C., 26, Brechin Place, South Kensington, London, S.W.

Robinson, Miss E. G., Mount House, Whitby.

Robson, Joseph, Smithfield and Argentine Meat Co., Yaratte, Argentine, S.A.

Robson, Henry, Surrey Road, Bournemouth.

Ross, J. G., M.B., C.M., 43, Flowergate, Whitby.

Rowland, L. G., 3, St. Hilda's Terrace, Whitby.

Ruff William, Kiora, West Cliff, Whitby.

S

Saunderson, Mrs., Holy Rood Cottage, Hedon, E. Yorks.

Sawdon, John R., 35, Abbey Walk, Halifax.

Sewell, J. T., Chubb Hill Road, Whitby.

Sherwood, Miss Rebecca N., 13, St. Hilda's Terrace, Whitby.

Simpson, Miss Clara, 24, Bagdale, Whitby.

Simpson, Miss, The Elms, Hull Road, York.

Simpson, Thos. H., 35, Via Colonna, Rome, Italy.

Smailes, Thos., Master Mariner, Victoria Square, Whitby.

Smailes, George, 100, Plymouth Road, Penarth.

Smailes, Richard, Master Mariner, 5, Hanover, Terrace, Whitby

Smith, Middleton, 45, Flowergate, Whitby.

Smith-Brodrick, G. B., Streonshalh, Birkdale.

Smithson, Ed., 10, Normanby Terrace, Whitby.

Smales, Charles, Magdala Place, Whitby.

Smales, Miss A. M., Magdala Place, Whitby.

Smales, Miss G. M., Magdala Place, Whitby.

Smales, Harold W., Magdala Place, Whitby.

Smales, Chas. B., Magdala Place Whitby.

Smales, Miss F. E., Magdala Place, Whitby.
Smales, Edward H., Arundel Howe, Whitby.
Snowdon, Mrs. Matthew, The Carrs, Ruswarp, Nr. Whitby.
Spanton, Robert, Flowergate, Whitby.
Spokes, Mrs. Russell, 22, Denmark Terrace, Brighton.
Stonehouse, John, 23, Silver Street, Whitby.
Stonehouse, Wm. J., 10, West Terrace, Whitby.
Storm, Jacob, Master Mariner, Leeside, Robin Hood's Bay.
Sturdy, Jacob, 11, John Street, Whitby.
Suggit, A. Neville, Rosslyn, Bagdale, Whitby.
Surridge, Miss, 12, Bagdale, Whitby.

T

Tattersfield, Mrs., Villette, Whitby.
Taylor, Miss Jane, Ingleside, Whitby.
Thistle, Miss Mary, 6, Belle Vue Terrace, Whitby.
Thistlethwaite, B. F., Laurel Bank, Nantwich.
Thistlethwaite, Rev. C. W., M.A., Tarporley, Cheshire.
Thistlethwaite, Capt. T. V. C., Nantwich, Cheshire.
Thompson, Mrs., 33, Gray Street, Whitby.
Thompson, Gilbert, Master Mariner, 2, Hanover Terrace, Whitby.
Thursfield, Mrs., Cranford Rectory, Kettering.
Tinley, T. Tinley, 2, Havelock Place, Whitby.
Towgood, Mrs., Saintfoins, Little Shelford, Cambridge.
Tose, T. W., Master Mariner, Poplar Row, Whitby.
Trowsdale, J., Master Mariner, Ocean Road, Whitby.
Turnbull, Thomas, Airy Hill, Whitby.
Turnbull, John, J.P., Golden Grove, Whitby.
Turnbull, Philip, Fairmead, Newport Road, Cardiff.
Turnbull, L. R., Raisdale, Penarth.
Turnbull, Wilfrid O., Fairmead, Whitby.
Turnbull, E. O., 22, Bagdale, Whitby.
Turner, Ed., 43, Fargate, Sheffield.

U

Urwin, W. E. G., 42, Fleetham Street, Middlesboro'.
Usherwood, Mrs., Bagdale House, Whitby.
Usherwood, T. E., 179, St. James' Court, Buckingham Gate, London, S.W.

V

Varley, Ernest W., Blackburn Yard, Whitby.
Vasey, Chris., Master Mariner, 16, John Street, Whitby.
Vause, F., West Cliff Station, Whitby.
Veazey, Rev. David, 27, Rectory Place, Woolwich, S.E.

W

Walker, Mrs. Herbert, Stakesby Vale, Whitby.
Walker, W. Ness, J.P., Ainthorpe, Danby.
Watson, H., Master Mariner, Istancia La Virginia, Isla Verde, Argentine.
Watson, W. C., 10, Lyndhurst Road, Hampstead, London.
Watson, Ed., Leeds House, Castleford.
Watson, Miss, 12, Bagdale, Whitby.
Ward, J. H., Scaling Mill, Grinkle, Loftus, R.S.O.
Wear, W. Carver, 13, Falcon Terrace, Whitby.
Weatherill, Miss, 4, Park Terrace, Whitby.
Weatherill, Miss Elizabeth, 4, Park Terrace, Whitby.
Weatherill, J.B., Master Mariner, Chubb Hill Road, Whitby.
Weatherill, John, 6, Ailesbury Road, Dublin.
Weatherill, W., Master Mariner, Eglinton Villa, Saltburn.
Webster, Hugh, L.R.C.S., 89, Lady Pit Lane, Leeds.
Wedgwood, Wm. R., 4, Gray Street, Whitby.
Wedgwood, Thos., 4, Gray Street, Whitby.
Weighill, Mrs. John, Brunswick House, Whitby.
Wellburn, Mrs. R., Hillgarth, Sleights.
West, F. C., Bawnmore, Bilton, Rugby.
West, Mrs. Mary M., 11, Northmoor Road, Oxford.
Wharton, Miss, 1, Union Place, Whitby.
Whitby Subscription Library, The Pier, Whitby.
White, Robert W., Whitby.
Whiteley, Mrs., Belthorpe, Whitby.
Wilson, W. H., M.B., Flowergate, Whitby.
Willison, G., Rosslyn Gardens, London, N.W.
Wilson, Miss, 12, Hanover Terrace, Whitby.
Willis, Mrs. Charles, Lyndhurst, Argyle Road, Whitby.
Woodwark, T. H., 16, Bagdale, Whitby.
Wright, Mrs. Wm., Flowergate Cross, Whitby.
Wright, Wm., Flowergate Cross, Whitby.
Wright, Charles, Flowergate Cross, Whitby.

Wright, Richard C., Flowergate Cross, Whitby.
Wright, Noel, Flowergate Cross, Whitby.
Wright, Theodore, Flowergate Cross, Whitby.

Y

Yeoman, F. W. K., 12, Bagdale, Whitby.
Yeoman, T. E., Ballarpur, Chanda District, Central Provinces, India.
Young, T. H., 36, Church Street, Whitby.

CPSIA information can be obtained at www.ICGtesting.com
Printed in the USA
BVOW09s0102311214

381483BV00017B/233/P